the inclusive hebrew scriptures

volume i: the torah

the inclusive hebrew scriptures

volume i: the torah

Co-sponsors' edition

PRIESTS FOR EQUALITY
Brentwood, Maryland

PRIESTS FOR EQUALITY
P.O. Box 5243
W. Hyattsville, MD 20782-0243

Printed in the United States of America
01 02 03   5 4 3 2nd printing

Original cover illustration by Melissa Cooper
Book designed by Craig R. Smith
Typeset in Book Antiqua and FC American Uncial

Library of Congress Catalog Card Number: 99-74682
ISBN 0-9644279-6-6

table of
contents

the torah

dedication

To all who have struggled to find their
own voice inside of their religious institutions and who, with courage, have
dared to speak out prophetically for equality; and to those still searching
for their own voice inside of repressive structures: this volume is dedicated
to you.

> Hear the voice of the Bard!
> Who Present, Past, & Future sees,
> Whose ears have heard
> The Holy Word
> That walk'd among the ancient trees,
>
> Calling the lapsed Soul,
> And weeping in the evening dew:
> That might controll
> The starry pole,
> And fallen, fallen light renew!
>
> "O Earth, O Earth return!
> Arise from out the dewy grass;
> Night is worn,
> And the morn
> Rises from the slumberous mass.

"Turn away no more:
Why wilt thou turn away?
The starry floor
The wat'ry shore
Is giv'n thee till the break of day."

William Blake (1757–1827)
Songs of Innocence and of Experience:
Shewing the Two Contrary States of the Human Soul, 1794

acknowledgments

July 24th, 2000, marked the 25th anniversary of Priests for Equality. We were the first project of the Quixote Center, which for the past twenty-five years, has struggled to build more just and loving structures in our church and in society.

The Quixote Center has been a good home for us and has been with us through the years as we have worked toward the full and equal participation of women and men in the church and in society. They have supported and encouraged us as we have worked to develop these inclusive language translations. So, first we would like to thank the board, staff and volunteers of the Quixote Center whose tireless work for justice continues to be an inspiration to us:

Polly Alonso (staff—Nicaraguan Cultural Alliance), Tony Banout (former staff—Equal Justice, USA), Carol Binstock (staff—Business Manager), John Boynton (consultant—Priests for Equality), Jack Bresette (board), Jim Burchell (part-time staff—Quest for Peace), Joseph Byrne (part-time staff—web weaver), Bill Callahan (staff—Quixote Center/Quest for Peace), Rose Marie Canty (volunteer), Charity Carbine (Intern—Haiti Reborn), Nick Carroll (volunteer), Peter Cerutti (part-time staff—Computer Operations), John Clark (staff—Computer Operations Manager), Marie Clarke (staff—Quest for Peace), Mary Ann Coyle (board), William D'Antonio (board), Caleb Downin (part-time staff—Equal Justice, USA), Jack Engle (volunteer), Maureen Fiedler (staff—Faith Matters), Pablo Giron (part-time staff—Quest for Peace), Abby Graf (Intern—Quest for Peace), Dylan Grimes (former staff—Equal Justice, USA), Jane Henderson (staff—Equal Justice, USA), Mary Virginia Herr (volunteer), Rea Howarth (part-time staff—Catholics Speak Out), John Judge (part-time staff), Trisha Kendall (staff—Equal Justice, USA), Sara Klemm (part-time staff—Equal Justice, USA), Ellen Lynch (part-time staff/ volunteer), Scot McGraw (volunteer), Therese Mele (volunteer), Alan Michel (consultant—Accountant), Melinda Miles (staff—Haiti Reborn), Ervin Murfree (staff—Equal Justice, USA), Harold Nielsen (board), Jerry Pederson (volunteer), Joel Polin (board), Dolly Pomerleau (staff—Quixote Center/Quest for Peace), Jane Quinlan (part-time staff—Data Entry), Linda Rabben (consultant—Faith Matters), Carol Ries (part-time staff—Quest for Peace), Dee Riley (volunteer), Tim Scanlon (former staff—Business Manager), Shari Silberstein (staff—Equal Justice, USA), Meredith Sommers (board), Shirley Tung (board) Neerja Vasishta (staff—Nicaraguan Cultural Alliance) and Tammy Williams (staff—Quixote Center/Quest for Peace). We would also like to acknowledge Alexander Henderson-Clark (age 6) and Guthrie Henderson-Clark (age 1½) for the joy and wonder they bring to the lives of everyone at the Quixote Center.

Next, we would like to thank our readers who reviewed this translation. Each of these women possesses a profound commitment to equality and love of language. They made sure that we were true to our purpose of producing a truly inclusive text that read smoothly:

❖ **Mary Ahearn** (Feminism) brought a close editor's eye to the texts and ensured that they read smoothly.

❖ **Kate Barfield** (Feminism) once again brought her careful attention to detail and sensitivity to the nuances of language to the task.

❖ **Mary Dougherty** (Feminist Theology, Ecumenism) gave us many insights into how inclusive language is being used in a number of faith traditions.

❖ **Barbara Marian** (Feminist Theology, Liturgy) again brought her expertise as a liturgist and her keen sensibilities with the cadence of the spoken word to help craft the text.

❖ **Gail Rekers** (Psychology) is a psychologist who joined our team of scripture on people and offered many useful observations and suggestions on how to make the text more inclusive.

❖ **Anne Patrick Ware, SL** (Feminist Theology) provided a sharp theological and grammatical reading to the texts.

And finally, we celebrate the gifts of talent and commitment that came together in the team that produce this book. From the very beginning, we have been blessed with a very special group of people who have been directly involved in the creation of this text. These people came together from many walks of life and who represent a variety of disciplines:

❖ **Rev. Joseph A. Dearborn** (Pastoral Theology) is PFE's national secretary and oversees the Inclusive Language Project. He helped create the raw text that was used in this translation.

❖ **Mark D. Buckley** (Scriptural Theology, Editor) worked on the initial drafts of each of the books. His vast knowledge of scholarly biblical commentaries as well as the latest linguistic research added much insight to both the translation and the footnotes.

❖ **The Rev. Elizabeth Anderson** (Feminist Theology, Editor) joined us once again, bringing to the text the meticulous attention of an expert editor and insights of a feminist scholar. She made sure that the text read smoothly and cross-checked each verse of the text to make sure that nothing was left out.

❖ **Nick Vittum** (Poet, Editor) edited the drafts of these texts and provided the voice of a gifted poet to many of the most beloved scripture passages.

❖ **Craig R. Smith** (Scripture Translation, Layout and Design) continued to serve as both our independent scripture scholar and this book designer. Words cannot begin to describe what an invaluable resource Craig is. Craig's encyclopedic knowledge and love of scripture translation, as well as his creative design of this book, is reflected on each and every page.

CO-SPONSORS

It is with great gratitude that we recognize those who have helped to make this book possible, those named and those unnamed:

❖ Bernardine & Joseph Abbott ❖ Lorraine & Peter Ackerman ❖ Sr. Fran Acton, OSF & Sr. Maracella Francis, OSF ❖ Joyce M. Albro ❖ The Alverno ❖ S. G. Anderson ❖ Robert L. Anstey ❖ Robert Anthony ❖ Elizabeth Anton ❖ Mary Arroyo ❖ Jane Audrey-Neuhauser ❖ Marsha Bade ❖ Elizabeth Baldini ❖ Susan J. Barnes ❖ Lucy Basler ❖ Brendan M. Bass ❖ Gary B. Beebe ❖ Maurine Behrend ❖ Sue Bell ❖ Roy Bender ❖ Abigail M. Benkeser ❖ Raymond Bernabo ❖ David & Christine Bernklau Halvor ❖ Martin J. Biglin ❖ In Memoriam: Francis MacIntyre Cleary (1906-1997) ❖ Joanne R. Bobek ❖ Rev. Adrian B. Boone ❖ Teresa Bowden ❖ Good Shepherd Parish MCC ❖ Laurene Brady ❖ Gerardo Brambila ❖ John & Peg Bruggeman ❖ Douglas L. Brunk ❖ Joseph F. Buckley ❖ Helen Buswinka ❖ Ann Carberry & James E. Brown ❖ Sr. Nic Catrambone, BVM ❖ Robeana Chaffiot ❖ Kate Chambers ❖ Monica & Rudy Cerniak ❖ Rosalie E. Cieply ❖ Tine & Peter ❖ James F. Clay ❖ Rev. Francis T. Connolly ❖ Sisters of Loretto ❖ Mary M. Crimmin ❖ Santa M. Cuddihee ❖ Kate Cudlipp ❖ Tom & Rosemary Daily ❖ Jean M Daniels ❖ Gail Davis ❖ Declan Deane ❖ Chris & Dan Delany ❖ Richard Paul Demlow ❖ Peter K. Dennis ❖ Anonymous ❖ Maureen D. Douglas ❖ Grace M. Drake ❖ Mary Ellen & Dan Duran ❖ Ms Glenn Ellefson-Brooks ❖

Rosemary English ❖ Mafalda Faillace ❖ Tommy Fiske ❖ Cecilia T. Flores ❖ Sr. Victoria Forde ❖ Jacqueline Gagnon ❖ Patricia Reilly Gamache ❖ Michelle L. Gaugy ❖ Mary Gehrke ❖ Rev. B. J. George ❖ Meg Gloger ❖ Mary Glover ❖ Anonymous ❖ Pacific School of Religion ❖ Colonel Rosanne M. Greco ❖ Lucille Grow, Ph.D. ❖ Sandra Gilian ❖ Alexandra Guliano ❖ Roberta Guthrie ❖ Rev. Anne Hall ❖ In Memoriam: Edward J. Halpin ❖ Judith Hansen ❖ Relma Hargus ❖ Joan T Harrigan, CSJ ❖ Emily Albrink Fowler Hartigan ❖ Judy & Steve Hayes ❖ Nancy M. Healy, SFCC ❖ Margaret L. Herman ❖ Rosemary R. Hobson ❖ Posy Jackson ❖ Maureen Jessnik, RSM ❖ Janet Johnson ❖ Mary Beth Jones ❖ Dr. Donna M. Kane ❖ Diane T. Kay ❖ Anonymous ❖ Nancy Lou Kelly ❖ Anna M. Kelly ❖ Maureen M. Kennedy ❖ Arleen Kerrigan ❖ Ruth Keys ❖ Rev. Eugene M. Kilbride ❖ Elsie Kilpatrick ❖ Ruth & Robert Kremer ❖ Rev. Joseph G. Kromenaker ❖ Rev. & Mrs. Edmund & Shirley Kurth ❖ Rev. K. Larsen & Mike Sittaso ❖ Jon & Hanna Laven ❖ Cheryl Huber Lee ❖ David Lee ❖ Katherine McNeil Leighton ❖ Betty & Fred Leone ❖ Dr. Eleanor V. Lewis—In Memory of Bea Mills, Ed.D. ❖ Mary & John Lindstrom ❖ Valinda D. Littfin ❖ John J. Lobell ❖ Mary Lopata ❖ Anony-mous ❖ Sue Malone ❖ Betty Mannlein ❖ Sr. Marie V. Marnell ❖ James B. & Margaret W. Martin ❖ Angelia C. Martin ❖ Martha T. Martson ❖ Steve Martson ❖ Michael Mass & Daniel Morris ❖ Sam Mason ❖ Mary McGladry ❖ Carol E. McGuire ❖ Joseph W McLaughlin ❖ Bridget Mary Meehan— SOFIA: Spirituality of the Femi-nine in Action ❖ Lois A. Michelin ❖ Mary L. Mild ❖ Arthur V. Milholland ❖ Rick Mitchell ❖ Joan Mitchell ❖ Dr. Virgina Ramey Mollenkott ❖ The Rev Grace Jones Moore ❖ Rev. Eleanor S. Morrison ❖ Neil & Judy Mulock ❖ Mary Jo Neal ❖ Micaela Grace Bueno ❖ Patricia Nemec ❖ Suzanne Nightengale ❖ Mary Jo Nocero ❖ Rev. Tilda Norberg ❖ Lisa Norman ❖ Susan B. P. Norris ❖ Margaret O'Herron ❖ Kathy & Joel Olah ❖ John O'Leary ❖ Walter R. O'Neil ❖ Anonymous ❖ Tom Ozanne ❖ Barbara Parsons ❖ Monica & Bob Peiffer ❖ Sheila Peiffer ❖ Miguel Perez-Gibson ❖ Elizabeth Baldwin Phillips ❖ Irene M. Piekarski ❖ Noella Poinsette, OSF ❖ J. William Potter, Jr. ❖ Rebecca Propst ❖ Anne Province ❖ Mildred Lange Ranzini ❖ Aaron Raulerson ❖ Karen Ray ❖ Joyce A. Recker & Lambert Zuidevaart ❖ Kathy & Robert Redig ❖ Steve Reed ❖ Lawrence A. Reh, First Light Ministries ❖ Katherine Rhoda ❖ Sr. Frances Roberts, SSJ ❖ In Memoriam: David Rose ❖ Liane Rozzell & Linda Kaufman ❖ Joan Ryder ❖ Therese E. Sachnik ❖ Louise

& Donald Sandercock ❖ Rev. Kenneth J. Schaefer ❖ A Happy and Thankful Daughter and Sister ❖ In Memoriam: Rev. Frank Norris, SS ❖ Susan Scherer ❖ Lisa Senuta ❖ Rebecca A. Shaw ❖ Michael J. Sheehan ❖ Barbara M. Sitko, HM ❖ The Rev. Jane G. Smith ❖ Margaret M. Snell ❖ The Sonntag Family Trust ❖ Jerome G. Sowul ❖ Ruth L. Steach ❖ Margaret Sterchi ❖ Stan Stewart ❖ Ed Stieritz ❖ Rhoda Swanner ❖ Bernadine Tackowiak ❖ Robert F. Taylor ❖ Thayer C. Taylor ❖ Anonymous ❖ In Memory of Deceased Helpers ❖ Anonymous ❖ Anonymous ❖ Geraldine Butler Trost ❖ Dr. & Mrs. Raymond J. Trybus ❖ Rev. Irvin Udulutsch ❖ Fr. Will Votrow ❖ Britt Wanta ❖ Paul Wehner ❖ Annmarie & Henry Weiler ❖ John V. & Heather J. Westra ❖ Martha J. Wicklund ❖ Susan Widman ❖ Joyce Wilkerson ❖ Martha Willi ❖ Chaz Williams ❖ Anonymous ❖ Faye Wilson ❖ Mary & Newell Witherspoon ❖ Kirk Woodliff ❖ Rev. Julie Yarborough ❖ Dave Yenko ❖ Marie & Deacon Don Zirkel

introduction

Ít is a difficult task to write an "introduction" to the Torah, just as it is difficult to write an introduction to a great work of art. Great art speaks for itself, as the saying goes, and the rest is commentary. And the Torah is indeed a work of art—a large and splendid tapestry, rich in color, intricate in detail, panoramic in scope, and endless in the depth of its teachings. The lessons of the Torah are new for each generation.

Looking closely at the Torah, one can see the intricate threads that form the whole, interlaced together: tradition and law, poetry and prose, genealogy and legend. Looking from a distance, one can see the story of God's work unfold in splendor. The stories and images not only tell a story, but draw the reader in, inviting participation in the divine plan. The Torah is the foundation for the rest of the Hebrew scriptures, as well as for the New Testament. In a nutshell, it defines and explicates three things: Israel as the people of God; God's relationship with Israel; and Israel's relationship with God.

In the broadest sense, the word *torah* means "instruction," such as the instruction a parent gives to a child, or a teacher gives pupils. Here, it is the divine Instruction, the revelation to Moses concerning the will of God. It is not simply a collection of laws; it is *the* Law.

More specifically, however, the Torah refers to the first five books of the Hebrew scriptures: *Genesis, Exodus, Leviticus, Numbers* and *Deuteronomy*— the books containing the teaching of the Mosaic revelation, together with the laws and commandments. In the ancient Greek translation of the Hebrew scriptures, they were collectively known as the Pentateuch, from the

Greek *pent teuchos,* or "five-volumed (book)," following the Jewish designation, "the five-fifths of the Law."

Origin of the Torah

There was a time when the Mosaic authorship of the Torah was undisputed—Moses wrote the entire work, as God dictated it. This is a venerable tradition that goes back to the Torah itself. In Exodus 17:14 and Numbers 33:1-2, God instructs Moses to write accounts of battles as a reminder to Joshua and the people. In Exodus 24:4,7 and Exodus 34:27ff, God commands Moses to record all the divine laws and dictates. Other parts of the Bible also contain references to Mosaic authorship. The eighth of the thirteen articles of faith formulated by Maimonides and incorporated into the Jewish prayer book reads: "I believe with full faith that the entire Torah as it is in our hands is the one that was given to our teacher Moses, to whom be peace."

Over time, questions have been raised about Mosaic authorship. In early Christianity, Clement of Rome objected to some of the stories in the Torah, such as that about Noah's drunkenness, and claimed that another person must have written them. Ibn Ezra (1089-1164) believed the Torah contained material that had originated at various times but was compiled at a later date.

Discrepancies in the text are easy to spot. Different styles of writing are present in the Torah—the repetitive style of Genesis 17 differs from the dynamic flow in Genesis 15, both passages concerning God's making the Covenant with Abraham. Use of names and facts from later times (such as "land of the Philistines" in Genesis 21:32; "before any ruler reigned over the Israelites" in Genesis 36:31) imply that at the very least, the Torah was edited at a later date. Stories are repeated, such as Abraham's passing off Sarah as his sister twice (Genesis12:20), or Isaac's presenting Rebecca as his sister (Genesis 26). Different names are used for the same place (Mt. Sinai and Mt. Horeb) and for the same people (Jethro and Reuel). There are two creation accounts in Genesis, with significant variations: Are human beings created after the animals, as in chapter 1, or before, as in chapter 2? Does God speak humankind into existence, or mold them from clay? The two accounts of the Flood disagree over totals for the number of clean animals taken into the ark. The Torah refers to God by different names. Moses is frequently referred to in the third person, and Deuteronomy 34 gives an account of his death, which casts additional doubt on his authorship.

Scholars throughout the years worked to resolve such discrepancies. Using the two accounts of creation, Genesis 1:1–2:4a and 2:4b–3:24, which differ in style and in the names they use for God, H.B. Witter in 1711 and Jean Astruc in 1753 presented initial evidence of two different literary sources. In 1875, building upon their work and the work of scholars such as Karl Heinrich Graf, Julius Wellhausen gathered and organized the earlier theories and presented them as a coherent whole. He identified four source documents of *Genesis*, each reflecting its own social and historical conditions and concerns. This schema became known as the Graf-Wellhausen or Documentary Hypothesis.

Using criteria such as subject matter, use of divine names (YHWH vs. Elohim), duplications of material (doublets and triplets), similarity of vocabulary and style, uniformity of theological outlook, and priestly concerns, Wellhausen labeled the four source documents Yahwist (abbreviated J, after the German spelling), Elohist (E), Deuteronomist (D) and Priestly (P).

The Yahwist (J) is so named for the frequent use of the divine Name YHWH, even before Exodus 3:14, where God first reveals the Name to Moses. This source seems to have been written during the time of the Davidic/Solomonic monarchies (ca. 950 BCE). By the time of David and Solomon, the promises God made to Abraham (Gen. 12:1-3) had come true. The question that concerned the writer was whether success would cause the people to forget God. The writer collected accounts and traditions to teach Israel not to be overcome by success, wealth and power, but to avoid temptation and obey God. Israel is to be a blessing to the nations (Gen. 12:1-3).

The Elohist (E) is named for the frequent use of the term El or Elohim to refer to God. Written in the northern part of Israel sometime in the eighth or seventh centuries BCE, it uses terms common in that region—Amorites instead of Canaanites, Horeb in place of Sinai. The Elohist downplays the role of Moses and other leaders, but stresses the people of Israel. God is less personal, more distant, and speaks to the people through dreams, angels and prophets, instructing them through tests of faith. Even as the prophets called Israel to obey the unseen God who demanded their exclusive worship, so does the Elohist call the people to stand in awe before God.

The Deuteronomist (D) is so named because its style is restricted, in all but a few instances, to the book of *Deuteronomy*. *Deuteronomy* has a particular history. Its old traditions and legal code (12-26) are put forth in the form of "discourses" by Moses before his death. The extraordinarily intense and hortatory tone fits the mood of a discourse. The book possibly contains the preaching of the Levites in the northern part of Israel before its fall in 721 BCE. If the book of *Deuteronomy* is placed in its proper historical perspective, its true impact may be more vividly appreciated. It is the blueprint of the great "Deuteronomic" reform under Josiah (640-609 BC). This was an attempt to galvanize the people into a wholehearted commitment to the Covenant's ideals, into an obedience motivated by the great commandment of love (Deut. 6:4ff): If it obeys, Israel has another chance. The people are poised between life and death, and they are exhorted to choose life.

The Priestly (P) reflects the concerns of the period during and after the Babylonian exile and represents an effort to preserve traditions, counter Babylonian religious views and practices, rekindle hope among the Jewish people and encourage the rebuilding of what was lost in the exile. For example, the story of Creation in Genesis 1:1–2:4 gives hope that out of the chaos—the topsy-turvy world of exile—God can create order and purpose for the people. In much the same way, the stories of Noah and the Exodus give hope of new beginnings provided by God. Faithfulness to the Law offers the way for the people to recover heritage and create a structure for their lives after the exile. A subset of the Priestly tradition, identified by more recent scholars, was the **Holiness Code (H)**, which contained the bulk of the ceremonial and ritual procedures.

These four traditions were then woven together by a later team of redactors, or editors, to form the whole of the Torah as we know it today.

Themes of the Torah

The five books of the Torah trace a chronological and theological progression: from the implementation of the divine plan in creation, to the founding of the theocracy as Israel prepares to claim its inheritance in the Promised Land.

Genesis recounts the origins of the world and the founding of the theocracy through the Covenant with Sarah and Abraham—with the promised blessing that the descendants of Sarah and Abraham will outnumber the stars.

Exodus tells of the liberation from slavery of the children of Sarah and Abraham and the formation of this people to be a nation with a constitution.

Leviticus sets out Israel's culture by providing a manual of ordinances to help with their needs when they approach God, who is going to live among the people in holiness (Lev 26:11-12).

Numbers recounts God's bringing order to Israel (the military arrangement, census of the tribes, transport of the sacred ark), and Israel's disruption of God's order. Nevertheless, the promised blessing cannot be frustrated from within or without.

Deuteronomy is presented as the last will and testament of Moses. It gives a summary of history and law and presents a new interpretation of the law as a covenant renewal in legal-prophetic form, as Israel prepares to enter the Promised Land.

Patriarchy and Monotheism: Defining a People

Much of the Torah deals with the tension between the older polytheistic cultures that inhabited the region and this new monotheistic religion of Israel: God, through Moses, gives a constant call for holiness—which, at its heart, is separateness: separate cultures, dietary laws, customs, and methods of worship. A strong distinction is made between clean and unclean, order and chaos, light and darkness.

At the same time, one can see in these books the polemic between the new patriarchy and the older goddess-centered religions. In the tension between light and darkness, darkness may not be evil, but it's close: the One God is now the only Mystery, not the wilderness or the sea, or birth and death, or Nature or womankind. All other mysteries, like all other gods, must now bow to the Most High.

Beneath this tension, however, decidedly feminine aspects of the divine continue to break through: the Spirit, the *shekinah* or Presence of God, the Rock in the desert—in fact, where divinity is immanent and manifest, rather than transcendent, that manifestation has a more feminine quality (and, in the Hebrew, it usually takes the feminine pronoun). This does not minimize the overt desire of the patriarchy of that era to wipe out any remnant of matriarchal cultures or to relegate women to a very low status in the society—both of which are clearly portrayed in the Torah. Yet a loving and powerful resistance to those strictures is also perceptible, as if to say that the divine Mystery is not so easily codified and contained.

Getting Our Attention: Defining God's Relationship with Israel

Another theme in the Torah is God's persistent attempt to bring humankind into relationship with the Holy One, and to keep us there despite our recalcitrance. This dance—toward God, then away, then back again—is repeated throughout the Bible, but never is it clearer than in these first five books. God uses a multitude of techniques to get and keep our attention, usually in escalating intensity. As C.S. Lewis wrote in his book *The Problem of Pain*, "God whispers to us in our pleasures, speaks in our conscience, but shouts in our pains: it is [God's] megaphone to rouse a deaf world."

A perfect case in point is the "plague narrative" in the book of *Exodus* (chapters 5 through 11). God's battle with Pharaoh is a powerful illustration of the way that God teaches us lessons in cycles, with each successive cycle getting more serious. And only after that lesson is learned can true liberation—in this case, the Passover, and the escape from Egypt at the crossing of the Sea of Reeds—take place.

In each of the ten plagues, which the Hebrew calls "blows," the same pattern is followed: Moses tells Pharaoh, "Let my people go!"; Pharaoh's heart is hardened; and a plague is unleashed. There are five different motifs to the plagues: the first two plagues deal with the Nile (the river turns to blood, and frogs come out of the river to cover the land); the second two feature insects (gnats, and a mixture of insects, perhaps flies); the third pair deals with disease (pestilence on livestock, and boils on humans); in the fourth group, people must cope with airborne disaster (hail, and locusts); and the fifth pairing brings darkness and death. Each plague is worse than the one before, and each pairing is "higher" than the one before: from the water's edge, to the insects on the land, to animal and human afflictions, to the surrounding air, to the numinous.

Another arrangement of the plague narrative may be particularly helpful toward seeing the cycle of God's dealing with stiff-necked humanity. The story is told in three groups of three.

The first cycle is Moses' battle with the magicians of Pharaoh, in which God is proved more powerful than the gods of Egypt—essentially a battle between monotheism and polytheism. Within that cycle are three confrontations with Pharaoh: "Confront Pharaoh in the morning," informally, while he is bathing at the river, after which comes the first plague; "go to Pharaoh" and meet him in a more formal setting at his royal court, then the second plague; and finally, a third plague, without warning, to show that God's patience has been exhausted.

The cycle begins again, with the next three contests designed to draw a distinction between Israel and Egypt, and to separate God's people from their captors. And again there are the same three confrontations: a plague after an informal morning meeting; a plague after a formal meeting at the royal court; and then a plague without warning.

The final cycle of three plagues follows the same arrangement, though these plagues are the heaviest. The cycle concludes with the cataclysmic tenth plague: the death of the firstborn—and the deliverance of the Israelites through the Passover.

In each cycle, God tries to get Pharaoh's attention, to use Lewis' analogy, first by whispering, then by speaking plainly, then by shouting. And throughout the Torah, when God is dealing with a rebellious Israel, a similar pattern is followed again and again.

The Sacrificial System: Defining Israel's Relationship with God

A third major theme in the Torah is the ceremonial and ritual life of Israel, which was the people's principal avenue of access to God. Particular emphasis was put on the system of animal sacrifice. For many people, the whole issue is troubling—nearly as upsetting as the "warrior God" mentality seen elsewhere in the Bible. But the rationale for the practice, placed in its proper context makes the idea of sacrifice, if not entirely acceptable, at least understandable.

Theologian Roland DeVaux sees three separate motives for animal sacrifice among ancient cultures:

❖ **Gift**, in which the worshiper brings something of value to the deity. The animal is killed, which sets it apart for sacred use; then the animal is burned, becoming an invisible substance which can rise to heaven. The gift may be a means either of giving thanks, or of assuaging the demonic powers that many societies (particularly Mesopotamia, Abraham's homeland) felt controlled everyday life. In general, the gift assures reciprocity on the part of the god, establishes relationship, and maintains the social order; in Israel, the focus was clearly on relationship with God.

❖ **Communion**, wherein the model of the meal is crucial: humans and gods share a great repast, cementing kinship the way business deals are celebrated by drinks and dinner.

❖ **Atonement or expiation**, where sin, communal or individual, is purged away by the act of sacrifice; the gods receive life as a substitute for the sinner's own, which is symbolized by the victim's blood. In the Bible, sacrifice for the sake of atonement is almost always in reference to unintentional sins, whereas deliberate wrongdoing may not be atoned for through this system.

Scholar and translator Everett Fox, in his groundbreaking volume *The Five Books of Moses*, writes:

The fact that this reconciliation, as it were, takes place against a background of slaughter should not be as upsetting to moderns as it is usually felt to be. In ironic contrast to our mechanized and mass-produced society, where the killing of animals for food takes place at a remove from our consciousness and from our direct participation, the sacrificial system in fact involved worshiper and priest alike, and the symbolic value of the operation, whatever it may have been in specific cases, lay in its directness, in its *consciousness of the taking of life*. Some would even maintain that in societies where the practice and rationale for sacrifice has broken down, there is inevitably an increase in intrahuman violence.

The book of *Leviticus* describes five types of sacrifices; they articulate the five ways of approaching God. The **whole burnt offering** represented complete self-surrender on the part of the worshiper. The **grain offering** was voluntary and usually spontaneous, an expression of joy and thanksgiving. The **fellowship sacrifice** was for communion, to create and celebrate a good relationship between the individual and God. The **purification offering** was given to cleanse individuals or groups from unintentional sins. And the **reparation offering** was for repairing and repaying a transgression.

It is notable that there are five principal sacrifices, just as there are five books of the Law: five, the number of fingers and toes, represents ability. In *Leviticus* the entire sacrificial system represented both the desire and the ability of Israel to effect and maintain a strong and healthy relationship with God.

CR CR CR

Inclusive Language

Human beings are creatures of language, born into a world of language. It is in and through language that we come to know ourselves, others and the world. Language gives structure and shape to our experience. It not only gives us the means to describe our experience, but also prescribes our views, values and norms of the world as we think it should be. Through language, we also perpetuate biases, resentments, fears and frustrations. Sexism, racism and classism are perpetuated in our language, and words are often used as weapons.

In developing scripture translations today, translators still bring the biases of their own culture. For two millennia, standard biblical translations have reflected Western, male-centered attitudes and prejudices. Words and phrases, such as "brotherhood of man," which are claimed to include all people, carry with them the implication that maleness is the standard for being human. The language used in such translations does not merely describe sexual biases and prejudices; it also prescribes a course of behavior that follows from such an understanding. Biblical translations have been used to justify patriarchal and exclusionary practices and oppressive measures against women.

This is changing rapidly in our own culture as a consciousness of equality grows and develops. As women of faith have become more conscious of their exclusion, they have sought to recover their place in religious traditions. For them, inclusive language—using words and phrases that are not sexist, racist or classist—is a vital and attitude-changing tool in the church. And as inclusive language becomes more accepted in general use, particularly in the media and public discourse, the need for inclusive language in religious texts becomes clearer than ever.

With this shift in consciousness has come a shift in language. Inclusive language is more than a corrective to the language of patriarchy—it is a form of language that expresses a vision of inclusion. Inclusive language is an issue of social justice, as well as a means of achieving it. To use inclusive language is to challenge deeply ingrained biases and educate people in the habit of equality. In short, inclusive language is an essential consciousness-raising tool that can foster change in the church and in society at large.

Developing Inclusive Language Translations

When Priests for Equality first started working on inclusive-language texts in 1987, we struggled with learning to speak the language of inclusion. We faltered and fell many times in our initial efforts—and we sometimes still do. Thanks primarily to the encouragement and suggestions of women and men who share our vision of equality, we began to develop a degree of confidence. We now feel more at ease with the language of equality.

Along the way, we have developed a set of guiding principles to ensure that we are consistent in our use of inclusive language. These principles are:

❖ **To create a "critical feminist biblical interpretation" of sacred Scripture that is inclusive in both content and style.** From the beginning of the project, our efforts have involved grassroots feedback, the guidance of feminist theology and scripture scholars and an editorial process that involves women and men skilled in both the theological and the social aspects of feminist, pastoral and scriptural critique.

❖ **To present the text in a layout that enhances the flow of the text, emphasizing the particular literary form that the text uses, while retaining the traditional chapters and verses.** The modern divisions of the Bible into chapters most likely happened in the 13th century; separating the text into numbered verses occurred in the 16th century. While we have retained the traditional chapter and verse numbering throughout the Torah, we have sought to present the text in its appropriate literary style: Poetry looks like poetry, stories look like stories, genealogies are recognizable as genealogies, etc.

❖ **To make a clear distinction between linguistic convention and overt bias in passages that appear sexist, and to distinguish between passages that simply exclude women and those that actively vilify women.** This is probably the most difficult problem we have had to face in our translation work. Nonetheless, we have sought to determine whether the text is using a mere linguistic convention that seems sexist to modern sensibilities, or whether the underlying meaning of the text is inherently sexist.

In all circumstances, we seek to recover the original meaning of the text without perpetuating sexist or classist idiom. To do this, we have employed some of the most up-to-date biblical scholarship and feminist critique available.

❖ **To use terminology that acknowledges the many forms in which God appears in our lives and to restore the role of women and of feminine images of God in Scripture.** Through our many surveys and countless written responses, people who use our inclusive-language texts have told us that the biggest concern in inclusive scripture is "God language"—words and images that describe the divine mystery. God is spirit, and the words and images we use to describe God are approximations, drawn from our experience, to describe a mystery. Drawing upon imagery that is exclusively male violates both our experience and the divine mystery. We do not rely on exclusively male models as the standard for human experience—why then limit God to exclusively male images?

❖ **To maintain a preferential option for those relegated to society's margins.** It is becoming fairly standard to avoid characterizing people by a particular accident of birth or fortune. Our goal is to humanize individuals and declare God's preferential option for those on the margins of society. To that end, we strive to acknowledge the dignity of each individual by the way we address that person.

One way we do this in our translation is to prefer terms that emphasize social justice over moral rectitude. For example, the same Hebrew word can be translated as "justice" and "righteousness"; "wickedness" can just as easily be translated as "corruption." While traditional translators have preferred terms underscoring morality and virtue (or lack thereof), we believe the original Hebrew concepts are more correctly translated by terms that describe personal ethics, the quality of interpersonal relationships and just (or unjust) social structures.

❖ **To stress an underlying mutuality and equality in human relationships.** Another area of the translation work that proved somewhat problematic was handling what is often referred to as "power language." This is language that reflects power relations among human beings and between human beings and the divine. Such language has been used to perpetuate injustices such as sexism, classism and ethnocentrism. Use of power language reflects the inequalities in societies where individuals and groups dominate other individuals and groups.

The ancient world was filled with inequalities reflected in the scriptural text: There were kings and servants, masters and slaves. God was portrayed as a ruler very much like the despots of the ancient world. Over the past few years, however, concern has grown about the role of power language in the perpetuation of sexist, racist and classist structures. People of conscience have begun to work with substitutes, many of which we have incorporated in our translation.

We have attempted to eradicate power language that might be used to perpetuate forms of injustice such as sexism and racism and to find ways of mitigating it in other circumstances. In our text, we have attempted to find "functional" substitutes for social roles—terms that describe what a person does but do not define who the person is. For example, we have in most cases translated "kings" as "rulers" or "leaders." "Masters" and "servants" frequently become "employers" and "laborers."

However, in describing historical conditions and events, we tried to reflect these circumstances as they were—including the inequalities built into the society. We attempted to use language that would describe the social roles and conditions then present, rather than prescribe the way things ought to be. Even here, we may not have done this to the extent that would make everyone happy: some wish we would use the harsher terms to underscore how deeply patriarchal and classist a world it was, while others feel we should downplay the ugliness and violence of those times. Our intention is always to provide a text that is both faithful to the original *and* reflective of the values of justice and equality that we hold so dear. We humbly leave it to the reader to determine whether we have fulfilled our intention.

The Continuing Task

The tranlsation of scripture into inclusive language is not an easy task, but it is a necessary one. For people today to hear the liberating word of scripture, the words used in translation must themselves be liberated from the shackles of sexism. We cannot deny our sexist past, but we must not perpetuate it in either word or deed.

As noted scripture scholar Phyllis Trible put it, "Since no exegesis is exempt from the experience of the exegete, no interpretation is fixed once and for all. Clearly the hermeneutical task requires understanding the Bible as dynamic literature engaged with continued experience." Every translation is an interpretation and reflects the views and experiences of the translators. What we have presented in *The Inclusive Hebrew Scriptures* is guided by our commitment to make them accessible to women and men today. Our dedication to produce quality texts is what impels us to study the texts carefully and uncover the intention behind each passage, so that we might faithfully render it. Our bond of solidarity with women and men struggling to build just religious and social structures has been our touchstone. If this book can help deepen faith, open eyes or strengthen commitment to effect change, our labors will not have been in vain.

The Genesis of This Project

Priests for Equality began in 1975 as a group of seventy-five Catholic priests, who committed themselves to working on issues of equality in the church and society. In the early days, priests signed a seventeen-point charter calling for full equality of women and men in church and society. Within the first year, more than 1,000 priests signed the document.

Considerable water has passed under the bridge since those early days. The original gathering of priests grew into a larger and stronger movement. People from all walks of life soon joined our ranks—women and men, religious and lay—as interest in our work broadened. We are now a very diverse group of women and men from a variety of faith traditions, and we are committed to making our faith communities and society approach greater equality and mutuality.

Our program has also changed with the times. In the 1970s, with the spirit of optimism in the Catholic Church following the Second Vatican Council, our emphasis was on direct action and institutional change. There was a growing openness in the church to respond to the needs of the people. During this time, we worked hard on issues like women's ordination and the Equal Rights Amendment to the U.S. Constitution. It may sound naïve today, but back then it seemed that all we needed was a committed group of people to organize efforts around the key issues, and we could bring about major structural change.

We have accomplished much together over the years. We challenged the U.S. Catholic bishops to address the real issues of sexism and equality in their pastoral letter on women's concerns and were part of a coalition that effectively lobbied the bishops to cease work on their hopelessly watered-down pastoral. In 1983, we wrote our own pastoral letter on equality, *Toward a Full and Equal Sharing*, which has been translated into Spanish and French. We helped make the writings of significant feminist theologians more accessible with our tabloid series, *Miriam's Song*. We have worked with other organizations, such as the Women's Ordination Conference, to promote the equality of women.

Even as institutions in both the church and society began to close ranks in the 1980s, we did not stop in our commitment to build a culture of equality. With the advent of the papacy of John Paul II and the failure of the Equal Rights Amendment, we realized that significant changes in eliminating sexism would need to come from the grassroots. Our focus changed from trying to change church and society from the top down, to working to bring about these changes from the bottom up.

Consistent with this shift was a change in program. We had always considered inclusive language to be an important element of our work. Our charter calls on the church to use inclusive language in all its official documents and in worship. We surveyed our supporters in the late 1980s, asking what they considered the vital issues in equality, and they echoed the need for more inclusive language resources.

Our work on inclusive language scriptures began in 1988, when we received permission to distribute a collection of lectionary readings produced by Dignity/San Francisco. We initially offered the readings at cost to our supporters, asking only that they use the texts and let us know what they thought of them. Feedback about the texts—from both spontaneous and formal surveys conducted by PFE—flooded in, prompting us to revise the texts. The surveys told us that one of the major concerns about inclusive language was the revision of the "God language."

As we continued to work on the texts, the work took on a life of its own. We formed a four-person editorial committee, with each member having an area of expertise either in scripture, feminist theory, theology or pastoral ministry. We then moved from revising already existing texts to doing our own translation work from the original languages. As our work progressed, we began to replace existing revised texts with fresh, original, inclusive translations. Since then, PFE has produced inclusive language lectionaries, which are used in parishes, religious houses, intentional communities and campus ministries in the United States and throughout the world.

From the very beginning of our translation work, we dreamed of producing a complete inclusive language Bible. This dream remained on the back burner for a few years as we produced the lectionary texts. At some point in early 1994, however, we realized that we had translated significant portions of the New Testament, and we began to see our dream as an achievable task. At that point, the editorial committee set about the task of translating the remaining passages of the New Testament. By December 1994, PFE had produced the first all-inclusive New Testament text.

The initial response to *The Inclusive New Testament* was enthusiastic. To date, the book has gone through three printings. Along with these positive responses, more and more people began to ask us when we were going to finish "the rest of the Bible." Our dream—and the dream of many others—had merged into a mission, and we set about the task of translating the Hebrew Scriptures.

Our first installment of *The Inclusive Hebrew Scriptures*, published in 1997, was a stand-alone edition of the Psalms that could be used for personal and public prayer. In the lectionaries, we had used *Psalms Anew*, by Nancy Schreck and Maureen Leech. These texts served us well as responsorial psalms, which are used in liturgies throughout the world. Our intention, however, was to create our own translation—one that was fresh and vivid, and steered away from traditional liturgical rhythms.

We are publishing the Hebrew Scriptures in three volumes, using the categories in which the books are arranged in Jewish tradition: the Law (*Torah*), the Prophets (*Nevi'im*) and the Writings (*Ketuvim*). Because we already had the Psalms finished, and because so many wanted the complete books of the wisdom literature, we decided to publish the third volume, *The Writings*, first; it came out in 1999. The current volume, *The Torah*, will appear at the end of 2000, with *The Prophets* planned for 2002.

Mark D. Buckley   Craig R. Smith

genesis

In the beginning*
God created
the heavens
and the earth.

2   But the earth became
chaos and emptiness,
and darkness came over
the face of the Deep—
yet the Spirit of God
was brooding
over the surface of the waters.**

---

* The books of Hebrew scripture in general, and of the Torah in particular, are named for the first few words of the text; the Hebrew name for *Genesis* is "In the Beginning." Some translators feel that the etymological construction of this phrase indicates that "the beginning" is not a time, but a process—thus rendering it "At the beginning of God's creating...."

** Hebrew rarely uses the verb *to be* in its sentence construction, and where it occurs, it is usually to make a point. Here the intensity of the verb suggests *becoming*, indicating that the original creation became a ruination; indeed, the phrase *tohu va-bohu*, usually translated "formless and void," we have rendered as "chaos and emptiness"—the closest English rendering of the Hebrew might be "topsy-turvy"—and every other time the phrase is used in the Bible, it describes a scene of ruination and desolation. Biblical scholars Robert Graves and Raphael Patai have pointed out the linguistic connection between *tohu*, or chaos; *tehom*, the word here translated "the Deep"; and the Babylonian goddess Tiamat. Here we find a remnant of Goddess imagery in the mysterious, watery chaos from which all life is created, echoed by the feminine Spirit of God (*ruach Elohim*) hovering over the waters the way a bird broods over the eggs in her nest. The phrase could also be rendered "mighty wind" or "breath of God"; in either case, it represents the divine power to recreate and restore that which has been spoiled and destroyed.

³ Then God said, "Light: Be!" and light was. ⁴ God saw that light was good, and God separated light from darkness. ⁵ God called the light "Day" and the darkness "Night." Evening came, and morning followed—the first day.

⁶ Then God said, "Now, make an expanse between the waters! Separate water from water!"* So it was: ⁷ God made the expanse and separated the water above the expanse from the water below it. ⁸ God called the expanse "Sky." Evening came, and morning followed—the second day.

⁹ Then God said, "Waters under the sky: be gathered into one place! Dry ground: appear!" So it was. ¹⁰ God called the dry ground "Earth" and the gathering of the waters "Sea." And God saw that this was good. ¹¹ Then God said, "Earth: produce vegetation—plants that scatter their own seeds, and every kind of fruit tree that bears fruit with its own seed in it!" So it was: ¹² the earth brought forth every kind of plant that bears seed, and every kind of fruit tree on earth that bears fruit with its seed in it. And God saw that this was good. ¹³ Evening came, and morning followed—the third day.

¹⁴ Then God said, "Now, let there be lights in the expanse of the sky! Separate day from night! Let them mark the signs and seasons, days and years, ¹⁵ and serve as luminaries in the sky, shedding light on the earth." So it was: ¹⁶ God made the two great lights, the greater one to illumine the day, and a lesser to illumine the night. Then God made the stars as well, ¹⁷ placing them in the expanse of the sky, to shed light on the earth, ¹⁸ to govern both day and night, and separate light from darkness. And God saw that this was good. ¹⁹ Evening came, and morning followed—the fourth day.

²⁰ God then said, "Waters: swarm with an abundance of living beings! Birds: fly above the earth in the open expanse of the sky!" And so it was: ²¹ God created great sea monsters and all sorts of swimming creatures with which the waters are filled, and all kinds of birds. God saw that this was good ²² and blessed them, saying, "Bear fruit, increase your numbers, and fill the waters of the seas! Birds, abound on the earth!" ²³ Evening came, and morning followed—the fifth day.

²⁴ Then God said, "Earth: bring forth all kinds of living soul—cattle, things that crawl, and wild animals of all kinds!" So it was: ²⁵ God made all kinds of wild animals, and cattle, and everything that crawls on the ground, and God saw that this was good.

²⁶ Then God said, "Let us make humankind in our image, to be like us.**

---

* That is, separate the "waters up there"—the literal translation of the word for sky or heaven—from those here below. The word translated "expanse" or, in other translations, "vault," means something hammered out, as a thinly beaten sheet of metal; the sky was often depicted as a vaulted dome.

**The common word for "God," *Elohim*, is actually a plural (literally, "gods"or "powers") but is usually treated as a singular noun. This verse and two others (3:22 and 11:7) are notable exceptions. The "us" has been explained as the majestic or imperial plural; others see it as God including the angelic hosts; still others, as a reflection of the more ancient polytheistic roots of the story.

Let them be stewards of the fish in the sea, the birds of the air, the cattle, the wild animals, and everything that crawls on the ground."

27   Humankind was created as God's reflection:
       in the divine image God created them;
       female and male, God made them.

28 God blessed them and said, "Bear fruit, increase your numbers, and fill the earth—and be responsible for it! Watch over the fish of the sea, the birds of the air, and all the living things on the earth!"* 29 God then told them, "Look! I give you every seed-bearing plant on the face of the earth, and every tree whose fruit carries its seed inside itself: they will be your food; 30 and to all the animals of the earth and the birds of the air and things that crawl on the ground—everything that has a living soul in it— I give all the green plants for food." So it was. 31 God looked at all of this creation, and proclaimed that this was good—very good. Evening came, and morning followed—the sixth day.

2:1 Thus the heavens and the earth and all their array were completed. 2 On the seventh day God had finished all the work of creation, and so, on that seventh day, God rested. 3 God blessed the seventh day and called it sacred, because on it God rested from all the work of creation.

4 These are the generations** of the heavens and the earth when they were created.

At the time when Our God made the heavens and the earth, 5 there was still no wild bush on the earth nor had any wild plant sprung up, for Our God had not yet sent rain to the earth, and there was no human being to till the soil.† 6 Instead, a flow of water would well up from the ground and irrigate the soil.

7 So Our God fashioned an earth creature out of the clay of the earth, and blew into its nostrils the breath of life. And the earth creature became a living being.

---

* This passage, because of its traditional translation—"subdue the earth, and have dominion over…every living thing on it"—has been used to excuse humankind's penchant for trampling the earth and subjugating its creatures. Unfortunately, the actual Hebrew is even more brutal, prompting traditional translations to soften the language somewhat. But this charge immediately follows the statement that we were created in God's image—that is, to be like God—so surely the idea of stewardship and caretaking, not violation and destruction, is inherent in that calling.

**"These are the generations" is a continuing refrain throughout Genesis—literally,"these are the begettings," but a more colloquial rendering would be, "This is the family history…."

† The first of many puns. "Human being" (or "earth creature") is *adâm*; soil is *adama*. A similar play on words in English, with a similar etymology, would be *human* and *humus*.

⁸ Our God planted a garden to the east, in Eden—"Land of Pleasure"—and placed in it the earth creature that had been made. Then Our God caused every kind of tree, enticing to look at and good to eat, to spring from the soil. In the center of the garden was the Tree of Life, and the Tree of the Knowledge of Good and Evil.*

¹⁰ A river flows through Eden to water the garden, after which it branches into four tributaries. ¹¹ The first stream is named Pishon, or "Spreader." It circles through Havilah, a land rich in gold, ¹² gold of the highest quality. There are gum resins there, and precious onyx stones. ¹³ The second stream is named Gihon, or "Gusher," and it flows through the entire land of Cush. ¹⁴ The third stream is the Tigris, which borders Assyria on the east. The fourth stream is the Euphrates.

¹⁵ Then Our God took the earth creature and settled it in the garden of Eden so that it might cultivate and care for the land. ¹⁶ Our God commanded the earth creature,

> "You may eat as much as you like
>   from any of the trees of the garden—
> ¹⁷ except the Tree of
>   the Knowledge of Good and Evil.
> You must not eat from that tree,
>   for on the day you eat from that tree,
>   that is the day you will die—yes, die."

¹⁸ Then Our God said, "It is not good for the earth creature to be alone. I will make a fitting companion for it." ¹⁹ So from the soil Our God formed all the various wild beasts and all the birds of the air, and brought them to the earth creature to be named. Whatever the earth creature called each one, that became its name. ²⁰ The earth creature gave names to all the cattle, all the birds of the air, and all the wild animals.

But none of them proved to be a fitting companion, ²¹ so Our God made the earth creature fall into a deep sleep, and while it slept, God divided the earth creature in two, then closed up the flesh from its sides. ²² Our God then fashioned the two halves into male and female, and presented them to one another.**

---

* The two trees represent the tension between unity, seeing all things as interconnected (the Tree of Life), and dualism, seeing things as right or wrong, black or white (the Tree of the Knowledge of Good and Evil). Paradise is here depicted as the state of living in unity with all things; eating the fruit of dualism—seeing all things as separate, and ourselves as alone—is indeed death.

** The literal translation is, "…and while the earth creature (the *adâm*) slept, God took one of its sides [or possibly, ribs] and closed up the flesh in its place. ²² Then Our God made the part that was taken from the *adâm* into a woman and brought her to the *adâm*." But if the earth creature is without gender before woman is created, then surely it becomes gendered when the split takes place—hence our rendering of the passage.

When the male realized what had happened, ²³ he exclaimed,

> "This time, this is the one!
> Bone of my bone and flesh of my flesh!
> Now, she will be Woman, and I will be Man,
> because we are of one flesh!"*

²⁴ This is why people leave their parents and become bonded to one another, and the two become one flesh.

²⁵ Now, the woman and the man were both naked, though they were not ashamed. **3:1** But the snake was even more naked: the most cunning** of all the animals that Our God had made.

The snake asked the woman, "Did God really tell you not to eat from the trees in the garden?"

² The woman answered the snake, "We may eat fruit from all the other trees in the garden. ³ But of the fruit from the tree in the middle of the garden, God said, 'Don't eat it and don't touch it, or you will die.'"

⁴ The snake said to the woman, "Die? You won't die! ⁵ God knows well that on the day that you eat it, your eyes will be opened and you will be like gods, knowing good and evil!"

⁶ The woman knew that the tree was enticing to the eye, and now saw that the fruit was good to eat—that it was desirable for the knowledge it could give. So she took some of its fruit and ate it. She gave some also to the man beside her, and he ate it.

⁷ Then the eyes of both of them were opened, and they realized that they were naked. So they sewed fig leaves together and made loincloths for themselves.

⁸ When they heard the sound of Our God walking in the garden in the cool of the evening, the man and the woman hid from Our God's presence among the trees of the garden. ⁹ Our God called to the man: "Where are you?"

¹⁰ "I heard you walking in the garden," replied the man. "I was afraid because I was naked, and I hid."

¹¹ "Who told you of nakedness? Have you eaten from the tree whose fruit I forbade you to eat?"

¹² The man replied, "It was the woman you put beside me; she gave me the fruit, and I ate it."

¹³ Then Our God asked the woman, "What is this that you have done?"

---

* Literally, "She will be called Woman (*isha*) because she was taken from Man (*ish*)...."

** Another pun. The Hebrew word for "naked" (literally, "smooth," as unclothed skin) is the root of the word for "cunning" (literally, "smooth," as in the phrase "smooth operator").

The woman replied, "The snake tempted me, so I ate."

14 Then Our God said to the snake,

> "Because you have done this, you are accursed:
>   lower than the cattle, lower than the wild beasts,
> you will crawl on your belly and eat dust
>   every day of your life.
>   15 I will make you enemies of one another,
>   you and the woman, your offspring and hers;
> Her offspring will wound you on the head,
>   and you will wound hers in the heel."

16 To the woman God said,

> "I will greatly multiply your pains in childbearing;
>   you will bear your children in pain.
> You will desire union with your man,
>   but he will be bent on subjugating you."

17 To the man God said,

> "Because you listened to your woman
>   and have eaten from the tree which I forbade you,
> when I said, 'You are not to eat from it,'
>   the earth will be cursed because of you!
> With painstaking labor you will eat of it
>   all the days of your life.
>   18 It will yield thorns and thistles
>   when you try to eat the plants of the field.
>   19 By the sweat of your brow
>   you will eat bread,
> until you return to the earth,
>   just as you were taken from it.
> You are dust,
>   and to dust you will return."

20 Adam, or "Humanity," named the woman Eve, or "Lifegiver," because she became the mother of all the living.

21 Our God made clothes of animal skins for the woman and the man to wear.

22 Then Our God said, "Look—these humans have become like one of us, knowing both good and evil. They must not be allowed to take in their hands the fruit from the Tree of Life as well, or they will eat of it, and live forever." 23 So Our God drove them from the garden of Eden, and sent them to till the soil from which they had been taken. 24 Once they were

banished, winged sphinxes* with fiery, ever-turning swords were placed at the entrance to the garden of Eden to guard the way to the Tree of Life.

4:1 Adam and Eve knew each other,** and Eve conceived and gave birth to Cain. "With the help of Our God," she said "I have gotten a child." 2 She also gave birth to a second child, his brother Abel.†

Now Abel became a shepherd, and kept flocks, but Cain tilled the soil. 3 In the course of time Cain brought an offering to Our God from the fruit of the soil, 4 while Abel, for his part, brought one of the finest of the firstborn of his flock. Our God looked with favor on Abel's offering, 5 but had no regard for Cain's offering.

At this, Cain was filled with rage and despair. 6 Our God asked Cain, "Why are you filled with rage? Why are you downcast? 7 If you intend good, you can hold up your head; if you don't intend good, then sin is a demon haunting your doorway, and it wants you—but you can conquer it."

8 Cain said to Abel, "Let us go out in the field." When they were in the field, Cain turned on his brother Abel and killed him.

9 God asked Cain, "Where is Abel your brother?"

Cain answered, "I don't know. Am I my brother's keeper?"

10 God said to Cain, "What have you done? Listen! I hear Abel's blood crying to me from the earth! 11 You will be cursed by the earth, which opened its mouth to receive Abel's blood from your hand. 12 If you till the soil, it will no longer give you its produce. You will be a restless wanderer on the earth."

13 Cain answered, "This punishment is too great to bear! 14 Since you have banished me from the soil—since I must leave your presence to be a restless wanderer on the earth—anyone I encounter can kill me!"

---

* "Cherubim," the traditional translation, are far from the baby angels portrayed in sentimental art. Rather, they are gigantic mythic creatures represented on the Ark of the Covenant and found throughout ancient iconography of the Near East. Buddhist philosophy names these two angels Fear and Desire, the two manifestations of ego which must be overcome before we can re-enter our own Eden.

**This traditional euphemism for sexual intercourse is particularly apt; in Hebrew, "to know" bears a wide range of meanings, from intellectual understanding to complete union with the divine. In the case of sexual union, it emphasizes the sanctity rather than the "carnal knowledge" to which this term later degenerated. To *know* someone in this way implies the deepest and most spiritual understanding of that person's soul, of a sort quite comparable to knowing God.

† Another pun: though Cain means a smith or ironworker, the phrase "I have gotten" in Hebrew sounds like "Cain"—rather as if we were to say, "I have 'gained' a son." And Abel's name indicates something transitory, as indeed his life proves to be. In the strife between the two brothers we see the ancient tension between the agriculturalists and the hunter-gatherers. In this story, God rejects an offering from the ground which has been cursed, but accepts an offering which involves sacrifice, possibly an expression of the turning from goddess worship toward the worship of a (male) god.

genesis 3

¹⁵ "No!" said Our God. "Whoever kills Cain will face sevenfold vengeance!" Then Our God put a mark on Cain, so that no one who came across him would kill him. ¹⁶ So Cain left God's presence, and settled in the land of Nod—"Wandering"—which is east of Eden.

¹⁷ Cain knew his wife, and she conceived and gave birth to Enoch. Cain built a city where they lived, and named it after their son Enoch. ¹⁸ Enoch begot Irad; and Irad begot Mehujael; and Mehujael begot Methushael; and Methushael begot Lamech.

¹⁹ Lamech had two wives; one was named Adah, and the other, Zillah. ²⁰ Adah gave birth to Jabal, the ancestor of those who live in tents and raise livestock. ²¹ His brother was Jubal, the ancestor of all those who play the harp and the flute. ²² Zillah gave birth to Tubal-Cain, the forebear of blacksmiths and coppersmiths. His sister was Naamah.

²³ Lamech said to his wives:

"Adah and Zillah, listen to my voice,
    spouses of Lamech, hear what I say:
I killed a man who wounded me—
    a youth who merely struck me!
²⁴ If Cain's deed will be avenged sevenfold,
    then Lamech's will be avenged seventy-seven times!"

²⁵ Eve and Adam again had relations with each other, and she gave birth to a another child, whom she called Seth, "One Who Is Given"—for she said, "God has granted me another child in the place of Abel, whom Cain killed." ²⁶ Seth had a son, who was named Enosh, "Mortal." It was at this time that people began invoking the Name of Our God.

5:1 This is the record of the generations of humankind.

When God created humankind,
    they were made to be like God.
² They were created female and male, given a blessing,
    and named "Humankind" on the day they were created.

³ When Adam had lived 130 years,* he and Eve had a child who was like them, made in their image, whose name was Seth. ⁴ After Seth was born,

---

* The extraordinarily long lives of individuals who lived before the Flood has received much focus. Many commentators see the ages as a measure of respect and a sign of God's favor—the older, the better. Others see the numbers as primarily symbolic, as with Enoch's 365 years, or Lamech's 777.

Adam lived another 800 years and fathered other daughters and sons. ⁵ Adam was 930 years old when he died.

⁶ Seth was 105 when Enosh was born. ⁷ After Enosh was born, Seth lived another 807 years and had other daughters and sons. ⁸ Seth was 912 years old when he died.

⁹ Enosh was 90 when Kenan was born. ¹⁰ After Kenan was born, Enosh lived another 815 years and had other daughters and sons. ¹¹ Enosh was 905 years old when he died.

¹² Kenan was 70 years old when Mahalalel was born. ¹³ After Mahalalel was born, Kenan lived another 840 years and had other daughters and sons. ¹⁴ Kenan was 910 years old when he died.

¹⁵ Mahalalel was 65 years old when Jared was born. ¹⁶ After Jared was born, Mahalalel lived another 830 years and had other daughters and sons. ¹⁷ Mahalalel was 895 years old when he died.

¹⁸ Jared was 162 years old when Enoch was born. ¹⁹ After Enoch was born, Jared lived another 800 years and had other daughters and sons. ²⁰ Jared was 962 years old when he died.

²¹ Enoch was 65 years old when Methuselah was born. ²² After Methuselah was born, Enoch walked in accord with God for another 300 years and had other daughters and sons. ²³ In all, Enoch lived 365 years. ²⁴ Enoch walked in accord with God, and then he was no more, for God had taken him.

²⁵ Methuselah was 187 years old when Lamech was born. ²⁶ After Lamech was born, Methuselah lived another 782 years and had other daughters and sons. ²⁷ Methuselah was 969 years old when he died.

²⁸ When Lamech was 182 years old, he begot a son. ²⁹ Lamech called him Noah, or "Relief," saying, "He will comfort our sorrow from our toil, and our painful struggle to make a living from the soil, which Our God has cursed." ³⁰ After Noah was born, Lamech lived another 595 years and had other daughters and sons. ³¹ Lamech was 777 years old when he died.

³² When Noah was 500 years old, Shem, Ham and Japheth were born.

CR CR CR

6:1 When humankind began to grow in numbers and to spread over the earth, and women became more plentiful, ² divine beings* saw how beautiful

---

* Literally, "sons of God" or, perhaps, "godlings." Many cultures explain the presence of great heroes and heroines, people who seem "more than human," with a myth of angels or gods mating with humans and producing demigods or gods in human form; however, some commentators believe the passage refers to the godly descendants of Seth, or to people of power (judges were often called *elohim*).

the human women were, and chose women to marry with, whomever they chose.

³ Our God said, "I will not allow my spirit to dwell within humankind for such long periods, because they are only flesh. From now on, they will not live more than 120 years."

⁴ The Nephilim were on the earth in those days, and afterward as well, when divine beings had intercourse with mortal women, who bore children by them. These were the Gibborim of old, individuals of great renown.*

⁵ Our God saw the great wickedness of the people of the earth, that the thoughts in their hearts fashioned nothing but evil. ⁶ Our God was sorry that humankind had been created on earth; it pained God's heart. ⁷ Our God said, "I will wipe this human race that I have created from the face of the earth—not only the humans, but also the animals, the reptiles, and the birds of the heavens. I am sorry I ever made them."

⁸ But Noah found favor in the eyes of Our God.

⁹ These are the generations of Noah:

Noah was just and blameless among his contemporaries, and walked in accord with God.¹⁰ Noah had three children: Shem, Ham, and Japheth.

¹¹ It was clear to God that the world was corrupt and full of violence. ¹² God looked at the earth, and saw that it had gone to ruin: all flesh had defiled its way upon the earth. ¹³ So God said to Noah, "The end of all flesh has come before me, for they are the cause of all its violence. I will destroy them, and the earth as well.

¹⁴ "Build an ark** for yourself out of cypress. Build rooms in the ark, and coat it with pitch, both inside and out. ¹⁵ Its dimensions are to be 450 feet long, 75 feet wide, and 45 feet tall. ¹⁶ Put a roof over it, with an overhang of eighteen inches. Put a door on the side, and give it a lower deck, and a second and a third deck below that.

¹⁷ "What I have decided to do is to flood the earth and to destroy all flesh under heaven that has the breath of life in it. Everything on earth will die. ¹⁸ But I will establish my covenant with you: you and your wife will go into the ark, with your children and their spouses. ¹⁹ Bring with you two of every living thing—one male and one female—of all flesh, to preserve them. ²⁰ Every kind of bird, every kind of animal, and every kind of thing

---

* A difficult passage. *Nephilim* is often translated "giants," but the word may derive from the words for "fallen" or "miscarriage." The passage may be hinting that they were the offspring of the divine/human unions. *Gibborim* means "mighty ones"; the passage could be referring to valiant and heroic individuals, or to violent people, in which case "renown" should be translated "infamy."

** The word describes a box or chest.

that creeps on the ground—two of each—are to come to you, to keep alive. ²¹ You must also store up all kinds of food to eat—food for yourselves, and food for all the creatures with you." ²² Noah did as he was instructed; he did everything that God commanded.

7:1 Our God said to Noah, "Come aboard the ark, you and your household; you alone among this whole generation do I see as righteous. ² Of all the ritually clean animals you must take seven pairs of each kind, a female and a male. Of the unclean animals you must take one pair, a female and a male. ³ Of the clean birds of heaven also, seven pairs of each kind, a female and a male, to propagate their kind over the earth. ⁴ For in seven days' time I will bring rain to the earth; it will rain for forty days and forty nights, and I will rid the earth of every living thing that I have made." ⁵ Noah did everything that Our God commanded.

⁶ Noah was 600 years old when the flood waters came over the earth. ⁷ So Noah and his wife, together with their sons and spouses, entered the ark to escape the flood waters. ⁸ With them came the clean and the unclean animals, birds and creatures that move on the ground, ⁹ two by two came to Noah into the ark, male and female as God had commanded.

¹⁰ Seven days later the waters of the flood appeared on the earth. ¹¹ In Noah's 600th year, on the seventeenth day of the second month, all the well-springs of the Deep burst, and the windows of heaven opened, ¹² and it rained for forty days and forty nights. ¹³ On that day Noah, his wife, their children Shem, Ham, Japheth, and their spouses entered the ark. ¹⁴ Every kind of wild animal, every kind of cattle, every kind of slithering creature that crawls on the ground, every kind of bird—anything that chirps or has wings— ¹⁵ came to Noah and entered the ark, two by two from all flesh in which the breath of life resides. ¹⁶ There was one male and one female of every form of life. They came to Noah as God commanded, and Our God closed the door of the ark upon them.

¹⁷ For forty days the flood continued, and the rising water lifted the ark so that it rose high above the earth. ¹⁸ The waters rose and rose throughout the whole earth, and the ark rose with them. ¹⁹ The waters rose so high over the earth that all the high mountains under heaven were covered— ²⁰ the waters rose above the mountaintops by more than 250 feet.* ²¹ All life on the earth perished—birds, domestic animals, wild animals, all swarming

---

* Some commentators feel the story of the Flood speaks of the ending of the last ice age, when the melt from the receding glaciers raised the sea level high enough to submerge much of what had before been dry land, occurring long before recorded history, but recently enough in the history of the human race to remain as tribal memory. Others believe there was a devastating flood in more recent prehistory, but one which was perhaps not global in nature. Still others see it as symbolic, with mythic power but little historical veracity.

creatures, and all humankind. ²² Everything that had once had the breath of life in its nostrils, everything on the earth, died. ²³ God destroyed all living things that existed on earth, from humans to animals, from things that crawled to things that flew; all were wiped out throughout the world. Only Noah and those with him in the ark survived. ²⁴ The waters rose for 150 days.

⁸⁺¹ God did not forget Noah and all the animals in the ark, and sent a mighty wind* over the earth so that the waters began to subside. ² The springs of the Deep and the windows in the heavens were closed up. The rain from the heavens stopped. ³ The water covering the earth gradually dropped, until at the end of 150 days it was gone.

⁴ On the seventeenth day of the seventh month the ark rested on the mountains of Ararat. ⁵ The water continued to go down until the tenth month. On the first day of the tenth month the tops of the mountains came into view.

⁶ At the end of forty days Noah opened the porthole he had made in the ark ⁷ and sent out a raven. It would fly off and return to him as the waters were drying up from the earth. ⁸ Then Noah sent out a dove to see if the waters had subsided on the earth. ⁹ The dove, finding nowhere to perch, returned to the ark, for there was still water over the whole earth. Putting out his hand for the dove he brought it back into the ark. ¹⁰ Noah waited seven more days, and again sent out the dove from the ark. ¹¹ In the evening, the dove returned with a freshly plucked olive branch in its beak, and Noah knew that the waters were receding from the earth. ¹² After seven more days, he again sent out the dove, and this time it did not return.

¹³ In Noah's 601st year, on the first day of the first month, the waters had dried up on the earth. Noah opened the door on the side of the ark and saw that the ground was drying. ¹⁴ By the twenty-seventh day of the second month the earth was dry, ¹⁵ and God said to Noah, ¹⁶ "Leave the ark, with your wife and your children and their spouses. ¹⁷ Bring out all the living things with you—the birds, animals, and all the slithering things of the earth—so they may spread throughout the earth, bear fruit, and become many on the earth." ¹⁸ So Noah with his wife and his children with their spouses, ¹⁹ and every kind of bird, animal, and crawling thing that moves on the ground, left the ark, one family at a time.

---

* The parallels to the creation story are unmistakable, with the breath/wind/spirit present in the beginning once again hovering over the face of the Deep, bringing order and life out of chaos and destruction.

²⁰ Noah built an altar to Our God, and choosing from every clean animal and every clean bird, offered burnt offerings on it. ²¹ Our God smelled the sweet fragrance and said, "Never again will I curse the earth because of humankind, since the evil their hearts contrive begins from infancy. Never again will I strike down every living thing as I have done.

> ²² So long as the earth lasts,
>   sowing and reaping,
> cold and heat,
>   summer and winter,
> day and night
>   will never cease."

9¹ God blessed Noah and his family and said to them, "Bear fruit and be many, and fill the earth. ² Now, however, all the earth's wildlife, all the birds of the air, and all that crawls on the ground or swims in the sea, will be afraid of you. But remember that they are your responsibility: they are in your hand. ³ You may now eat anything that moves and lives, just as it had been with the green plants: I now give them all to you.

⁴ "However, you are not to eat flesh with its lifeblood still in it. ⁵ At the same time, I will demand an accounting from your own lives, your own blood: from every animal I will demand it, and from every member of the human race in regard to one another, I will demand an accounting of human life.

> ⁶ "If anyone sheds the blood of another,
>   by others will their blood be shed;
> for in the image of God
>   has the human race been created.

⁷ "Now go, bear fruit and be many—abound on the earth and increase your numbers!"

⁸ God then said to Noah and his family, ⁹ "I hereby establish my covenant with you and with your descendants after you, ¹⁰ and with every living creature that is with you—birds, cattle, and the earth's wildlife—everything that came out of the ark, everything that lives on the earth. ¹¹ I hereby establish my covenant with you:

> All flesh will never again be swept away
>   by the waters of the flood;
> never again will a flood
>   destroy all the earth."

¹² God said, "Here is the sign of the covenant between me and you and every living creature for ageless generations: ¹³ I set my bow in the clouds, and it will be a sign of the covenant between me and the earth. ¹⁴ When I bring clouds over the earth, my bow will appear in the clouds. ¹⁵ Then I will remember the covenant that is between me and you and every kind of living creature, and never again will the waters become a flood to destroy all flesh. ¹⁶ Whenever my bow appears in the clouds I will see it, and remember the everlasting covenant between God and every living creature on the earth."* ¹⁷ God said to Noah, "This is the sign of the covenant that I have established between me and all living things on the earth."

☙ ☙ ☙

¹⁸ The sons of Noah who came out of the ark were named Shem, Ham, and Japheth. Ham was the father of Canaan. ¹⁹ These three were the offspring of Noah, and from them sprang all the inhabitants of the earth.

²⁰ Noah—the first tiller of the soil—planted a vineyard. ²¹ Once, when he had made wine, he drank so much that he lay naked in his tent. ²² Ham, the father of Canaan, saw his father's nakedness** and went out and told his brothers. ²³ So Shem and Japheth took a garment, put it on their shoulders, and walking backwards, covered their father's naked body. Each kept his face averted so that they could not see their father's nakedness.

²⁴ When Noah awoke from his drunken slumber and learned what his youngest had done to him, ²⁵ he said,

> "Cursed be Canaan!
> You will be the lowest of subordinates to your siblings."

²⁶ He also said,

> "Blessed is Our God, the God of Shem;
> and may Canaan be subject to Shem!"
> ²⁷ May God expand Japheth's territories;
> may you dwell in Shem's tents
> with Canaan as your subordinate."

²⁸ After the flood Noah lived 350 years. ³⁰ He was 950 years old when he died.

---

* The bow (i.e., rainbow) may depict God as the divine Hunter, and underscore once again the conflict between agriculturalists and hunter-gatherers.

** To "see [someone's] nakedness" is a common biblical euphemism for sexual contact. The passage is most likely metaphorical, not literal, and is an allusion for the sexual practices of the Canaanites, which included both homosexuality and incest; this explains the why the curse falls on Canaan, progenitor of the Canaanites, rather than on Ham.

10:1 These are the generations of the sons of Noah—Shem, Ham, and Japheth—whose children were born after the flood.

2 The descendants of Japheth: Gomer, Magog, Madai, Javan, Tubal, Meshech, and Tiras. 3 The descendants of Gomer: Ashkenaz, Riphath, and Togarmah. 4 The descendants of Javan: Elishah, Tarshish, Kittim, and Dodanim. 5 From these the maritime people branched out into their own lands, each with its own language, divided into nations and family clans.

6 The descendants of Ham: Cush, Egypt, Put, and Canaan. 7 The descendants of Cush: Seba, Havilah, Sabtah, Raamah, and Sabteca. The descendants of Raamah: Sheba and Dedan.

8 Cush begot Nimrod, the first great warrior. 9 Nimrod was a mighty hunter before Our God; hence the saying, "Like Nimrod, a mighty hunter before Our God." 10 From the beginning, Nimrod's realm included Babel, Erech, and Accad, all three located in the land of Shinar. 11 Asshur came from this land; he built Nineveh, Rehobothir, Calah, 12 and Resen, a large city between Nineveh and Calah.

13 The descendants of Egypt were the Ludim, Anamim, Lehabim, Naphtuhim, 14 Pathrusim, Casluhim and Caphtorim, the predecessors of the Philistines. 15 Canaan's descendants were Sidon, the firstborn, and Heth, 16 as well as the Jebusites, the Amorites, the Girgashites, 17 the Hivites, the Arkites, the Sinites, 18 the Arvadites, the Zemarites, and the Hamathites. Eventually the families of the Canaanites scattered, 19 and their territory extended from Sidon toward Gerar, all the way to Gaza, then toward Sodom, Gomorrah, Admah and Zeboim, as far as Lasha. 20 These were the descendants of Ham, with their families, languages, lands and nations.

21 Shem, ancestor of the Everites and the older brother of Japheth, also had descendants. 22 These were Elam, Asshur, Arpachshad, Lud, and Aram. 23 The descendants of Aram were Uz, Hul, Gether and Mash. 24 Arpachshad begot Shelah, and Shelah begot Eber. 25 Eber begot Peleg, "Splitting"—so named because the inhabited world was split up during his lifetime*—and Joktan. 26 Joktan begot Almodad, Sheleph, Hazarmaveth, Jerah, 27 Hadoram, Uzal, Diklah, 28 Obal, Abimael, Sheba, 29 Ophir, Havilah, and Jobab. 30 The territory in which they dwelt extended from Mesha all the way to Sephar. 31 These were the descendants of Shem, with their families, their languages, and their nations and lands.

32 These were the families of the descendants of Noah according to their genealogies within their nations, and from these nations came the peoples who inhabited the earth after the flood.

---

* A reference to the incident in the next chapter in which God scatters humankind throughout the world to stop them from building the tower of Babel.

11:1 Throughout the earth, people spoke the same language and used the same words. ² Now, as they moved eastward, they found a valley in the land of Shinar and settled there. ³ They all said to one another, "Let us make bricks and bake them in the fire." They used bricks as building stones, and bitumen for mortar. ⁴ Then they said, "Let us build ourselves a city, and a tower* whose top can reach to heaven. Let us make a name for ourselves, to keep us from being scattered over the face of the whole earth."

⁵ Our God came down to see the city and the tower these mortals had built. ⁶ "They are a single people with a single language," Our God said. "And this is but the beginning of their undertakings! Now there will be nothing too hard for them to do. ⁷ Come, let us go down and baffle their language so that they can no longer understand one another." ⁸ So Our God scattered them over the face of the earth, and they had to stop building the city. ⁹ It was named Babel, because Our God made humans babble different languages throughout the world. It was from there that Our God scattered them over the whole earth.

¹⁰ These are the generations of Shem: Shem's heir, Arpachshad, was born when Shem was 100 years old, two years after the flood. ¹¹ Shem lived another 400 years and had other daughters and sons.

¹² Arpachshad's heir, Shelah, was born when Arpachshad was 35 years old. ¹³ After Shelah's birth Arpachshad lived another 400 years, and had other daughters and sons.

¹⁴ Shelah's heir, Eber, was born when Shelah was 30 years old. ¹⁵ After Eber's birth Shelah lived another 400 years, and had other daughters and sons.

¹⁶ Eber's heir, Peleg, was born when Eber was 34 years old. ¹⁷ After Peleg's birth Eber lived another 400 years and had other daughters and sons.

¹⁸ Peleg's heir, Reu, was born when Peleg was 30 years old. ¹⁹ Peleg lived another 209 years and had other daughters and sons.

²⁰ Reu's heir, Serug, was born when Reu was 32 years old. ²¹ Reu lived another 207 years and had other daughters and sons.

²² Serug's heir, Nahor, was born when Serug was 30 years old. ²³ Serug lived another 200 years and had other daughters and sons.

²⁴ Nahor's heir, Terah, was born when Nahor was 29 years old. ²⁵ Nahor lived another 119 years and had other daughters and sons.

---

* Probably a ziggurat, a type of terraced pyramid built by the Assyrians, Babylonians, and Chaldeans as the base for a temple.

²⁶ Terah lived for 70 years and had three descendants: Abram, Nahor and Haran.

²⁷ These are the generations of Terah: the children of Terah are Abram, Nahor, and Haran. Haran begot Lot. ²⁸ Haran died in the presence of Terah his father, in Ur of the Chaldeans, the land of his birth.

²⁹ Both Abram and Nahor married. Sarai was the spouse of Abram, and Milcah, the daughter of Haran, married Nahor. Haran's other daughter was Iscah. ³⁰ Sarai and Abram were unable to have children.

³¹ Terah took Abram and Sarai, his son and daughter-in-law, together with his grandson Lot, and left Ur of the Chaldeans to go to Canaan. When they arrived at Haran, they decided to settle there.* ³² Terah, who died in Haran, was 205 at the time of his death.

12:1–25:18

OUR God said to Abram, "Leave your country, your people, and the home of your parents, and go to a place I will show you. ² I will make of you a great people. I will bless you and make your name so great that it will be used in blessings. ³ I will bless those who bless you, and I will curse those who curse you. And all the people on the face of the earth will be blessed through you."

⁴ Abram, who was 75 years old when he left Haran, began the journey as Our God had instructed, and his nephew Lot went with them. ⁵ Abram took Sarai his spouse, Lot, all their possessions, and all the dependents they acquired in Haran, and set out for Canaan.

When they arrived in Canaan, ⁶ Abram and his family traveled through the land until they arrived at the sacred place at Shechem and came to the oak grove of Moreh.** The Canaanites occupied the land at that time.

---

* "Ur of the Chaldeans" is a deliberate anachronism; at this time there was barely a Babel, let alone a Babylon which would grow from it, or a Chaldea which would later supplant it. But the Chaldeans are invoked here to underscore the magico-religious emphasis of area; both Ur, which they leave, and Haran, in which they settle, were important cities and centers of Goddess worship. The name Haran means "crossroads."

** It is clear that oak groves were held as sacred places to many ancient peoples, not only the Celts. It is likely that Abram found that these places had already been sites of worship by the Canaanites, and set up altars to God there; it is not uncommon for new cultures to piggyback their traditions, places of worship, and holidays onto those of the cultures that precede them.

⁷ Our God appeared to Abram and said, "I will give this land to your descendants." Abram built an altar where Our God appeared to him. ⁸ Then they moved off toward the hill country east of Bethel and set up camp, with Bethel toward the sea and Ai to the east. Abram built an altar to Our God and invoked the Name of Our God.

⁹ After that they traveled in stages toward the Negev.

¹⁰ At this time there came a famine to the land. The famine was so severe that Sarai, Abram, and Lot went down to Egypt to live a while.

¹¹ As they neared Egypt, Abram said to Sarai, "Look here. I know how beautiful a woman you are, ¹² and this is a fact that won't be lost on the Egyptians. When they learn that you're my wife, they'll murder me, so that you'll be free to marry one of them. ¹³ Tell them that you're my sister;* then it will go well for me—and I won't be killed because of you."

¹⁴ When they came to Egypt, the Egyptians did indeed see how beautiful Sarai was. ¹⁵ When the officials of the Pharaoh** saw her, they spoke highly of her to the Pharaoh, and she was taken into the ruler's house. ¹⁶ Because of her the Pharaoh treated Abram generously and gave him sheep, oxen, donkeys, female and male attendants, jennies and camels.

¹⁷ Our God inflicted Pharaoh and Pharaoh's household with severe illnesses because of Abram's spouse, Sarai. ¹⁸ Pharaoh summoned Abram saying, "What have you done to me? Why didn't you tell me you two were married? ¹⁹ Why did you say, 'She is my sister' and let me take her as a spouse? Here, take her, and be gone!"

²⁰ Then Pharaoh ordered the officials to see that Sarai, Abram, and their entourage left immediately.

13:1 So Sarai and Abram left Egypt with all their possessions, and Lot went with them. ² Abram was by now very rich in livestock, silver and gold. ³ From the Negev they traveled in stages toward Bethel, toward the place between Bethel and Ai where they had pitched their tents before, ⁴ where they had built an altar. There Abram invoked the Name of Our God.

⁵ Lot, who was with them, also had many flocks and cattle and tents. ⁶ The land was not adequate to accommodate them both, for they had too many possessions between them to live together. ⁷ Quarrels broke out

---

* This is the first of three nearly identical stories in *Genesis* in which an honored man of God seeks to save his own skin by passing off his spouse as his sister. Some see this as the "Trickster motif" that finds its apex in the story of Jacob in chapter 25; others see in it a reference to Mesopotamian law, in which a wife can be elevated to the status of "sister" as one element in the expansion of her status.

** A title meaning "Sovereign of the Great House," applied to Egyptian rulers regardless of gender.

between the herders of their livestock. At this time the Canaanites and the Perizzites were occupying the land.

⁸ Abram said to Lot, "Let there be no quarrel between us, nor between your herders and mine, for we are relatives. ⁹ The whole land is open before us. Let us part company: if you go to the left, I'll go to the right. If you take the right, I'll go left."

¹⁰ Lot looked around and saw the fertile plains which the Jordan River watered so well everywhere. This was before God had destroyed Sodom and Gomorrah. It was like the Garden of God, or the land of Egypt as far as Zoar. ¹¹ So Lot chose the whole Jordan valley and moved off eastward, and they parted company.

¹² Abram stayed in the land of Canaan, while Lot settled among the cities of the plain, pitching his tents near Sodom. ¹³ But the people of Sodom were extremely corrupt and sinful in Our God's sight.

¹⁴ After Lot left, Our God said to Abram, "Look around you. From where you stand, look to the north and to the south, the east and the west. ¹⁵ All the land within your sight, I give to you and to your descendants forever. ¹⁶ I will make your descendants like the dust on the ground: if someone could count the specks of dust, only then could your descendants be numbered. ¹⁷ Travel through the length and the width of the land, which I intend to give to you." ¹⁸ Abram took his tents and settled near the oak groves of Mamre, near Hebron, and there Abram built an altar to God.

14:1 In these days, Amraphel ruler of Shinar, Arioch ruler of Ellasar, Kedorlaomer ruler of Elam, and Tidal ruler of Goyim, ² went to war against Bera ruler of Sodom, Birsha ruler of Gomorrah, Shinab ruler of Admah, Shemeber ruler of Zeboiim, and Zoar the ruler of Bela. ³ These joined in battle in the Valley of Siddim, or "Limestone"—the area around the Dead Sea.

⁴ For twelve years these five had been subjects of Kedorlaomer, and in the thirteenth year they rebelled. ⁵ Then in the fourteenth year, Kedorlaomer and his allies made war on—and defeated—the Rephaim in Ashteroth-karnaim, the Zuzites in Ham, the Emites in the plain of Kiriathaim, ⁶ and the Horites in the hill country of Seir, on the edge of the desert near El-paran. ⁷ Upon their return they came to En-mishpat, "Judgment Spring," which is now Kadesh, and took possession of the territories of the Amalekites and of the Amorites dwelling in Hazazon-tamar.

⁸ Then the rulers of Sodom, Gomorrah, Admah, Zeboiim and Bela, which is now Zoar, marched out with their armies into the Valley of Siddim ⁹ against the armies of Kedorlaomer of Elam, Tidal of Goiim, Amraphel of Shinar, and Arioch of Ellasar—thus, four rulers against five. ¹⁰ Now the

valley of Siddim is laced with tar pits, and when Sodom and Gomorrah retreated, some of their troops fell into these pits, and the rest fled into the hills. ¹¹ The four rulers captured all the flocks and herds of Sodom and Gomorrah and all their provisions before they withdrew. ¹² They took Abram's nephew Lot prisoner, for he was living in Sodom at the time, and took all his flocks and herds as well.

¹³ One of Lot's household fled to Abram the Hebrew and told him everything that had happened. Abram was dwelling by the oaks of Mamre the Amorite; Mamre was the brother of Eshcol and Aner, and the three of them were allies of Abram.¹⁴ When Abram learned that his nephew was a prisoner, he gathered all those of the clan who were able-bodied and fit for battle—318 in all—and pursued them as far as Dan. ¹⁵ In the night, he split his forces and attacked from opposing directions. He pursued them as far as Hobah, north of Damascus. ¹⁶ They recovered all the captured possessions, and freed Lot, as well as the women and the other hostages.

¹⁷ When Abram returned from the defeat of Kedorlaomer and his allies, the ruler of Sodom came to meet him in the Valley of Shaveh—that is, the Ruler's Valley.

¹⁸ The ruler of Salem, Melchizedek,* who was a priest of the Most High God, brought out bread and wine ¹⁹ and blessed Abram, saying,

> "Blessed be Abram by the Most High God,
>   Creator of Heaven and Earth!
> ²⁰ And blessed be the Most High God,
>   who delivered your oppressors into your hands."

Abram then gave Melchizedek one tenth of everything.

²¹ Then the ruler of Sodom said to Abram, "Give the women and men to me and take the property for yourself."

²² But Abram told the ruler of Sodom, "I have sworn to Our God, the Most High, creator of heaven and earth, ²³ that I would not take one thread or sandal thong that belongs to you, so that you could never say, 'I have made Abram rich.' ²⁴ I will take only that which my fighters have eaten, and the share that belongs to the three who accompanied me—Aner, Eshcol and Mamre—for they have earned their share."

15:1 After these events, the word of Our God came to Abram in a vision:

---

* Melchizedek, which means "Ruler of Justice," is both a priest and the ruler of Salem, believed to be an early settlement which would become Jerusalem. This mysterious individual appears out of nowhere, interrupting the narrative flow, and is never mentioned again in the Hebrew scriptures.

"Fear not, Abram!
  I am your shield;
  I will make your reward very great."

² Abram said, "But my Sovereign, My God, what good are these bless-ings to me, so long as Sarai and I will die in disgrace? My only heir is a foreigner who lives in my household, Eliezer of Damascus. ³ Since you have given me no offspring," Abram continued, "an attendant in my house will be my heir."

⁴ Then the word of Our God came to Abram and said, "This person will not be your heir. Your heir will be of your own flesh and blood." ⁵ Then God took Abram outside and said, "Look up at the sky and count the stars, if you can! As many as that, you will have for descendants." ⁶ Abram believed Our God, and God accounted it to Abram as righteousness.

⁷ Our God then said to Abram, "I am Your God who brought you from Ur of the Chaldeans to give you this land as a possession."

⁸ Abram asked, "Sovereign God, how am I to know that I will possess it?"

⁹ God answered Abram, "Bring me a heifer, a goat, and a ram, each three years old, and a turtledove, and a young pigeon." ¹⁰ Abram brought all of these, cut them in half, and placed each half opposite the other—except the birds, which he did not cut up. ¹¹ Birds of prey swooped down on the carcasses, but Abram drove them away. ¹² As the sun was about to set, a trance fell over Abram, and a deep, terrifying darkness enveloped him.

¹³ Then Our God said to Abram, "Know this: your descendants will be aliens in a land that is not their own; they will be enslaved in that place and oppressed for 400 years. ¹⁴ But I will punish the nation that enslaves you, and in time you will leave that place with great possessions. ¹⁵ As for you, you will go to your ancestors peacefully, and be buried in your old age. ¹⁶ Your descendants will return here in the fourth generation, for the iniquity of the Amorites is not yet done."

¹⁷ When the sun had set and it was dark, a smoking brazier and a flam-ing torch appeared, which passed between the halves of the sacrifices.* ¹⁸ On that day Our God made this covenant with Abram: "To your descendants I give this land, from the River of Egypt to the Great River, the Euphrates: ¹⁹ the land of the Kenites, the Kenizzites, the Kadmonites, ²⁰ the Hittites, the Perizzites, Rephaim, ²¹ the Amorites, the Canaanites, the Girgashites, and the Jebusites."

---

* In Hebrew, the word "covenant" is derived from the verb "to cut." Usually both parties cut the sacrifice jointly, as if to say, "May this happen to me if I violate our agreement." Here, however, Abram prepares the sacrifice, but God alone "ratifies" it by passing between the pieces, indicating that the covenant is unconditional and unilateral.

16:1 Now Sarai and Abram were childless. However, Sarai had an Egyptian attendant named Hagar. 2 Sarai said to Abram, "Since Our God has made me childless, go to Hagar. Perhaps I will get children through her."

Abram agreed to Sarai's suggestion, 3 and so Sarai took Hagar and gave her to Abram as a concubine. Sarai and Abram had been living in the land of Canaan for ten years by this time. 4 Abram had relations with Hagar, and she became pregnant.

Once Hagar became pregnant, she looked with disdain on Sarai. 5 So Sarai said to Abram, "This wrong being done to me is your fault! It was I who put Hagar into your arms, but now that she has conceived, you allow me to count for nothing in her eyes! Let Our God judge between you and me!"

6 Abram told Sarai, "She is your attendant. Treat her as you will." Sarai then treated Hagar so badly that she ran away.

7 The angel* of Our God found Hagar in the desert near a spring, the spring on the road to Shur. 8 The angel asked, "Hagar, attendant of Sarai, where have you come from, and where are you going?"

"I am running away from Sarai," she replied.

9 The angel said to her, "Go back to Sarai and submit to her. 10 I will make your descendants too numerous to count." 11 The angel continued,

> "You are now pregnant and you will bear a child;
> you will name it Ishmael—"God hears"—
> for God has heard you in your sorrow.
> 12 He will be like a wild donkey,
> with his hand against everyone,
> and everyone's hand against him,
> living in strife even with his own siblings."

13 Recognizing God as the one who spoke to her, Hagar said to Our God, "You are the God of Seeing!" adding, "Have I actually gone on seeing—and living—after God has seen me?" 14 That is why the well is called Beer-lahai-roi, or "Well of the Living One Who Sees Me." It exists to this day, between Kadesh and Bered.

15 Hagar bore Abram a child, and Abram named it Ishmael. 16 Abram was eighty-six years old when Hagar gave birth to Ishmael.

---

* The word means, simply, "messenger," and is used for emissaries human or divine. When the context indicates that a divine being has taken human form, we have used "messenger" instead.

17:1 When Abram was ninety-nine years old, Our God appeared and said, "I am the Breasted One.* Walk in my presence and be blameless. ² I will make a covenant between you and me, and I will increase your numbers exceedingly."

³ Abram fell on his face before God, and God said to him, ⁴ "This is my covenant with you: You will be the ancestor of many nations. ⁵ You are no longer to be called Abram, "Respected Parent," but Abraham, "Progenitor of a Multitude," for you are the progenitor of a multitude of nations. ⁶ I will make you most fruitful, and I will make nations of you, and rulers will spring from you. ⁷ I will establish my covenant as an everlasting covenant between me and you, and your descendants after you for generations to come. I will be your God, and the God of your descendants after you. ⁸ I will give to you and to your descendants after you, this land in which you are an alien, the land of Canaan; it will be yours and your descendants', and I will be their God as well."

⁹ God also said to Abraham, "For your part, you and your descendants must keep my covenant throughout the ages. ¹⁰ This is my covenant with you and your descendants after you that you must keep: every male among you must be circumcised. ¹¹ Circumcise the foreskin to serve as a sign of the covenant between me and you. ¹² Eight days after they are born, every male among you is to be circumcised, whether they are members of your family or attendants in your household or foreigners you buy with money; ¹³ they must be circumcised without fail, even the laborers you acquire, so that my covenant will be imbedded in your flesh as a covenant forever. ¹⁴ And any male—any who does not have himself circumcised—will be cut off from his people as a covenant-breaker!"

¹⁵ God continued, "As for Sarai,** her name will now be Sarah, "Noblewoman." ¹⁶ I will bless her, and I will give you a child by her. I will bless her, and she will become nations; rulers of peoples will come from her."

¹⁷ Abraham fell on his face and laughed, and said to himself, "Is a child to be born of a man who is 100 years old? And will Sarah bear a child at the age of ninety?" ¹⁸ But to God Abraham said aloud, "Oh, if only Ishmael might live before you!"

---

* The name El Shaddai is usually translated "the Almighty," under the assumption that it derives either from the word *shadad*, which means "burly" or "powerful," or from *shadah*, which means "mountain," making the name mean "God of the mountains." There is growing opinion, however, that Shaddai may derive from the word *shad* or "breast"—thus El Shaddai may be a feminine image of God meaning "the Breasted God." Then again, since mountains are frequently shaped like breasts, these two interpretations are not mutually exclusive.

**Sarai was the name of a barren mountain in the area. The test in verse 16 is usually translated "the mother of nations," but it literally says that she will become—i.e., embody—entire nations.

[19] God replied, "Nevertheless, it is your wife Sarah who will bear a child, and you are to name him Isaac—'Laughter.' I will establish my covenant with Isaac, an everlasting covenant, to be his God and the God of his descendants.

[20] "As for Ishmael, I have heard your request. I will bless Ishmael and make him fruitful and greatly increased in numbers. He will beget twelve leaders, and I will make them into a great nation. [21] However, it is with Isaac that I will establish my covenant, and Sarah will give birth to him at this time next year."

[22] So God finished speaking with Abraham, and left him.

[23] Then Abraham took his son Ishmael, and all those males born in his household or bought with money—that is, all the males in Abraham's household—and circumcised them as God had commanded. [24] Abraham was 99 years old when he was circumcised, [25] and Ishmael was 13. [26] On that very day Abraham and Ishmael were both circumcised, [27] and every male in his household, even the foreign-born, was circumcised as well.

18[1] Our God appeared to Abraham by the oak grove of Mamre, while Abraham sat at the entrance to his tent in the heat of the day. [2] Looking up, Abraham saw three travelers standing nearby.

When he saw them, Abraham ran from the entrance of the tent to greet them; and bowing to the ground, said, [3] "If I have found favor in your eyes, please do not pass by our tent. [4] Let some water be brought, that you may bathe your feet, and then rest yourselves beneath this tree. [5] As you have come to your faithful one, let me bring you a little food, that you may refresh yourselves. Afterward, you may go on your way."

"Very well," they replied, "do as you have said."

[6] Abraham hurried into the tent to Sarah and said, "Quick—take a bushel of fine flour and knead it into loaves of bread." [7] Abraham then ran to the herd, selected a choice and tender calf, and sent a worker hurrying to prepare it. [8] Then Abraham took cheese and milk and the calf which had been prepared, and placed it before the travelers; and he waited on them under the tree while they ate.

[9] "Where is Sarah?" they asked.

"There in the tent," Abraham replied.

[10] One of them said, "I will surely return to you this time next year, and Sarah will then have a child." Sarah was listening at the entrance of the tent, just behind him.

¹¹ Now Sarah and Abraham were old, well on in years, and Sarah no longer had her periods. ¹² So Sarah laughed to herself and said, "Now that I am so old and my husband even older, is pleasure to come my way again?"

¹³ Our God said to Abraham, "Why does Sarah laugh and say, 'Will I really deliver a child, at my age?' ¹⁴ Is anything too extraordinary for God to do? At the appointed time, at this time next year, I will return to you, and Sarah will have a child."

¹⁵ Sarah was afraid, and said, "I didn't laugh."

God said, "Oh, but you did indeed laugh!"

¹⁶ The travelers then set on their way. and came to where they could view Sodom, with Abraham accompanying them as an escort. ¹⁷ Now Our God reflected, "Should I hide from Sarah and Abraham what I am about to do? ¹⁸ For they will become a great nation, and will be a source of blessings among all nations of the earth. ¹⁹ I have known them, so that they may command their family and their progeny after them to maintain my way by doing what is right and just; in this way, I will carry out for Sarah and Abraham what I promised them."

²⁰ So Our God said to Abraham, "The outcry against Sodom and Gomorrah is terrible, and their sin is so grave ²¹ that I must go down and see for myself. If they have done what her cry against them* accuse them of, I will destroy them. If not, I need to know that, too."

²² While the travelers walked along toward Sodom, Abraham remained in Our God's presence. ²³ Then Abraham drew closer and said, "Will you sweep away the innocent and the guilty? ²⁴ Suppose there were fifty innocent people in the city; would you wipe out the place, rather than spare it for the sake of the fifty innocent within it? ²⁵ Far be it from you to do such a thing, to make the innocent die with the guilty! Should the innocent and the guilty be treated the same way? Heaven forbid it! Shouldn't the Judge of the earth act with justice?"

²⁶ Our God replied, "If I find fifty innocent people in the city of Sodom, I will spare the whole place for their sake."

²⁷ Abraham spoke up again: "See how I presume to speak to my Sovereign, though I am only dust and ashes! ²⁸ What if there are forty-

---

* Judith S. Antonelli, in her book *In the Image of God: A Feminist Commentary on the Torah,* says that "her cry" is meant literally: "The cry of Sodom is the cry of a woman—'a certain young woman whom they put to death in an unnatural manner because she had given food to a poor person,' according to [medieval Jewish scholar] Rashi. There were actually several women who did this and were caught."

five innocent people? Will you destroy the whole city for the lack of those five?"

"I will not destroy it," God answered, "if I find forty-five there."

²⁹ Abraham persisted, and said, "What if only forty are found there?"

God replied, "For the sake of the forty, I will not destroy it."

³⁰ Then Abraham said, "Let not my Sovereign grow impatient if I go on. What if only thirty are found there?"

God replied, "For the sake of the thirty, I will not destroy it."

³¹ Still Abraham went on, "Since I have thus dared to speak to my Sovereign, what if there are no more then twenty?"

"For the sake of the twenty, I will not destroy it," God answered.

³² Abraham persisted: "Please, do not be angry if I speak up this last time. What if there are only ten there?"

"For the sake of the ten," God replied, "I will not destroy it."

³³ After speaking with Abraham, Our God departed, and Abraham returned home.

19:₁ The two messengers arrived at Sodom in the evening, and found Lot sitting by the city gate. When he saw them, he rose to meet them, then bowed so deeply that he touched the ground, ² saying, "Please, honorable travelers, come to your faithful one's house. Wash your feet, and refresh yourselves and spend the night. You can continue your journey in the morning.

"No," they answered, "we will spend the night in the square."

³ But Lot urged them so strongly that they agreed to come to his house. Lot prepared a meal for them, baking unleavened bread, which they ate.

⁴ Before they had retired to the sleeping quarters, the men of Sodom surrounded the house, young and old, down to the last man in town, ⁵ yelling to Lot, "Where are these travelers who entered your house today? Bring them out to us, and let us 'know' them too!"

⁶ Lot went out before the crowd, closing the door behind him, and pleaded with them, ⁷ saying, "No, friends, don't do such a wicked thing. ⁸ Look, I have two young daughters who are virgins—take them and do whatever you want with them, but do nothing to these travelers, for they are enjoying the protection of my hospitality."*

---

* It is frankly shocking, and a powerful indictment of the patriarchal interpretation of the scriptures, that so much has been made of the actions of the inhabitants of Sodom, and so little of Lot's offer to let the crowd rape his daughters. Jesus, and the vast majority of ancient rabbinical tradition, states unequivocally that the sin of Sodom and Gomorrah was their lack of hospitality, one of the gravest transgressions in the ancient world—particularly ironic in light of the church's institutional lack of hospitality to gay and lesbian people.

⁹ But the crowd yelled, "Stand aside!" They said, "This fellow Lot came into our community as a foreigner, and now he would play the judge. We will treat him to worse than his visitors!" They crowded around Lot and pressed close in order to break down the door. ¹⁰ But the travelers reached out and pulled Lot inside, shutting the door behind him. ¹¹ Then all the men who were at the door, great and small, were blinded by a dazzling light so that they were unable to find the entrance.

¹² Then the two travelers asked Lot, "Do you have anyone else here— daughters, sons, their spouses, or anyone else in the city? Get them out of this place, ¹³ for we are about to destroy it. The clamor against its people is terrible before Our God, who sent us to destroy it."

¹⁴ So Lot went to his future sons-in-law, who were betrothed to his daughters, and said, "Get out of the city, for Our God is about to destroy it!" But the young men treated the warning as a jest.

¹⁵ When dawn broke, the travelers urged Lot, "Come, flee with your spouse and your two daughters, or you will be swept away in the punishment of Sodom." ¹⁶ Lot hesitated, but because Our God was merciful, the travelers took Lot, his spouse, and their two daughters by the hand and led them out and left then outside the city. ¹⁷ When they were safely away from the city, the travelers told them, "Now, run for your lives! Don't look back or stop anywhere on the plain. Head for the hills, or you will all be swept away."

¹⁸ "No, please," Lot rejoined, ¹⁹ "you have already shown us, your faithful ones, great kindness by intervening to save our lives. But we cannot flee to the hills in time to keep disaster from overtaking us, and so we will die. ²⁰ Look, this town ahead is near enough to escape to, and it's so tiny. Let us take refuge there—see how tiny it is?—so that our lives can be spared."

²¹ The travelers replied, "This favor is granted. The town you speak of will be spared. ²² Now hurry! Nothing can happen until all of you are safe." This is why the town is known as Zoar—"Tiny."

²³ The sun was rising over the land by the time Lot's family reached Zoar. ²⁴ Then Our God rained brimstone and fire down from heaven on Sodom and Gomorrah, ²⁵ destroying those cities and the whole plain, with all the inhabitants of the towns, and everything that grew on the land.

²⁶ Lot's spouse was behind him, and she stopped and looked back— and became a pillar of salt.

²⁷ Early the next morning Abraham went out to the place where he had stood in Our God's presence. ²⁸ As he looked down toward Sodom and Gomorrah and the whole region of the plain, he saw dense smoke over the land, rising like smoke from a furnace.

²⁹ And so it was that God, in destroying the cities of the plain, was yet mindful of Sarah and Abraham by rescuing Lot and his family from the destruction of the place where Lot's family had lived.

³⁰ Lot and his two daughters left Zoar—he was afraid to stay there—and settled in the hill country. He and his daughters lived in a cave. ³¹ The elder daughter said to the younger, "Our father is old, and there is no one anywhere to lie with us, as is done everywhere else in the world. ³² Why don't we ply him with wine and then lie with him so that we can have children by our father?" ³³ That night they gave him wine and got him drunk. The elder daughter went in to his bed after he was asleep and rose before he awakened.

³⁴ The next day the elder daughter said to her sister, "Last night I lay with him. Let us ply him with wine again so that you can lie with him as well, so that we can keep our family name alive." ³⁵ So they got their father drunk with wine again that night, and the younger daughter went and lay with him, but he knew nothing of her lying down or getting up again. ³⁶ In this way both daughters became pregnant through their father.

³⁷ The elder daughter gave birth to a child she named Moab—"By Father." Moab is the ancestor of the present day Moabites. ³⁸ The younger daughter gave birth to a child she named Ben-Ammi—"Child of My Kinspeople." Ben-ammi is the ancestor of the present-day Ammonites.

20:1 Eventually Sarah and Abraham moved on from there to the Negev, and settled between Kadesh and Shur at a place called Gerar. ² While they were there, Abraham again referred to Sarah as his sister. Abimelech, the ruler of Gerar, sent for her and made her part of his harem. ³ But God came to Abimelech in a dream at night and said, "You will die because of this women you took. She is married."

⁴ Now Abimelech had not yet slept with Sarah, so he said to God, "Will you destroy innocent people? ⁵ Didn't he say to me, 'She is my sister'? And didn't she say to me, 'He is my brother'? I did this in good faith and with a clear conscience."

⁶ Then God said to the ruler in a dream, "Yes, I know that you did act in good faith and with a clear conscience. So it was I who kept you from lying with her. I did not let you touch her. ⁷ Now, return her to her husband. He is a prophet, and he will intercede for you. You will not die. But if you do not return her, I tell you that you will die, you and all your household."

⁸ Abimelech rose early the next day and called together all who served under him, told them of what had happened, and they were afraid. ⁹ Then

Abimelech called for Abraham and asked him, "Why have you done this to me? How have I offended you, that you would bring such guilt on me and on my realm? What you did to me should not have been done." ¹⁰ Abimelech asked Abraham, "Why did you do these things?"

¹¹ Abraham replied, "I did it because I said to myself, 'There is surely no reverence for God in this place; they will kill me because of my spouse.' ¹² She really is my sister—the daughter of my father, but not of my mother—but she is also my spouse. ¹³ When God told me to leave my family's household and wander, I said to her, 'You will do me a great kindness if, wherever we travel, you say that I am your brother.'"

¹⁴ Then Abimelech took sheep and cattle, and female and male attendants, and gave them to Abraham, and restored Sarah his spouse to him. ¹⁵ Abimelech said, "My land is open to you. Settle wherever you choose." ¹⁶ To Sarah Abimelech said, "Look, I have given your 'brother' twenty-five pounds of silver; let's forget this ever happened. Everyone who is with you—and everyone else—will see that you were blameless in this."

¹⁷ Abraham prayed to Our God to heal Abimelech's wife and his concubines, and they gave birth; ¹⁸ for every woman in Abimelech's household had been unable to give birth because of Sarah, Abraham's wife.

21:1 Our God was gracious to Sarah as it had been foretold, and did what had been promised. ² Sarah conceived and gave birth to a child for Abraham, who was now in old age, at the very time God had promised. ³ They named the child Isaac, ⁴ and Abraham circumcised the child Isaac when he was eight days old, according to God's command. ⁵ Abraham was 100 years old when Sarah gave birth to Isaac, "Laughter," ⁶ for Sarah said,

> "Now God has given me laughter,
>   and all who hear of this will laugh with me."

⁷ She also said,

> "Who would have said to Abraham
>   that Sarah would suckle children?
>   Yet I have given Abraham a child in his old age."

⁸ The child grew, and on the day of weaning, Sarah and Abraham held a great feast. ⁹ But Sarah noticed the child that Hagar the Egyptian had borne for Abraham, playing with her child Isaac. ¹⁰ She demanded of Abraham, "Send Hagar and her child away! I will not have this child of my attendant share in Isaac's inheritance."

¹¹ Abraham was greatly distressed by this because of his son Ishmael. ¹² But God said to Abraham, "Don't be distressed about the child or about Hagar. Heed Sarah's demands, for it is through Isaac that descendants will bear your name. ¹³ As for the child of Hagar the Egyptian, I will make a great nation of him as well, since he is also your offspring."

¹⁴ Early the next morning Abraham brought bread and a skin of water and gave it to Hagar. Then, placing the child on her back,* he sent her away. She wandered off into the desert of Beersheba. ¹⁵ When the skin of water was empty, she set the child under a bush, ¹⁶ and sat down opposite him, about a bow-shot away. She said to herself, "Don't let me see the child die!" and she began to wail and weep.

¹⁷ God heard the child crying, and the angel of God called to Hagar from heaven. "What is wrong, Hagar?" the angel asked. "Do not be afraid, for God has heard the child's cry. ¹⁸ Get up, lift up the child and hold his hand; for I will make of him a great nation."

¹⁹ Then God opened her eyes, and she saw a well of water. She went to it and filled the skin with water, and she gave the child a drink.

²⁰ God was with the boy as he grew up. He lived in the desert and became a fine archer. ²¹ He made his home in the desert of Paran, and his mother found a wife for him in Egypt.

²² At about that time Abimelech, with Phicol, Abimelech's army commander, visited Abraham and said, "God is with you in everything you do. ²³ Swear to me in the Name of God here and now that you will never deceive me, nor any of my offspring or my descendants. ²⁴ As I have kept faith with you, so also must you keep faith with me—with me and this land where you have sojourned."

Abraham answered, "I swear to it," ²⁵ but he then wanted to discuss the matter of a well which Abimelech's soldiers had seized.

²⁶ Abimelech averred, "I did not know that this had happened. No one told me of it."

²⁷ So Abraham brought sheep and cattle and gave them to Abimelech, and the two made a covenant. ²⁸ Abraham set seven ewe lambs aside, ²⁹ and when Abimelech asked him the meaning of this, ³⁰ Abraham said, "I give you these seven ewe lambs as proof that I dug this well." ³¹ That is why the place is called Beersheba—"Well of the Seven-Swearing"—for the two of them swore an oath there. ³² Once they had made their pact at

---

* Genesis 17:24 says Ishmael was 13, yet here is a child young enough to be carried on Hagar's back or "set under a bush" (v. 15). Continuity problems lend further support to the Documentary Hypothesis (see the Introduction for more information).

Beersheba, Abimelech left with Phicol, the army commander, and returned to the land of the Philistines. ³³ Abraham planted a tamarisk tree* at Beersheba, and there Abraham invoked the Name of Our God, the Eternal God. Abraham lived in the land of the Philistines for many years.

22·¹ After these events, God tested Abraham.**

"Abraham!" God called.

"Here I am," Abraham replied.

² "Take your son," God said, "your only child Isaac, whom you love, and go to the land of Moriah, "Seeing." Offer him there as a burnt offering, on a mountain I will point out to you."

³ Rising early the next morning, Abraham saddled a donkey and took along two workers and his son Isaac. Abraham chopped wood for the burnt offering, and started on the journey to the place God showed them. ⁴ On the third day, Abraham looked up and saw the place in the distance. ⁵ Then Abraham said to the workers, "Stay here with the donkey. The boy and I will go over there; we will worship and come back to you."

⁶ Abraham took wood for the burnt offering and gave it to Isaac to carry. In his own hands he carried the fire and the knife. Then the two of them went on alone.

⁷ Isaac said, "Father!"

"Here I am, my child," Abraham replied.

"Here are the fire and the wood, but where is the lamb for the burnt offering?"

⁸ Abraham answered, "My child, God will provide the lamb for the burnt offering."

Then the two of them went on together. ⁹ When they arrived at the place God had pointed out, Abraham built an altar there, and arranged wood on it. Then he tied up his son Isaac and put him on the altar on top of the wood. ¹⁰ Abraham stretched out his hand and seized the knife to kill the child.

¹¹ But the angel of God called to him from heaven: "Abraham! Abraham!"

"Here I am!" he replied.

¹² "Do not raise your hand against the boy!" the angel said. "Do not do the least thing to him. I know now how deeply you revere God, since you did not refuse me your son, your only child."

---

* The tree may indicate a holy place, similar to the oaks where Abraham dwelled earlier.

**This famous incident, according to commentator B. W. Anderson, was included to explain a sacred place name, and to justify the Israelites' break with other ancient cultures' practice of child sacrifice.

[13] Then looking up, Abraham saw a ram caught by its horns in a bush. He went and took the ram, and offered it up as a burnt offering instead of his child. [14] Abraham called the place "God Provides," and so it is said to this day: "On this mountain Our God provides."

[15] The angel of God called Abraham a second time from heaven and said,

[16] "I swear by myself—
it is Your God who speaks—
because you have done this,
because you have not refused me your son, your only child,
[17] I will shower blessings on you;
I will make your descendants as many
as the stars of heaven
and the grains of sand on the seashore.
Your descendants will possess
the gates of their enemies,
[18] and in your descendants
all the nations of the earth will find blessing—
all this because you obeyed my command."

[19] Abraham then returned to his attendants, and they set out together for Beersheba, where Abraham made his home.

[20] Some time after this Abraham was told that his sister-in-law Milcah had also become a mother, bearing sons to Nahor, Abraham's brother. [21] Uz was the firstborn, then Buz, Kemuel—who would later beget Aram— [22] Kesed, Hazo, Pildash, Jidlaph, and [23] Bethuel, who would beget Rebecca. These eight were the children Milcah had with Nahor, Abraham's brother. [24] Nahor also had four children with his concubine Reumah: Teban, Gaham, Tahash, and Maacah.

23[1] Sarah lived 127 years. [2] She died at Kiriath-arba—that is, Hebron—in the land of Canaan, and Abraham performed the customary mourning rites for her. [3] Then, standing beside her body, he said to the Hittites, [4] "Although I am a foreigner living here among you, sell me from your holdings a piece of property for a burial ground, so that I may bury my dead wife."

[5] The Hittites replied, [6] "Listen to us, Abraham: You are a leader who speaks with authority. Bury your spouse in the choicest of our burial sites. There is none among us would dare to deny you their burial place for your dead."

[7] Abraham rose and, bowing to the ground, [8] said to the people of that place, the Hittites, "If it is your will to allow me to bury my dead, repre-

sent me to Ephron, begot of Zohar. ⁹ Ask him for a cave he owns, the cave of Machpelah. It sits at the end of his field. Tell Ephron I will pay the full price for it. Let the transaction take place in your presence, so that I may have a burial place."

¹⁰ As it happened, Ephron was present among the Hittites, and he spoke up in the hearing of the other Hittites who had gathered at the city gate. ¹¹ "I won't hear of it. I give you the field, and I give you the cave at the end of the field. I give them to you in the presence of all my people. The field and the cave are yours for a burial ground."

¹² Abraham bowed to the ground before all the gathered people, ¹³ and said to Ephron, "Can this be true? I am willing to pay for the field. Please accept payment from me, so that I may have a burial place."

¹⁴ Ephron replied to Abraham, ¹⁵ "Please listen to me. A piece of land worth ten pounds of silver—what is that between you and me? Bury your dead." ¹⁶ Abraham agreed with Ephron, and he weighed out the price named in the presence of the Hittites—ten pounds of silver, according to the weights current among merchants.

¹⁷ So Ephron's field in Machpelah, to the east of Mamre, the field with its cave, as well as all the trees on the land, ¹⁸ became the property of Abraham in the presence of the Hittites and all those gathered at the city gate. ¹⁹ After the transaction, Abraham buried Sarah in the cave of the field of Machpelah, facing Mamre—that is, Hebron—in the land of Canaan. ²⁰ So the field and the cave in it passed from the Hittites into Abraham's possession as a burial place.

24:1 Abraham was now very old, and God blessed him in every way. ² Abraham said to the oldest retainer of the household, the steward of all his property, "Place your hand under my thigh,* ³ for I would have you swear to Our God, the God of heaven and earth, that you will not choose a spouse for my son, Isaac, from the daughters of the Canaanites among whom I live, ⁴ but will go to my own land. to my own kindred, to find a spouse for him there."

⁵ The steward said, "What if a woman doesn't want to come with me to this country? Must I take the boy back to the country from which you came?"

⁶ Abraham answered, "Do not take Isaac back there on any account. ⁷ Our God, the God of heaven and earth, took me from my ancestral home,

---

* "Thigh" is a euphemism. It was a common gesture when swearing an oath, amounting to swearing on the lives of one's children and grandchildren.

and from the land of my kinfolk, and swore to me that I would be given this country for my descendants. God will send an angel ahead of you, and ensure that you will find a spouse for my son there. ⁸ If the woman is unwilling to follow you, you will be released from this oath. But never take my son back there."

⁹ So the steward placed his hand under the thigh of Abraham the elder, and swore to carry out this oath.

¹⁰ Then the steward took ten of Abraham's camels and set out on the journey, taking with him many gifts from Abraham. He came to Aram-of-Two-Rivers, and the city of Nahor, ¹¹ and tethered the camels outside the city near a well. It was evening, at the time of the day when women came to the well to draw water. ¹² The steward prayed, "My God, the God of my elder Abraham, grant me success today and be kind to Abraham whom I honor. ¹³ I stand here near this spring of water, as the women of the town come out to draw water. ¹⁴ Let it be that when I ask a woman, 'May I have a jar of water, please?' and she answers, 'Yes, and I will water your camels as well'—let her be the woman whom you have chosen to marry your faithful one Isaac. By this I will know you have shown kindness to my elder."

¹⁵ Even before he had finished praying, Rebecca approached the well shouldering a water jar. She was the daughter of Bethuel, begot of Milcah the wife of Nahor, who was Abraham's brother. ¹⁶ This beautiful young woman, who had never lain with a man, went to the spring, filled her jar and moved off. ¹⁷ The steward then approached her, asking, "Please, let me have a drink of water from your jar."

¹⁸ "Drink, sir," she replied, and lowered the jar from her shoulder and offered it to him. ¹⁹ When he had drunk, she offered, "I'll draw water for your camels until they have had their fill." ²⁰ Then she quickly emptied her jar into the trough and ran to the spring to draw more water for the camels. ²¹ The steward watched in silence to see if God had made his journey successful or not.

²² When the camels had drunk their fill, the steward gave her a gold nose ring weighing a fifth of an ounce, and two gold bracelets weighing four ounces. ²³ He asked her, "Whose daughter are you, and is there a place for me to spend the night in your house?"

²⁴ She said, "I am the daughter of Bethuel, begot of Milcah and Nahor." ²⁵ She added, "We have plenty of straw and fodder, and a room for you to stay in."

²⁶ The steward bowed low and worshipped God ²⁷ saying, "Blessed be God, the God of my elder Abraham, for constant and unfailing faithfulness to my elder, and for guiding me to the house of Abraham's kin!"

²⁸ The girl ran and told her mother's household what had happened. ²⁹⁻³⁰ Rebecca's brother, Laban, saw the nose-ring, and the bracelets on his sister's arms, and hearing her account of what had happened at the spring, he immediately ran to the spring. There he saw the steward, standing by the camels.

³¹ Laban said, "Come to our house, blessed one of Our God. Do not stand here in the open, for we have prepared places for you and your camels."

³² So the steward went to the house, where the camels were unloaded and provided with straw and fodder, and the travelers were given water to wash their feet. ³³ But when food was set before them, the steward forestalled them: "I cannot eat until I deliver my message."

Laban said, "Then speak to us."

³⁴ "I am Abraham's steward," he said. ³⁵ "Our God has greatly blessed Abraham. He is now a wealthy person. God has given him flocks, herds, silver, gold, attendants, camels, and donkeys. ³⁶ Sarah, Abraham's spouse, bore a son late in life, and he is Abraham's heir. ³⁷ Abraham swore me by an oath, saying, 'You must not allow my son to marry any of the Canaanites, in whose land we live. ³⁸ Go to the land of my mother and father, to my kin, to find a spouse for Isaac.' ³⁹ I asked, 'What if the woman won't come with me?' ⁴⁰ Abraham answered, 'Our God, in whose presence I live, will send an angel with you and make your journey a success. You must find a spouse for Isaac from my family and from my father's house. ⁴¹ Only then will you be relieved from the oath you swore. But once you come to my family, if they refuse to let her go with you, then you are freed from the oath.'

⁴² "Today, when I came to the spring, I prayed, 'O God of my elder Abraham, let my journey be a successful one. Let it happen like this— ⁴³ here I am at the spring, and when a young woman comes to draw water, I will ask her, 'Please let me have a drink of water from the spring.' ⁴⁴ If she answers, 'Have a drink, and I will water your camels as well,' let it be that she is the woman whom Our God has chosen to become the spouse of Abraham's heir Isaac.' ⁴⁵ Before I had finished praying, I saw Rebecca approaching the spring, shouldering her water jar. She went down to the spring to draw water, and I asked her, 'May I please have a drink of water?' ⁴⁶ She immediately put the jar into the spring and said, 'Drink, and I'll water your camels as well.' So I drank while she watered the camels.

⁴⁷ "Then I asked her about her parentage. She replied, 'I am the daughter of Bethuel, begot of Milcah and Nahor'; whereupon I put the ring in her nose and the bracelets on her arms, ⁴⁸ and I bowed down and worshipped Our God. I praised Our God, the God of my elder Abraham, who led me to the right place to find the granddaughter of Abraham's brother for Isaac.

⁴⁹ Please tell me that you will show this kindness and loyalty to Abraham! If not, just say so, and I will go to other places."

⁵⁰ Laban and Bethuel replied, "But this is from Our God; there is nothing we can do against it! ⁵¹ Rebecca will go with you to marry Isaac, Abraham's heir, as Our God has decreed."

⁵² The steward, hearing this, fell to the ground before Our God. ⁵³ He then brought out silver and gold ornaments and articles of clothing and gave them to Rebecca, and gave gifts to her mother and brother. ⁵⁴ They ate and drank and spent the night there.

When they rose in the morning, the steward said, "Give me leave to return to the honorable Abraham."

⁵⁵ Rebecca's mother and brother replied, "Let Rebecca remain for a few days—no more than ten—before she leaves us."

⁵⁶ The steward said, "Let me not be delayed. You see that it is Our God who granted us this success. Give me leave to return to the honorable Abraham."

⁵⁷ They said, "Let us call Rebecca to see how she feels."

⁵⁸ They called Rebecca and put the question to her. She replied, "Yes, I am ready to leave." ⁵⁹ So Rebecca and her attendant went with Abraham's steward and his entourage.

⁶⁰ They blessed Rebecca and said to her:

> "You are our sister, and you will increase
>   to thousands and tens of thousands!
> May your descendants take possession
>   of the gates of their foes!"

⁶¹ Rebecca and her attendants got ready, then mounted their camels to follow Abraham's steward. The steward took Rebecca, and they set off on their journey.

⁶² Isaac had gone to live in the region of the Negev, and came to the Well of the Living One Who Sees Me. ⁶³ One day toward evening he went out in the field to meditate, and as he looked around, he saw that camels were approaching.

⁶⁴ When Rebecca saw Isaac, she alighted from her camel ⁶⁵ and asked the steward, "Who is that man out there, walking through the field toward us?"

"That is indeed Isaac," he replied. She then covered herself with her veil.

⁶⁶ The steward recounted to Isaac all that had been done. ⁶⁷ Then Isaac led Rebecca into Sarah's tent, and she became his wife, and he loved her. That is how Isaac was comforted after the loss of his mother.

25:1 Abraham married again, to a woman named Keturah. 2 Her children were Zimran, Jokshan, Medan, Midian, Ishbak, and Shuah. 3 The children of Jokshan were Shebah and Dedan. The descendants of Dedan were the Asshurim, Letushim and Leummim. 4 The heirs of Midian were Ephah, Epher, Enoch, Abida, and Eldaah. All these were descended from Keturah.

5 Abraham gave all his possessions to Isaac. 6 He had already provided for the children of his concubines and sent them away to the east, out of Isaac's way.

7 These are the days and years of the life of Abraham: 8 he was 175 years old when he was gathered to his ancestors, and having lived a full and abundant life, he breathed his last. 9 His heirs Isaac and Ishmael buried him in the cave at Machpelah, in the field of Ephron begot of Zoar the Hittite, east of Mamre— 10 the plot which Abraham had bought from the Hittites. Abraham was buried there with Sarah, his wife. 11 After Abraham's death, God blessed Isaac, who had settled near the Well of the Living One Who Sees Me.

12 These are the generations of Ishmael, begot of Hagar, Sarah's Egyptian attendant, 13 listed in order of birth: Nebaioth, Ishmael's firstborn; then Kedar, Adbeel, Mibsam, 14 Mishma, Dumah, Massa, 15 Hadad, Tema, Jetur, Naphish, and Kedemah. 16 These names of Ishmael's heirs are also the names of the twelve tribal rulers, according to their settlements and encampments. 17 Ishmael lived 137 years when he breathed his last and was gathered to his ancestors. 18 Ishmael's heirs dwelt on the land from Havilah to Shur, east of Egypt on the way to Asshur. Ishmael dwelt to the east of his brothers.

25:19–37:1

*t*hese are the generations of Abraham's son Isaac.

Isaac was the son of Abraham. 20 At the age of forty Isaac married Rebecca, daughter of Bethuel the Aramean from Paddan-aram, and sister of Laban the Aramean.

21 Isaac prayed to Our God on behalf of Rebecca, for they had no children. God listened to the prayers and Rebecca conceived. 22 The babies in her womb struggled with each other. Rebecca said, "If this is the way it is to

be, why go on living?" She asked for divine guidance and ²³ Our God said to her,

> "Two nations are in your womb,
>> two tribes in your belly who will be rivals.
> One will be stronger than the other,
>> and the older will serve the younger."

²⁴ When the time came for her to deliver, she gave birth to twin boys. ²⁵ The first to enter the world was very ruddy, and had so much hair on his body that he looked as if he was wearing a fur coat. So they named him Esau, "Rough One." ²⁶ When the second came out, he was grasping Esau's heel, so they named him Jacob, "Heel-Grabber."* Isaac was sixty years old when Rebecca delivered the twins.

²⁷ The children grew up. Esau became a skilled hunter and enjoyed the open country, while the quiet Jacob preferred to stay at home. ²⁸ Isaac, who especially enjoyed wild game, favored Esau while Rebecca favored Jacob.

²⁹ One day, when Jacob was cooking a stew,** Esau came in from hunting, famished. ³⁰ He said to Jacob, "I'm starving—let me have some of the red stuff, that red stew." This is why he was also called Edom, "Red One."

³¹ Jacob replied, "Not until you sell me the rights you own from being firstborn."

³² Esau replied, "Here I am ravenous for food. What good is my birth-right to me now?"

³³ Jacob said, "Swear to me first!"

So Esau swore to Jacob and sold his birthright. ³⁴ Only then did Jacob give Esau some bread and the lentil stew. He ate and drank, then got up and left. This is how little Esau valued his birthright.†

26:1 Around this time the land was struck with famine—not the famine that struck in Abraham's time—and Isaac moved back to the territory of Abimelech, ruler of the Philistines at Gerar.

---

* Yaakov, the Hebrew form of the name Jacob, may have originally meant "May God Protect," but the popular reinterpretation, "Heel-Grabber," implies deceit—someone who intentionally trips others. Jacob fulfills the Trickster archetype much the way Coyote does in Native American stories. Indeed, the Trickster is a prevalent theme in *Genesis* and throughout Jewish literature. Often it is both an expresion of the Jewish sense of humor, and an adaptive response of a persecuted people.

** The Hebrew phrase connotes plotting. Jacob is "cooking up something," or "stirring up" trouble.

† It is interesting to note that the food for which Esau, the hunter, sells his birthright is the food not of the hunt, but of the plowed land—another echo of the tension between the agriculturists and the hunter-gatherers, seen first in the enmity between Cain and Abel.

² Our God appeared to Isaac and said, "Do not go down into Egypt. I say to you: stay here and live in this land. ³ Stay in this land and I will dwell with you and bless you. I will give all this land to you and your descendants, to fulfill the oath which I swore to Abraham. ⁴ I will make your descendants as numerous as the stars in the heavens. I will give your descendants all these lands. All the nations of the world will be blessed through your descendants, ⁵ for Abraham obeyed me and kept my charge, my commandments, my statutes and my laws."

² So Isaac stayed in Gerar. ⁷ When the men of Gerar inquired about Rebecca, he told them they were brother and sister.* He was afraid that if it was known she was his wife, he could be murdered because of her, because she was very beautiful.

⁸ Now when they had been there for some time, Abimelech the ruler, peering out the window, spied Isaac and Rebecca laughing and cavorting with one another. ⁹ The ruler summoned Isaac and said, "So she is your spouse after all! Why did you say she was your sister?"

Isaac replied, "I feared for my life because of her!"

¹⁰ Enraged, Abimelech said, "What have you done to us! What if one of us had lain with her? You would have brought guilt upon us!" ¹¹ Abimelech warned all the people that whoever harmed this woman or this man in any way would be put to death.

¹² Isaac sowed grain on the land and reaped a hundred times the amount of seed he sowed. ¹³ Our God blessed Rebecca and Isaac, and they prospered tremendously until they were exceedingly wealthy. ¹⁴ Rebecca and Isaac had flocks of sheep, herds of oxen, and a large household of attendants, and the Philistines grew envious. ¹⁵ They filled with dirt the wells that Abraham's workers had dug in his day. ¹⁶ Finally Abimelech said to Rebecca and Isaac, "We want you to leave. You now outnumber us."

¹⁷ So Rebecca and Isaac left, and settled in the valley of Gerar. ¹⁸ Their workers reopened the wells that had been dug there in the time of Abraham, which the Philistines filled in after Abraham died, and he restored their original names. ¹⁹ Isaac's workers dug in the valley and discovered another well of fresh water, ²⁰ but the shepherds dwelling there claimed the water as theirs. They called the well Esek, "Bickering," for they disputed with him. ²¹ The workers dug another well, and this incited yet another quarrel. ²² Isaac moved again and dug still another well, which was not

---

* Like father, like son! Abimelech has already been stung by that ruse once; he's not about to fall for it again, which perhaps explains his anger in verse 10 and his hostility in verse 16.

disputed. So he called it Rehoboth, "Space," saying, "Now Our God has given us space so that our people can prosper on the land."

²³ From there Isaac went up to Beersheba. ²⁴ That same night God appeared to him and said, "I am the God of your father Abraham. Don't be afraid, for I am with you. I will bless you, and you will increase the number of your descendants for the sake of my obedient Abraham." ²⁵ Isaac built an altar there and invoked the Name of Our God. He then pitched his tent there, and had the workers dig a well.

²⁶ Abimelech came to Isaac from Gerar with his advisor Ahuzzath and the army commander Phicol. ²⁷ Isaac asked them, "Why do you come here, after you were so hostile to me and expelled me?"

²⁸ They answered, "We now are convinced that Your God is with you. We wish to have a formal treaty between us, to bind us together with an oath and a pact—²⁹ that you will do us no wrong, just as we have never harmed you, and as we let you leave in peace. Your God has blessed you."

³⁰ So Isaac set up a huge banquet for them, and they feasted and drank. ³¹ Early the next morning the two parties swore their oath. Then the visitors departed in peace.

³² That same day Isaac's well diggers came to tell him, "We have struck water!" ³³ Isaac named the well Sheba, and to this day the name of the place is called Beersheba—"Well of Sheba."

³⁴ Esau, in his fortieth year, married two Hittite women: Judith, the daughter of Beeri the Hittite, and Basemath, the daughter of Elon the Hittite. And that brought bitterness of spirit to Rebecca and Isaac.

27:1 When Isaac was so old that his eyesight had failed, he summoned his older child Esau and said, "My child!"

"Here I am," answered Esau.

² Then Isaac said, "As you can see, I am so old that I could die at any time. ³ Take your gear, your quiver and bow, and go out into the country and hunt me some game. ⁴ Prepare a tasty dish for me, the kind I like, and bring it to me to eat, and I will give you my special blessing before I die."

⁵ Rebecca overheard the conversation while Isaac was talking to Esau. So when Esau left for the wilds to hunt for game for Isaac, ⁶ she said to Jacob, "I just overheard Isaac tell Esau, your brother, ⁷ 'Bring me some game and make a tasty dish for me to eat. I intend to bless you in Our God's presence before I die.' ⁸ Now listen closely, Jacob, and do what I tell you. ⁹ Go to the flock and bring me two choice kids, and I'll cook them especially for Isaac. ¹⁰ You then take it to your father so that he will give you his blessing before he dies."

¹¹ Jacob said to Rebecca, "But Esau is hairy, and I am smooth-skinned. ¹² What if Isaac touches me? I'll be a trickster in his eyes, and I'll bring down a curse on myself instead of a blessing."

¹³ Rebecca answered, "Let your curse fall on me, my son. Now do as I say—go fetch the kids." ¹⁴ So Jacob fetched the kids and gave them to Rebecca, and she prepared a delicacy, just as Isaac liked it. ¹⁵ Then Rebecca took Esau's clothes, the best clothes she could find in the house, and gave them to her younger son Jacob to wear; ¹⁶ then she took the skins of the young goats and covered his hands and the hairless parts of his neck. ¹⁷ Then she handed her younger son Jacob the tasty dish and the bread she had prepared, and Jacob carried the tasty dish and the bread to Isaac.

¹⁸ Jacob said, "Father!"

"Here I am," replied Isaac. "Which of my sons are you?"

¹⁹ "I am Esau, your firstborn," Jacob replied. "I have done as you told me. Here, sit up and eat some of the game, so that you may give me your special blessing."

²⁰ "How did you find it so quickly, my child?" asked Isaac.

Jacob replied, "It was the Most High God, your God, who let things turn out in my favor."

²¹ Isaac told Jacob, "Come closer, then, and let me touch you, so I can tell if you really are Esau or not."

²² Jacob moved close to Isaac, who touched him. "The voice is Jacob's," said Isaac, "but the hands are Esau's." ²³ Isaac was confused, because Jacob's hands were hairy like Esau's, and in the end Isaac gave Jacob his blessing.

²⁴ "Are you really Esau?" Isaac asked.

Jacob replied, "I am."

Isaac said, ²⁵ "Then bring me the game to eat, and I will give you my blessing." Jacob took Isaac the game to eat and some wine to drink. ²⁶ Then Isaac said, "Come closer, Esau, and kiss me." ²⁷ Jacob approached Isaac and kissed him on the cheek; and when Isaac smelled Esau's scent on the clothes, he gave Jacob his blessing.

Isaac said:

> "The scent of my heir
>   is like the smell of a fertile field
>   blessed by Our God.
> ²⁸ May God give you dew from heaven
>   and the richness of the earth,
>   an abundance of grain and wine!
> ²⁹ May nations serve you
>   and peoples bow down before you!

Rule over your brothers and sisters,
  and let your mother's children bow down before you!
Cursed are those who curse you;
  blessed are those who bless you!"

³⁰ When Isaac finished the blessing, Jacob left his father's presence—just as Esau was returning from his hunting. ³¹ He too had prepared a tasty dish which he took to Isaac, saying, "Isaac, sit up and eat the tasty dish I have prepared for you, so that you may give me your blessing."

³² "Who are you?" Isaac asked.

"I am Esau, your firstborn."

³³ Isaac, trembling greatly, said, "Then who was it that hunted game and brought it to me? I ate it just before you came in from hunting, and I blessed him! Now that blessing must remain on him!"

³⁴ When Esau heard this, he cried bitterly and loudly. "Father, bless me too!" he said.

³⁵ Isaac said, "Your brother came deceitfully and took your blessing."

³⁶ "He isn't called 'Heel-Grabber' for nothing!" said Esau. "This isn't the first time he has deceived me. He usurped my right as the firstborn, and now he robs me of my blessing. But do you have no blessing for me?"

³⁷ Isaac replied, "I have made Jacob elder over you and set all his sisters and brothers under him. I provided him with wine and grain. What can I give you, Esau?"

³⁸ Esau said, "Do you have only one blessing? Bless me as well, father!" and Esau wept loudly.

³⁹ Isaac replied to Esau,

"Your dwelling place must be far from the earth's riches,
  far from the heaven's dew above.
⁴⁰ You will live by your sword,
  and you will serve Jacob.
But the time will come
  when you will brandish that sword,
  and you will tear Jacob's yoke from your neck."

⁴¹ Esau hated Jacob because of the blessing Isaac had given him. He thought, "It won't be long before we will be mourning Isaac. Then I will kill Jacob."

⁴² When Rebecca learned what Esau was planning, she called Jacob, "Esau is making plans to murder you. ⁴³ Now, Jacob, listen to me: Leave at once for Haran, where my brother Laban lives. ⁴⁴ Stay there for a few days until Esau's anger cools. ⁴⁵ When his anger turns away from you and he

forgets what you did to him, I will send word for you to return. Why should I lose both of you on the same day?"

⁴⁶ Then Rebecca said to Isaac, "I am wearied to death of these Hittite women that Esau married. If Jacob marries a Hittite woman like one of these, one of the women of this country, my life will not be worth living."

28:¹ So Isaac called Jacob to him and blessed him, and charged him with these words: "You must not marry a Canaanite woman. ² Go immediately to Paddan-aram, to the house of Bethuel, your mother's father; find a spouse there among the daughters of Laban, your mother's brother. ³ May the Breasted One bless you; may God make you fruitful and increase your descendants until they become a family of nations. ⁴ May God give to you and to your offspring the blessing given to Abraham, that you may possess the land of your sojournings, the land that was given to Abraham." ⁵ Then Isaac dismissed Jacob, and Jacob went to Paddan-aram to Laban, begot of Bethuel the Aramean, who was the brother of Rebecca, the mother of Jacob and Esau.*

⁶ Esau learned that Isaac had given his farewell blessing to Jacob and sent him to Paddan-aram to find a spouse; that Jacob had been forbidden to marry a Canaanite woman; ⁷ and that he had obeyed his parents and gone to Paddan-aram. ⁸ Moreover, learning that his parents did not like Canaanite women, ⁹ Esau went to Ishmael, and, in addition to his other spouses, married Mahalath, the sister of Nebaioth and daughter of Abraham's son Ishmael.

¹⁰ Jacob left Beersheba and set out for Haran. ¹¹ When he reached a certain place, he passed the night there. He took a rock and used it for a headrest and lay down to sleep there. ¹² During the night he had a dream: there was a ladder, standing on the ground with its top reaching to heaven; and messengers of God were going up and coming down the ladder. ¹³ Our God was there, standing over him, saying, "I am Your God, the God of Sarah and Abraham, and the God of Rebecca and Isaac. ¹⁴ Your descendants will be like the specks of dust on the ground; you will spread to the east and to the west, to the north and to the south, and all the tribes of the earth will bless themselves by you and your descendants. ¹⁵ Know that I am with you. I will keep you safe wherever you go, and bring you back to this land; I will not desert you before I have done all that I have promised you."

---

* The younger son has already begun to supersede the elder, as seen from the order in which they are now listed.

¹⁶ Then Jacob woke and said, "Truly, Our God is in this place, and I never knew it!" ¹⁷ He was filled with trembling and said, "How awe-inspiring this place is! This is nothing less than the house of God; this is the gate of heaven!" ¹⁸ Jacob rose early the next morning, and took the stone he had used as a headrest and set it up as a monument, and anointed it with oil. ¹⁹ Jacob named the place Bethel—"House of God"—though before that, the town was called Luz.

²⁰ Jacob then made this vow: "If you go with me and keep me safe on this journey which I am making, and give me bread to eat and clothes to wear, ²¹ and if I return home safely to my parents' house, you will be my God. ²² This stone that I have set up as a memorial pillar will be a place of worship, and I promise to give back to you one tenth of everything you give me."

29:1 Jacob continued his journey, and headed to the land of the eastern tribes. ² He arrived at a well in a field that had three flocks of sheep lying beside it, for the well provided water to the sheep. A huge stone covered the mouth of the well. ³ When all the flocks were gathered there, the shepherds would roll the stone off the mouth of the well to water the flocks, and then they would replace the stone over the mouth of the well.

⁴ Jacob asked the shepherds, "Friends, where are you from?"

They replied, "We are from Haran."

⁵ He asked if they knew Laban, the heir of Nahor.

They answered, "Yes, we do."

Jacob asked, "Is he well?"

They answered, "Yes, he is. There's his daughter Rachel coming with his sheep."

⁷ Jacob said, "But look, it's broad daylight. This is not the time to bring the sheep in. They should be watered and taken back to their pastures."

⁸ They said, "We can't do that until all the shepherds gather here to remove the stone from the mouth of the well. Only then can we water our flocks."

⁹ While he talked to them, Rachel arrived with Laban's sheep, which she tended. ¹⁰ The moment Jacob saw Rachel, daughter of Laban, his mother's brother, with her sheep, he went to the well, removed the stone and watered Laban's sheep. ¹¹ Then he kissed Rachel, and he was moved to tears. ¹² When he told her he was Rebecca's son and was related to her father, Rachel ran to tell Laban what had happened.

¹³ As soon as Laban learned about Jacob, Rebecca's son, he ran to the well, and embraced and kissed Jacob, and welcomed him to their house. Jacob told Laban of all that had happened, ¹⁴ to which Laban replied, "Truly, you are my flesh and blood!"

¹⁵ When Jacob had been with them for a month, Laban said, "Why do you work for me without wages just because we are related? Tell me your worth, and I'll hire you."

¹⁶ Now Laban had two daughters: the older one was Leah, and the younger one was Rachel. ¹⁷ Leah was near-sighted; but Rachel was lovely and graceful, and ¹⁸ Jacob was in love with her. He said, "I will work for seven years for the hand of your younger daughter, Rachel."

¹⁹ Laban answered, "I would rather that she marry you than give her hand to another. I accept this offer."

²⁰ So Jacob worked for seven years for the right to marry Rachel, but to him it felt as if it were a few days—that was how much he loved Rachel. ²¹ When seven years were up, Jacob said to Laban, "I have worked for you for seven years. Let me now marry Rachel."

²² So Laban brought together all the local people for a wedding feast, and there was a great deal of drinking. ²³ That night, however, he brought his daughter Leah to Jacob, and Jacob slept with her. ²⁴ Laban also gave Leah his maid Zilpah, to attend her that night.

²⁵ In the morning Jacob woke up—and it was Leah beside him! Jacob said to Laban, "What is this you have done to me? Didn't I work for you for seven years for Rachel's hand? Why have you deceived me?"

²⁶ Laban answered, "It is not our custom here to let the younger child marry first. ²⁷ Finish this wedding week with the elder, and I will let you marry the younger for another seven years' work." ²⁸ Jacob agreed to finish the wedding week with Leah.

When the week was finished, Laban allowed Rachel and Jacob to marry. ²⁹ And Laban assigned his maid Bilhah to Rachel. ³⁰ So Jacob lay with Rachel too, and he loved her more than Leah. Then Jacob worked for Laban seven more years.

³¹ Seeing that Leah was unloved, Our God granted her a child, while Rachel remained childless. ³² Leah conceived and gave birth to a son. She named it Reuben—"See, a Son!"—for she said, "God saw my humiliation, but now Jacob will love me." ³³ She conceived a second time, saying, "Our God, hearing that I am unloved, gave me this child too," so she called it

Simeon, "Hearing." ³⁴ She conceived again. She said, "Now that I have given Jacob three sons, surely he will become attached to me," so she called the child Levi, "Joining." She conceived a fourth time saying, "This time I will praise Our God," so she named it Judah, "Praise." This was her last child.

30:1 Rachel was unhappy that she had no children, and she became deeply jealous of her sister and complained to Jacob, "Give me children before I die!"

² Jacob grew angry and replied, "Am I in the place of God, the One who denies you children?"

³ Rachel replied, "Let Bilhah, my maid, lie with you, so that she will bear children, and through her I too will have a growing family." ⁴ Then Bilhah went to Jacob, and he slept with her. ⁵ She conceived and gave birth. ⁶ Then Rachel said, "God has given me justice—God has heard my plea." So she named the child Dan, "Justice." ⁷ Rachel's maid Bilhah conceived again. ⁸ Rachel said, "I struggled mightily with my sister, and I have prevailed." So she named the child Naphtali, "My Struggle."

⁹ Now when Leah stopped bearing children, she took Zilpah, her maid, to Jacob, ¹⁰ and Zilpah bore Jacob a son. ¹¹ Leah said, "Good fortune has come my way," and so she named the child Gad, "Fortune."* ¹² Zilpah gave birth again, ¹³ and Leah said, "I am so happy, and the women will see that I am happy," and so she named this child Asher, "Happiness."

¹⁴ One day during the wheat harvest Reuben went out into the open country to gather plants that had aphrodisiac powers, and brought them to his mother Leah. Rachel asked Leah for some of Reuben's plants, ¹⁵ but she replied, "Isn't it enough that you took away my husband? Would you take away Reuben's plants, as well?"

"Very well," Rachel replied, "Let Jacob sleep with you tonight—in exchange for Reuben's aphrodisiac plants."

¹⁶ As Jacob came in from the fields, Leah went out halfway to meet him. "You must sleep with me tonight, for I hired you in exchange for Reuben's aphrodisiac plants." Jacob slept with her that night, ¹⁷ and God answered Leah's prayer, for she conceived and bore Jacob another child. ¹⁸ Leah said, "God has paid me my wages, because I gave my worker to Jacob." So she named the child Issachar, "Wages." ¹⁹ Leah conceived once more and bore a sixth child. ²⁰ She said, "God has given me a precious gift. Now Jacob will honor me for I have given him six heirs." She named him Zebulun, "Hon-

---

* "Gad" can also mean "Troop"; Leah may be saying, "A troop is coming!"— an exclamation perhaps in response to severe labor pains.

ored." ²¹ Some time later she gave birth to a daughter, and the daughter she named Dinah, "Justice."

²² Then God took note of Rachel, and listening to her, opened her womb. ²³ She conceived and gave birth to a child saying, "God has removed my disgrace." ²⁴ She named him Joseph,* saying, "May Our God add another child to me."

²⁵ After Rachel gave birth to Joseph, Jacob went to Laban, saying, "Let me leave this place so that I can return to my country. ²⁶ Let me take my spouses and my children, for whom I have worked for you, and I will be on my way. You know very well the work I have done for you."

²⁷ Laban said, "Yes, I have prospered through you, and God has blessed me through you, too. ²⁸ What do I owe you?" Laban asked. "I will pay whatever you say."

²⁹ "You know how I served you," replied Jacob, "and how your livestock prospered under my care. ³⁰ The little you had when I came has grown abundantly, and Our God has blessed you wherever I turn. But now it is time to provide for my own family."

³¹ Laban asked, "Then what do I owe you?"

"Not a thing," Jacob replied. "When I return, I will again tend your livestock and be in charge of them, if you will do this: ³² let me go through the herds today and pick from them every speckled and spotted sheep, all the black lambs, and every spotted or speckled goat. That will be my payment. ³³ My honesty will speak for itself on a future day: when you come to look at those that I have taken, you'll be able to see at a glance what I have; you'll know that any goat among mine that is not speckled or spotted, and any lamb that is not black, has been stolen."

³⁴ Laban replied, "Agreed. Let it be as you say."

³⁵ But later that same day Laban removed all the male goats that were spotted or speckled and all the female goats that were spotted and speckled and all the black lambs, and turned them over to his sons.

³⁶ Immediately thereafter, he went on a three-day journey. He wanted to put as much distance as possible between himself and Jacob.

All the time Laban was doing this, Jacob was tending Laban's herds. ³⁷ Aware of Laban's deceit, Jacob took fresh-cut branches from poplar, almond, and plane trees, and stripped off pieces of the bark to expose the

---

* Joseph means "May God add," but also sounds like the word for "removed" in the previous verse, prefiguring his destiny as a child both lost and found.

white of the branches. ³⁸ He placed the peeled branches upright in the watering troughs so that they were directly in front of the flocks when they came to drink. He knew that some of the females that came to drink would be in heat, ³⁹ and that they would mate in front of the branches, and so give birth to young that were spotted or speckled or striped.*

⁴⁰ Jacob separated out the rams, and let the ewes mingle with those rams in Laban's herds that were striped and black. In this manner he created separate herds—with his herd growing, but Laban's maintaining its original size. ⁴¹ Whenever the stronger females were in heat, Jacob placed the branches in the troughs in front of them so that they mated before the branches. ⁴² He did not place them there for the weaker animals. By doing this the weaker animals went to Laban, and the strong went to Jacob. ⁴³ In this manner Jacob became immensely prosperous with very large herds, as well as a multitude of attendants, camels, and donkeys.

31:1 Jacob learned that Laban's sons were saying, "Jacob has taken everything that our father owned, and all of Jacob's wealth comes from Laban's possessions." ² Jacob also knew from Laban's disposition that he was no longer in Laban's favor.

³ It was at this time that God said to Jacob, "Return to the land of your ancestors and to your relatives. I will go with you." ⁴ So Jacob sent word to Rachel and Leah to come out to the pastures where the herds were, ⁵ and said to them, "I see from Laban's disposition that I am no longer in his favor; but the God of our ancestors has been with me. ⁶ You yourselves well know that I have given my best to Laban, ⁷ yet he cheated me ten times by changing my wages. But God did not let him harm me. ⁸ When Laban said, 'The speckled will be your wages,' all the herd dropped speckled young. And when Laban said, 'The spotted will be your wages, ' all the herd dropped spotted young. ⁹ In this manner God took the livestock from Laban and gave them to me.

¹⁰ "In the mating season I once had a dream in which the males mating with the females were streaked, speckled and spotted. ¹¹ Then the angel of God in the dream said to me, 'Jacob!' and I answered, 'Here I am!' ¹² It said, 'Look up and you will see that all the males that are mating with the herd are striped, speckled and spotted. For I see all that Laban is doing to you. ¹³ I am the God of Bethel, where you anointed the pillar and made your vow to me. It's time to leave this land immediately and return to your homeland.'"

---

* An old folk tradition, and an example of sympathetic magic, held that what animals see when they mate will influence the color of their offspring

¹⁴ Then Rachel and Leah spoke up: "We no longer have an inheritance in our father's house. ¹⁵ Aren't we regarded as foreigners, now that he has effectively sold us and used up the purchase price? ¹⁶ Surely all the wealth that God has taken from Laban belongs to us and to our children! So then: do now what God has told you to do!"

¹⁷ So Jacob then loaded his spouses and their children on camels, ¹⁸ and with all the livestock and all the goods he had accumulated in Paddan-aram, he set off for the land of Canaan, where Isaac had dwelt.

¹⁹ Now while Laban was out among the herds shearing, Rachel stole his household idols;* ²⁰ and Jacob outwitted Laban the Aramean by not telling him of his plans to depart. ²¹ So Jacob took all that he had and left, crossing the Euphrates and turning toward the hill country of Gilead.

²² Laban learned that Jacob had left a full three days after his departure. ²³ So he and his relatives pursued Jacob for seven days until they caught up to them in the hill country of Gilead.

²⁴ God came to Laban the Aramean in a dream that night and said, "I warn you: do not to say one word to Jacob, whether good or evil!"

²⁵ When Laban overtook Jacob's caravan they were camped in the hill country. ²⁶ Laban said to Jacob, "What are you doing? You deceived me! You carried off my daughters like prisoners of war! ²⁷ Why did you leave without letting me know? I would have sent you away with a celebration—with merriment and singing, with tambourines and lyres! ²⁸ Why did you deny me a fitting farewell to my daughters and my grandchildren? You have acted like a fool. ²⁹ I could hurt you, but the God of your ancestors told me last night, 'I warn you: do not say one word to Jacob, whether good or evil!' ³⁰ I know that you longed for your ancestors' homeland—but why did you steal my household idols?"

³¹ Jacob responded to Laban, "I left as I did because I feared you would take your daughters from me by force. ³² But the person you find in possession of your household idols will be put to death. In the presence of our sisters and brothers, look for yourself for anything of yours that is with us. You may have whatever you find." Jacob did not know that Rachel had stolen the household idols.

³³ So Laban searched Jacob's tent and Leah's tent, then the tent of their two maids, but did not find them. Then he left Leah's tent and entered Rachel's tent. ³⁴ Now Rachel had taken the household idols and put them

---

* Even though the Hebrews were monotheistic, they frequently took on the worship practices of neighboring cultures; this was a particular problem during periods of intermarriage, and is a frequent area of concern throughout the Bible.

in her camel's saddlebag, and now she sat on it. Laban rummaged all through the tent and did not find them. ³⁵ Rachel, remaining seated, said, "Please don't be angry that I can't stand up before you, father, for I am having my period." So he rummaged the more, but still did not find the idols.

³⁶ Now Jacob grew angry and took Laban to task. He said, "What wrong have I done? Have I sinned, that you pursue me like a thief? ³⁷ Here you are going through my belongings, and what have you found that is yours? Place it here before your relatives, so that they may decide between us.

³⁸ "I served you for twenty years. Your ewes and nannies never miscarried. I never ate your rams. ³⁹ When any were killed by wild beasts, I did not bring it up to you—I bore the expense myself. Yet you demanded payment from me for any animals stolen by day or by night. ⁴⁰ Heat consumed me during the day, and cold during the night. I slept little.

"For twenty years I served like this in your household. I labored for twenty years for your two daughters and six years for your flocks, and you changed my wages ten times. ⁴² If the God of my ancestors—the God of Sarah and Abraham, the Awesome One of Rebecca and Isaac—had not been with me, you most certainly would have sent me away empty-handed. God saw my plight and the calluses of my hands, and judged you last night."

⁴³ Laban replied to Jacob, "The daughters are my daughters, the children are my children, the herds are my herds. All that you see here belongs to me. What can I do here and now about my daughters, or about the children whom they bore? ⁴⁴ Come now, we will make a covenant, you and I, and may it be a witness between us."

⁴⁵ So Jacob took a huge stone and set it up as a monument. ⁴⁶ He said to his relatives, "Gather stones," and they gathered stones into a large pile, and they ate there by the pile of stones. ⁴⁷ Laban called it Yegar-Sahadutha, but Jacob called it Gal-Ed.*

⁴⁸ Laban said, "This pile of stones serves as a sign between you and me today." This is why it is called Gal-Ed, "Witness Mound." ⁴⁹ It was also called Mizpah, "Watchtower," because he said, "May Our God keep watch over us when we are away from each other. ⁵⁰ If you mistreat Rachel or Leah or if you have other spouses, even if no one is with us, remember that God witnesses between us."

⁵¹ Then Laban said to Jacob, "Take note of this pillar and this monument which I have set between us. ⁵² This pillar and this monument witness that

---

* Both names mean "Witness Mound," but Laban's is in Aramaic, a form of Hebrew that in later years became the common language in the area.

I will not go beyond this pile to your side, nor will you pass beyond this pile and this pillar to my side, either of us, to do harm. 53 May the God of Abraham and the God of Nahor—the God of our ancestors—judge between us."

Jacob swore an oath in the name of his father Isaac. 54 Then Jacob offered a sacrifice on the mountain and told his kinfolk to join in the feast. They ate the meal and spent the night on the mountain.

55 Early the next morning Laban kissed his daughters and granddaughters, and blessed them, and left for home.

32:1 As Jacob left that place, angels of God accompanied him. 2 When he saw them, he said, "This is the encampment of God." It is for this reason that the place is called Mahanaim, "Two Camps."

3 Jacob sent messengers ahead to Esau, his brother, in the Seir region, which is in Edomite territory, telling them, 4 "Say this to the honorable Esau: tell him Jacob says, 5 'I lived with Laban until now, and have acquired livestock, donkeys, sheep, goats and indentured workers. I send this message ahead of my arrival, asking for your approval.'"

6 The messengers returned to Jacob, saying, "We delivered your message to Esau, and he is coming to meet you—with 400 riders!"

7 This news greatly upset Jacob, and filled him with fear and dread. Jacob then split his caravan into two groups, and the livestock, the herds and camels as well, 8 reasoning, "If Esau comes to destroy us, at least one group could survive. "

9 Jacob then prayed, "O God of my ancestors Sarah and Abraham, the God of Rebecca my mother and Isaac my father, the God who reminded me, 'Go back to your homeland and to your kin, and I will bless you'— 10 I am unworthy of the smallest part of your constant love and the faithfulness you showed to me, your faithful one. When I originally crossed the Jordan, I had only my walking stick. Now I have grown to two caravans. 11 Please deliver me from my brother, from the clutches of Esau. For I fear that Esau is coming to attack me, and my children and their mothers as well. 12 Yet you said, 'I will make you prosper greatly, and will make your descendants like the sand of the sea, which cannot be counted because of its numbers.'"

13 Jacob spent the night there, and from his possessions he chose a gift for Esau: 14 200 female and twenty male goats; 200 ewes and twenty rams; 15 thirty female camels with their young; forty cows and ten bulls; and twenty-five female donkeys and ten male donkeys. 16 He put each herd or

flock into the hands of a drover, and told them, "Move to the front and keep a space between each herd or flock."

To the lead drover, he said, "When my brother Esau meets you and asks, 'Whom do you represent? What is your destination? Whose animals are you herding?' ¹⁸ you are to say, 'They belong to your brother Jacob, who is offering them as a gift to your honor. Jacob himself is behind us.'" ¹⁹ Jacob gave these same instructions to the second and third herds and then to all the rest of them, telling them to say the same thing to Esau when they met with him, ²⁰ and that they must add, 'Your attendant Jacob is behind us.'" Jacob reasoned, "I will put him at ease with these gifts I send on ahead, so that when I see him later, maybe he will accept me." So the gifts moved on ahead and Jacob himself spent the night in camp.

²² In the course of the night, Jacob arose, took the entire caravan, and crossed the ford of the Yabbok River.* ²³ After Jacob had crossed with all his possessions, he returned to the camp, ²⁴ and he was completely alone.

And there, someone** wrestled with Jacob until the first light of dawn. ²⁵ Seeing that Jacob could not be overpowered, the other struck Jacob at the socket of the hip,† and the hip was dislocated as they wrestled.

²⁶ Then Jacob's contender said, "Let me go, for day is breaking."

Jacob answered, "I will not let you go until you bless me."

²⁷ "What is your name?" the other asked.

"Jacob," he answered.

---

* Yabbok means "crossroads." The name is also significant in its similarity in sound to Yaakov (Jacob) and the word *yaabok*, "to wrestle or struggle."

** Literally, "a mortal." Tradition has called this mysterious stranger an angel, or God in human form. But the Hebrew in the following passage is almost completely lacking in proper names—each line of dialogue begins, "And he said," without any indication of who is speaking, a dizzying construction which gives the reader the idea that Jacob and the Other are mirror images of one another—Jacob in effect wrestling with himself, or figuratively wrestling with his twin, Esau, whom he is about to confront. Indeed, in the next chapter Jacob says of Esau, "Seeing your face is like seeing the face of God," which of course is what he names the site of the encounter in verse 30.

† "Socket"—literally, "hollow"—figuratively means power or essence; "hip," or "thigh," euphemistically refers to the genitals, and figuratively means the seat of one's being; and the word "dislocated" can also mean overpowered or alienated. So in saying that Jacob's hip was dislocated, the writer is indicating that he was struck at the center of his being, and that he was changed—losing his own power, but gaining God's.

†† The name may actually mean "God Wrestles" or "God Rules." "Overcomer of God" is a *double entendre*: God, in the form of a mysterious being, is overcome, yet Jacob himself becomes God's overcomer or valiant one. Another translation might be "Dominion-Getter." This is one of two biblical explanations for the name Israel; the other is "One Who Sees God," an etymology referred to later in *Genesis*.

²⁸ The other said, "Your name will no longer be called 'Jacob,' or 'Heel-Grabber,' but 'Israel'—'Overcomer of God'††—because you have wrestled with both God and mortals, and you have prevailed."

²⁹ Then Jacob asked "Now tell me your name, I beg you."

The other said, "Why do you ask me my name?"—and blessed Jacob there.

³⁰ Jacob named the place Peniel—"Face of God"—"because I have seen God face to face, yet my life was spared."

³¹ At sunrise, Jacob left Peniel, limping along from the injured hip. ³² That is why, to this day, the Israelites do not eat the sciatic muscle that is on an animal's hip socket, because Jacob's hip socket was struck at the sciatic muscle.

33·1 Jacob looked up and saw Esau approaching with 400 riders. So he divided the children between Leah, Rachel, and their two maids. ² He placed the maids and their children first, Leah and her children next, and Rachel and Joseph in the rear. ³ Jacob went on ahead and bowed to the ground seven times as he approached Esau.

⁴ But Esau ran to Jacob and embraced him, throwing his arms around him and kissing him. And they wept.

⁵ Esau looking at the women and children, asked, "Who are all these people?"

⁶ Jacob replied, "These are our children, which God has so graciously given us." Then the maids and children approached and bowed down. ⁷ Next came Leah and her children, who also bowed down. Last came Rachel and Joseph, who bowed down as well.

⁸ Esau asked, "What is the meaning of all your company that met me?"

"It was intended to find favor in your eyes."

⁹ He replied, "I have more than enough, my brother. Keep what is yours!"

¹⁰ Jacob insisted, "No, please! If I have found favor in your eyes, please take these gifts from my hand. Seeing your face is like seeing the face of God, and you have graciously welcomed me. ¹¹ Please accept this gift which I set here before you, for God has blessed me and I have everything." Jacob insisted so strongly that Esau accepted the gifts.

¹² Then Esau said, "It is time for us to move on. I will go with you."

¹³ Jacob said, "The children are still young, and the cows and ewes are nursing. It is better that you go on ahead, while I drive the herds at their own pace. We will lose livestock if we drive them too fast. ¹⁴ If you would,

your honor, please cross on ahead of us. We will move slowly—more to the children's pace—and we will meet up in Seir."

¹⁵ Esau said, "Please let me put some of my attendants at your disposal, to accompany you."

Jacob replied, "Why should you be so kind to me?"

¹⁶ So Esau returned to Seir, ¹⁷ and Jacob set out for Succoth, where he built a house and built shelters for the livestock. This is why the place is called Succoth—"Shelters."

¹⁸ Jacob arrived safely in the city of Shechem in Canaan on his trip home from Paddan-aram, and set up camp east of the city. ¹⁹ He purchased the land where he pitched his tent from the descendants of Hamor, who was Shechem's father, for 100 lambs. Then Jacob set up an altar there, and called it "El, the God of Israel."*

34·1 Now Dinah, the daughter of Leah and Jacob, was out visiting the women of the area ² when Shechem, begot of Hamor the Hivite, the ruler of the area, saw her, and seized her and raped her. ³ He fell deeply in love with Dinah, regretted his act and spoke tenderly to her. ⁴ So Shechem talked to his father Hamor, and said, "Arrange for me to marry her."

⁵ When Jacob learned that Dinah had been raped, his sons were in the pastures with the cattle, so he kept quiet until they came home. ⁶ Hamor, Shechem's father, came out to speak with Jacob ⁷ just as Dinah's brothers were coming in from the pastures. They were shocked and enraged and horrified when they heard the news, for in raping Dinah, Shechem had done an abominable thing in Israel—a thing that must never be done.

⁸ Hamor reasoned with them, "Shechem deeply loves Dinah. Let there be a marriage. ⁹ Let there be marriages between our daughters and your sons, and between your daughters and our sons. ¹⁰ Settle among us, and our land will be open to you. Live on it, move about freely, and acquire your own land."

¹¹ Shechem also spoke to Jacob and his sons: "Accept me favorably and I will give whatever you ask! ¹² Set the marriage gift and the dowry as high as you like. I will give whatever you ask, if only you will let me marry Dinah."

¹³ Jacob's children responded to Shechem and Hamor with cunning, for their sister had been defiled. ¹⁴ They said to them, "We cannot let our sister

---

* El, which means God or a god, is also the formal name of the Canaanite deity, represented in iconography as a bull. Here Jacob is saying that the God worshipped by the inhabitants of that land is the same God whom he reveres.

marry one who is not circumcised. This would disgrace us. ¹⁵ We will let this marriage happen only on one condition. We will consent to the marriage if you are circumcised, and every male among you too. ¹⁶ Only then will our daughters marry you, and your daughters marry us. Only then will we live among you and become one people. ¹⁷ If you don't accept this condition and accept circumcision, we will take Dinah and leave this place."

¹⁸ Hamor and Shechem accepted the offer. ¹⁹ Shechem, the most respected in Hamor's household, was circumcised immediately, for he desired Dinah greatly. ²⁰ Then Hamor and Shechem stood up before the city gate and spoke to the leaders gathered there. ²¹ "These people are friendly people. Let's let them settle our land and travel about freely. There's room enough for all of us. Let our daughters and sons marry each other. ²² There is only one condition they have set for settling among us and becoming one with us—all of our men must be circumcised just as theirs are circumcised. ²³ All their herds, livestock, and property—won't they also become ours, then? We only have to agree with them, and they will be free to live among us." ²⁴ All those at the city gate agreed with Hamor and Shechem, and all those at the city gate were circumcised.

²⁵ On the third day, while the men were still in pain, Simeon and Levi, Jacob's sons—Dinah's brothers—stole into the city with their swords, and killed all the men. ²⁶ They killed Hamor and Shechem, removed Dinah from Shechem's house, and left. ²⁷ When the other children of Jacob came upon the scene, they plundered the city because their sister had been defiled. ²⁸ They removed herds, flocks, donkeys—anything of value in the city and in the fields. ²⁹ They carried off their wealth, captured the women and children, and looted all the buildings.

³⁰ Jacob said to Simeon and Levi, "You have brought me trouble by making me odious to the people of this land, the Canaanites and the Perizzites. We are few in number, and if they join forces to attack us, I and my entire household will be destroyed."

³¹ They simply replied, "Should our sister be treated like a prostitute?"

35⁻¹ God said to Jacob, "Go now up to Bethel and settle there. When you get there, build an altar to the God who appeared to you when you fled from your brother Esau."

² Jacob said to his household and to all who were with him, "Get rid of any foreign gods among you, purify yourselves and change your clothes. ³ Then come with me; we will go up to Bethel. I am to set up an altar there to the God who answered me in the day of my distress—to the God who has been with me wherever I have gone."

⁴ Then they all turned over to Jacob their household gods and the sacred jewelry they wore in their ears. Jacob hid them under the oak at Shechem.

⁵ As they moved on, the towns along the way were so terror-stricken by God that no one pursued them. ⁶ Jacob arrived with the caravan in Luz—now called Bethel—which is in the land of Canaan. ⁷ He built an altar there and called the place "El of Bethel," because it was the place where God had appeared to Jacob as he fled from Esau.

⁸ Then Rebecca's nurse Deborah died and was buried under the oak near Bethel. Jacob called the place "Oak of Tears."

⁹ God appeared to Jacob once more when they had come home from Paddan-aram, and blessed him. ¹⁰ God said, "Your name is Jacob. Now you no longer will be called Jacob—Israel will be your name." So God called him Israel. ¹¹ God said to him,

> "I am the Breasted One.
>> Bear fruit, and increase your numbers!
> A nation—a host of nations!—will descend from you,
>> and rulers will also spring from you.
> ¹² I give you the land I gave to Abraham and Isaac;
>> I also give this land to your descendants.

¹³ Then God left the place where they met. ¹⁴ Jacob erected a pillar at the place where God spoke to him, a pillar of stone. He poured a drink offering on it, and then an offering of oil. ¹⁵ So this place where God and Jacob met, Jacob called Bethel—"House of God."

¹⁶ Then the caravan left Bethel. When they were still some distance from Ephrath, Rachel went into labor. It was a terrible labor. ¹⁷ When she was in the worst of her labor, the midwife said to her, "Don't be afraid—you will have another son." ¹⁸ As her life was slipping away—for she was dying—she named the child Ben-oni, "Son of My Woe." But Jacob called the baby Benjamin, "Son of My Right Hand."

¹⁹ Then Rachel died, and she was buried on the way to Ephrath, which is now called Bethlehem. ²⁰ Jacob set up a pillar at her grave. It is the pillar of Rachel's tomb, and it is there to this day.

²¹ Israel's caravan journeyed on, and they pitched their tents beyond the tower of Eder. ²² While Israel dwelt in that land, Reuben went to bed with Bildah, his father's concubine, and Israel learned of it.*

---

* This tiny fragment presages Reuben's fall as firstborn, which occurs later in *Genesis*. The act was symbolic, a sign both of rebellion and of a desire to attain the parent's authority.

²³ By this time, Jacob had twelve children. ²³ The children of Leah were Reuben, Jacob's firstborn; then Simeon, Levi, Judah, Issachar, and Zebulun. ²⁴ The children of Rachel were Joseph and Benjamin. The sons of Bilhah, Rachel's maid, were Dan and Naphtali. ²⁶ The children of Zilpah, Leah's maid, were Gad and Asher. These were the heirs of Jacob who were born in Paddan-aram.

²⁷ Jacob came home to his father Isaac, to the region of Mamre, to the town of Arba—now known as Hebron—where Abraham and Isaac had sojourned; ²⁸ Isaac was 180 when he died ²⁹ and was gathered to his ancestors, old and full of years. His sons, Esau and Jacob, buried him.

36₁ These are the generations of Esau—that is, Edom.

² Esau married Canaanite women—Adah, daughter of Elon the Hittite, and Oholibamah, daughter of Anah begot of Zibeon the Horite, ³ and Basemath, daughter of Ishmael and sister of Nebaioth. ⁴ Adah gave birth to Eliphaz by Esau; Basemath gave birth to Reuel; ⁵ and Oholibamah gave birth to Jeush, Jalam, and Korah. These offspring of Esau were born in the land of Canaan.

⁶ Esau took his three spouses, their daughters and sons, all the household and field workers, the cattle and livestock, and all their assets acquired while in Canaan, and he moved away from Jacob, ⁷ for their possessions were far too many for them to live near one another. The land in Canaan could not support their combined herds and flocks. ⁸ So Esau, that is Edom, moved to the hill country of Seir.

⁹ The following are the descendants of Esau, ancestor of the Edomites, in the hill country of Seir: ¹⁰ Eliphaz, begot of Esau's wife Adah; and Reuel, begot of Esau's wife Basemath. ¹¹ The offspring of Eliphaz are Teman, Omar, Zepho, Gatam, and Kenaz. ¹² Eliphaz, begot of Esau, also had a concubine named Timna, who gave birth to Amalek. So all these are descended from Esau's wife Adah. ¹³ The offspring of Reuel are Nahath, Zerah, Shammah, and Mizzah. These are descended from Basemath, Esau's wife. ¹⁴ And these are the offspring of Esau's spouse, Oholibamah, daughter of Anah, begot of Zibeon: she gave birth to Jeush, Jaalam, and Korah.

¹⁵ These are the leaders of clans descended from Esau:

The clans descended from Esau's firstborn, Eliphaz: Teman, Omar, Zepho, Kenaz, ¹⁶ Korah, Gatam, and Amalek. They are the clan leaders descended from Eliphaz in Edom. They are descended from Adah.

¹⁷ The clans descended from Esau's heir Reuel: Nahath, Zerah, Shammah, and Mizzah. They are the clan leaders descended from Esau's spouse Basemath.

¹⁸ These are the clans descended from Esau's wife Oholibamah: Jeush, Jalam, and Korah. They are the clan leaders descended from Oholibamah, daughter of Anah, Esau's wife.

¹⁹ All these, then, are offspring of Esau—that is, Edom—and these are their clans.

²⁰ The offspring of Seir, the Horite who originally inhabited the land: Lotan, Shobal, Zibeon, Anah, ²¹ Dishon, Ezer, and Dishan. They are the clan leaders of the Horites, the offspring of Seir in Edom.

²² The heirs of Lotan were Hori and Hemam. Lotan's sister's name was Timna.

²³ These are the heirs of Shobal: Alvan, Manahath, Ebal, Shepho, and Onam.

²⁴ These are the heirs of Zibeon: Aiah and Anah. Anah is the one who found hot springs in the wilderness while tending donkeys for Zibeon. ²⁵ The offspring of Anah are Dishon, and Oholibamah daughter of Anah. ²⁶ The offspring of Dishon are Hemdan, Eshban, Ithran, and Cheran.

²⁷ There are the heirs of Ezer: Bilhan, Zavan, and Akan. ²⁸ The heirs of Dishan are Uz and Aran.

²⁹ These, then, are the clan leaders descended from the Horites: Lotan, Shobal, Zibeon, Anah, ³⁰ Dishon, Ezer, and Dishan. These are the leaders descended from the Horites according to their clans in the hill country of Seir.

³¹ These were the rulers who reigned in Edom before the Israelites had rulers. ³² Bela begot of Beor became the ruler in Edom; the capital city was called Dinhabah. ³³ When Bela died, Jobab begot of Zerah of Bozrah, ruled the realm. ³⁴ When Jobab died he was succeeded by Husham the Temanite. ³⁵ When Husham died, Husham was succeeded by Hadad begot of Bedad, who defeated Midian in the country of Moab. Hadad ruled from the city of Avith. ³⁶ Hadad died and was succeeded by Samlah of Masrekah. ³⁷ When Samlah died, Samlah was succeeded by Saul of Rehoboth-on-the-Euphrates. ³⁸ When Shaul of Rehoboth-on-the-Euphrates died, Shaul was succeeded by Baal-hanan begot of Akbor. ³⁹ When Baal-hanan died, Baal-hanan was succeeded by Hadar, who ruled from Pau. The ruler's spouse, Mehetabel, was the daughter of Matred, who in turn was the daughter of Me-zahab.

[40] These are the names of the clan leaders descended from Esau, as found in their family records and places: Timna, Alvah, Jetheth, [41] Oholibamah, Elah, Pinon, [42] Kenaz, Teman, Mibzar, [43] Magdiel, and Iram. All are clan leaders of Edom based on their cities in the land they possessed—and Esau is the progenitor of the Edomites.

37:[1] Then Jacob took up residence in the place where Isaac had settled, the land of Canaan.

37:2–50:26

*t*hese are the generations of Joseph.

When Joseph was seventeen years old, he used to accompany his siblings, the children of Bilhah and Zilpah, Jacob's spouses, as they herded the flocks. Joseph would tattle on the others to Jacob while they tended the animals, always presenting them in a negative light.

[3] Now, Israel doted on the youth, because he was a child of his old age; he loved Joseph more than the others. And Israel gave Joseph a richly ornamented robe.*

[4] When the brothers saw that Israel loved him best, they were jealous and had nothing but words of contempt for the boy.

[5] Joseph had a dream, and when he told it to his brothers, they hated Joseph all the more. [6] Joseph had said to them, "Listen to my dream. [7] We were all out in the field binding sheaves, when all at once my sheaf straightened itself and remained standing upright, and your sheaves circled around my sheaf, bowing down as if paying homage to my sheaf."

[8] The brothers rejoined, "So you want to play the sovereign with us? Do you really intend to rule over us?"—and they hated Joseph that much more because of the dream and how he interpreted it.

[9] Then Joseph had another dream, which he told to his father and the brothers: "Listen to me, I had a second dream. In this dream the sun, the moon, and eleven stars bowed down to me."

[10] When he told them the dream, Israel scolded him. He said, "What is all this dream business? Are you saying that I, your mother, and the rest of

---

* The Hebrew is obscure. The word may mean "many-colored," "full-length," or simply "long-sleeved"—but at any rate, it is clear that the coat is a symbol of his father's favoritism. On the other hand, it is probably Joseph's own behavior as a tattletale that brought on his abuse by his brothers.

the family will bow down and pay homage to you?" ¹¹ The siblings were jealous, but Israel did not forget the incident.

¹² The brothers had gone to tend the herds at Shechem. ¹³ Israel said to Joseph, "Your brothers are tending to the herds at Shechem. I will send you to them."

Joseph replied, "I am ready."

¹⁴ Israel told Joseph to see if things were going well and to report back to him. So Joseph set off from the valley of Hebron. ¹⁵ When he arrived at Shechem ¹⁶ and was wandering in the fields in search for the herds, ¹⁷ someone asked, "What are you looking for?"

Joseph answered, "I am looking for my brothers. Can you tell me where they are tending sheep?"

¹⁷ The person said, "They have moved on. I heard them say they were going to Dothan." So Joseph left that place and caught up with the herd at Dothan.

They saw Joseph approaching in the distance, and before he reached them, they plotted to murder the lad. ¹⁹ They said to one other, "Here comes that dreamer. ²⁰ Now's our chance! Let's kill Joseph and throw his body in one of these pits. We'll say a wild animal devoured him. Then we'll see what becomes of Joseph's dreams!"

²¹ Reuben intervened and saved the boy from their hands, saying, "No bloodshed! Throwing him into a pit in the wilderness is one thing, but let's not lay a hand on him." Reuben's intention was to rescue Joseph and return him to Israel.

²³ So when Joseph came upon his brothers, they stripped him of his robe, the ornamented robe he wore, ²⁴ and picked him up and threw him into a pit. The pit was empty, and there was no water in it.

²⁵ Then they sat down to eat. As they were eating, they noticed an Ishmaelite caravan coming from Gilead, with loads of gum, balm and resin, on its way down to Egypt. ²⁶ Judah said to the others, "What is to be gained by murdering Joseph and concealing his death? ²⁷ Why not sell Joseph to these Ishmaelites? He is, after all, our flesh and blood, and in that way his blood will not be on our hands." The others agreed.

²⁸ Meanwhile, some Midianite traders passed by, and pulled Joseph out of the pit. They sold him for eight ounces of silver to the Ishmaelites, who took Joseph with them into Egypt.

²⁹ When Reuben came back to the pit to rescue Joseph, he found Joseph gone, and he tore his clothes in grief. ³⁰ Returning to the others, Reuben said, "The boy is gone! Now what will I do? What will become of me?"

³¹ So they took Joseph's robe, slaughtered a goat, and dipped the robe in the blood. ³² Then they took the ornamented robe and brought it to Israel, saying, "Look what we found! Do you recognize it? Isn't it Joseph's robe?"

³³ Israel recognized the robe. "It is Joseph's! A wild animal has devoured him. Joseph was surely ripped to pieces!" Jacob tore his clothes, dressed in sackcloth, and mourned Joseph's death for a long time. ³⁵ His daughters and sons tried to comfort Israel, but he refused to be comforted, saying, "I will go to my grave mourning for Joseph."

³⁶ Meanwhile, the Midianites had sold Joseph in Egypt to Potiphar, one of Pharaoh's court officials and captain of the guard.

38:1 It happened at about that time that Judah went south, and moved away from his brothers to stay with an Adullamite named Hirah. While there, he became attracted to Shua, the daughter of a Canaanite. He married her and knew her, ³ and she conceived and gave birth to a son whom she named Er. ⁴ She conceived again and gave birth to another son, whom she named Onan. ⁵ She conceived again and gave birth to a third son, whom she named Shelah. This took place at Kezib.

⁶ Judah found a spouse named Tamar for Er, his firstborn. ⁷ However, Judah's firstborn Er was corrupt in Our God's sight, so Our God caused Er's death.

⁸ Then Judah told Onan, "You must sleep with your brother's spouse to fulfill the duty of a brother-in-law to her.* You must raise the offspring of your brother."

⁹ Onan knew the offspring would not be his, so whenever he would lie with her, he would ejaculate on the ground to avoid begetting an offspring for his dead brother. ¹⁰ But what Onan did was bad in Our God's sight, so Our God took away his life too.

¹¹ Judah said to Er's wife, Tamar, "Remain a widow in your parent's house until Shelah is grown." Judah feared that Shelah might die like the others. So Tamar went and lived with her parents.

¹² Eventually Judah's wife, Shua, died. When Judah completed the time of mourning, he and Hiram the Adullamite went up to Timnah to supervise the sheep-shearing. ¹³ When Tamar learned that her father-in-law was visiting the sheep-shearing, ¹⁴ she removed her widow's clothes, covered her face with a veil, and sat down at the entrance to Enaim, "Two Wells,"

---

* If a man died without leaving an heir, it was the obligation of his nearest relative, usually his brother, to marry the widow and beget a son, who would then continue the lineage of the deceased family member. Onan's sin was not simply *coitus interruptus* or even masturbation, but was a betrayal of his brother, his family, and their cultural customs.

which is on the road to Timnah. She did this because even though Shelah was now grown, she had not been allowed to marry him.

15 When Judah saw her sitting there, he thought she was a temple prostitute,* for her face was veiled. 16 As Judah passed Tamar, he turned to her and said, "Let me lie with you," not realizing she was his daughter-in-law.

She answered, "What will you give me in return?"

17 Judah answered, "I will send you a young goat from my herd."

She said, "I agree, but you will have to give me a pledge until you send it."

18 "What kind of pledge do you want?" he asked.

She said, "Your seal, its cord, and the staff in your hand."

He handed them over to her, and lay with her. Tamar became pregnant. 19 She then returned home, took off her veil, and once more put on her widow's clothes.

20 Judah sent Hiram the Adullamite to take the young goat to the woman and to retrieve the pledge from her, but he could not find her. 21 He asked the people living there, "Where is the temple prostitute who was at the fork in the road to Enaim?"

22 "There was no temple prostitute around here," they answered.

22 So the Adullamite returned to Judah and reported, "I did not find her, and the locals said, 'There haven't been any temple prostitutes around here.'"

23 Then Judah commented, "Let her keep the pledge—I fear that I will be ridiculed if this gets out. After all, I kept my promise to send a young goat, but you couldn't find her."

24 About three months later Judah was told, "Tamar, your daughter-in-law, has played the wanton—she's pregnant!"

Judah said, "Bring her out! Let her be burned to death."

25 As she was being brought out, she sent a message to Judah. "I am pregnant by the man who owns these," she said. "Take note, please, who owns this seal, cord and staff."

26 Judah recognized them, saying, "She is more in the right than I, since I wouldn't let my son Shelah marry her." He did not have intercourse with her again.

27 When her time came to give birth, they discovered that she was having twins. As Tamar was in labor, one of the babies put out its hand. The midwife tied a crimson thread to its wrist, saying, "This one came out first." But when the baby drew back its hand, his brother came out, and

---

* In Canaan and throughout the Middle East, prostitute-priestesses ministered at shrines and temples as representatives of the Goddess, and were revered as healers of the sick. The word in Hebrew simply means "sacred" or "consecrated one," but was meant derogatorily.

the midwife said, "So! It was you who broke out first!" And it was named Perez, "Breaking Out." ³⁰ Then the baby with the crimson thread came out and it was named Zerah, "Crimson."

39·¹ When Joseph was taken down to Egypt by the Ishmaelites, he was sold to an official of the Pharaoh—Potiphar, a captain of the guard. ² Our God was with Joseph, so he became a success: while he lived in the Egyptian's household, ³ the official saw that Our God was with Joseph and brought him success in everything he did. ⁴ Potiphar was so impressed by what he witnessed that he put Joseph in charge of the household and made him overseer of everything he owned. ⁵ From the time Potiphar put Joseph in charge of the household and of all his holdings, Our God blessed the household of Potiphar because of Joseph. Our God blessed everything Potiphar owned, from house to fields. ⁶ So the Egyptian left everything in Joseph's hands and never worried about anything while Joseph was there, except what to eat.

Now Joseph was a handsome youth, and well-built, ⁷ and in time Potiphar's spouse noticed him and said, "Come to bed with me."

⁸ But he refused, saying, "Look, Potiphar doesn't need to worry about anything to do with the household with me here. I am entrusted with everything you and he possess. ⁹ He has made me his equal, and nothing has been withheld from me except you, for you are his wife. How could I do such a monstrous thing? I would be sinning against God to do so!" ¹⁰ And though she pursued Joseph day after day, Joseph refused to have intercourse with her, or even listen to her.

¹¹ One day when Joseph came into the house to carry out his duties, he noticed there were no workers in the household. ¹² Potiphar's spouse grabbed Joseph's loincloth, saying, "Come to bed with me!" But he left the loincloth in her hands and ran from the house.

¹³ When she saw that he had left his loincloth and fled, ¹⁴ she called for the household workers, and said, "Would you look at this! This Hebrew has come into our house to insult us! He came in to rape me, but I screamed, ¹⁵ and he panicked and ran out of the house, leaving his loincloth behind." ¹⁶ She kept the loincloth beside her until Potiphar came home. ¹⁷ She then related her version of the incident: "That Hebrew you brought us tried to rape me, ¹⁸ but as soon as I screamed for help, he left this loincloth and ran from the house!"

¹⁹ When Potiphar heard what his wife was telling him—"This is what your worker did to me!"—he was furious. ²⁰ He had Joseph thrown into prison—the prison where Pharaoh's prisoners are kept.

While Joseph was there in the prison, ²¹ Our God was with Joseph and showed him kindness, so that he soon won the favor of the warden. ²² Joseph was put in charge of the other inmates, supervising their work; whatever needed to be done, he was the one to do it. ²³ The warden trusted him so much he hardly supervised his work, because Our God was with Joseph and made him successful in all his work.

40·1 Some time later it happened that the Pharaoh's cupbearer and baker offended their ruler, the Pharaoh of Egypt. ² Pharaoh was so angry with the two, the chief cupbearer and the chief baker, ³ that he jailed them in the house of the captain of the guard, in the guardhouse where Joseph was imprisoned. ⁴ The captain of the guard assigned Joseph to them, and Joseph waited on them.

After they had been imprisoned for some time, ⁵ both of them—the cupbearer and the baker of the Pharaoh of Egypt—had a dream on the same night, but each dream had its own meaning. ⁶ When Joseph came to them in the morning, he noticed they were dejected. ⁷ He asked the two officials of Pharaoh who were in custody with him, "Why are you so downcast this morning?"

⁸ They replied, "Each of us had a dream during the night, and there is no one to interpret them for us."

Joseph said, "Don't interpretations come from God? Tell me your dreams."

⁹ So the chief cupbearer told Joseph the dream: "I saw a vine before me in my dream, ¹⁰ with three branches on it. As soon as it budded, it blossomed and its clusters ripened into grapes. ¹¹ I held Pharaoh's cup in my hand, took the grapes, squeezed them into the cup, and handed the cup to Pharaoh."

Joseph said, ¹² "Here is what the dream means: the three branches represent three days. ¹³ In three days Pharaoh will restore you to your position, and you will hand the cup to Pharaoh, just as you did when you were the ruler's cupbearer before. ¹⁴ Remember me when all is well with you, and do me this favor—mention me to Pharaoh and get me out of this place. ¹⁵ For I was forcibly taken away from the land of the Hebrews, and even here I have done nothing to deserve being put in a dungeon."

¹⁶ When the chief baker saw that Joseph's interpretation for the cupbearer was a positive one, he said to Joseph, "I, too, had a dream. I had three baskets of bread on my head. ¹⁷ The uppermost basket held all kinds of baked goods for the Pharaoh. But the birds kept eating them out of the uppermost basket."

¹⁸ Joseph said "Here's what it means: the three baskets represent three days. ¹⁹ Within three days Pharaoh will lift your head from you and hang your body on a tree, and the birds will eat the flesh off your body."

²⁰ Now on the third day, because it was his birthday, Pharaoh gave a feast for all the officials. He brought the chief cupbearer and the chief baker before the assembled officials. ²¹ The Pharaoh restored the chief cupbearer to his position, and he handed the cup to Pharaoh once again. ²² But Pharaoh hanged the chief baker, just as Joseph had prophesied.

²³ The chief cupbearer did not remember Joseph as he had promised, but forgot him.

41:1 Two full years later it happened that Pharaoh had a dream: while the ruler was standing at the edge of the Nile River, ² seven handsome, fat cows came up out of the Nile and grazed in the reed grass. ³ Shortly after this, seven gaunt and ugly cows came up out of the Nile and stood beside the first seven who were grazing in the reed grass. ⁴ Then the gaunt and ugly cows ate the handsome and fat cows. Pharaoh woke up with a start. ⁵ He fell asleep again and had a second dream: seven ears of plump and ripe corn were growing on a single stalk. ⁶ Then seven thin and blighted ears of corn, scorched by the east wind, sprouted. ⁷ And the thin ears of corn swallowed up the plump ears of corn. Then Pharaoh woke up and remembered the dream.

⁸ In the morning Pharaoh's spirit was so agitated that he sent for all the magicians and sages in Egypt. He described his dream to them, but not one could interpret it for the ruler. ⁹ Then the chief cupbearer spoke to Pharaoh: "Today I am reminded of my faults. At one time Pharaoh was so angry with some of his staff that he imprisoned the chief baker and me in the house of the captain of the guard. ¹¹ Both of us had a dream on the same night, and each dream had its own meaning. ¹² There was a young Hebrew imprisoned with us, an attendant of the captain of the guard. We told him our dreams, and the Hebrew interpreted them for us. He gave each dream its own interpretation. ¹³ His interpretations turned out exactly as the Hebrew foretold: I was restored as cupbearer, and the baker was hanged."

¹⁴ So Pharaoh called for Joseph, who was quickly released from the dungeon. When he had shaved and dressed himself in clean clothes, Joseph came in before the Pharaoh. ¹⁵ The ruler said to Joseph, "I have had a dream, and no one could interpret it for me. I have been told that when you hear a dream, you can interpret it."

¹⁶ Joseph replied, "I cannot interpret your dream. It is God who will bring peace back to Pharaoh's mind."

¹⁷ Then he said to Joseph, "In my dream I was standing at the edge of the Nile, ¹⁸ and suddenly seven handsome, fat cows came up out of the Nile and grazed in the reed grass. ¹⁹ Shortly after this seven other cows came up—gaunt and very ugly and wretched. I have never seen such unhealthy-looking cows in all of Egypt. ²⁰ The gaunt and ugly cows ate the handsome, fat cows that had come up first. ²¹ But even after they ate them, no one could tell that they had eaten. They looked just as gaunt and ugly as before. Then I woke up.

²² "I fell asleep again and this time I saw seven ears of plump and ripe corn growing on a single stalk. ²³ Then seven thin and blighted ears of corn, scorched by the east wind, sprouted, ²⁴ and the thin ears of corn swallowed up the seven ripe ears of corn. I told all this to the magicians, but there was none among them who could explain it to me."

²⁵ Joseph said to Pharaoh, "Both of Pharaoh's dreams have the same message. God has revealed to Pharaoh what is about to happen. ²⁶ The seven good cows represent seven years, and the seven good ears represent seven years. The two dreams are one dream. ²⁷ The seven gaunt and ugly cows that came up after them represent seven years. It is the same with the seven thin and blighted ears of corn scorched by the east wind. They represent seven years of famine.

²⁸ "It is as I told Pharaoh. God has shown Pharaoh what is about to happen. ²⁹ Seven years of great abundance will come to all the land of Egypt. ³⁰ After that, a seven-year famine will ravage the land, ³¹ and all the prosperity will be forgotten because of the severity of the famine. ³² The reason Pharaoh's dream has two versions is that God's mind is firm. God will make it happen soon.

³³ "Therefore, Pharaoh must select a discerning and wise person to be put in charge of the land of Egypt. ³⁴ Pharaoh must appoint overseers for the land of Egypt, and set aside one-fifth of the harvest during each of the seven years of plenty. ³⁵ They will collect this food during these good years ahead and store the grain under the authority of the Pharaoh to feed the cities— ³⁶ this food will be held in reserve for the land of Egypt, and it is to be used during the seven years of famine. This will save Egypt in the famine years."

³⁷ This plan seemed wise to Pharaoh and to all his officials. ³⁸ Pharaoh asked them, "Where can we find another person like this, who bears the spirit of a god?" ³⁹ So Pharaoh said to Joseph, "Because God has revealed all this to you, there is no one else as discerning and wise as you. ⁴⁰ You will be my chancellor, and all my people will obey your orders. Only in matters of the throne will I be above you."

⁴¹ Then Pharaoh said to Joseph, "I hereby appoint you governor of the whole land of Egypt." ⁴² Pharaoh removed the signet ring from his own finger and placed it on Joseph's finger. He then dressed Joseph in fine linen robes and placed a gold chain around his neck. ⁴³ The ruler had him ride in the chariot of the second-in-command, and attendants shouted before him, "Make way!" In this manner Pharaoh placed Joseph in charge of the whole of Egypt.

⁴⁴ Then the ruler said to Joseph, "I am Pharaoh, but without your word no one will lift a hand or a foot in all of Egypt." ⁴⁵ Pharaoh named Joseph Zaphenath-Paneah, "The God Speaks, and He Lives,"* and married him to Asenat, daughter of Potiphera, priest of On. Joseph's authority extended to all of Egypt.

⁴⁶ Joseph was thirty years old when he became chancellor under the Pharaoh, ruler of Egypt. When he left the Pharaoh, he made an inspection tour of the land of Egypt. ⁴⁷ During the seven years of plenty, the harvests were abundant. ⁴⁸ Joseph supervised the collection of the food grown in the fields in the seven years of plenty in Egypt and stored it in the cities. In each city he stored the harvested food from the fields around it. ⁴⁹ Joseph stored up huge quantities of grain, as much as the sand of the sea. It was so much that he stopped keeping records because the produce was immeasurable.

⁵⁰ Prior to the years of famine, Joseph and Asenat, daughter of Potiphera, priest of On, had two children. ⁵¹ They named the first Manasseh, "The One Who Lets Us Forget"—because, Joseph said, "God let me forget all my troubles and my former home." ⁵² The second child was named Ephraim, "Fruitful"—because, Joseph said, "God made me fruitful in the land of my suffering."

⁵³ The seven years of abundance in Egypt came to an end, ⁵⁴ and the seven years of famine began, just as Joseph had prophesied. The famine spread to every country, but in Egypt there was food. ⁵⁵ When the whole country began to feel the famine, the people cried out to Pharaoh for bread. Pharaoh told all the Egyptians, "Go to Joseph and do whatever he tells you."

⁵⁶ When the famine had spread throughout the land, Joseph opened all the granaries and rationed their supplies to the Egyptians. The famine grew worse; ⁵⁷ soon people were coming to Egypt from all over the world

---

* This Egyptian name is particularly appropriate. Because God speaks through him, Joseph lives; and because Joseph lives, so does Egypt, Joseph's family, and the people of Israel.

to buy grain from Joseph, for the famine had grown severe throughout the world.

42:1 When Jacob learned that Egypt had grain to sell, he said to the sons, "Don't just stand there staring at each other! 2 I am told there is grain in Egypt. Go down there to buy some for us. Otherwise we will die of starvation."

3 So ten of Joseph's brothers traveled down to Egypt to buy grain there. 4 Jacob did not send Joseph's brother Benjamin with the others, for he feared some harm might come to him. 5 So the children of Israel went to Egypt to buy grain, for there was famine in the land of Canaan.

6 Now as the country's governor, Joseph himself sold grain to all buyers. So Joseph's brothers came and bowed down before him, their faces to the ground. 7 Joseph saw his brothers and recognized them, but he pretended not to, and spoke harshly to them. "Where do you come from?" he demanded.

They said, "From the land of Canaan, to buy food."

8 Though Joseph recognized his brothers, they did not recognize him. 9 He recalled the dreams he had had about them. He said, "You are spies! You came here to learn where our defenses are weak!"

10 "No, sir!" they replied. "We have come to buy food. 11 We are all born of one man. We are honest people! We are not spies!"

12 "No!" Joseph maintained. "You have come to find our weaknesses!"

13 "We are twelve brothers, begot of one man, who lives in the land of Canaan. The youngest is now with our father; one other is no more," they said.

14 Joseph said to them, "I'll say it again: you are spies! 15 I will test you: as Pharaoh lives, you will not leave here unless your youngest brother comes here. 16 One of you must go and bring your brother to me. The rest will remain in prison until the truth of your words is tested, whether there is truth in you or not. No, as Pharaoh lives, you are spies!" 17 Then he put them all in prison for three days.

18 On the third day Joseph said to them, "Follow my instructions and you will live, for I am God-fearing. 19 If you have been honest, only one of your brothers needs to be confined in this prison; the rest of you may go and take the grain to relieve the famine of your families. 20 You will bring me your youngest brother. Thus your words will be verified, and you will not have to die." They agreed to this arrangement.

²¹ To one another, however, they said, "Surely we are being called to account for our brother Joseph. We saw the anguish of his heart, when he pleaded with us, yet we paid no heed, and now this anguish has come home to haunt us."

²² Reuben said, "Didn't I tell you not to wrong the boy? You didn't listen, and now we are brought to account for his blood."

²³ They did not know that Joseph understood what they had said, for he had been speaking to them through an interpreter. ²⁴ Joseph turned away from them and wept, but then turned back to them again. He selected Simeon and had him bound before their eyes.

²⁵ Joseph gave orders to fill their containers with grain, and to hide the money each had paid for the grain in their bags; then they were given provisions for their journey. When this had been done, ²⁶ they loaded the grain on their donkeys and left. ²⁷ Stopping for the night, one of them opened a sack of grain to feed the donkey, and discovered the money in the top of his pack. ²⁸ "My silver has been returned!" he said to the others. "It's here in my pack!" In panic and trembling they said to each other, "What has God done to us?"

²⁹ When they returned to the land of Canaan, they related to Jacob all that had happened: ³⁰ "The one who rules over the land there spoke harshly to us and accused us of spying on the country. ³¹ But we denied it—we told him, 'We are not spies, we are honest people. ³² We are twelve brothers begot of the same parent. One of us is no more, and the youngest is here in Canaan with you now.'

³³ "The one who rules over the land then said to us, 'This is how I will learn if you are honest or not: leave one of you with me, then take food for your starving households and go. ³⁴ But bring your youngest brother to me, and I will know that you are honest people and not spies.'"

³⁵ As they emptied their sacks they found out that each one of them had a bag of silver. They were frightened at the discovery, and so was their father.

³⁶ Jacob said to them, "You are robbing me of my children. Joseph is no more, Simeon is no more, and now you want me to let you take Benjamin. Everyone is against me."

³⁷ Then Reuben said, "You can put both of my children to death if I do not bring Benjamin back. Entrust him to me and I will return the boy to you."

Jacob said, "No, Benjamin will not go back with you! Joseph is dead and Benjamin has no brother. If the boy is harmed on this trip you are taking, you will send me with my gray hairs down to a sorrowful grave."

43:1The famine persisted in the land of Canaan, 2 and when the grain they brought up from Egypt ran out, Israel said to them, "Go back and buy more grain for us to eat."

3 Judah said to Israel, "The official there gave us a solemn warning, 'You will not be admitted into my presence if you are without your brother.' 4 If you allow our brother to accompany us, we will go down and buy food for you. 5 So if you don't let him go with us, we can't go, for the official clearly stated, 'You will not be admitted into my presence unless your brother is with you.'"

6 Israel said, "Why did you treat me so badly, telling the official you had another brother?"

They replied, "The official carefully questioned us about our family: 'Is your father alive?' and 'Do you have another brother?' We just answered the questions. How were we to know that he would tell us to bring Benjamin down there?"

8 Judah told Israel, "Let the boy come with me, and let this journey be delayed no longer so that we might save all of our lives—ours, yours, and our dependents'. 9 I will personally guarantee his safety, and you may hold me personally responsible for the boy. If I don't bring him back to you and stand him in front of you, the blame will be on me forever. 10 Indeed, if we had not wasted so much time, we could have gone and come back twice."

11 Then Israel said to them, "If it must be, do it. Take some choice fruits of our land to the official—some balsam, a little honey, some spices and myrrh, pistachio nuts and almonds. 12 Take twice as much silver, for you must return the silver that was put into your sacks. It might have been an oversight. 13 Take Benjamin, too, and return to the official at once. 14 May the Breasted One be merciful to you before the official, so that he will allow both the one you left behind and Benjamin to return with you. As for me, if I must grieve, I will grieve."

15 So they took the gifts and twice the amount of silver as before, and Benjamin, as well. They made their way to Egypt as quickly as they could and presented themselves to Joseph. 16 When Joseph saw Benjamin with them, he said to the steward of the house, "Take these people to my house, slaughter an animal and prepare a meal, for they will eat the noon meal with me."

17 The steward did as ordered and took the brothers to Joseph's house. 18 Now the brothers were frightened as they were taken to Joseph's house. They speculated, "We were brought here because of the silver put into our

bags the last time. He intends to attack us, enslave us, and seize our donkeys."

¹⁹ So they spoke to Joseph's steward when they got to the house. "We came down here the first time to buy food. ²¹ But at the place we stopped the first night we opened our bags and each of us discovered silver—the exact amount we had paid—just inside the bag. We brought it back with us this time, ²² as well as additional silver for more food. We don't know how the silver got into our bags."

²³ "It's all right," the steward said, "don't be afraid. Your God, the God of your ancestors, put the silver in your sacks. I received full payment for the grain." Then the steward released Simeon to them.

²⁴ The steward led them into Joseph's house, gave them water to bathe their feet and had their donkeys fed. ²⁵ They set out their gifts for Joseph's midday arrival, for they understood that they were to eat there together.

²⁶ When Joseph arrived, they presented him with the gifts they brought from Canaan, bowing low to the ground. ²⁷ He asked them how they were, and then inquired, "How is your father, the old one? Is he well? Is he still living?"

²⁸ They said, "Our father is alive and well." And they paid homage to Joseph, bowing low.

²⁹ Joseph looked about and spotted Benjamin, his own mother's child, and inquired, "Is this the youngest, the one you told me about?" He added, "May God be gracious to you, my boy!" ³⁰ Joseph, deeply moved by the sight of Benjamin, left quickly, and went to his private chambers to weep.

³¹ Eventually he controlled himself and washed his face, and then returned to the visitors and ordered the meal to be served. ³² They served Joseph alone at his table, the brothers at another table, and the Egyptians separately at other tables—for Egyptians find it an abomination to eat with Hebrews. ³³ When the brothers were seated before Joseph, they found their seats arranged in order of their ages, from firstborn to the youngest, and they looked at each other in amazement. ³⁴ Their portions were served to them from Joseph's table, and Benjamin's portion was five times larger than the others. So they feasted and drank heartily with Joseph.

44¹ Joseph instructed the steward, "Fill each bag with as much food as they can carry, and put the money they paid in the top of each bag. ² Then put my silver goblet in the top of the young one's bag along with the silver he paid for the grain." ³ The steward did as instructed.

⁴ At first light the brothers loaded their donkeys and set out. They had traveled only a small distance from the city when Joseph said to the steward, "Go after those Hebrews immediately, and when you reach them, ask them, 'Why did you repay good with evil? ⁵ Isn't this the cup the governor drinks with and uses for divination? What an evil thing to do!'"

⁶ When the steward caught up to the caravan, he repeated the words to them.

⁷ They replied, "Why does your governor say such things? Far be it from us to do something like this! ⁸ We even returned the silver from our homeland in Canaan that we discovered in our bags after our first trip. So why would we steal silver or gold from your chancellor's house? ⁹ Search our bags, and if any of us is guilty, he will die, and the rest of us will be indentured for life to your governor."

¹⁰ "Very well," the steward said, "let it be as you say. The one found with the silver cup comes back with us, but the rest will not be blamed."

¹¹ Each of them lowered his bag to the ground and opened it. ¹² Then the steward began searching, starting with the oldest and continuing down to the youngest. The cup was found in Benjamin's bag, ¹³ and when it was discovered, they tore their clothes in grief. Then they loaded their donkeys and returned to the city.

¹⁴ Joseph was still at home when Judah and the others arrived, and they threw themselves to the ground before the governor. ¹⁵ Joseph said, "Why have you done something like this? Don't you realize that a person such as myself discovers things by divination?"

¹⁶ Judah said, "What can we say? What can we do or say to prove our innocence? God has revealed our guilt! We are indentured to you—we ourselves, as well as the one in whose bag the silver cup was found!"

¹⁷ Joseph said, "I cannot do such a thing! Only the one in whose bag the cup was found will be indentured to me. The others, all of you, may return to your homeland in peace."

¹⁸ Then Judah approached Joseph and said, "Sir, let me have just one word with you, and do not be angry with me—you are the equal of the Pharaoh. ¹⁹ When you asked us, 'Do you have a father or another brother?' ²⁰ we replied, 'We do, we have an aged father and a younger half-brother, the child of his old age. His full brother is dead, and since he is the only child left by that mother, the aged father dotes on him.' ²¹ Then you told us, 'Bring him down to me that my eyes may look on him.' ²² Then we said to you, sir, 'The boy must stay with the father. If he leaves the father will die.' ²³ But you said to us, 'Unless the youngest brother comes back with

you, you will not come into my presence again.' ²⁴ When we returned to our father, we reported to him your words.

²⁵ "Later, our father told us to come back to you and buy some food for the family. ²⁶ So we reminded him, 'We cannot go down there; only if our youngest brother is with us can we go, for we won't be allowed to see the Egyptian official unless our youngest brother is with us.' ²⁷ Then our father said to us, 'You well know that my wife bore two sons. ²⁸ One of them has disappeared, and he surely must have been torn to pieces by wild beasts, for I have not seen him since. ²⁹ If you now take this Benjamin from me too, and some disaster befalls him, you will send me to my grave with my gray head bowed in misery.'

³⁰ "So now, if the boy is not with us when we return to our father, and if our father, whose life is bound up with the boy's life, ³¹ does not see the boy, he will die. We will have brought the gray head of our father to his death. ³² I guaranteed the safety of the lad to our father. I said, 'If I do not bring him back to you, I will bear the blame before you, father, for my whole life!' ³³ Please, then, let me remain here in your service in place of the boy, and let him return with our brothers. ³⁴ How could I return to our father if the boy does not return? No! Don't let me see the misery my father would suffer."

45:1 Then Joseph was no longer able hold back his feelings in front of his attendants, and he cried out to them, "Leave me!" So no one was present when Joseph made himself known to his brothers—² but he wept so loudly that all of his Egyptian attendants heard him, and the news of it reached the Pharaoh's palace. ³ Joseph said to his brothers, "It is I—Joseph! Is my father really still alive?" The brothers could not answer, so dumbfounded were they.

⁴ Then Joseph said to the brothers, "Come closer to me." When they had come closer he said to them, "I am your brother Joseph, whom you sold into Egypt! ⁵ Please don't rebuke yourselves for having sold me here. God sent me here ahead of you so that I could save your lives. ⁶ There has been famine in the land for two years, and for the next five years there will be no tilling and no harvesting. ⁷ But God sent me ahead of you to guarantee that you will have descendants on earth and to keep you alive as a great body of survivors.

⁸ "So it was not you who sent me here, but God! God has made me Pharaoh's chief counselor, the head of his household and governor of all Egypt. ⁹ Hurry back to our father and give him this message from Joseph: 'God has made me governor of all of Egypt. Come to me here at once! Do

not delay. ¹⁰ You will live here near me in the territory of Goshen, you, your children, your grandchildren, your flocks and herds, and all your possessions. ¹¹ I will provide for you here—for the next five years will be years of famine—so that you and your children and all that you own will be spared from destitution.'

¹² "You can see for yourselves, and so can my brother, Benjamin, that it is I who speak to you. ¹³ Report to our father about how I am honored here in Egypt, and about everything you have seen. Go quickly, now, and bring my father to me!" ¹⁴ Joseph threw his arms around Benjamin and wept, and Benjamin embraced him and wept too. ¹⁵ Then he kissed his other brothers, weeping over them as well, and then he and his brothers talked.

¹⁶ When word reached Pharaoh that Joseph's brothers had arrived, the Pharaoh and court officials were pleased. ¹⁷ Pharaoh told Joseph to tell his brothers, "Tell your brothers, 'Load your donkeys and return to the land of Canaan, ¹⁸ and bring your father and your families back to me. I will give you land with the best soil in Egypt so that you can enjoy the fat of the land.' ¹⁹ You are also charged to say to them: 'Do this: Take wagons from Egypt for your children and your spouses. Bring your father. Please come. ²⁰ Don't worry about your belongings, for the best that is in Egypt will be yours.'"

²¹ So the children of Israel did as they were instructed. Joseph provided them with wagons, by Pharaoh's orders, and furnished them with provisions for the trip. ²² To each of them he gave a set of new clothes. But to Benjamin he gave nearly eight pounds of silver and five sets of new clothes. ²³ To their father Joseph sent ten donkeys loaded with fine gifts from Egypt, and ten jennies loaded with bread and grain, and more provisions for his father's return trip. ²⁴ Then he sent them on their way, admonishing them as they left, "Don't argue along the way!"

²⁵ They set off and traveled from Egypt to their father up in the land of Canaan. ²⁶ They told him, "Joseph is alive! He is ruling over Egypt!"

Jacob was stunned; he could hardly believe what he heard. ²⁷ When he heard all that Joseph had told the others, and when he saw the wagons Joseph had sent for the return trip, his spirit soared. ²⁸ Israel said, "Yes! I believe! My son Joseph is alive. Now I must go to see him before I die."

46:1 Jacob set out with all his belongings, and when he reached Beersheba, he offered sacrifices to the God of their forebears, Rebecca and Isaac. ² God spoke to Jacob in a vision that night: "Jacob, Jacob!"

Jacob replied, "Here I am!"

God said, "I am El, the God of your ancestors. Don't be afraid to go down to Egypt, for there I will make you a great nation. ⁴ Not only will I go down to Egypt with you, I will also bring you back here after Joseph has closed your eyes."

⁵ So Jacob departed from Beersheba, and the children of Israel took Jacob their father, their wives and young ones, and filled the wagons that Pharaoh had provided for their transport. ⁶ They took with them their livestock and all the possessions they had acquired in Canaan. So Jacob and all his descendants went to Egypt. ⁷ Daughters and sons, granddaughters and grandsons—all his descendants—went with Jacob to Egypt.

⁸ These are the descendants of Jacob and his spouses who went into Egypt, led by Reuben, Jacob's firstborn:

⁹ Reuben's children, Hanoch, Pallu, Hezron, and Carmi; ¹⁰ Simeon's children, Jemuel, Jamin, Ohad, Jakin, Zohar, and Shaul, who was begot of a Canaanite woman; ¹¹ Levi's children, Gershon, Kohath and Merari; ¹² Judah's children, Er, Onan, Shelah, Perez, and Zerah, though Er and Onan had died in Canaan; Perez's children, Hezron and Hamul; ¹³ Issachar's children, Tola, Puvah, Jashub, and Shimron; ¹⁴ and Zebulun's children, Sered, Elon, and Jahleel— ¹⁵ all these grandchildren came from the sons born to Leah and Jacob in Paddan-aram, but they also had one daughter, Dinah; their daughter, sons, and grandchildren numbered thirty-three in all.

¹⁶ Then there were Gad's children, Ziphion, Haggi, Shuni, Ezbon, Eri, Arodi, and Areli; ¹⁷ Asher's children, Imnah, Ishvah, Ishvi, and Beriah, and their sister Serah; Beriah's children, Heber and Malkiel— ¹⁸ these grandchildren came from the sons born to Zilpah and Jacob; she was the maid Laban had given to his daughter Leah—bringing their total to sixteen.

¹⁹ Rachel and Jacob had two children: Joseph and Benjamin. ²⁰ Joseph and Asenat, daughter of Potiphera, priest of On, had two children, Manasseh and Ephraim, both of whom were born in Egypt. ²¹ Benjamin's children were Bela, Beker, Ashbel, Gera, Naaman, Ehi, Rosh, Muppim, Huppim, and Ard. ²² These were the descendants born to Rachel and Jacob. They came to a total of fourteen.

²³ Dan's child was Hushim. ²⁴ Naphtali's children were Jahzeel, Guni, Jezer and Shillem. ²⁵ These were the children born to Bilhah and Jacob; she was the maid whom Laban had given to his daughter Rachel. They came to a total of seven.

²⁶ So all the direct descendants accompanying Jacob into Egypt, excluding the children's spouses, numbered sixty-six; ²⁷ but with Asenat and Joseph

and their two children included, there were seventy members of Jacob's family who entered Egypt.

²⁸ Now Israel sent Judah ahead to meet Joseph in Goshen. When Judah arrived in the region of Goshen, ²⁹ Joseph hitched the horses to his chariot and rode ahead to meet Israel, his father. As soon as he saw him, he flung his arms around his father and wept for a long time in his arms. ³⁰ Israel said, "Now I can die, for I have seen with my own eyes that Joseph, my child, is still alive."

³¹ Then Joseph said to his brothers and his father's household, "I will go up and tell Pharaoh, 'My brothers' and my father's households, who formerly resided in the land of Canaan, have arrived. ³² They are shepherds who own their flocks and herds, and they have brought these flocks and herds here along with all their other possessions.' ³³ Now when the Pharaoh calls for you and asks your occupation, you are to say, 'We are keepers of livestock, and have been all our lives, as our forebears were before us.' You must say this in order to settle in Goshen, for shepherds are detested by Egyptians."

47:1 Joseph then went to Pharaoh and said, "My family have arrived from the land of Canaan, with all their possessions, including their flocks and herds. They are now in Goshen."

² Joseph chose five brothers to present to Pharaoh, ³ and Pharaoh asked them, "What is your occupation?"

"We keep livestock," they replied, "just as our ancestors did." ⁴ They said, "We have come here to live for awhile, for the famine is severe in Canaan, and our flocks and herds have no place to graze. So we ask of you, sir, to let us settle in Goshen."

⁵ Pharaoh said to Joseph, "Jacob and your brothers have come to you, ⁶ and the land of Egypt is open to you. Settle your family in its best parts, in Goshen. If among them there are some whom you know are especially skilled, place them in charge of my livestock."

⁷ Then Joseph presented Jacob to Pharaoh. Jacob greeted the ruler with a blessing.

⁸ "How old are you?" Pharaoh asked.

⁹ Jacob replied, "I have lived on this earth for 130 years—few and hard those years have been, and they are nothing compared to those of my ancestors." ¹⁰ Jacob blessed the Pharaoh once more and withdrew.

¹¹ Joseph settled the family in Egypt and did as Pharaoh had said: he gave them prime farmland, in the district of Rameses. ¹² Joseph also provided Jacob and all his family and their households with as much food as they needed.

¹³ Throughout the whole region, however, there was no food because of the severity of the famine. Egypt and Canaan wasted away because of it. ¹⁴ Joseph collected all the funds he could find in Egypt and Canaan in exchange for the grain the people purchased, and placed the funds in the Pharaoh's treasury.

¹⁵ When the funds of Egypt and Canaan ran out, the Egyptians came to Joseph. "Give us grain," they pleaded, "or we will perish before your very eyes. We have no money."

¹⁶ Joseph answered, "If your money is gone, give me your livestock and I will give you food." ¹⁷ So they brought their livestock to Joseph, who provided them food in exchange for their horses, sheep, goats, cattle, and donkeys. And he got them through the year with food in exchange for their livestock.

¹⁸ When that year ended, the people came to him once more, saying, "We cannot hide from you that our money is gone and our livestock is already in your hands. The only thing left is our lives and our land. ¹⁹ Must we perish before your very eyes, we and our land? Take us and take our land in exchange for food. We and our land will be bonded to Pharaoh. Give us corn to survive on; otherwise, we will die, and our land will turn into desert."

²⁰ So Joseph took possession of all the land of Egypt for Pharaoh. One and all, the Egyptians sold their land because of the severity of the famine. ²¹ Once the land belonged to the ruler, Joseph reduced the people to indenture from one end of Egypt to the other. ²² He did not purchase the land of the priests, for they received a stipend from Pharaoh and had enough food from what the ruler gave them, and so they did not have to sell their land.

²³ Then Joseph said to the people, "Now that I have purchased your land for Pharaoh, I will provide you with seed. Plant the land. ²⁴ When you reap the corn, you will give one-fifth of the harvest to Pharaoh. The other four-fifths will be yours for seed for planting and for food for yourselves, your households and your children."

²⁵ "You have saved our lives," the people said. "May we find favor in your eyes! We will serve the Pharaoh."

²⁶ Then Joseph made it a law in Egypt that one-fifth of the crop goes to the ruler—a law that is still in force to this day. Only the priests were exempt from this law.

²⁷ Thus the Israelites settled in Egypt in the region of Goshen. They gained possession of the land and various holdings, and their families grew and prospered. ²⁸ Jacob lived in Egypt for seventeen years, to the age of 147.

²⁹ As the time of his death drew near, Israel called for Joseph and said, "If I have favor in your sight, put your hand under my thigh and swear that you will be loyal and faithful to me: do not bury me in Egypt! ³⁰ Once I am at rest with my forebears, take my body up from Egypt and bury me with my ancestors."

"I will do as you say," Joseph replied.

³¹ "Swear to me," Israel said. Joseph swore to him, and Israel laid his head on the bed.

48¹ Some time later Joseph was told that Jacob was ill. With his two sons, Manasseh and Ephraim, Joseph went to Jacob. ² When he was told, "Joseph is here to see you," Israel gathered his strength and sat up in bed.

³ Jacob said to Joseph, "The Breasted One appeared to me at Luz in the land of Canaan and blessed me. ⁴ God told me, 'I will make you bear fruit and I will increase your descendants until they become a multitude of nations, and I will give this land to your descendants to have forever.'

⁵ "Now then, your two children born to you in Egypt before I came here will be considered as mine. Ephraim and Manasseh will be mine just as Reuben and Simeon are mine. ⁶ The children born to you after them will be yours, and they will be recorded under the names of their siblings for the purpose of their inheritance. ⁷ Up in Canaan when I was returning from Paddan-aram—there was still a long way to travel to Ephrath—your mother Rachel died. We buried her beside the road to Ephrath, that is, Bethlehem."

⁸ Then Israel saw Joseph's children and he asked, "Who are these?"

⁹ "They are my sons, given to me by God," Joseph replied.

Then Israel said, "Bring them to me so I may bless them."

¹⁰ Now Israel's vision was cloudy in his old age, and he could hardly see. So Joseph brought the two of them up close, and Jacob kissed them and embraced them. ¹¹ Israel said to Joseph, "I had given up hope of ever seeing your face again. Now God allows me to see your two children as well!"

¹² Joseph took them from Israel's knees, and then bowed down with his face to the ground. ¹³ As Joseph lifted the two—Ephraim with his right

hand so that he was on Israel's left, and Manasseh with his left hand so that he was on Israel's right—and brought them closer to him. ¹⁴ But Israel reached out his right hand and put it on Ephraim's head, who was the younger, and crossing his arms put his left hand on Manasseh's head, who was the firstborn. ¹⁵ Then he blessed Joseph saying,

> "May the God in whose presence
> my ancestors Sarah and Abraham
> and Rebecca and Isaac walked,
> the God who shepherded me
> all the days of my life,
> ¹⁶ the angel who rescued me
> from all misfortune,
> bless these two children;
> let my name live in and through them,
> and the names of my ancestors
> Sarah and Abraham
> and Rebecca and Isaac;
> let them grow into a great people
> on this earth."

¹⁷ When Joseph saw that Israel was placing his right hand on Ephraim's head, it distressed him, and he took Israel's hand to move it from Ephraim's head to Manasseh's. ¹⁸ Joseph said to Israel, "No, my father, this one is the firstborn. Put your right hand on his head."

¹⁹ Israel refused, saying, "I know, Joseph, I know. Yes, he also will become a people, and he will be famous. Nevertheless, the younger will become greater than the firstborn, and his descendants will become a multitude of great nations." So Israel blessed them that day, saying,

> "When a blessing is spoken in Israel
> people will use your name, saying,
> 'May God make you
> like Ephraim and Manasseh.'"

So Israel put Ephraim before Manasseh.

²⁰ Then Israel said to Joseph, "I am dying, but God will be with you and bring you back to the land of your ancestors. I give to you one portion of land more than to your siblings—the portion I took from the Amorites with my sword and my bow."

49:1 Then Jacob called all his children together and said, "Gather round so I can tell you what will happen to you in the future:

2 Gather and listen, heirs of Jacob—
    listen to me!

3 Reuben, my firstborn,
    my life and the firstfruit of my energy,
excelling in honor,
    excelling in might,
4 wild as a flood,
    you will no longer excel—
for you crept into my bed,
    and you defiled my couch.

5 Simeon and Levi, such brothers!
    their bonds of kinship are weapons of violence.
6 May I not enter their counsel;
    may I not join their assembly,
for they have killed men in their anger,
    and tortured oxen on a whim.
7 Cursed be their anger for its viciousness;
    cursed be their rage for its ruthlessness!
I will divide them in Jacob;
    I will scatter them in Israel.

8 Judah, your sisters and brothers will praise you;
    your hand will grip the neck of the enemy;
    your parents' children will bow down to you.
9 You are a lion's cub, Judah,
    fresh from the kill, my son.
He crouches and stretches out like a lion—
    like a lioness no one dares to disturb.
10 The scepter will never leave Judah,
    nor the ruler's staff from between his feet,
so that tribute will come to him*
    and the obedience of the people will be his.
11 You tether your donkey to the vine,
    your colt to the choice vine,

---

* The Hebrew is difficult; as one commentator puts it, "The phrase is an old and unsolved problem for interpreter and translator alike." The phrase literally reads, "until he comes to Shiloh," or possibly, "until Shiloh comes." But an old Midrash, following Isaiah 18:7, reads *shiloh* as two words, *shai loh*, "tribute to him," or "belongs to him." This has caused some Christian translators to render the passage, "until the coming of the one to whom it belongs, the one the nations will obey."

and wash your garments in wine,
    your robes in bloody grapes.
¹² Darker than wine are your eyes,
    whiter than milk are your teeth.

¹³ Zebulun will live on the shore of the sea
    and be a safe harbor for ships,
    with a border extending to Sidon.

¹⁴ Issachar has the strength of a donkey,
    lying at ease among the paddocks;
¹⁵ he took a liking to the settled life
    and the pleasantness of the land,
he leaned into the burden
    and fitted himself to the yoke.

¹⁶ Dan will mete out judgment
    to all the branches of Israel.
¹⁷ Dan is a snake on the road,
    a viper along the footpath,
that bites the horse's heel,
    and the rider is thrown off backward.

¹⁸ I yearn for your salvation, My God!

¹⁹ Gad will be raided by troops of marauders,
but he will attack them at their heels.

²⁰ Asher will have rich food
    and will provide delicacies fit for a ruler.

²¹ Naphtali is a doe set free
    who gives birth to beautiful fawns.

²² Joseph is a fruitful vine,
    a healthy vine close to water,
    with branches climbing the wall.
²³ Vicious archers attacked Joseph;
    they pressed the attack fiercely.
²⁴ But Joseph's bow stayed taut;
    Joseph's tireless arms prevailed
by the hands of the Strong One of Jacob,
    through the Name of the Shepherd, the Rock of Israel,

²⁵ through the God of your ancestors who aids you,
 by the Breasted One who blesses you:
the blessings of Heaven on high,
 the blessings of the Deep down below,
the blessings of breasts and womb,
²⁶ and the blessings of Jacob,
stronger than the blessings of eternal mountains,
 wider than the everlasting hills:
may they all rest on Joseph's head,
 on the brow of the one set apart from his brothers.

²⁷ Benjamin is a ravenous wolf;
 devouring prey in the morning,
 dividing plunder in the evening."

²⁸ These are the twelve tribes of Israel, and these are the things that their father said to them at the time of their blessing, when he gave each a fitting blessing.

²⁹ Jacob gave them these instructions: "I am about to be gathered to my ancestors. Bury me with them in the cave that lies in the field of Ephron the Hittite, ³⁰ the cave in the field of Machpelah, the field that Abraham bought from Ephron the Hittite for a burial ground. ³¹ There Sarah and Abraham are buried, and Rebecca and Isaac, and there I buried Leah—the field and the cave in it were purchased from the Hittites."

³³ When Jacob had finished giving these instructions, he drew up his feet into the bed, breathed his last, and was gathered to his ancestors.

50¹ Then Joseph threw himself onto his father's body, weeping over him and kissing him. ² Then he gave orders to the doctors to embalm Israel's body, ³ which, as was their custom, took over forty days to complete. The Egyptians mourned Jacob for seventy days.

⁴ When the days of mourning were over, Joseph spoke to the members of the Pharaoh's court. Joseph said, "If I have favor in your sight, please tell Pharaoh this for me: ⁵ 'When he was dying, Jacob made me swear an oath that I would bury his body in the tomb which he dug for himself in Canaan.' Ask Pharaoh to allow me to travel to Canaan to bury Jacob, and I will return after the burial."

⁶ "Go up and bury Jacob, as he made you swear by an oath," Pharaoh said.

⁷ So Joseph went up to bury Jacob, accompanied by Pharaoh's attendants, the court officials, and all the elders of the land of Egypt, ⁸ together with his own household and the households of his siblings and of Jacob.

Only their children and their herds and flocks remained at Goshen. ⁹ Chariots and mounted troops accompanied them. It was a very large caravan.

¹⁰ When the caravan reached Goren Ha-Atad, beyond the Jordan, they held sorrowful and solemn lamentation, and Joseph observed seven days of mourning for Jacob. ¹¹ When the local people, the Canaanites, witnessed the mourning at Goren Ha-Atad, they commented, "Such a solemn mourning for Egypt!" This is why the place beyond the Jordan is called Meadow of Egypt.*

¹² So the children of Israel carried out Jacob's wishes. ¹³ They carried his body to the land of Canaan and buried it in the cave in the field of Machpelah, near Mamre, which Abraham had purchased as a burial place from Ephron the Hittite. ¹⁴ After the burial, Joseph, the brothers and all the others in the caravan returned to Egypt.

¹⁵ Pondering their father's death, Joseph's brothers said, "What if Joseph is angry with us and repays us for all the wrong we did him?" ¹⁶ So they approached Joseph, saying: "Before Jacob died he said to us, ¹⁷ 'You must say to Joseph: I beg you, please forgive your brothers their crime and their sin and all the wrong they did you.' Now therefore, we ask you, forgive the crime of us who are faithful to the God of your parents." Joseph wept when he heard this. ¹⁸ Then the brothers wept also, and fell down before him, saying. 'We present ourselves before you, as your attendants."

¹⁹ Joseph replied, "Don't be afraid; is it for me to put myself in God's place? ²⁰ You planned evil for me, but God planned it for the good, as it has come to pass this day—to bring about the survival of many people. ²¹ So you need not be afraid. I myself will provide for you and your little ones." In this manner he assured them with words that touched their hearts.

²² Joseph remained in Egypt with his father's family, and lived to be 110 years old. ²³ He saw Ephraim's children to the third generation, and the children of Machir, begot of Manasseh, also sat upon Joseph's lap.

²⁴ At the last, Joseph said to his family, "I am about to die. God will surely take care of you and lead you out of this land to the land promised on oath to Sarah and Abraham, Rebecca and Isaac, and Leah and Rachel and Jacob." ²⁵ Joseph made the children of Israel swear an oath, saying, "God will come to your aid, and then you must carry my bones up from this place."

²⁶ Joseph died at the age of 110. They embalmed him and laid his body in a sarcophagus in Egypt.

---

* The Hebrew words for "mourning" and "meadow" sound very similar.

exodus

these are the names* of the children of Israel and their families, who migrated to Egypt with Jacob: ² Reuben, Simeon, Levi and Judah; ³ Issachar, Zebulun and Benjamin; ⁴ Dan and Naphtali; Gad and Asher. ⁵ The direct descendants of Jacob numbered seventy; Joseph was already in Egypt. ⁶ Then Joseph and his brothers died, and, one by one, all the members of that generation passed away; ⁷ but the children of Israel were fruitful, and they became a veritable swarm—their numbers increased so much that they filled the land and became powerful.

⁸ A new Pharaoh—one who did not know Joseph—came to power in Egypt. ⁹ Pharaoh said to the Egyptians, "Look at how powerful the Israelites have become, and how they outnumber us! ¹⁰ We need to deal shrewdly with their increase, against a time of war when they might turn against us and join our enemy, and so escape out of the country."

¹¹ So they oppressed the Israelites with overseers who put them to forced labor; and with them they built the storage cities of Pitom and Ra'amses. ¹² Yet the more the Israelites were oppressed, the more they multiplied

_____

* *These Are the Names* is the Hebrew title for the book of *Exodus*.

and burst forth, until the Egyptians dreaded the Israelites. ¹³ So they made the Israelites utterly subservient with hard labor, brick-and-mortar work, and every kind of field work. ¹⁴ The Egyptians were merciless in subjugating them with crushing labor.

¹⁵ Pharaoh spoke to the midwives of the Hebrews*—one was Shiphrah, and the other Puah—¹⁶ and said, "When you assist the Hebrew women in childbirth, examine them on the birthing-stool. If the baby is a boy, kill it. If it is a girl, let it live."

¹⁷ But the midwives were God-fearing women, and they ignored the Pharaoh's instructions, and let the male babies live. ¹⁸ So Pharaoh summoned the midwives and asked why they let the male babies live. ¹⁹ The midwives responded, "These Hebrew women are different from Egyptian women; they are more robust, and deliver even before the midwife arrives." ²⁰ God rewarded the midwives, and the people increased in numbers and in power. ²¹ And since the midwives were God-fearing, God gave them families of their own.

²² The Pharaoh then commanded all those in Egypt, "Let every boy that is born to the Hebrews be thrown into the Nile, but let every girl live."

2·¹ There was a man from the house of Levi who had married a Levite woman, ² and she conceived and gave birth to a boy. And she saw that the baby was good,** so she hid it for three months. ³ When she could hide the baby no longer she took a papyrus basket, daubed it with bitumen and pitch, and put the child in it, and placed the basket among the reeds by the banks of the Nile. ⁴ The baby's sister watched from a distance to learn what would happen.

⁵ Pharaoh's daughter came down to the Nile to bathe, while her attendants walked along the river bank. She noticed the basket among the reeds, and sent her attendant to fetch it. ⁶ Opening it, she saw the baby—and how it wept! She was moved to pity and said, "This must be one of the Hebrews' children!"

⁷ Then his sister said to Pharaoh's daughter, "Do you want me to go and find a nurse for you among the Hebrews to suckle the child for you?"

⁸ "Yes, go," she answered. So the sister went off and brought the baby's

---

* Despite their Semitic names, these midwives were likely Egyptian; Hebrew women would not be likely to heed the Pharaoh's command to kill Hebrew babies, which is why their disobedience in verse 17 is significant.

**Others translate "beautiful" or "healthy," though the author is clearly alluding to the creation in *Genesis*: "And God saw that the light was good."

own mother. ⁹ Pharaoh's daughter said to her, "Take this child with you and suckle it for me, and I myself will pay you." The woman took the child and nursed it. ¹⁰ After the child was weaned, she brought it to Pharaoh's daughter, who adopted it as her own. She called him Moses—"He Who Pulls Out"—for she said, "I pulled him out of the water."*

ও ও ও

¹¹ Some years later, when Moses had grown up, he went out among his own people and witnessed firsthand their forced labor. He saw an Egyptian beating a Hebrew, one of Moses' kindred. ¹² Looking around, and seeing no one, Moses beat the Egyptian to death, and hid the body in the sand.

¹³ The next day he went out again, and this time he saw two Hebrews fighting with each other. Moses said to the one who was in the wrong, "Why do you strike a fellow Hebrew?"

¹⁴ He replied, "Who appointed you ruler and judge over us? Do you intend to kill me the way you killed the Egyptian?"

Moses was frightened, thinking, "Clearly, this business has come to light." ¹⁵ Pharaoh, too, heard of the affair, and sought to put Moses to death.

Moses fled from Pharaoh's court, and settled in the wilderness of Midian.

One day, Moses was sitting by a well. ¹⁶ The priest of Midian had seven daughters, and they came to draw water to fill the troughs for his flocks. ¹⁷ Some shepherds happened along and drove them away, but Moses rose up and came to their rescue, and watered their flock.

¹⁸ When the daughters returned, their father Re'uel** inquired, "Why are you back so soon?"

---

* The name is packed with meaning. Moses, or *Mss*, is an old Egyptian name meaning "child of," as in Ra'amses—"child of Ra"—so Pharaoh's daughter is simply naming him "my son." But the name in Hebrew, Moshe, is a deliberate pun. Pharaoh's daughter thinks the name Moshe recalls her act of "pulling out" the baby from the Nile. But, as commentator Everett Fox points out, "the verb for *moshe* is active, not passive, and thus it is Moshe himself who will one day 'pull out' Israel from the life-threatening waters of both slavery and the Sea of Reeds."

** The priest of Midian is known by two different names, Re'uel and Jethro. As noted in the Introduction, several different literary sources were later combined to create the version of the Torah we have today. As with the dual stories of creation and the Flood, little effort was taken to edit out contradictions. At the same time, Jethro means "pre-eminence" or "excellence," and may be a title similar to "your Excellency," whereas Re'uel ("friend of God") may have been his personal name.

[19] They answered, "An Egyptian defended us from the shepherds. He even watered the flock."

[20] "Where is this Egyptian now?" asked the priest. "Why did you leave him at the well? Go back and invite him to supper."

[21] Moses agreed to settle down with the family, and eventually married one of the daughters, Zipporah. [22] Zipporah gave birth to a child they named Gershom, "Sojourner There"—so named because Moses said, "I have become a sojourner in a foreign land."

[23] Many years later, the ruler of Egypt died, but the Israelites still groaned under oppression. They cried out from the depths of their bondage to God, [24] who heard their moaning, and remembered the covenant that had been made with Sarah and Abraham, with Rebecca and Isaac, and with Leah and Rachel and Jacob. [25] God saw the children of Israel. And God knew.

෨ ෨ ෨

3:1 Moses was tending the flock of his father-in-law Jethro, the priest of Midian. Leading the flock deep into the wilderness, Moses came to Horeb, the mountain of God.*

[2] The messenger of Our God appeared to Moses in a blazing fire from the midst of a thornbush. Moses saw—"The bush is ablaze with fire, and yet it isn't consumed!" [3] Moses said, "Let me go over and look at this remarkable sight—and see why the bush doesn't burn up!"

[4] When Our God saw Moses coming to look more closely, God called out to him from the midst of the bush: "Moses! Moses!"

Moses answered, "I am here."

[5] God said, "Come no closer! Remove the sandals from your feet, for the place where you stand is holy ground!

[6] "I am the God of your ancestors," the voice continued, "the God of Sarah and Abraham, the God of Rebecca and Isaac, the God of Leah and Rachel and Jacob!"

Moses hid his face, afraid to look at the Holy One.

[7] Then Our God said, "I have seen the affliction of my people in Egypt; I have heard their cries under those who oppress them; I have felt their sufferings. [8] Now I have come down to rescue them from the hand of

---

* Another name for Sinai. In the next verse, the word for "thornbush" is s'neh, which sounds like Sinai.

Egypt, out of their place of suffering, and bring them to a place that is wide and fertile, a land flowing with milk and honey*—the land of the Canaanites, the Hittites, the Amorites, the Perizzites, the Hivites, and the Jebusites. ⁹ The cry of the children of Israel has reached me, and I have watched how the Egyptians are oppressing them. ¹⁰ Now, go! I will send you to Pharaoh, to bring my people, the children of Israel, out of Egypt."

¹¹ But Moses said to God, "Who am I, that I should go to Pharaoh and lead the children of Israel out of Egypt?"

¹² God answered, "I will be with you, and this is the sign by which you will know that it is I who have sent you: after you bring my people out of Egypt, you will all worship at this very mountain."

¹³ "But," Moses said, "when I go to the children of Israel and say to them, 'The God of your ancestors has sent me to you,' if they ask me, 'What is this god's name?', what am I to tell them?"

¹⁴ God replied, "I AM AS I AM. This is what you will tell the Israelites: 'I AM has sent me to you.'"**

¹⁵ God spoke further to Moses: "Tell the children of Israel: 'The Most High, the 'I AM,' the God of your ancestors, the God of Sarah and Abraham, of Rebecca and Isaac, of Leah and Rachel and Jacob, has sent me to you.' This is my Name forever; this is the name you are to remember for all generations.

¹⁶ "Now go. Gather the elders of the Israelites and tell them, 'I AM, the God of your ancestors, appeared to me—the God of Sarah and Abraham, the God of Rebecca and Isaac, the God of Leah and Rachel and Jacob—and said: 'I have heard you and I have seen the way you are being treated in Egypt. ¹⁷ I tell you now that I will lead you out of your oppression in Egypt into the land of the Canaanites, the Hittites, the Amorites, the Perizzites, the Hivites and the Jebusites, to a land flowing with milk and honey.' "

¹⁸ "They will hear your message. And together with the elders of Israel, you will go to the ruler of Egypt and say, 'Our God, the God of the

---

* Milk and honey—literally, "goats' milk and date syrup"—are ancient euphemisms for the male and female sexual fluids, respectively; when the Israelites were to enter "a land flowing with milk and honey," the peace and joy of such a land was depicted in terms of the full expression of physical love.

**In the ancient world, knowing the true name of a person or a god meant that one could understand the other's true essence—possibly for the purpose of coercion or manipulation. Here God resolutely refuses to be controlled, yet is completely self-revelatory. The phrase we have translated "I am as I am," *Ehyeh asher Ehyeh,* is difficult, and may mean "The One who brings things into being," "the One who is," or "I will be however I will be." The phrase "I am" (*Ehyeh*) may also mean "I will be" or "I will be there": the verb indicates presence, "being there" for Moses and the people of Israel. The revered, unpronounceable (and unpronounced) Name of God revealed in verse 15, usually translated "Our God" in this version, derives from the same root: "to be" or "to become."

Hebrews, met with us. Permit us, therefore, to make a three days' journey into the desert to offer sacrifice to Our God.' ¹⁹ However, I know that the ruler of Egypt will not allow you to go except by the force of a mighty hand. ²⁰ So I will stretch out my hand, and strike Egypt with all the wonders I am going to work there. After that the Pharaoh will set you free.

²¹ "And I will make the Egyptians look with favor on you, so that when you leave you will not go empty-handed. ²² Each of the women will borrow objects of silver and gold from her neighbors and any people renting from them; they will borrow clothes from them as well, which you will then put on your daughters and sons. In this way you will plunder Egypt."

4:1 Moses asked, "But what if they do not believe me or even listen to me? What if they say, 'God has not appeared to you!'?"

² Then God asked Moses, "What do you have in your hand?"

"My staff," Moses replied

³ God said, "Throw it on the ground."

Moses threw it to the ground, and it became a snake. Moses recoiled from it in horror.

⁴ Then Our God said to Moses, "Reach out your hand and grab it by the tail." Moses reached out his hand, grabbed the snake, and it became a staff in his hand once again. ⁵ "This is how they will trust that God, the God of their ancestors—the God of Sarah and Abraham, of Rebecca and Isaac and of Leah and Rachel and Jacob—has appeared to you."

⁶ Then Our God said, "Put your hand inside your tunic." Moses did as instructed, putting his hand inside the tunic; and when he pulled it out the hand was snowy white with leprosy. ⁷ God said, "Put your hand back into your tunic." Moses put it back into the tunic, and when he took it out again it was restored, and like the rest of his skin.

⁸ Then God said, "If they disbelieve you, and do not believe the message of the first sign, they might believe the second. ⁹ But if they disbelieve both miraculous signs and don't even listen to your message, take some water from the Nile and pour it on the ground. It will turn into blood."

¹⁰ Then Moses said to the Holy One, "Please, my God, I am not good with words. I wasn't yesterday, nor the day before, nor am I now, even after you spoke to me. I speak slowly, and with a wooden tongue."

¹¹ Our God replied, "Who taught people to speak in the first place? Who makes them deaf or mute? Who makes them see, or be blind? Who, if not I, Your God? ¹² Now go! I myself will be with you when you speak. I will teach you what to say."

¹³ But Moses said, "Please, my God, please send someone else. Not me."

¹⁴ Then God's anger flashed out against Moses. "If you can't do it, I know someone who can—Aaron the Levite, your brother! He can speak, and speak well. He is coming to meet you this minute, and his heart will leap to see you. ¹⁵ He will do the speaking for you, and you will put the words in his mouth. I myself will be there, with your mouth and with his mouth, and I will show both of you what to do. ¹⁶ He will speak on your behalf to the people; Aaron will be a mouth for you, and you will be a god for him.* ¹⁷ And take that staff in your hand; with it you will perform the signs."

ℭℛ   ℭℛ   ℭℛ

¹⁸ Then Moses returned to Jethro his father-in-law and said, "Give me permission to return to my own people in Egypt. I need to know if they are still alive."

Jethro said, "Go in peace."

¹⁹ While he was in Midian, Our God had said to Moses, "Go back to Egypt. All those who wanted to kill you are dead." ²⁰ So Moses put Zipporah and their two children on donkeys and started for Egypt, and carried God's staff in his hand.

²¹ Then Our God said to Moses, "Once you arrive in Egypt, go to Pharaoh and perform all the wonders with which I empowered you. I will harden Pharaoh's heart so that he won't let the people go. ²² Then you will say to Pharaoh, 'Our God says: Israel is my firstborn, ²³ and I told you, "Let my firstborn go to worship me freely." But you refused to let Israel go. Therefore I will kill your firstborn.'"

²⁴ On the journey, where they had stopped for the night, Our God came to Moses, and sought to kill him.** ²⁵ But Zipporah grabbed a flint knife, cut off their son's foreskin, and touched it to Moses' feet.† "What a bridegroom of blood you are to me!" she exclaimed, ²⁶ whereupon God released Moses. She then said "Bridegroom of blood!" over their son's circumcision.

---

* Aaron, the firstborn, will speak Moses' words as a prophet speaks the words of God.

**Likely through illness. It is interesting to note that the daughter of a pagan priest understood God's intentions better than Moses did, and intuitively knew the remedy. The incident, which brings Moses into full compliance with all the terms of God's covenant with Abraham (all the males in the household were to be circumcised), also foreshadows the ceremonial smearing of blood at the Passover.

† "Feet" was a common euphemism for the genitals.

²⁷ Our God said to Aaron, "Go into the desert to meet Moses."

Aaron met Moses at the mountain of God and embraced him warmly. ²⁸ There Moses told Aaron all the words with which Our God had sent him, and all the signs which were to be performed.

²⁹ Then Aaron and Moses went, and brought together all the elders of the Israelites. ³⁰ Aaron spoke all the words that Our God spoke to Moses, and Moses did the signs before the people's eyes. They believed, and when they had heard that Our God had compassion on the plight of the children of Israel, and had seen their misery, they bowed down in worship.

ଓଃ   ଓଃ   ଓଃ

5:1 After this Aaron and Moses went to Pharaoh and said, "These are the words of Our God, the God of Israel: 'Let my people go, for they wish to observe a pilgrimage festival* in the wilderness.'"

² Pharaoh asked, "Who is this god of yours, and why should I listen to any demand to let Israel go free? I do not know this god, and I will not let Israel go."

³ They replied, "The God of the Hebrews has met with us. Let us travel a three days' journey into the wilderness, where we will offer sacrifices to Our God, or we will be confronted by plagues, or the sword!"

⁴ But the ruler of Egypt said, "Aaron and Moses, who are you to take these people from their work? All of you, get back to your work!" ⁵ Pharaoh continued, "Look at all the people in this land—and you're holding up their work!"

⁶ That same day Pharaoh gave instructions to the slave-drivers of the people and the overseers. ⁷ "You will not gather straw any longer for the workers making bricks. Let them gather their own straw. ⁸ But don't lower their brick quota. They are to make as many bricks as before. These people are lazy, and this is why they whine, 'Let us go to offer a sacrifice to Our God.' ⁹ Let them have more work, more servitude! If they work hard enough, they'll stop listening to false messages!"

¹⁰ Then the slave-drivers and the overseers went to the people and said, "Pharaoh says, 'I will not give you any more straw. ¹¹ Go out and find your own straw wherever you can. But not one load of bricks will be subtracted from your daily quota.'" ¹² So the Hebrews scattered throughout the coun-

---

* The Hebrew word for pilgrimage festival, *hag*, is echoed in the great pilgrimage of Islam, the *hajj*, in which worshippers make (sometimes long) journeys to Mecca.

try scavenging for stubble out of which to make straw. ¹³ The overseers harassed the workers, telling them, "You must meet your daily quota, just as you did when we provided you with straw every day!" ¹⁴ The Israelite officials, who had been appointed by Pharaoh's overseers, were beaten, and asked, "Why haven't you met your quota of bricks as you did yesterday and the day before? As yesterday, so today!"

¹⁵ Then the Israelite officials complained to Pharaoh. "Why do you treat your subjects the way you do? ¹⁶ We are not provided with straw, but we're still told, 'Make bricks!' We are beaten, but it is not we who are at fault—the fault is with you!"

¹⁷ Pharaoh replied, "Lazy! You people are lazy! That's why you keep saying, 'Let us go into the wilderness to worship Our God.' ¹⁸ Now get out of here! Go to work. Find your own straw, and fill your quota of bricks."

¹⁹ When the Israelite officials were told again that they must fulfill their daily quota of bricks and find their own straw, they knew they were in trouble. ²⁰ When they left Pharaoh, they waited for Aaron and Moses to come by, and they confronted them. ²¹ They said, "May Our God see what you are doing and judge you! You have made us reek in the nostrils of the Pharaoh and the court officials! You have given them a sword with which to kill us!"

²² Moses returned to the Holy One and asked, "O God, why have you added to the oppression of this people? Why did you ever send me? Ever since I first came to Pharaoh to speak in your name, the ruler has treated this people worse, but you—you have done nothing to deliver your people!"

6¹ Our God said to Moses, "It is time for you to see what I will do to Pharaoh: By the power of my hand, the ruler will set them free. By the power of my hand, Pharaoh will drive my people from the country."

² God also said to Moses, "I am Your God. ³ I appeared to Sarah and Abraham, to Rebecca and Isaac, and to Leah and Rachel and Jacob, as 'El Shaddai,' but by the name 'I AM' I did not reveal myself. ⁴ I also established my covenant with them to give them the land of Canaan, where they lived as foreigners. ⁵ And now I have heard the groaning of the Israelites, whom the Egyptians enslaved, and I have not forgotten my covenant. ⁶ Say to the Israelites: 'I am your God, and I will free you from the yoke of the Egyptians. I will free you from the bondage you are subjected to, and I will redeem you with my arm outstretched and with overwhelming acts of judgment. ⁷ I will make you as my own, and I will be your God. Then you will always know that I am Your God who brought you out of the bondage of the Egyptians. ⁸ I will lead you to the land I

vowed to give to Sarah and Abraham, Rebecca and Isaac, and Leah and Rachel and Jacob. I will give it to you for your own possession. I am Your God.'"

⁹ Moses took this message back to the Israelites, but they would not listen; they were too dispirited, broken by the weight of their cruel bondage.

¹⁰ Then Our God said to Moses, ¹¹ "Go tell Pharaoh the ruler of Egypt to let my people leave this country."

¹² But Moses appealed to Our God, "The Israelites won't listen to me; why would Pharaoh? After all, I speak so poorly!"

¹³ So Our God spoke to both Moses and Aaron, ordering them to go together to the Pharaoh, the ruler of Egypt, and bring the Israelites out of the land of Egypt.

¹⁴ These are the heads of the tribal units:

The heirs of Reuben, Israel's firstborn, were Hanoch and Pallu, Hezron and Carmi. These were the clans of Reuben.

¹⁵ The heirs of Simeon were Jemuel, Jamin, Ohad, Jachin, Zohar, and Shaul, whose mother was a Canaanite. These were the clans of Simeon.

¹⁶ The heirs of Levi, according to their records, were Gershon, Kohath and Merari. Levi lived for 137 years. ¹⁷ The heirs of Gershon were Libni and Shimei; these were their clans. ¹⁸ The heirs of Kohath were Amram, Izhar, Hebron, and Uzziel. Kohath lived for 133 years. ¹⁹ The heirs of Merari were Mahli and Mushi. All of these were the clans of Levi, according to their records.

²⁰ Amram married his aunt, Jochebed—Kohath's sister—and had two heirs, Aaron and Moses.* Amram lived for 137 years.

²¹ The heirs of Izhar were Korah, Nepheg and Zichri. ²² The heirs of Uzziel were Mishael, Elzaphan and Sithri. ²³ Aaron married Elisheva, who was the daughter of Amminadab and the sister of Nahshon. She gave birth to Nadab and Abihu, Eleazar and Ithamar. ²⁴ The heirs of Korah were Assir, Elkanah and Abiasaph. These were the clans of Korah.

²⁵ Eleazar begot of Aaron married one of Putiel's daughters. Phinehas was their child.

These were the heads of the Levite tribal units, clan by clan. ²⁶ It was to two of that number, Aaron and Moses, that Our God said, "Lead the Israelites out of Egypt, division by division." ²⁷ It was this Moses and this Aaron who told Pharaoh to allow the Israelites to leave Egypt.

---

* They also had one girl, Miriam. She became a prophet and later served together with Moses and Aaron.

²⁸ Our God spoke to Moses in Egypt, and said, "I am Your God. Tell Pharaoh, the ruler of Egypt, all that I say to you." But Moses appealed to God, saying, "I cannot speak well. Why should Pharaoh listen to me?"

7¹ Our God said to Moses, "Look, I have made you like a god to Pharaoh, with Aaron, your brother, as your prophet. ² Tell Aaron everything I command you to say, and your brother will tell Pharaoh, so that he will let the Israelites leave Egypt. ³ I, for my part, will harden Pharaoh's heart, and I will show many signs and omens in Egypt. ⁴ When the ruler does not heed your warnings, I will lay my hand on Egypt with mighty acts of judgment. I will take my people the Israelites, clan by clan, from the land of Egypt. ⁵ When I have shown my power against Egypt and freed all the Israelites, the Egyptians will know that I am Your God."

⁶ Aaron and Moses acted just as God instructed them. ⁷ Aaron was eighty-three years old and Moses was eighty when they confronted Pharaoh.

03   03   03

⁸ Our God said to Aaron and Moses, ⁹ "If Pharaoh says to you, 'Show me a miracle,' then you, Moses, are to tell Aaron to throw his staff at Pharaoh's feet, and let it turn into a serpent."*

¹⁰ Aaron and Moses went to the ruler and did as God had told them. Aaron threw down the staff before Pharaoh and the court officials, and it turned into a serpent.

¹¹ Then Pharaoh summoned the magicians and the sorcerers. The Egyptian magicians and sorcerers did the same thing through their sorcery. ¹² Each one threw down a staff and it turned into a serpent. But Aaron's serpent swallowed all the others. ¹³ Pharaoh's heart was hardened, however, and the ruler refused to listen to them, as God had foretold.

¹⁴ Then Our God said to Moses, "Pharoah's heart is heavy and stubborn, and he refuses to release my people. ¹⁵ In the morning, go to the bank of the Nile, when he comes down to the water to bathe. Have with you the staff you turned into a serpent.

¹⁶ "Tell him, 'Our God, the God of the Hebrews, sent me to say to you: Let my people go, so that they may worship me in the wilderness! Until now you have refused. ¹⁷ So now Our God says to you: By this you will

---

* The word used here for serpent is different from the common word for snake, and carries mythic overtones. The author may be alluding to ancient cosmologies in which God conquered the great archetypal Dragon in the battle for creation.

know that I am Your God—with this staff I will strike the water of the Nile and it will turn into blood! ¹⁸ The fish in the river will die, the water will stink, and it will not be fit for drinking.'"

¹⁹ Then Our God said to Moses, "Tell Aaron, 'Take your staff and stretch your hand over the waters of Egypt—over its rivers, over its streams, over its canals, ponds and cisterns—and they will turn into blood. Blood will be everywhere in Egypt, even in wooden vats and stone jars.'"

²⁰ Aaron and Moses did as God told them. In the presence of Pharaoh and all the officials, Aaron raised the staff and struck the water. The entire river turned into blood. ²¹ The fish in the Nile died, and the river stunk so badly that the people could not drink it. Everything in Egypt was bloody.

²² But the Egyptian sorcerers and magicians did the same thing with their secret arts. So Pharaoh's heart remained hardened, and he refused to listen to Aaron and Moses, just as Our God had foretold. ²³ The ruler went back into into the royal residence and took none of this seriously. ²⁴ All the Egyptians had to dig for drinking water along the banks of the Nile, for they could not drink the river water.

²⁵ Seven days passed after God struck the Nile.* ²⁶ Our God then told Moses to go to Pharoah and say, "Let my people go so that they may worship me! ²⁷ If you refuse I will release a plague of frogs over all your country. ²⁸ The river will swarm with frogs. They will be everywhere: in your royal residence, in your bedrooms and in your beds, in the houses of the officials and all the people, in your ovens and in your kneading-bowls. ²⁹ They will climb all over you, your people, and your officials."

8:1 Then God told Moses what to say to Aaron. "Tell Aaron to stretch the staff out over Egypt's waters—the rivers, the streams, the canals, the ponds—and make frogs come up out of the water throughout all Egypt." ² So Aaron held out the staff over Egypt's waters, and the frogs came out and covered the land. ³ But the Egyptian magicians and sorcerers did the same thing through their sorcery; they too made frogs come up out of the water throughout Egypt.

⁴ Pharaoh summoned Aaron and Moses and said, "Pray to Your God to remove the frogs from me and from my people, and I, in return, will let you and your people go to offer sacrifices to Your God."

⁵ Moses said, "Here I will give you the advantage over me. I will plead for you, and I will let you determine the exact time that the frogs will leave

---

* Though here we follow the verse numbering used in the Hebrew texts, many English versions begin chapter 8 at this point; i.e., our verse 26 is 8:1 in other versions. The four-verse discrepancy in the numbering continues through the end of chapter 8.

you, your officials, your people, and your houses; the only place frogs will be is in the Nile."

⁶ Pharaoh said, "Tomorrow."

"It will be as you say," responded Moses. "By this you will know that there is no one like Our God. ⁷ The frogs will leave you and your houses, your officials and your people. They will remain only in the Nile."

⁸ So Aaron and Moses left the ruler, and Moses entreated Our God to remove the frogs that had invaded Pharaoh. ⁹ Our God did as Moses had asked. The frogs died where they were—in the houses, in the yards, in the open fields. ¹⁰ The people put them in piles, heaps upon heaps, and the land reeked with their stench. ¹¹ But once the Pharaoh had breathing room, his heart hardened again, and again Aaron and Moses were ignored, just as Our God had predicted.

¹² Then Our God told Moses to tell Aaron, "Stretch out your staff and strike the dust on the ground. Throughout all of Egypt the dust will turn into gnats."

¹³ They did so; and when Aaron struck the dust of the ground with the staff, gnats swarmed over the people and animals. All the dust throughout the land of Egypt turned into gnats. ¹⁴ When the sorcerers and magicians tried to create gnats by their sorcery, they failed. And the gnats covered everything—people and animals alike.

¹⁵ The sorcerers and magicians said to Pharaoh, "This is the finger of a god!" But the ruler remained obstinate, and as Our God had predicted, the Pharaoh would not listen

¹⁶ Then Our God said to Moses, "Arise early tomorrow and meet Pharaoh as he goes down to the water. Say, 'Our God says: Let my people go, so that they may worship me. ¹⁷ If you do not do this, I will send insects* upon you, your officials, your people and your houses. All the residences of Egypt will be filled with insects, as will the ground on which they stand. ¹⁸ But in the land of Goshen, where my people dwell, there will be no insects, so that you will know that I, the Most High, am in this land. ¹⁹ I will make a distinction between my people and your people. This sign will appear tomorrow.'" ²⁰ The Almighty did as promised, and dense swarms of insects invaded the royal residence, and the residences of the officials. The swarms of flies spread out, blanketing the land of Egypt.

---

* The Hebrew term literally means "mixture," and may be a mixture of insects such as flies and mosquitoes; some ancient Hebrew commentaries suggest a mixture of wild animals.

²¹ Then Pharaoh summoned Aaron and Moses and said, "Go, make your sacrifices to your god, but stay here in Egypt."

²² But Moses replied, "That would not be fitting. The sacrifices we offer to Our God are considered an abomination to Egyptians. And if they saw us offering sacrifices that they consider abominable to them, they would certainly stone us. ²³ We must go a three days' journey into the desert to offer sacrifices to our Most High God, as we are commanded."

²⁴ Pharaoh said, "You can go into the desert to offer sacrifices to your God. But you must not go too far. Now pray for me!"

²⁵ And Moses answered, "As soon as I leave you I will intercede with Our God, and tomorrow the swarms will leave you, your officials and your people. But you must not deceive us again and refuse to let our people leave to offer sacrifices to Our God."

²⁶ Then Moses left the ruler and prayed to the Holy One. ²⁷ Our God answered Moses' prayers: the insects left Pharaoh, his officials, and his people. Not a single insect remained. ²⁸ But Pharaoh grew obstinate once more, and would not let the people go.

9₁ Then Our God said to Moses, "Go to Pharaoh and say, 'The Most High, the God of the Hebrews, says this: Let my people go to worship me! ² If you refuse to let them go, and hold them under your power, ³ my hand will fall upon your livestock with a terrible plague—on your horses, your donkeys, and your camels and cattle, sheep and goats. ⁴ But I will make a distinction between your livestock and our livestock so that none of the livestock of the Israelites will die in the plague.'"

⁵ Then Our God appointed a time: "By this time tomorrow Our God will do this throughout the land." ⁶ And so God did: all the Egyptians' livestock died, and the Israelites lost none. ⁷ The ruler made a general inquiry, and found that none of the livestock of the Israelites had died. But the Pharaoh's obstinate heart would not yield, and he would not let the Israelites go.

⁸ Then Our God said to Aaron and Moses, "Take handfuls of soot from a furnace—when Moses throws it into the air in the presence of Pharaoh, ⁹ it will turn into a fine dust throughout Egypt and create festering boils on both people and animals."

¹⁰ So they took soot from a furnace, and standing before Pharaoh, threw the soot into the air. Festering boils broke out on animals and on people. ¹¹ The sorcerers and magicians could not face Moses because they were covered with boils, as were all the people.

¹² But Our God made Pharaoh's heart obstinate once more. The ruler would not listen to Aaron and Moses, just as God had told Moses.

¹³ Then Our God said to Moses, "Get up early in the morning and stand before Pharaoh and say, 'Our God of the Hebrews says: Let my people go so that they can worship me! ¹⁴ This time I will strike with the full force of my blows, against you as well as against your officials and your people. You will understand that there is no one like me in all the earth. ¹⁵ For by now I could have stretched out my hand and struck you and your people with plague, and you would have vanished from the earth. ¹⁶ But I have allowed you to live so that my power and my Name would be proclaimed throughout the earth. ¹⁷ You continue to set yourself high over my people, and you refuse to let them go. ¹⁸ So tomorrow—at this very hour—I will send the worst hailstorm that Egypt has ever seen since its beginning. ¹⁹ Prepare now: have your livestock and everything else that is out in the open brought under shelter. For the hail will fall on every person and every animal, and anything which is not under shelter will surely die.'"

²⁰ Those officials of the Pharaoh who feared God's word hurried to have their workers and livestock under cover. ²¹ But those who ignored the admonition of God left their workers and livestock out in the open.

²² Then Our God said to Moses, "Stretch out your arm to the sky to make hail fall on all of Egypt—on people and on livestock and on everything growing in Egypt's fields." ²³ When Moses held out the staff toward the sky, Our God sent thunder ²⁴ and hail, with lightning flashing through it. It was the worst storm that had been seen in the land of Egypt since its beginning as a nation. ²⁵ All over Egypt hail tore down everything standing in the fields—people and animals. It beat down everything growing in the fields and stripped the trees. ²⁶ The only place that did not suffer from the hailstorm was the land of Goshen, where the Israelites resided.

²⁷ Then Pharaoh summoned Aaron and Moses. "This time I have sinned," Pharaoh said to them. "Your God is right. I, and my people, are wrong. ²⁸ Intercede with Your God. For we cannot bear any more of this thunder and hail."

²⁹ Moses said, "As soon as I leave the city I will spread out my arms in prayer to Our God. The thunder will cease and the hail will cease. And you will then know that the earth belongs to Our God. ³⁰ I know, however, that you and your officials do not yet revere Our God."

³¹ The flax and the barley had been ruined, ripening on their stalks; ³² but the wheat and the spelt were not ruined, because they sprout late in the

year. ³³ Moses left the Pharoah and the city, and stood with arms raised, praying to Our God, and the thunder and the hail stopped, and the rain stopped pouring down on the land. ³⁴ But when Pharaoh learned that the thunder and the hail and rain had stopped, the ruler continued to sin, and made his heart obstinate. ³⁵ Pharaoh and his officials steadfastly refused to let the Israelites go, just as God had predicted through Moses.

10:1 Then Our God said to Moses, "Go to Pharaoh and his officials. I have made their hearts obstinate, so that I could work these wonders for you— ² so that you could tell your children and your grandchildren about how harshly I treated the Egyptians and about the signs I have worked among them—and so that you would know that I am Your God."

³ So Aaron and Moses said to Pharaoh, "Our God, the God of the Hebrews, asks, 'How much longer will you refuse to submit yourself before me? Let my people go to worship me! ⁴ If you refuse to release them, I will cover your country with locusts tomorrow. ⁵ I will cover the country with locusts so thick that the ground will be invisible. They will devour the little that is left from the hailstorm, and the leaves of every tree in the country. ⁶ Your house, the houses of the officials and your people will be filled with locusts. Such a thing as this has never been seen, since the time of your parents and your grandparents until now.'" Then Moses left the ruler.

⁷ Pharaoh's officials turned to him, "How long will this Moses trouble us? Let those people go to worship their God! Can't you see that Egypt is in ruins?"

⁸ So Aaron and Moses were summoned back. Pharaoh told them, "You may go to worship your God. But who will go?"

⁹ Moses answered, "Everyone, our young and our old, our daughters and our sons, our flocks and our herds. We have to keep Our God's feast."

¹⁰ Pharaoh replied, "May Your God be with you, indeed! Do you think I would let you leave with your entire families? You are planning some evil—it is written on your faces! ¹¹ Never! Only your men may go and worship your God. That is what you asked for!" Then Aaron and Moses were thrust out of Pharaoh's chamber.

¹² So Our God said to Moses, "Stretch out your hand over the land to let the locusts swarm over Egypt and devour every growing thing—everything that remains after the hail."

¹³ Moses stretched his hand out over Egypt, and Our God sent a roaring eastern gale. It blew all day and all night, and when the dawn arose it revealed that the gale had brought locusts. ¹⁴ Hordes of locusts covered all

of Egypt, settling everywhere. Never before had there been a plague of locusts in such numbers, nor will it ever be again. ¹⁵ The land was black with the horde. They consumed everything left from the hail, every growing thing in the fields, all the fruit on the trees. Nothing green remained throughout Egypt, neither trees nor crops.

¹⁶ Pharaoh quickly summoned Aaron and Moses, saying, "I sinned against the Most High, your God—and against you. ¹⁷ Forgive me once more. Pray to Your God to remove this deadly plague from me."

¹⁸ Then Moses left the ruler and prayed to God. ¹⁹ And God brought the wind whipping out of the west, and it caught up the locusts and blew them out over the Sea of Reeds.* Not one locust was to be seen anywhere in Egypt.

²⁰ But God made the Pharaoh's heart obdurate once more, and again he refused to let the Israelites go.

²¹ Then God said to Moses, "Stretch out your arms toward the sky to make it dark over all of Egypt—darkness so dense that it can be felt."

²² Moses held out his arms to the sky. For three days it was a terrible darkness in Egypt. ²³ People could not even see each other or leave their homes for three days. But where the Israelites lived, there was light in their settlements.

²⁴ So Pharaoh again summoned Moses and said, "Go, worship your God with your women, your men, and your children. But you must leave your herds and flocks here."

²⁵ Moses replied, "You must not prevent us from offering sacrifices and burnt offerings to Our God. ²⁶ Our livestock must accompany us. Not one hoof is to be left behind! We must choose from among them in our worship of Our God, and we won't know until we get there which ones we must offer to God."

²⁷ But Our God made Pharaoh obstinate once more, and would not agree to let them go. ²⁸ The ruler said to Moses, "Get out of my sight! You are not to appear before me ever again! The day that you see my face again, it will be your death!"

²⁹ Moses answered, "It will be as you say. Never again will I stand before you."

11·¹ God said to Moses, "I will bring one last plague on the Pharaoh and on

---

* Throughout *Exodus*, the great sea of Egypt is the Sea of Reeds—not, as is commonly thought, the Red Sea, which derived from a mistranslation of the Hebrew *Yam Suf.*

Egypt. When it happens you will be released, and when the ruler lets you go, you will be completely driven out. ² Tell your people, the women and the men alike, to ask their Egyptian neighbors for articles of silver and gold."

³ God made the Egyptians favorably disposed to the Israelites. Moses, especially, became highly esteemed in Egypt by Pharaoh's officials and by the citizenry.*

⁴ Then Moses said, "Our God says: At midnight I will pass throughout Egypt. ⁵ Every firstborn in Egypt will die, from the firstborn of the Pharaoh who sits on the judgment seat, to the firstborn of the lowest household worker working at the hand-mill, and every firstborn of the livestock as well. ⁶ Egypt will wail with a cry that has never heard before and will never be heard again. ⁷ But silence will reign—not even a dog will bark—among the Israelites. Then you will all know that Our God distinguishes between Israel and Egypt. ⁸ All your officials will come to me, bowing low to say, 'Go, you and all those who follow you!' Only then will I leave." Then Moses, hot with anger, left the Pharaoh's presence.

⁹ Then God said to Moses, "The ruler will not listen to you so that my wonders will be multiplied throughout Egypt." ¹⁰ Aaron and Moses worked these wonders in the presence of Pharaoh, but Our God made Pharaoh obstinate, so he would not let the Israelites leave Egypt.

ෂ   ෂ   ෂ

12:¹ Our God said to Aaron and Moses in the land of Egypt, ² "This month will be the first of all months to you. You will count it as the first month of the year.** ³ Say this to the whole community of Israel: On the tenth day of this month, every family in Israel will take an animal from the flock, one for each household. ⁴ If your household is too small for a whole animal, join with your next door neighbor, and divide the animal as the number of persons requires. ⁵ The animal must be a year-old male without

---

* Throughout this story, though no time frame is explicitly mentioned, the implication has been that each new plague happened on the heels of the last one, perhaps over a period of a few weeks. This little paragraph, with its "Moses, especially, became highly esteemed," suddenly lends a human face to it: human nature being what it is, no one becomes "highly esteemed" in a matter of weeks, especially when he is raining such calamities upon everyone involved. It appears more likely that the events described were in fact spread out over many years; and if they are understood in that light, they suddenly become much more believable. The "hardening of Pharaoh's heart"over and over again likewise seems more realistic, with time between each event to forget, and to slip back into habitual avarice and obstinacy.

** In the Hebrew calendar, the civil year begins in the fall, with Rosh Hashanah and Yom Kippur. However, the ritual year begins in the spring, at the vernal equinox. Several commentators have noted how significant it is for Israel's birth to coincide with "nature's new year."

blemish. You may take it from either the sheep or the goats. ⁶ You must keep it until the fourteenth day of the month,* then the whole community of Israel is to slaughter it at sunset. ⁷ Some of the blood must then be taken and applied to the two doorposts and the lintel of every house where the animal is eaten.

⁸ "That night you will eat the roasted flesh with unleavened bread and bitter herbs. ⁹ Do not eat any of it raw or boiled, but roasted over the fire— the head, feet and entrails. ¹⁰ You must not leave any over until morning. Whatever is left in morning you are to burn.

¹¹ "This is how you are to eat it: with your belt buckled, your sandals on your feet, and a staff in your hand; you will eat it in haste. It is the Passover of Our God. ¹² For I will pass through the land of Egypt that night and strike down all the firstborn in the land of Egypt, both humans and animals. I will execute this judgment on all the gods of Egypt: I am Your God. ¹³ The blood will mark the houses where you live. When I see the blood I will pass over you, and no harm will come to you when I strike the land of Egypt.

¹⁴ "This day will be for you a memorial day, and you must celebrate it as a feast to Your God. All generations are to observe it forever as a feast day.

¹⁵ "Then you are to eat unleavened bread for seven days.** Remove the yeast from your homes on the first day. Those who eat leavened bread from the first day through the seventh day will be expelled from Israel. ¹⁶ Hold a sacred assembly on the first day and a second one on the seventh day. Do no work on any of these days with the exception of preparing food for all to eat. That is the only exception.

¹⁷ "Keep this Feast of the Unleavened Bread, for it was on this day I led your ranks out of Egypt. This feast is to be celebrated as a perpetual ordinance from generation to generation. ¹⁸ Beginning on the evening before the fourteenth day of the first month until the evening before the twenty-first day, you will eat unleavened bread. No yeast is to found in your homes for seven days. ¹⁹ Those who eat leavened bread will be expelled from the Israel—be they native-born or alien. ²⁰ Eat nothing with yeast; wherever you live, eat unleavened bread."

²¹ Then Moses gathered all the elders of Israel and said to them, "Go immediately to select animals for your families and slaughter them. ²² Take a sprig of hyssop, dip it in the pan of blood, and sprinkle the lintel and the

---

* That is, until the full moon.

**This command is an interpolation from a later period. Clearly the tradition of eating unleavened bread comes from verse 34, where it is stated that the Israelites left in such haste that there was no time to let their bread rise; the seven-day festival arose later to commemorate the event.

two doorposts with it. No one is to leave the house until morning. ²³ When Our God goes through the land to strike down Egypt, the blood on the lintel and posts of your door is the sign to pass over that place. The destroyer will not enter your place to strike you down.

²⁴ "You will keep this ritual as a perpetual observance for yourself and for your descendants. ²⁵ Observe this ritual when you enter the land which Our God has promised to give you. ²⁶ When your children ask you, 'What does this ritual mean?' ²⁷ tell them, 'It is the Passover sacrifice to Our God, who passed over our homes in Egypt, when God struck down Egypt but saved our homes.'" The Israelites bowed to the ground in worship, ²⁸ and they went to do exactly as Aaron and Moses had told them.

²⁹ At midnight Our God struck down the firstborn in Egypt, from the firstborn of Pharaoh, who sat on the judgment seat, to the firstborn of the prisoner in the dungeon, to the firstborn of all livestock. ³⁰ Pharaoh, the officials and all the Egyptians rose from their beds that night, and the air was filled with loud wailing throughout the land of Egypt, for there was death in each Egyptian dwelling.

³¹ In the course of the night Pharaoh summoned Aaron and Moses and said, "Go! Leave us! You and your Israelites! Leave! Worship your God as you requested! ³² Take your herds and flocks, as you said, and go! And bless me as well!"

³³ The Egyptians urged them to leave the country quickly, saying, "We're all going to die!" ³⁴ So they shouldered their bowls of unleavened dough, wrapped in cloaks. ³⁵ The Israelites, as Moses had told them, had asked their neighbors for items of gold, silver and clothing. ³⁶ Because God had made the Egyptians favorably disposed to the Israelites, they readily gave them whatever they asked for. In this way they plundered Egypt.

³⁷ That night, the Israelites, about six hundred thousand families, set out from Rameses for Succoth. ³⁸ A mixed crowd* accompanied them, as well as numerous flocks and vast herds. ³⁹ They baked cakes with the unleavened dough they had brought out of Egypt—there had been no time to bring leavening, because they had rushed out of Egypt without even opportunity to prepare food for their journey.

⁴⁰ The length of time the Israelites had stayed in Egypt was 430 years.

---

* The Hebrew suggests "riffraff." These are likely Egyptians who had fallen into disfavor with Pharoah, or who felt similarly oppressed and sought freedom with the Hebrews; they may also be individuals of mixed ancestry, the offspring of Hebrew-Egyptian intermarriage.

⁴¹ And on the last day of the 430th year, all the hosts of Our God's people left the land of Egypt.

> ⁴² This is a night for Our God to keep watch,
> to bring the Israelites out of the land of Egypt;
> that is this night for Our God,
> to be kept as a night of vigil to God
> by all Israelites in every generation.

⁴³ God said to Aaron and Moses, "These are the regulations governing Passover:

"Foreigners are not to eat it, ⁴⁴ but all indentured workers may eat the Passover, provided they first enter into the covenant with God. ⁴⁵ A bond-laborer or a hired worker may not eat the Passover.

⁴⁶ "The Passover must be eaten within one house only. None of the meat can be taken outside the house. No bones are to be broken. ⁴⁷ The whole community of Israel must keep the feast.

⁴⁸ "A foreigner living among the Israelites who desires to celebrate the Passover must first have all males in the household circumcised. Then they may celebrate it, and will be treated as natives in that place; but uncircumcised males may not eat the Passover. ⁴⁹ This same regulation applies both to the native-born and to the foreigners living among you."

⁵⁰ All the Israelites lived by what Our God commanded Aaron and Moses.

⁵¹ On that very day, when Our God delivered the Israelites out of Egypt by their ranks, **13:**1 Our God said to Moses, ² "Consecrate every firstborn to me. The firstborn out of every womb among the Israelites is to be mine, whether human or animal."

³ Then Moses said to the people, "Commemorate this day, the day you left Egypt and left your bondage, for Our God liberated you with a powerful hand. Eat nothing with yeast in it on this day, ⁴ for this day, in the month of Aviv,* is the day of your liberation. ⁵ When Our God brings you into the land of the Canaanites, Hittites, Amorites, Hivites and Jebusites—a land flowing with milk and honey, the land Our God swore to your ancestors to give to you—you are to keep this ceremony in this month. ⁶ You are to eat bread without yeast for seven days, and celebrate a feast honoring Our God. ⁷ Eat only bread without yeast for those seven days.

---

* Literally, the month of Ripe Grain. Later, during the Babylonian captivity, all of the months in the Hebrew calendar took on the Babylonian names by which they are known today; Aviv is today known as the month of Nissan.

Nothing with yeast in it is to be among you; nothing with yeast in it is to be seen within your territory. ⁸ On that day tell your firstborn, 'We do this because of what Our God did for us when we came out of Egypt.' ⁹ Observing this day is to be like a sign on your hand and a memento on your forehead, to guarantee that the law of Our God is always on your lips, for Our God delivered you from Egypt with a mighty hand. ¹⁰ You must keep this statute every year at the appointed time.

¹¹ "After Our God brings you into the land of Canaan that was promised to you and to your ancestors, and gives it to you, ¹² you are to give to Our God the first offspring of the womb. All firstborn of your livestock are to be given to Our God. ¹³ Every firstborn donkey is to be redeemed with a lamb. If you do not redeem it, you must break its neck. Likewise, the firstborn among your children must be redeemed.*

¹⁴ "In the future, when your children ask, 'What does this mean?' say, 'Our God brought us out of Egypt, out of bondage, with a mighty hand. ¹⁵ When Pharaoh refused to let us go time and time again, Our God killed every firstborn of that land, people and animals. This is why I sacrifice to God the every firstborn of my flock, and why I redeem the firstborn among my children.' ¹⁶ It is to be like a sign on your hand and a memento on your forehead that by the powerful hand of Our God you were delivered out of Egypt."

ଉ ଉ ଉ

¹⁷ When Pharaoh let the people go, God did not lead them the short way, through the country of the Philistines, for God thought: "If they are confronted with war, they are more likely to lose heart and return to Egypt." ¹⁸ So God led them through the desert toward the Sea of Reeds. Even so, the Israelites left Egypt armed.

¹⁹ Moses brought with him the bones of Joseph, for Joseph had made the Israelites swear an oath, saying, "It is certain that God will take account of you. When that happens, carry my bones with you."

²⁰ After they left Succoth, they traveled to Etham, at the edge of the wilderness, where they camped. ²¹ Our God guided them with a pillar of cloud in the day, and with a pillar of fire to give them light after dark. They

---

* When an animal or a person was "given" to God, it was designated as *cherem*, or dedicated so utterly that it was unfit for any other use. In general, what was given was sacrificed. They were not, however, to sacrifice their children, so they were to pay a price—literally, a ransom or redemption price. Even today, many religious Jews "redeem" their firstborn sons thirty days after their birth, and give the money to charity.

were able to travel by day and by night, ²² and neither the pillar of cloud nor the pillar of fire failed to lead the people.

14:1 Then Our God spoke to Moses, ² "Tell the Israelites that they are to turn back and set up camp at Pi-hahiroth, halfway between Migdol and the sea. They are to set up camp by the sea, on the other side of Baal-zephon. ³ Pharaoh will think, 'They are wandering around confused and hemmed in by the desert.' ⁴ I will harden Pharaoh's heart, so that he pursues you. Then I will glorify myself at the expense of the ruler and the army. And the Egyptians will know that I am Your God." The Israelites did as God told them.

⁵ When the ruler of Egypt learned that the people had fled, he and his followers changed in their feelings toward them. "What have we done," they exclaimed, "allowing the Israelites to leave our service?" ⁶ So Pharaoh ordered the chariots harnessed and with an army of ⁷ 600 of the best chariots and all the other chariots in Egypt, with warriors on them, ⁸ pursued the Israelites even as they made their triumphant escape. ⁹ The Egyptians gave chase—the whole army, with horses, chariots, and charioteers—and caught up with them as they lay encamped by the sea, at Pi-hahiroth, facing Baal-zephon.

¹⁰ As Pharaoh drew near, the Israelites looked back and saw the Egyptians pursuing them, and cried out in terror to God. ¹¹ They turned on Moses, asking, "Were there no graves in Egypt that you must lead us out to die in the desert? What have you done to us? Why did you bring us out of Egypt? ¹² Didn't we tell you in Egypt, 'Leave us alone. Let us serve the Egyptians'? It would have been better to work for the Egyptians than to die here in the desert!"

¹³ But Moses told the people, "Don't be afraid! Stand your ground, and you will see the victory Our God will win for you today. Though you see Egypt today, you will never see it again. ¹⁴ Our God will do the fighting for you; you have only to keep still!"

¹⁵ Then Our God said to Moses, "Why are you crying out to me? Tell the Israelites to march on. ¹⁶ And you, lift up your staff and stretch out your hand over the sea, and split the sea in two, that the Israelites may pass through it on dry land. ¹⁷ I will make the hearts of the Egyptians so stubborn that they will come in after you, and I will glorify myself at the expense of Pharaoh and all the army, chariots and charioteers. ¹⁸ The Egyptians will know that I am Your God, when I glorify myself over Pharaoh and his chariots and charioteers."

¹⁹ Then the angel of God, who was leading the Israelites, moved to their rear—the pillar of cloud left the front of their number and took up position

behind them, ²⁰ between the Israelites and the Egyptians. All during the night the cloud provided light to one side and darkness to the other side, so that there was no contact between them.

²¹ Then Moses stretched his hand over the sea, and Our God swept the sea with a strong east wind throughout the night and so turned it into dry land. When the water was thus divided,* ²² the Israelites marched into the midst of the sea on dry land, with the water walled up on their right and on their left.

²³ The Egyptians followed in pursuit; all Pharaoh's horses and chariots and charioteers went after them into the midst of the sea. ²⁴ At dawn, Our God looked down upon the Egyptian forces from the column of fiery cloud, and threw the army into confusion and panic, ²⁵ clogging their chariot wheels so that they could hardly turn. The Egyptians turned to flee from the Israelites, saying "Their God fights for them against us!"

²⁶ Then Our God told Moses, "Stretch out your hand over the sea, and let the water flow back upon the Egyptians, over their chariots and their charioteers." ²⁷ So at sunrise, Moses stretched out his hand over the sea, and the waters rolled back in. As the Egyptians fled, Our God hurled them into its midst. ²⁸ As the water flowed back, covering the chariots and the charioteers—Pharaoh's whole army, who had followed the Israelites into the sea—not one of them survived. ²⁹ But the Israelites passed through, walking dry-shod in the sea, with the water like a wall, on their right and on their left. ³⁰ Thus Our God saved Israel on that day from the power of Egypt. When Israel saw the Egyptians lying dead on the seashore ³¹ and beheld the great power that Our God had shown against them, the people held Our God in awe; and put their faith in Our God and in Moses, God's trusted servant.

15:1 Then Moses and the Israelites sang this song to Our God:

> "To you, O God, I sing:
>> you have triumphed powerfully;
> horse and charioteer
>> you have flung into the sea!
> 2 Our God is our strength and our courage;
>> you have become our deliverance.
> You are Our God—we will praise you;
>> the God of our ancestors—we exalt you!
> 3 Our God is a warrior;
>> 'I AM' is your Name!

---

* An echo of the Creation, when God "separated water from water."

4 Pharaoh's chariots and army
    you has hurled into the sea,
  Pharaoh's choicest warriors
    sank in the Sea of Reeds.
5 The deep waters consumed them;
    they sank to the bottom like a stone.
6 Your right hand, O Most High,
    is mighty in power.
  Your right hand, O Most High,
    shattered our foe.
7 In the splendor of your power
    you threw down those who defied you;
  you released your wrath like fire,
    which consumed them like stubble.
8 With a blast of your nostrils
    the waters piled up.
  The waves stood like a dam,
    waters congealing in the depths of the sea.
9 The foe boasted,
    'I will chase them,
  I will overcome them!
    I will divide the plunder;
  I will feast on the spoils.
    Armed with my sword
    I will destroy them handily!'
10 But you poured out your breath
    and the sea enveloped them.
  They sank like lead
    into the raging waters.
11 Who is like you among the gods,
    O Most High?
  Who is like you—
    majestic in holiness,
  awesome and praiseworthy
    wonder-worker?
12 You stretched out your hand
    and the earth swallowed them up.
13 You led your redeemed people
    with your unfailing love.
  With your strength you guided them
    to your holy pasture.

¹⁴ When the nations hear of these things, they tremble!
    Anguish grips the people of Philistia.
¹⁵ The chieftains of Edom are terrified,
    the rulers of Moab take to trembling;
    the Canaanites collapse in fear.
¹⁶ Terror and dread fall on them all;
    by the power of your arm
they are stilled like stone—
    while your people pass through, O God,
    while the people you delivered pass through.
¹⁷ You brought them and planted them
    upon your own mountain—
that place, O Most High God,
    that place where you take your seat,
that sanctuary you have created
    with your own hands.
¹⁸ Our God will reign
    forever and ever!"

¹⁹ Once Pharaoh's horses, chariots and charioteers came into the sea-bed, Our God let the water collapse back upon them. But the Israelites walked through the sea on dry land.

²⁰ Then Aaron's sister, the prophet Miriam, picked up a tambourine, and all the women, followed her, dancing, with tambourines, ²¹ while Miriam sang:

"Sing to Our God
    who has triumphed gloriously,
who has flung horse and rider
    into the sea!"

15:22–18:27

Moses led the Israelites from the Sea of Reeds into the desert of Shur. They traveled for three days in the desert without finding water.

²³ When they arrived at Marah they found the water bitter and undrink-able. This is the reason for the name Marah—"bitterness." ²⁴ The people complained to Moses. "We need water to drink!"

²⁵ Then Moses cried out to Our God, who showed Moses a piece of

wood. Moses threw the piece of wood into the water, and the water was sweetened

It was there that Our God made a law and a decree for them, and there they were tested. ²⁶ God said to the people, "If you listen carefully to my voice, and do what is right in my eyes, and if you will pay attention to my decrees and obey my commands, I will not bring upon you any of the sufferings I brought upon the Egyptians—I am Your God. I am the One who heals you."

²⁷ Next they reached Elim, where they found twelve springs and seventy palm trees. They set up camp near the water.

16:1 From Elim they set out again, and the whole community of the Israelites reached the wilderness of Syn, which is between Elim and Sinai, on the fifteenth day of the second month after they left Egypt.

² They began to complain against Moses and Aaron there in the wilderness. ³ The people of Israel said to them, "If only we had died by Our God's hand in the land of Egypt, when we sat next to pots of meat and ate our bread till we were filled! But now you have brought the whole community out into this wilderness to die of hunger!"

⁴ Then Our God said to Moses, "Look, I will rain down bread from heaven for you. The people will go out and gather a day's portion every day, so that I can test them to see if they will follow my instructions. ⁵ On the sixth day, when they prepare what they brought in, it will be twice as much as the daily gathering."

⁶ So Moses and Aaron said to the Israelites, "In the evening you will know that it was Our God who brought you up out of Egypt, ⁷ and in the morning you will witness the glory of God, the One to whom you directed your complaints—for who are we, that you should complain to us?"

⁸ Moses continued, "It is Our God who will give you meat in the evening for your meal, and all the bread you want in the morning, because Our God has heard your complaints. For it is not to us that you are complaining—who are we?—but to Our God."

⁹ Then Moses said to Aaron, "Tell the whole Israelite community, 'Present yourselves before Our God, who has heard your complaints.'"

¹⁰ As Aaron was speaking to the whole Israelite community, they looked toward the desert, and there was the glory of Our God appearing in the form of a cloud. ¹¹ Then Our God spoke to Moses and said, ¹² "I have heard the complaining of the people of Israel. Say this to them: 'In the evening you will eat meat, and in the morning you will have your fill of bread. Then you will know that I, the Most High, am your God.'"

¹³ So it came about that in the evening quail flew in and all around the camp. And in the morning there was a layer of dew all around the camp; ¹⁴ when the layer of dew evaporated, there on the surface of the desert were flakes of something: delicate, powdery, fine as frost.

¹⁵ When they saw this, the people of Israel said to each other, "What is it?" —not knowing what it was.* But Moses told them, "This is the bread Our God has given you to eat.

¹⁶ "This is the command Our God gave you," he continued. "Each one is to gather just enough to eat. Let everyone collect a two-quart measure of it for each person in your tent." ¹⁷ The Israelites did as they were told. Some took a large amount. Some took very little. ¹⁸ But when they measured it by the two-quart measure, those who took a large amount did not have too much, and those who gathered very little did not have too little. Each had just as much as they needed.

¹⁹ Moses told them, "No one is to keep it overnight." ²⁰ Some of the Israelites did not listen, and kept it overnight. It turned rotten and full of maggots, and Moses was angry with them.

²¹ Each morning the people gathered as much as they needed, and as the sun grew high, it melted away.

²² On the sixth day the people gathered twice as much—two measures for each person. The clan leaders came to Moses to report this. ²³ Moses said, "Our God commanded this, saying, 'Tomorrow is a day of rest, a holy Sabbath** to Our God. Bake what you need to bake and boil what you need to boil. The remainder is to be set aside and kept until the next day.'" ²⁴ The Israelites did as Moses instructed them, and it did not rot or have maggots.

²⁵ "Eat it today," Moses counseled, "for today is the Sabbath of Our God. There is none on the ground today. ²⁶ For six days you are to gather it, and on the seventh day, the Sabbath, it will not be there."

²⁷ On the next day, some of the them went out looking for it, but there was none. ²⁸ Our God said to Moses, " How long will you refuse to keep my commandments and my instructions? ²⁹ Remember, I gave you the Sabbath, and I give you food for two days on the sixth day. You are to stay where you are on the seventh day. No one is to go out on the seventh day!" ³⁰ So the people rested that day.

---

* The common English translation is "manna," for the Hebrew *mahn hu*, a playful slurring of the words *mah hu* ("what is it?"); a similar phrasing in English might be to say that they called it "Whatzit" or "Whatchamacallit." Later poets referred to it as "the bread of angels."

**Sabbath, or *shabbat,* means to cease or to rest.

³¹ The Israelites called the food "manna." It was white like coriander seeds and it tasted like wafers made with honey.

³² Moses said, "This is what Our God commands: Take a measure of manna and set it aside for your descendants, so that they will see the bread with which I fed you in the wilderness when I led you out of Egypt."

³³ Moses said to Aaron, "Fill a jar with a full measure of manna and set it before Our God. It is to be kept for our descendants."

³⁴ Aaron did as God instructed Moses, storing it before the Covenant for safekeeping. ³⁵ The Israelites ate manna for the forty years it took to come into the region of Canaan. ³⁶ The two-quart measure that they used is one-tenth the size of a five-gallon *ephah*.

17·1 The Israelites left the desert of Syn to travel by stages, as Our God had directed them. They camped at Rephidim, but found no drinking water.

² Again they turned on Moses, saying, "Give us drinking water."

Moses replied, "Why do you quarrel with me? Why do you test Our God?"

³ But the people were thirsty, and complained even more to Moses. "Why did you bring us out of Egypt only to make us and our children and our livestock die of thirst?"

⁴ Moses appealed to Our God. "What am I to do with these people? They are ready to stone me!"

⁵ Our God answered Moses, "Take some of the elders and move to the front of the people. Take with you the staff with which you struck the Nile. Go! ⁶ I will wait for you there by the rock of Horeb.* Strike the rock, and water will come out of it for the people to drink."

And Moses did so, in the sight the elders.

⁷ Moses named the place Massah, "Testing," and Meribah, "Quarreling," for the Israelites tested Our God when they said, "Is Our God with us or not?"

⁸ The Amalekites came into the area and attacked the Israelites at Rephidim.

⁹ Moses said to Joshua,** "Select some of the able-bodied to go out and fight the Amalekites. Tomorrow I will stand on top of the hill holding the staff of God."

---

* Site of Moses' first encounter with God in the burning thornbush.
**Yehoshua, or "God delivers," becomes Moses' assistant, and later, the leader of the people of Israel.

¹⁰ So Joshua did as Moses ordered and fought the Amalekites, while Moses, Aaron, and Hur* climbed to the top of the hill. ¹¹ So long as Moses kept his hands raised, Israel held the advantage, but whenever he lowered them, the Amalekites took the advantage. ¹² When Moses' hands grew weary they set up a stone for him to sit on. Aaron and Hur held his hands up, one on each side, so that they remained upright until dusk. ¹³ And Joshua prevailed against the Amalekites by the sword.

¹⁴ Our God said to Moses, "Put this in writing, and tell it to Joshua: I will totally wipe out the memory of the Amalekites from under heaven." ¹⁵ Moses built an altar and named it "Our God is my Banner," ¹⁶ and said, "Our hands held up the banner** of Our God. And God will make war against the Amalekites throughout the ages."

18¹ Jethro, the priest of Midian, Moses' father-in-law, learned all about what God had done for Moses and for Israel, God's people, and how Our God led the Israelites to freedom from Egypt. ² When Moses had sent his spouse Zipporah home to her parents, Jethro had welcomed her ³ and her two sons. The firstborn was named Gershom, "Sojourner There"—so named because Moses said, "I have become a sojourner in a foreign land," ⁴ and the other was named Eliezer, "God's Help," because Moses had said, "The God of my ancestor came to my aid and saved me from Pharaoh's sword."

⁵ Now Zipporah and the children accompanied Jethro to the desert where the Israelites were camped at the mountain of God. ⁶ Jethro sent this message to Moses: "I, your father-in-law Jethro, am journeying to meet you, as are your wife and two children."

⁷ Moses went out to greet them. Then he bowed low before Jethro and kissed him, and they inquired after each other's health. Then they all went into Moses' tent. ⁸ Moses told them everything that Our God had done to Pharaoh and to Egypt for Israel's sake. He told of their journey and its hardships, and how God had provided for them.

⁹ Jethro rejoiced in this good news of Our God's kindness to Israel, and their salvation from Egypt. ¹⁰ Jethro said, "Praise to Your God, who rescued you from the hand of Egypt and of Pharaoh, who has rescued the people from Egypt's power! ¹¹ Now I know that Your God is above all other gods, for this God has delivered our people from the Egyptians and their pride."† ¹² So Jethro, father of Zipporah, made a burnt offering and

---

* Aaron's assistant.

**The traditional Hebrew text has "throne," but this is almost certainly a scribal error: the two words in Hebrew are very similar.

† Recall that Jethro was a priest in Midian, and the people there were not monotheists. His offering of sacrifice is an indication that he would now be a priest of the Most High.

other sacrifices to God, and Aaron and the elders came to share their meal with Jethro in God's presence.

¹³ The next morning Moses served as a judge and resolved the people's disputes, and was surrounded by them from dawn until dusk. ¹⁴ When Jethro saw this, he asked, "What is this about, with all the people around you? Why do you sit there with the people from dawn until dusk?"

¹⁵ Moses replied, "The people come to me for God's advice. ¹⁶ If there is a dispute among them, they come to me to settle their differences, and I instruct them in the statutes and laws of God."

¹⁷ Jethro said, "This is not a good way. ¹⁸ You and your people will wear yourselves out. It is too great a burden. ¹⁹ Let me give you some advice, and God will help you. Have them bring their cases before God, and represent them before God in those matters. ²⁰ Teach them the laws and the statutes, and instruct them how to conduct themselves and what they should do. ²¹ At the same time, find able, God-fearing people, honest and incorruptible, and appoint them as officials over units of ten, of fifty, of hundreds and of thousands. ²² These can serve as judges for the people at all times. Let them handle the simple cases, and bring difficult cases to you. Thus your burden will be both lightened and shared. ²³ By doing it this way, when God requires more of you in the future, the strain will not bring you down, and the people will arrive at their destination in peace."

²⁴ Moses heard Jethro's counsel, and took it. ²⁵ He selected wise people from all of Israel and appointed them as officials over units of ten, of fifty, of hundreds and of thousands. ²⁶ They heard the simpler cases daily, and the difficult cases they brought before Moses.

²⁷ Then Moses bid his father-in-law farewell, and Jethro returned home.

19:1–31:18

*t*hree months to the very day after their departure from the land of Egypt, the Israelites came to the desert of Sinai. ² They had traveled from Rephidim into the desert of Sinai and camped there, in front of the mountain.

³ Then Moses went up to God, and Our God called out from the mountain and said, "This is what you are to say to the house of Jacob, what you are to tell the Israelites: ⁴ 'You saw for yourselves what I did to Egypt, how I carried you on eagles' wings and brought you to myself. ⁵ If you now listen to my voice and keep my covenant, then out of all people you will be

my cherished ones. Truly, the whole earth is my own, ⁶ but you will be a kindom of priests—a holy nation.' These are the words you are to say to the Israelites."

⁷ Moses descended from the mountain. Summoning the elders of the people, he laid down for them the things Our God said to him.

⁸ The people answered with one voice: "What Our God has said, we will do."

When Moses went up to God to deliver the response of the people, ⁹ Our God said to Moses, "I will come to you in a dense cloud, so that when the people hear me speaking with you, they will always have faith in you." Then Moses reported the people's response.

¹⁰ Our God said, "Go to the people and tell them to make themselves holy, today and tomorrow. Let them wash their clothing ¹¹ and hold themselves in readiness for the third day, for on the third day Your God will descend from the mountain of Sinai in the sight of the people. ¹² You must set limits on the people. Tell them: 'Take care that no one either goes up the mountain or sets a foot on it. ¹³ Anyone who touches the mountain will absolutely be put to death. No one may put a hand on that person, but he or she is to be stoned to death or shot with arrows. Whether it is an animal or a human being, it must be killed.' But when the ram's horn blows, then they may go up the mountain."

¹⁴ Moses came down from the mountain to the people. He sanctified them, and they washed their clothes. ¹⁵ Moses said, "Prepare yourselves. For three days, let there be no sexual contact among you."

¹⁶ On the third day, when morning came, there was thunder and lightning, and a dense cloud settled over the mountain. Then there was such a loud trumpet blast that all the people trembled in their camp. ¹⁷ Moses led the people out of the camp to meet God, and they huddled together at the base of the mountain. ¹⁸ The mountain of Sinai was shrouded in smoke, for Our God had descended in the form of fire. The plumes rose like smoke from a furnace, and the mountain quaked violently. ¹⁹ Louder and louder came the trumpet. Moses spoke out, and Our God answered with peals of thunder. ²⁰ Our God came down upon the mountain of Sinai, and called Moses to the top of the mountain, and Moses went up.

²¹ Then Our God said to Moses, "Go down and warn the people not to break through the boundaries to try to see me, or many of them might die. ²² Even the priests who approach God must purify themselves, or I will lash out against them."

²³ Moses replied, "The people cannot come up the mountain, for you solemnly warned us to set boundaries on the mountain and declare it sacred."

²⁴ Our God replied, "Go down, and bring Aaron up with you. But do not let either the priests or people break through to come up and see me, or I will lash out against them." ²⁵ Moses descended and told the people these things.

20·1 Then God spoke all these words,* and said, ² "I am Your God who brought you out of the land of Egypt, out of the house of bondage.

³ "Do not worship any gods except me!

⁴ "Do not make for yourselves any carved image or likeness of anything in heaven above or on the earth beneath or in the waters under the earth, ⁵ and do not bow down to them or serve them! For I, Your God, am a jealous God, and for the parents' fault I punish the children, the grandchildren and the great-grandchildren of those who turn from me; ⁶ but I show kindness to the thousandth generation of those who love me and heed my commandments.

⁷ "Do not utter the Name of Your God to misuse it, for Our God will not acquit anyone who utters God's Name to misuse it!**

⁸ "Remember the Sabbath day and keep it holy! ⁹ For six days you will labor and do all your work, ¹⁰ but the seventh day is a Sabbath for Your God. Do no work on that day, neither you nor your daughter nor your son, nor your workers—women or men—nor your animals, nor the foreigner who lives among you. ¹¹ For in the six days Your God made the heavens and the earth and the sea and all that they hold, but rested on the seventh day; this is why Your God has blessed the Sabbath day and made it sacred.

¹² "Honor your mother and your father, so that you may have a long life in the land that Your God has given to you!

---

* In the following, "you" is always singular: the commandments, which Jewish tradition calls "the Ten Words," are addressed to the individual, not to the nation. There is some controversy over the numbering of the commandments; Jewish tradition makes verse 2 the first "commandment" and groups verses 3 and 4 together as the second commandment; other traditions separate verse 14 into two separate commandments. Most commentators, however, see the commandments falling into two groups, verses 2 through 12 forming the first half, and verses 13 and 14 forming the second half. The language in the first half is markedly different from that in the second half; and many have noted that the first group deals with relationships to God and family, whereas the second group is more concerned with society.

**"Misuse" is more than mere cursing; it is to invoke the Name in false oaths, to delude others, or to use it for any wrong purpose.

¹³ "No murdering!*

¹⁴ "No adultery!

¹⁵ "No stealing!

¹⁶ "No giving false testimony against your neighbor!

¹⁷ "No desiring your neighbor's house! No desiring your neighbor's spouse, or worker—female or male—or ox, or donkey, or anything that belongs to your neighbor!"

¹⁸ When the people witnessed the thunder and lightning, and heard the sound like blaring trumpets, and saw the smoking mountain, they shook in fear. Keeping their distance, ¹⁹ they said to Moses, "Speak to us and we will listen, but do not let God speak to us, or it will surely be our death."

²⁰ But Moses said, "Don't be afraid. God's coming this way was simply a test for you, to give you a sense of awe and reverence, and to keep you from sinning." ²¹ The people kept their distance, while Moses went up into the darkness where God was.

ଔ   ଔ   ଔ

²² Our God said to Moses, "Tell the Israelites, 'With your own eyes you have witnessed that I have spoken to you from heaven. ²³ You must not make for yourselves gods of silver or gods of gold to be worshipped beside me. ²⁴ Build a simple altar of earth for the sacrifice of your whole burnt offerings** and your fellowship sacrifices,† your sheep, your goats, your cattle. Wherever I cause my Name to be honored, I will come to you and I will bless you. ²⁵ If you make an altar of stone for me, you must not use hewn stone, for if you use tools on it, you will defile it.‡ ²⁶ You must not climb to the altar by steps when you approach it, to keep your nakedness from being exposed on it.

---

* Not "killing" in general. The abrupt language here is deliberate, and evokes the sentence structure, rhythm, and stark informality of the Hebrew in these verses. The Hebrew text combines this verse and the following three into one, so the verse numbering differs from standard English versions through the end of the chapter.

** Heb. *olah*, ascending, from the idea of the smoke of the sacrifice ascending to God. The animal was burned completely on the altar, symbolizing the complete self-surrender and devotion of the sacrificer to God. The word is frequently translated "holocaust."

† Traditionally, "peace offerings," of which there were three types: the votive (in completion of a vow), thank (in gratitude during times of prosperity and success), and freewill offerings (given anytime, from a glad heart).

‡ Iron was thought to drive out the soul of the stone—i.e., rob it of its essence.

21:1 "Here are the rules you are to establish for the people:

2 "When you buy an indentured Hebrew worker,* the worker will be in your service for six years. In the seventh year the indentured worker is to be freed without having to purchase his or her freedom.

3 "Indentured workers who come to you unmarried are to leave by themselves; 4 those who come to you married are to leave with their spouses.

"If a worker marries while in your service, and they have children, the mother and the children stay with you, but the man must leave by himself. 5 But if he should protest and say, 'I love my wife and my children! I will refuse my freedom,' 6 bring the worker before God.** The worker will be taken to the sanctuary door or doorpost, and have his ear pierced with an awl, and he will stay in that household for life.

7 "If a daughter is sold into service,† she is not to be freed as a male worker would be. 8 If the one who has taken her for himself is not pleased with her, she is to be returned to her parents, for a fee. She is not be sold to foreigners, for the man has treated her unjustly by not marrying her. 9 If parents have purchased her to be given to their son, she will have the rights of a daughter. 10 If the one who has purchased her takes a second wife, the first is not to be deprived of her food allotment, her clothes, or her conjugal rights. 11 And if she is deprived of any of these things, she is to go free without payment of any money.

12 "Anyone who strikes another with a mortal blow is to be executed. 13 If the slayer did not lie in wait—that is, if God let the death happen‡—then the slayer may flee to one of the cities of refuge which I will designate. 14 But if a person deliberately murders another and kills with premeditation, the individual must be seized—even at the altar—and taken away for execution.

15 "Anyone who strikes a parent—mother or father—is to be executed.

---

* In these times, indentured workers were essentially serfs; and while the text accepts such service as a given, it was not considered a permanent situation: immediately, the conditions for the release of such a worker are discussed, in an attempt to soften the conditions and humanize the institution somewhat.

**Or "judges." The word for God is plural, and literally means gods or powers, and can refer to oracles—those who speak for God, whether as prophets or as judicial representatives interpreting God's laws.

† Poverty-stricken parents would sometimes sell their daughters as attendants, to be treated as wives or concubines, acquiring more rights than an indentured worker would have.

‡ I.e., if it was not premeditated murder. The idea of God "letting it happen" here applies both to accidents and to crimes of passion.

[16] "Anyone who kidnaps another is to be be executed, whether the victim has been put into bondage, or is still in the custody of the kidnapper.

[17] "Anyone who curses mother or father is to be executed.

[18] "If two people quarrel, and one hits the other with a stone or a fist, but it is not a mortal blow and only puts the person in bed, [19] and if the injured person recovers enough to walk around outside with a crutch, the person who caused the injury will incur no liability. The offender must, however, compensate the injured person for loss of time at work and must provide for a full recovery.

[20] "If someone strikes one's own indentured worker, male or female, and the worker dies on the spot, the worker is to be avenged. [21] However, if the indentured worker lingers for a day or two, the offender has incurred no liability, for legally the worker is property.

[22] "When a fight breaks out between two individuals, and in the course of their struggle, one of them hits a pregnant woman and causes a miscarriage, but there are no further harm done, the offender will pay a fine set by the woman and her spouse, and agreed upon by the judges. [23] But if there are injuries, the penalty is to be a life for a life, [24] an eye for an eye, a tooth for a tooth, a hand for a hand, a foot for a foot, [25] a burn for a burn, a bruise for a bruise, or a wound for a wound.*

[26] "If someone strikes one's own indentured worker in the eye and the person is blinded in that eye, the worker must go free to compensate for the eye. [27] If one knocks out the tooth of one's indentured worker, whether female or male, the individual must go free to compensate for the tooth.

[28] "If an ox gores a woman or a man to death, it must be stoned to death, and its flesh must not be eaten. The owner of the ox is not liable. [29] But if the ox had a reputation for viciousness, and the owner had been warned, but has neglected to corral the ox, and the ox kills a person, then both the ox and the owner must be put to death.

[30] "If payment is demanded instead to compensate for the death, the owner is to pay whatever fee is imposed, and consider it a ransom for his or her own life. [31] The same rules apply if an ox gores a daughter or son. [32] But if an ox gores someone's indentured worker, the owner of the ox

---

* This is in contrast to the Babylonian system of justice, where wealthy people could essentially pay their way out of such offenses. Here, then, we are not seeing vengeance (as this passage is commonly interpreted), but a fairness in which all, high or low, are accountable in a measure equal to their actions.

need only pay thirty shekels of silver* to the worker's owner, though the ox is still to be stoned to death.

³³ "When a donkey or an ox falls into an open pit, or a new pit without a cover, ³⁴ the one who dug the pit must compensate the owner for the loss, but may keep the dead animal.

³⁵ "When one person's ox injures the ox of another, and the other ox dies, the live ox is to be sold, and both owners are to share equally in the proceeds; they are to split the dead ox. ³⁶ On the other hand, if the ox that did the injury was known to be vicious, and its owner was negligent, this owner must compensate the owner of the dead ox, and the dead ox remains with its owner.

22:1 "A thief who takes an ox or a lamb, and eats it or sells it, must pay restitution—five head of cattle for the ox, four sheep for the lamb. ⁴ If an ox, a donkey, or a sheep is found in the thief's possession still alive, the thief need only repay two animals for the one that was stolen.**

² "In the case of someone who breaks into a home during the night, and is caught by the homeowner: If the thief is struck down, and dies, the homeowner will not be held guilty; ³ but if this happens in the daylight, the homeowner has committed murder. Otherwise, the thief must repay the owner in full; the thief who has no money is be made an indentured worker.

⁵ "If a landowner who keeps livestock lets the cattle wander into a neighbor's fields to graze, restitution must be made from the choicest of the landowner's fields or vineyards.

⁶ "If someone is burning a thornbush and the fire breaks out and spreads, burning up a neighbor's sheaves, standing grain, or even the entire field, the person who started the fire must pay in full.

⁷ "When one entrusts silver or goods to one's neighbors for safekeeping, and they are stolen from the neighbors' home, the thief, if caught, must pay double the value of what was stolen. ⁸ If no thief is caught or identified, the homeowners must appear before the judges to determine whether or not they are guilty of the theft.

---

* About twelve ounces. Essentially, "thirty pieces of silver" is not simply the value of a human life, but the value of someone on the bottom rung of society.

**We have moved verse 4 up, where it fits the context better. Verse 22:1 is numbered 21:37 in the Hebrew text; the verse numbering continues to be at variance through the end of chapter 22.

⁹ "Whenever there is any conflict over who owns an ox, a donkey, a sheep, a cloak, or any other "lost" property, both parties must appear before the judges. Whoever loses the case must pay double to the one who wins the judgment.

¹⁰ "When a person places a donkey, an ox, a sheep, or any another domestic animal in another's care, and the animal dies, or is injured or disappears—and there are no witnesses— ¹¹ if the one keeping the animal swears an oath before the Most High God to the owner that not a hand has been laid on the animal, the owner must accept this as proof, and no payment need be made. ¹² But if the animal is stolen while under the care of the neighbor, payment must be paid to the owner. ¹³ If a wild creature mauled the animal, the remains are to be brought to the owner as evidence; no restitution is due for a mauled animal.

¹⁴ "If a person borrows an animal from a neighbor, and the animal dies while the owner is not present, the borrower must pay the animal's full price. ¹⁵ But if the owner was present, the borrower need pay nothing; or if the animal was hired, the rental fee covers the loss.

¹⁶ "If a man seduces a young woman who is not spoken for and lies with her, her seducer must marry her and pay the marriage fee. ¹⁷ If her parents will not agree to the marriage, the man must still pay a marriage fee, equal to the fee for a virgin.*

¹⁸ "Do not allow anyone who practices sorcery to live.

¹⁹ "Whoever has sexual relations with animals must be put to death.

²⁰ "Whoever offers sacrifices to any god other than the Most High must be sacrificed in return.**

²¹ "Do not mistreat or oppress foreigners, for you once were foreigners in Egypt.

²² "You must not take advantage of widows or orphans. ²³ If you do afflict them, they will cry out to me—and be certain that I will hear their complaint. ²⁴ My anger will be like fire, like a sword that will kill you. Your

---

* In biblical society there was essentially a sliding scale the marriage fee or "bride price," a payment in the form of money, property, or other valuable asset made by a prospective husband to the bride's family, with virgins commanding the highest marriage fee of all.

**Or "must be declared *cherem*," that is, placed under the sacred ban. The word often referred to a sacred object or ritual item; it was something that had been dedicated irrevocably to God—frequently by completely destroying it, as with something placed on an altar. The concept included anything that was taboo, including a ruler's "harem"—the Arabic form of the same word.

spouses will become widows and widowers, and your children will become orphans.

²⁵ "When you loan money to my people, to the poor who live beside you, do not act as a moneylender to them, charging them interest.

²⁶ "If you take your neighbor's cloak as collateral for a loan, you must return in by sunset, ²⁷ for it may be your neighbor's only warmth in the night—what else would you neighbor sleep in? If your neighbor appeals to me, I will hear, for I am the Compassionate One.

²⁸ "Do not blaspheme against Your God, or revile your leaders.

²⁹ "Do not hold back the firstfruits of your grain or your wine.

"Give me your firstborn, ³⁰ and the same of your oxen and your sheep—they are to stay with their mother for seven days, and on the eighth day they are to be given to me.

³¹ "You are my holy people. You must not eat the flesh of anything that was mangled by wild animals. Throw it to the dogs.

23:1 "Do not spread rumors.

"Do not conspire with a corrupt person by offering false testimony.

² "Do not be drawn into evil simply because the majority is doing it.

"If you are giving evidence in a lawsuit, don't speak anything less than the complete truth, no matter what others think or say; to do otherwise is to subvert justice.

³ "Do not show partiality in lawsuits—not even toward the poor.

⁴ "When you come upon an ox or donkey belonging to your adversary that has strayed—return it.

⁵ "If you see the donkey of someone who hates you, and it is lying helpless beneath its load—come to its aid.

⁶ "Do not deprive the poor of just treatment in their lawsuits.

⁷ "Always distance yourself from any false charges, and do not execute the clear and innocent—I will hold the guilty accountable.

⁸ "Do not accept bribes—bribery blinds the vision of officials, and twists the words of the just.

⁹ "Do not oppress foreigners, for you know what it is to be a foreigner—you were foreigners in Egypt.

¹⁰ "You may sow your crops and reap them for six years, ¹¹ but in the seventh year let it rest and lie untilled. In that year the land will provide food for the poor, and what they don't take will go to the wild animals. Do the same with your vineyards and olive groves.

¹² "For six days you are to do your work, but on the seventh day you must not work. On that day the donkey and the ox are to rest as well, and so are your indentured workers and the foreigners who do your work.

¹³ "Listen to every word I am telling you!

"Invoke no other gods—their very names must not cross your lips.

¹⁴ "Three times a year, you are to keep a pilgrimage festival to me.

¹⁵ "You are to celebrate the Festival of Unleavened Bread: for seven days, as I commanded you earlier, you are to eat unleavened bread. Do this at the time in the appointed month of Aviv, when you came out of Egypt. No one is to come into my presence empty-handed. ¹⁶ You are to celebrate the Harvest Festival,* with the firstfruits of your work, with what you sowed in the soil. And you are to celebrate the Festival of Ingathering** at the end of the year, when you gather in your labor's harvest from the land.

¹⁷ "These are the three times of the year when all my people must gather in the presence of the Most High, your God.

¹⁸ "Do not offer to me the blood of a sacrifice with anything made of yeast.

"The fat of my festival offering must not remain overnight until morning.

¹⁹ "You must bring your very best firstfruits of the earth into the house of the Most High, your God.

"Do not boil a kid in its mother's milk.†

²⁰ "I will send you a messenger,‡ one who will go before you to guide you on your way. My angel will lead you to the place I prepared for you. ²¹ Give my messenger your fullest attention; heed what it tells you. Do not

---

* Also known as the Shavu'ot, the Feast of Weeks, or Pentecost. This is the wheat harvest, or the harvest of the firstfruits, which usually falls in early June.

** Also known as Sukkot, the Feast of Booths, or Tabernacles. This is the larger harvest festival—and the grape harvest in particular—which is held in late September or early October.

† Jewish mystical tradition in the Middle Ages understood this as the separation between milk (life-giving) and blood (life-taking).

‡ The same Hebrew word describes both human messengers and celestial angelic beings—and the Angel of Our God is frequently the manifestation of the presence of God. Here it could mean a power like the pillar of cloud or fire. The passage was quoted in the gospel of Mark to indicate John the Baptist.

disobey my angel, for it will not forgive such transgression; my Name lives with it. ²² But if you attend carefully to its words, and do as I say, I will be an enemy to your foes; I will oppose all who oppose you.

²³ "My messenger will lead you, and bring you to the Amorites, the Hittites, the Perizzites, the Canaanites, the Hivites, and the Jebusites—and I will make them all disappear. ²⁴ You are not to bow down to their gods; or follow their worship practices. You must obliterate all their images and smash their standing stones.

²⁵ "You must worship Your God, the Most High, and I will bless your bread and your water, and take all sickness from you. ²⁶ Women will not miscarry or be infertile in your land, and I will give each of you long life.

²⁷ "I will send my terror before you, and cause panic in every nation you pass through. I will make all your enemies turn and run from you. ²⁸ I will send despair* before you to drive out the Hivites, the Canaanites and the Hittites from your presence. ²⁹ I will not expel them all in one year, for the land would become a wasteland and the wild beasts would run rampant. ³⁰ I will expel them little by little, until you have grown in numbers and possess their territory. ³¹ Your frontiers will run from the Sea of Reeds to the sea of the Philistines, and from the desert to the river Euphrates. I will place those in the land at your disposal, and you will force them out before you. ³² Do not make covenants with them or their gods. ³³ They are not to remain in your land, for they will bring you into sin against me, and you will be trapped in the worship of their gods!"

ଔ   ଔ   ଔ

24₁ Our God said to Moses, "Come up to Your God, you and Aaron, Nadab, and Abihu, and seventy of the elders of Israel. While all of you are still at a distance, all of you are to bow down. ² Only Moses is to approach Your God, but none of the others, and the people will not approach with you."

³ When Moses came and told the people the commands of Our God, and the ordinances, they answered with one voice, "We will do everything that Our God has decreed." ⁴ Moses then wrote down all the commands of God.

Early the next morning he arose and built an altar at the mountain's base, with twelve standing stones, one for each of the twelve tribes of Israel. ⁵ Then Moses directed young people among the Israelites to make burnt offerings and to sacrifice young bulls as communion offerings to Our God.

---

* Other versions render the Hebrew as "the hornet"; both translations are valid.

⁶ Moses took half of the blood of the offerings and put it into bowls; the rest he splashed against the altar.

⁷ Then, taking the scroll of the Covenant, Moses read it aloud to the people. The people answered, "We will heed and do all that Our God has decreed."

⁸ Then Moses splashed the blood over the people, saying, "This is the blood of the Covenant which Our God made with you in giving you these words."*

⁹ Then Moses, Aaron, Nadab, Abihu and seventy of the Israelite elders went up the mountain, ¹⁰ and they saw the God of Israel. Beneath God's feet was something that looked like a pavement made of sapphire, clear as the heavens. ¹¹ God's hand did not touch the elders of Israel; instead, they saw God, and yet they ate and drank.**

¹² Then Our God said to Moses, "Come up to me on the mountain and wait there, and I will give you the Law and the commandments, which I have inscribed on stone tablets, for you to teach them with."

¹³ So Moses, and Joshua, his attendant, went up the mountain of God, ¹⁴ saying to the elders, "Wait here for us until we return. Aaron and Hur will be with you; if there is dispute among you, turn to them."

¹⁵ Then Moses went up the mountain to where the clouds engulfed it. ¹⁶ The glory of Our God then came to dwell on Mount Sinai. The cloud covered the mountain for six days; on the seventh day, God called to Moses out of the cloud. ¹⁷ To the Israelites the glory of Our God looked like an all-consuming fire at the top of the mountain. ¹⁸ Moses climbed the mountain until he disappeared into the cloud, and stayed there for forty days and forty nights.†

---

* This is the ratification of the Covenant at Sinai. It has three elements: one directed toward God, one encompassing both God and the people, and one directed toward the people. First, Moses faces God and offers atonement for the people's sins (splashing the blood against the altar). Then he reads the terms of the Covenant—the Ten Commandments and the statutes that followed—and gets the people's explicit consent. Finally, he sprinkles the rest of the blood on the people while using traditional covenant language (echoed in the words of the Last Supper). Splashing or sprinkling blood on people occurs only two other places in the Hebrew scriptures—in the consecration of a priest, and the cleansing of a leper. The meaning, in both cases, is the beginning of a new life, which is particularly appropriate in this scene.

** A direct encounter with God usually meant death—recall Jacob's amazement that "I have seen God face to face, yet my life was spared!" Here the statement that "God's hand did not touch the elders" means that God did not kill them. The phrase "they saw God" is complex. Here "saw" translates *hazoh*, often used in connection with prophetic vision rather than ordinary sight; and "God" might better be rendered "Godhood"—indicating an epiphany, an experience of the essence of God, rather than simply seeing some entity.

† This echoes both the Flood and the experience of Elijah many years later on the same mountain.

25:1 Then Our God said to Moses, 2 "Tell the Israelites to collect offerings for me; from all who are moved in their hearts to give, receive gifts for me. 3 Collect from them gifts of gold, silver, and bronze; 4 indigo, purple and scarlet yarn; fine linen, and goat's hair; 5 rams' skins dyed red, fine leather, and acacia wood; 6 oil for the lamps; spices for anointing oil and for fragrant incense; 7 onyx stones and other precious stones to be set in the ephod and the breastpiece.*

8 "Tell them to construct a sanctuary for me so that I may dwell among you. 9 Build the Tabernacle and all of its furnishings according to the following design:**

10 "The Ark† is to be made of acacia wood, 45 inches long, 27 inches wide, and 27 inches high. 11 Overlay it with pure gold inside and out, and make a molding of gold around the edge. 12 Forge four rings of gold for it and fasten them to its four feet, with two rings on one side and two on the other. 13 Make two poles of acacia wood, overlaid with gold, 14 and insert them into the rings on the sides of the Ark to carry it. 15 The poles are to remain in place in the rings of the Ark, and not removed. 16 Place the tablets of the Covenant that I will give you into the Ark.

17 "Make its Covering‡ out of pure gold, 45 inches long and 27 inches wide. 18 Make two winged sphinxes§ out of hammered gold, and place them at the ends of the Covering, 19 one at each end; the sphinxes are to be of one piece with the Covering. 20 The wings of the sphinxes are to spread over the Covering, forming a canopy over it; the two sphinxes are to face one another, and are to look downward toward the Covering. 21 Put the Covering on top of the Ark, and into it place the Covenant which I will give you.

---

* Priestly garments which will be described in greater detail in chapter 28. The ephod was a kind of apron worn by the high priest; the breastpiece was a woven pouch to which stones were affixed on the outside, and in which were kept the priest's oracular tools, the Urim and Thummim.

** The Tabernacle, also called the Tent or the Dwelling, was composed of two sections: the Sanctuary, or Holy Place; and the Holy of Holies, or Most Holy Place.

† The word simply means a chest or a box.

‡ The Hebrew word literally means "cover," but encompasses the idea of atonement or expiation, as in covering sins. Besides serving as a cover for the box, it was used as a place where the actual atonement was performed. The term is frequently translated "mercy seat."

§ Usually translated "cherubim," these were mythic creatures that stood as guardians in Mesopotamian temples, and guarded the way to the garden of Eden.

²² "This is where I will meet you; I will speak to you from above the Covering, from between winged sphinxes on the Ark of the Covenant, and will give you commands for the Israelites.

²³ "Build a table of acacia wood, 36 inches long and 18 inches wide. ²⁴ Overlay the table with pure gold, and make a molding of gold around it. ²⁵ Make a rim around the table, the width of your hand, with a gold molding around the rim.

²⁶ "Cast four gold rings for the table, and place the rings at each corner on the four legs of the table. ²⁷ The four rings to hold the poles for carrying the table must be parallel to the rim. ²⁸ Make the poles of acacia wood and overlay them with gold, to be used for carrying the table.

²⁹ "Make containers, ladles, pitchers and sacrificial bowls—all out of pure gold—for the drink offerings.

³⁰ "And make sure the Bread of the Presence is placed on the table, and is before me at all times.

³¹ "Make a lampstand of pure hammered gold, with a stem and branches, cups, buds and blossoms—all made of one piece.*

³² "The lampstand is to have six branches, three branches on one side and three on the other. ³³ Three cups shaped like almond blossoms with leaves and petals is to be on the first branch, and three cups shaped like almond blossoms with leaves and petals is to be on the second branch, and so on for each of the six branches. ³⁴ Attached to the stem itself are to be four cups shaped like almond blossoms with leaves and petals, ³⁵ with a bud under the first pair of branches, and a second bud under the second pair of branches, and a third bud under the third pair of branches—and so on for all the branches. ³⁶ The buds and branches are to be of one piece with the lampstand—all a single piece of pure hammered gold.

³⁷ "Make seven lamps and place them so that they light the space in front of the lampstand. ³⁸ Its snuffers and the trays are to be of pure gold. ³⁹ Seventy-five pounds of pure gold is to be used for the lampstand and its accessories. ⁴⁰ And be certain that it all conforms exactly to the design you are being allowed to see on this mountain.

26:1 "Build the Tabernacle with ten tapestries of linen, finely woven of indigo, purple and scarlet threads, and finely brocaded with winged sphinxes.

---

* The lampstand is constructed in the shape of an almond tree, and represents the Tree of Life, a potent symbol found in nearly every culture on earth. In the Middle East it connoted permanence, growth, majesty, and enlightenment.

² The tapestries must each be the same size, 42 feet long and 6 feet wide. ³ Five of the them are to be sewn together into one piece, and the other five are to be sewn together into a second piece.

⁴ "Sew loops of indigo material along the outer edge of the outer tapestry of one set, and do the same with the other. ⁵ Attach fifty loops to the first tapestry, and the same along the edge of the second, with the loops opposite each other. ⁶ Then make fifty golden clasps to join the two sets together, to make the Tabernacle into a single unit.

⁷ "For a tent over the Tabernacle, make eleven tapestries of goats' hair. ⁸ These tapestries are to be of the same size—45 feet long and 6 feet wide. ⁹ Sew five of these tapestries into one set, and six into a second set; fold the sixth tapestry double, making a door across the front of the tent. ¹⁰ Put fifty loops along the outer edge of the first set, and do the same along the outer edge of the second. ¹¹ Make fifty bronze clasps and put them into the loops to join the tent together as a single piece. ¹² The additional length of the tent, the half tapestry that remains, is to be extended over the back of the Tabernacle. ¹³ The tent tapestries must be 18 inches longer on each side, and what is left will hang over the sides of the Tabernacle to cover it. ¹⁴ Make a tent cover of rams' skins dyed red, and over that a cover of fine leather.

¹⁵ "Then build vertical frameworks for the Tabernacle from acacia wood. ¹⁶ Each frame is to be 15 feet long and 27 inches wide, ¹⁷ with two tenons on each frame, parallel to one another. Make all the frames of the Tabernacle in this manner. ¹⁸ Make twenty frames for the side of the Tabernacle that borders the Negev Desert on the south, ¹⁹ with forty silver bases to go under them—two bases for each frame. ²⁰ For the other side, the north side of the Tabernacle, construct twenty frames ²¹ and forty silver bases, or two under each frame. ²² Make six frames for the west end of the Tabernacle, toward the Sea.*

²³ "Make two frames for the corners of the Tabernacle at the far end. ²⁴ They must be separate beneath, but joined at the top, at the first ring. It is to be this way for each of them, for they will form the two corners. ²⁵ There will be eight frames with their sixteen bases of silver, with two bases under the first frame and two bases under the next frame, and so on.

²⁶ "Make horizontal bars of acacia wood, five for each frame on one side of the Tabernacle, ²⁷ and five bars for the frames on the other side of the Tabernacle, and five bars on the back side of the Tabernacle, toward the Sea. ²⁸ The middle bar, halfway up the frames, will pass through from end to end.

---

* There are no frames for the east side because the Tabernacle is to be covered only by the tapestries. The "Sea" here is the Mediterranean.

²⁹ The frames will all be overlaid with gold, and the rings that hold the crossbars are to be of gold. Overlay the crossbars with gold as well.

³⁰ "Set up the Tabernacle exactly according to the plan which you have seen here on the mountain.

³¹ "Make a curtain finely woven with indigo, purple and scarlet linen, and skillfully embroider winged sphinxes upon them. ³² Hang it with gold hooks on four posts of acacia wood, standing on four silver bases. ³³ Hang the curtain from the clasps and place the Ark of the Covenant behind the curtain, so that the curtain separates the Sanctuary from the Holy of Holies for you. ³⁴ Place the Covering on the Ark of the Covenant in the Holy of Holies. ³⁵ Place the table outside the curtain, and the lampstand at the south side of the Tabernacle opposite the table. The table is to be on the north side.

³⁶ "Make a screen for the entrance of the tent with indigo, purple and scarlet yarn and finely woven linen, embroidered with needlework. ³⁷ Make five posts of acacia wood for the screen, overlaid with gold and with golden hooks. Cast five bronze bases for the posts.

27:1 "Make the altar of acacia wood, and make it square: 7½ feet long and 7½ feet wide. It is to be 4½ feet high. ² Make horns* for each corner of the altar, which is to be inseparable from it, and all is to be overlaid in bronze. ³ Make bronze pots for removing the ashes, as well as shovels, sprinkling bowls, forks and fire pans, all made of bronze. ⁴ Make a bronze grating, a lattice, with bronze rings on each corner. ⁵ Set it below the ledge of the altar so that it reaches halfway up the altar. ⁶ Make poles of acacia wood for the altar, overlaid with bronze. ⁷ These are to be inserted into the four rings to carry it. ⁸ The altar is to be hollow, and made of wood planks; in building it you must follow exactly these instructions which you have seen here on the mountain.

⁹ "Build a courtyard for the Tabernacle. On the south side, facing the Negev, make hangings for the courtyard of finely woven linen 150 feet long, with twenty posts and twenty bases of bronze, ¹⁰ but with hooks of silver, and silver rods. ¹¹ The north side will have the same: hangings 150 feet long with twenty posts and twenty bases of bronze, and with silver hooks and silver rods. ¹² Along the western side of the courtyard, toward the Sea, make the hangings 75 feet long, and with ten posts and ten bases. ¹³ And along the front, the eastern side, toward sunrise, make it

---

* Excavations reveal that such horns decorated the altars of various cultures in the region. Generally these were shaped like the horns of bulls, which stood for strength, and may be a dim remembrance of pre-Israelite religious practices in which gods and goddesses such as El (Ugaritic), Asshur and Asherah (Assyrian and Babylonian), Ba'al (Canaanite), and Hathor (Egypt) were often manifested as bulls or cows.

75 feet long: ¹⁴ 22½ feet of hangings on one side of the entrance, with three posts and three bases; ¹⁵ and 22½ feet of hangings on the other side, also with three posts and three bases; ¹⁶ and, at the entrance to the courtyard, a screen 30 feet long, finely woven of linen, indigo and purple and scarlet threads, all finely embroidered; this will have four posts with their four bases. ¹⁷ All the posts around the courtyard will have silver bands and hooks, and bronze bases. ¹⁸ The courtyard will be 150 feet long and 75 feet wide, with curtains of finely woven linen, 7½ feet high, and with bronze bases. ¹⁹ All the other items used in the Tabernacle construction, whatever their use, even the tent pegs for the Tabernacle and for the courtyard, are to be made of bronze.

²⁰ "Tell the Israelites that they are to provide pure, pressed olive oil for the light, and to keep the lamp burning perpetually. ²¹ In the Tent of Meeting, outside the curtain that is in front of the Ark of the Covenant, Aaron and Aaron's heirs are to keep the lamp burning before Your God from evening until morning. This is a perpetual ordinance of Your God, for all of Israelite's generations to come.

28:¹ "From among all the Israelites, call Aaron your brother to you, and Aaron's heirs Nadab and Abihu, Eleazar and Ithamar. They are to serve as my priests. ² Make sacred vestments for Aaron your brother, to give him glory and honor. ³ You are to instruct those most skilled among you, to whom I gave such practical abilities, to make Aaron's vestments for the ceremony of consecration as my priest.

⁴ "The vestments are to be a breastpiece, an ephod, a mantle, a woven tunic, a turban, and a sash. Have them make these sacred vestments for Aaron and Aaron's heirs, when they serve as my priests, out of threads of gold, indigo, purple and scarlet finely woven into linen.

⁶ "The ephod is to be made of gold, indigo, purple and scarlet threads woven into linen, subtly worked, and with artistry. ⁷ It is to have two shoulder pieces with attachments at its ends to join it to the front and back. ⁸ The waistband is to be of the same fine workmanship and substance, of gold, indigo, purple and scarlet threads finely woven into linen.

⁹ "Take two onyx stones and engrave on them the names of the houses of Israel. ¹⁰ Put six of the names on one stone, and six on the other, in the order of their birth. ¹¹ With great skill, the way a jeweler engraves a seal, engrave the two stones with the names of the houses of Israel. Then mount them in gold filigree. ¹² Mount the two stones on the shoulder pieces of the ephod, stones to commemorate the houses of Israel. Aaron will bear their names upon his shoulders to bring their memory before Our God. ¹³ Set them in

gold filigree, ¹⁴ with two chains of pure gold worked into the form of a cord; work the chains into the filigree settings.

¹⁵ "Create a breastpiece to help decide important matters; make it equal in artistry to the ephod, of pure gold. Make it with indigo, purple and scarlet threads, finely woven into linen. ¹⁶ It is to be folded double to form a square, 9 inches long and 9 inches wide. ¹⁷ Set four rows of stones into it: in the first row a ruby, a topaz and an emerald; ¹⁸ in the second row a turquoise, a sapphire, and a diamond; ¹⁹ in the third row a jacinth, an agate and an amethyst; ²⁰ in the fourth row a beryl, an onyx and a jasper; and all are to be set in gold filigree. ²¹ The stones are to represent the twelve houses of Israel, name by name. They are to be engraved as if they were seals, with each bearing the name of one of the tribes of Israel.

²² "Make chains of pure gold, twisted like cords; ²³ and make two gold rings, fixed to each end of the breastpiece. ²⁴ Run the golden cords through the two golden rings, and ²⁵ fasten their other ends to the two settings, so as to bind them in front to the shoulder pieces of the ephod. ²⁶ Make two gold rings and fasten them to the two lower corners inside the breastpiece right beside the ephod. ²⁷ Then make two rings and attach them to the bottom of the two shoulder pieces on the front of the ephod, close to the seam just above the waistband of the ephod. ²⁸ Then the breastpiece is to be attached to the ephod by its rings to the rings of the ephod with blue cord, so that the breastpiece cannot separate from the ephod. ²⁹ This way, when Aaron enters the Holy of Holies bearing the names of the houses of Israel over his heart, their memory will be brought before Your God.

³⁰ "Finally, for deciding important matters, add the Urim and the Thummim* to the breastpiece so that they will be close to Aaron's heart when he enters into the presence of Your God. Whenever he comes before me, Aaron is to wear the breastpiece over his heart for making decisions on behalf of the Israelites.

³¹ "Make the robe of the ephod of a single piece of blue cloth, ³² with the opening for the head in its middle, and a woven binding around the collar like the collar of scale armor, so that it will not tear. ³³ On the vestment's hem embroider pomegranates of indigo, purple and scarlet thread, with gold bells between them,** ³⁴ alternating gold bells with pomegranates all

---

* These objects for divining the will of God were likely kept in a pocket in the breastpiece, though their appearance and use are a great mystery—perhaps deliberately so. *Urim* means "lights" or "manifestations," and *Thummim* means "perfections" or "the truth." Most scholars feel they were stones for casting lots, but in the book of *1 Samuel,* the Urim were equated with dreams and prophets as a means of answering questions, so they may have been some other oracular device. It is also possible, since the words begin with the first and last letters of the Hebrew alphabet, respectively, that the names are merely symbolic.

**Pomegranates sumbolized fertility; bells were thought to drive away evil.

around the hem of the vestment. ³⁵ Aaron will wear it when serving in the Tabernacle, and its sound will declare the presence of the high priest, entering the Holy of Holies before Our God, and leaving it, so that the high priest will not die.

³⁶ "Make a gleaming medal of pure gold, and engrave the words 'Holy to Our God' as one engraves a seal. ³⁷ Attach it to the front of the turban with a blue cord as a diadem ³⁸ so that it sits over Aaron's forehead, for Aaron is to bear any accidental violations of purity present in the sacrifices that the Israelites offer as holy. Aaron is to wear the medal on his forehead always so that Our God will accept him.

³⁹ "Weave the tunic and the turban from fine linen. The sash is to be the work of one skilled in embroidery.

⁴⁰ "Make tunics and sashes for Aaron's heirs, and make headdresses to give them dignity and honor. ⁴¹ Clothe them in these garments, anoint them, ordain them, and consecrate them so that they can serve me as priests. ⁴² Make linen undergarments for them, which reach to the thighs to cover their private parts. ⁴³ Aaron and Aaron's heirs are to wear these when they enter the Tent of Meeting or when they approach the altar to minister in the sanctuary; if they do not wear them, they will bring guilt on themselves and die. This is to be an irrevocable statute for Aaron and for all of Aaron's descendants.

29:1 "When you consecrate them to be my priests,* do so with the following ritual: Take a young bull from the herd, and two healthy rams. ² Take unleavened bread, unleavened cakes mixed with oil, and unleavened wafers spread with oil, all made with finely ground wheat flour. ³ Put them in a basket and bring them to me with the bull and the two rams.

⁴ "Bring Aaron and Aaron's heirs to the entrance of the Tent of Meeting and wash them with water. ⁵ Take the vestments and clothe Aaron in the tunic, the robe of the ephod, the ephod, and the breastpiece. Gird him with the embroidered waistband of the ephod. ⁶ Place the turban on his head, and the sacred diadem to the turban. ⁷ Take the anointing oil and pour it on his head; this is the anointing. ⁸ Then bring the heirs of Aaron forward, vest them in their tunics, ⁹ gird them with their sashes, and tie their headdresses on them. They will exercise the priesthood by an irrevocable ordinance for all time.

"Next, ordain Aaron and his heirs. ¹⁰ Bring the bull to the front of the Tent of Meeting, and have Aaron and his heirs place their hands on the

---

* Here Moses is serving as God's personal representative; in this chapter, his ordination of Aaron and the other priests is really God's creation of a priesthood who will minister to the Holy One.

bull's head. ¹¹ Slaughter the bull before Our God in front of the Tent of Meeting. ¹² Take some of its blood and smear it with your fingers on the horns of the altar, and pour out the rest of the blood at the base of the altar.* ¹³ Then take all of the fat covering the entrails, the fatty covering of the liver, and the two kidneys encased in their fat, and burn them on the altar.** ¹⁴ But the flesh of the bull, as well as its skin and its dung, you must burn outside the camp, for it is an offering for the purification from sins of ceremonial uncleanliness.

¹⁵ "Take one of the rams, have Aaron and his heirs lay their hands on its head, ¹⁶ and then slaughter it. Fling its blood on all sides of the altar. ¹⁷ Cut up the ram into pieces, wash its inner parts and its legs, and then, with its head and the rest, ¹⁸ burn the entire animal on the altar. It is a burnt offering, it is a pleasing odor, a food offering to Your God.

¹⁹ "Take the second ram, have Aaron and his heirs place their hands on its head, ²⁰ and then slaughter it. Put some of its blood on the lobe of Aaron's right ear and the lobes of his heirs' right ears.† Next put some blood on their right thumbs and on the big toes of their right feet. Fling the rest of the blood on the sides of the altar. ²¹ Then take some of the blood on the altar, and some anointing oil, and sprinkle it on Aaron's vestments, and on Aaron's heirs and their vestments. Then both they and their vestments—Aaron, and Aaron's heirs—will be holy.

²² "Take the fatty parts of the ram—around the tail, the fat that covers the entrails, the fatty covering of the liver, and the two kidneys encased in their fat—and the right leg, for this is a ram for ordination. ²³ Take also a round loaf of bread, a cake cooked in oil, and a wafer from the basket of unleavened bread sitting before Your God. ²⁴ Place these items into Aaron's hands and into the hands of Aaron's heirs, so that they may lift them up and present as a special offering held high to Your God. ²⁵ Take these items from their hands and burn them on the altar with the whole offering, for this is a pleasing odor, a food offering to Your God.

²⁶ "Take the breast of Aaron's ram of ordination and lift it up in presentation to Your God. This is to be your portion. ²⁷ Hallow the breast and the leg of the special offering that has been set aside for Aaron and for Aaron's

---

* Laying hands on the animal to be sacrificed makes one identified with the animal, so that its sacrifice is a symbol of one's own. The smearing of blood on the horns of the altar has a similar meaning, as if to say, "This is my own blood."

** Fat represents abundance and comfort; it is burned on the altar as a symbolic act of giving over all of one's possessions and security, and becoming completely dependent on God.

† Putting blood on the earlobes, thumbs, and big toes is a dual symbol. As the body's extremities, they represent the entire body, so symbolically they are being "baptized" in blood. But it is also a way of consecrating the priests so that they hear only God's words, do only what God commands, and walk only God's path.

heirs. [28] This is to be their allotment, a gift from the Israelites, for all time; it is given as a contribution from the Israelites, donated from their communion sacrifices to Your God.

[29] "The sacred vestments worn by Aaron are to be passed on for the anointing and consecrating of Aaron's heirs in the future; they are to wear them when they are anointed and consecrated. [30] The heir who succeeds him as priest is to wear the vestments for seven days, entering the Tent of Meeting to minister in the Holy of Holies.

[31] "Take the ram for the ordination and boil it in the sanctuary. [32] Aaron and his heirs are to eat the ram's meat and the bread that is in the basket at the entrance of the Tent of Meeting. [33] They are to eat what was used in making atonement for them at their ordination and consecration—it is sacred, and no one else may eat it. [34] Any of the meat of the ordination, or any of the bread that is left over, must be destroyed by fire. It is not to be eaten, for it is sacred.

[35] "Everything I have commanded is to be done to Aaron and his heirs. The ordination will take place over seven days.

[36] "Every day, offer a bull as an offering for the purification from sins of ceremonial uncleanliness. Purge the altar by making atonement offerings on it. Anoint it to consecrate it. [37] For seven days purify the altar and consecrate it. It is the holiest of holy things. Whatever touches the altar is to be considered holy.

[38] "Every day, offer two yearling lambs on the altar; [39] the first is to be offered at dawn, and the other at dusk. [40] With the one in the morning, offer two quarts of fine flour mixed with a quart of pure olive oil, and a quart of wine as a drink offering. [41] With the second ram, at twilight, offer the same grain offering and the same drink offering as at dawn, for a soothing odor, an offering to Your God by fire.

[42] "This burnt offering is to be made always, from generation to generation, at the entrance to the Tent of Meeting before Your God, where I will meet you and speak to you.

[43] "I will meet with the Israelites there, in that place consecrated by my glory. [44] I will make the Tent of Meeting and the altar holy. And I will make Aaron and his heirs holy, so they can serve me as priests. [45] I will dwell in the midst of the Israelites, and I will be their God, [46] so that they will know that I am the Most High, their God, who delivered them from Egypt so that I myself would dwell in their midst. I am Your God.

30[1] "Make an altar of acacia wood for burning incense. [2] It is to be square, 18 inches long and 18 inches wide, and 3 feet high, with horns an integral part of the altar. ³ Overlay the altar—its top, sides, and the horns—with pure gold, and put a molding of pure gold around it. ⁴ Make two pairs of gold rings and put them under the gold molding, two on each side, to hold the poles by which it will be carried. ⁵ The poles are to be of acacia wood, overlaid with gold. ⁶ Place the altar before the curtain that hangs before the Ark of the Covenant, in front of the Covering which covers the Covenant, where I will meet with you.

⁷ "Aaron is to burn fragrant incense on it as an offering. Every morning when the lamps are being polished, he will burn the incense, ⁸ and he will burn the incense again in the evening when the lamps are trimmed, a regular incense offering before Our God for all your generations to come.

⁹ "No incense that is not sanctified may be offered, nor any burnt offering or grain offering, nor any drink offerings.

¹⁰ "Once every year, Aaron is to perform the rite of atonement by pouring the purifying blood of the sacrifice on the horns of the altar. Once every year he is to perform this purifying rite for all your generations to come. This altar is the holiest of holy things for Your God."

***

¹¹ The Holy One said to Moses: ¹² "When you take a census of the Israelites, all those counted must pay a ransom to Your God for their lives, to avert a plague for having taken a census.* ¹³ Those who are counted will pay a half shekel—a fifth of an ounce of silver, based on the shekel of the sanctuary, which is twenty *gerahs*. This is to be set aside for Your God. ¹⁴ Everyone who is to be counted—that is, those twenty years or over—will pay this offering for Your God. ¹⁵ The wealthy will give no more, and the poor no less, than this half shekel, which you will offer to Your God to ransom your lives. ¹⁶ You will take this ransom money from the Israelites, and dedicate it to the support of the Tent of Meeting. It will stand as reminder to the Israelites in the presence of Your God, making atonement for their lives."

¹⁷ Our God said to Moses: ¹⁸ "Make a bronze basin with a bronze pedestal for washing. Place it between the Tent of Meeting and the altar, and put water in the basin. ¹⁹ Aaron and his heirs are to wash their hands and feet

---

* The peril was realized in *2 Samuel*, where a plague breaks out because David usurps God's authority in counting warriors: it encourages one to trust one's own resources instead of the power of God— or, as theologian Theodor Gaster wrote, "One who can number, can control." The Talmud suggests that the Israelites were not to be counted because of the promise to Sarah and Abraham—that their descendants would be as the grains of sand, or numberless. To that end, Rashi, the great 11th century rabbinical commentator, explains that a direct census was not taken. Rather, each person contributed a half-shekel coin, all of which were in turn counted to determine the number of people.

there. ²⁰ Whenever they enter the Tent of Meeting they will wash with water so that they do not die; and when they approach the altar to present a burnt offering to Your God, ²¹ they must wash their hands and feet so that they do not die. This is to be a perpetual ordinance for Aaron and his heirs for all generations to come."

²² Our God said to Moses: ²³ "Take the following finest spices: 13 pounds of liquid myrrh; half that amount of fragrant cinnamon, 6½ pounds; 6½ pounds of aromatic cane; ²⁴ and 13 pounds of cassia—all measured according to the shekel of the sanctuary—and a gallon of olive oil. ²⁵ Take all these and prepare a sacred oil for anointing, a fragrant oil blended with a perfumer's skill. This is to be the sacred anointing oil. ²⁶ Use it to anoint the Tent of Meeting, the Ark of the Covenant, ²⁷ the table and its utensils, the lampstand and its accessories, the altar of incense, ²⁸ the altar of burnt offerings and its utensils, and the basin with its stand. ²⁹ Consecrate them and make them the holiest of holy things, and whatever touches them will be holy as well.

³⁰ "Anoint Aaron and Aaron's heirs, consecrating them to become my priests. ³¹ Say to the Israelites, 'This oil is to be my sacred oil of anointing for all generations to come. ³² It must never be used for common anointing of your bodies; you must make it in those exact proportions, and you must never make any other oil like it. It is sacred and you are to consider it as such. ³³ Anyone who makes a perfume like it and anoints an ordinary person or an outsider with it is to be cut off from my people.'"

³⁴ Our God said to Moses: "Take equal amounts of fragrant spices—gum resin, onycha, galbanum, and pure frankincense—³⁵ and blend them with a perfumer's skill to make incense: salted,* pure, and sacred. ³⁶ Grind some of it into powder to be placed before the Ark of the Covenant in the Tent of Meeting where I will meet with you. It is to be the holiest of holy things to you. ³⁷ Do not use this formula to make incense for any common use. It is holy to Your God. ³⁸ Anyone who makes this incense for common use, just to enjoy the fragrance, is to be cut off from my people."

31:1 Our God said to Moses: ² "Know that I have singled out Bezalel, begot of Uri, begot of Hur, from the tribe of Judah, ³ whom I filled with the Spirit of God. Bezalel has skills, wisdom, and knowledge in all kinds of crafts—⁴ creating designs in gold, silver, and bronze, ⁵ cutting and setting precious

---

* Salt was seen as a purifying agent, both literally and figuratively. It preserved food, improved its taste, asborbed blood, and warded of demons; a sacred and perpetual pact was often called "a covenant of salt."

stones, carving wood, and artisanship of every sort. ⁶ I have also appointed Oholiab begot of Ahisamach, of the tribe of Dan, to be Bezalel's assistant. And I have given wisdom to all your artisans, so that they can make for you everything that I have commanded: ⁷ the Tent of Meeting, the Ark of the Covenant, the Covering, all of the tent's furnishings, ⁸ the table and its utensils, the pure gold lampstand and its accessories, the altar of incense, ⁹ the altar of burnt offerings and all its utensils, the basin with its stand, ¹⁰ as well as the skillfully woven garments—the sacred vestments for the priest Aaron and the sacred vestments for Aaron's heirs when they serve as priests—¹¹ and the anointing oil and fragrant incense for the holy offerings. They will make these things just as I have laid them out for you."

¹² Then Our God said to Moses: ¹³ "Tell the Israelites, 'No matter what, you must keep my Sabbaths. They will stand as a sign between you and me through all the generations to come, so you will know that I, Your God, make you holy. ¹⁴ Keep the Sabbath, for it is holy to you. Anyone who desecrates it must be put to death. Anyone who works on that day must be cut off from the community. ¹⁵ You have six days for work; on the seventh day you have a Sabbath of rest, sacred to Your God. Anyone who works on the Sabbath must be put to death.' ¹⁶ All Israelites are to observe the Sabbath, celebrating it for all generations to come as an eternal covenant. ¹⁷ This will be an everlasting sign between the Israelites and me: I made the heavens and the earth in six days, and on the seventh day I rested and paused for breath."

¹⁸ When Our God finished speaking to Moses on Mount Sinai, Moses received the two tablets of the Covenant, stone tablets written by the finger of God.

32:1–34:35

moses was an extremely long time in returning from the mountain, and when the people saw this, they turned to Aaron and said, "Come and make a god for us, someone who will lead us. We don't know what has happened to that Moses, who brought us up from the land of Egypt."

² Aaron replied, "Remove the gold earrings you are wearing*—wives

---

* Part of the spoils they took when they left Egypt.

and husbands, sons and daughters alike—and bring them all to me."
³ All the people brought their gold earrings to Aaron. ⁴ Aaron took the
gold, melted it down and cast it in a mold, and made it into a calf, a
young bull.

Then the people said, "Israel, here is your God, who brought you up
from the land of Egypt!"

⁵ When Aaron saw this, he built an altar before the idol, proclaiming,
"Tomorrow we will have a feast in honor of the Most High, Our God!"*

⁶ In the morning the people rose early, sacrificing burnt offerings and
bringing communion offerings, and then they sat down to eat and drink,
and lost themselves in debauchery.

⁷ Our God said to Moses, "Go down, now! These people whom you led
out of Egypt have corrupted themselves! ⁸ In such a short time, they have
turned from the way that I have given them, and made themselves a
molten calf. Then they worshipped it and sacrificed to it saying, 'Israel,
here is your God, who brought you up from the land of Egypt!'

⁹ Our God then said to Moses, "I look at these people—how stubborn
they are! ¹⁰ Now leave me to myself so that my anger may pour out on
them, and destroy them! But you I'll make into a great nation."

¹¹ Then Moses soothed the face of the Most High, his God. "But why, my
God, should you let your wrath pour out on these people whom you
delivered from Egypt with great might, with a strong hand? ¹² Why should
the Egyptians say, 'Their God intended to destroy them all along, to kill
them in the mountains, to erase them from the earth?' Turn your back on
your rage; reconsider the disaster you intended for your people. ¹³ Do not
forget Sarah and Abraham, Rebecca and Isaac, and Leah and Rachel and
Jacob, your chosen ones, to whom you promised, 'I will make your descendants as numerous as the stars in the sky; I will give to you all this
land which I have promised—I will give it to your descendants, and they
will enjoy its inheritance forever.'"

¹⁴ So Our God relented, and the disaster that threatened the Israelites
was forestalled.

¹⁵ Then Moses made his way down from the mountain, bearing in his
hands the two tablets of the Covenant, inscribed on both the front and

---

* As opposed to a feast in honor of the idol. Aaron seems to view the calf not as a rival god, but as a
  symbol of the divine—as noted earlier, many gods and goddesses were represented as bulls or cows.
  Here the bull particularly represents fertility, an idea borne out in the following verse.

back. ¹⁶ These tablets were the work of God's hand, and the writing that was engraved on them was God's writing.

¹⁷ When Joshua heard the noise of the people celebrating, he said to Moses, "It sounds like a battle in the camp."

¹⁸ But Moses replied,

> "Those are not the shouts of victory,
>   nor the cries of defeat.
> The sounds that I hear
>   are sounds of debauchery."

¹⁹ As Moses and Joshua drew near the camp, they saw the calf and the dancing. Moses' anger raged, and he threw the tablets down and smashed them at the base of the mountain. ²⁰ Seizing the calf that they had made, he threw it into the fire and melted it. What came out of the fire he ground to a powder, and this he sprinkled on the water, and made the Israelites drink it.

²¹ Moses then asked Aaron, "What did these people do to you, for you to bring such terrible sin on them?"

²² Aaron replied, "Please, my sovereign, do not let your anger rage. You yourself know these people, and how they are inclined to wickedness. ²³ They came to me saying, 'Make us a god to lead us! We don't know what has happened to this fellow Moses who led us out of Egypt.' ²⁴ So I said to them, 'Who has gold?' Then they removed their jewelry and gave it to me. I threw it into the fire—and out came this calf!"

²⁵ When Moses saw the people so out of control—Aaron had let them run riot, until they were a joke among their enemies all around them— ²⁶ he stood at the gate of the camp, saying, "All who would stand with Our God, come to me!"

The entire tribe of Levi came and stood with Moses, ²⁷ and Moses said to them, "The Most High, the God of Israel, says this: 'Every one of you, take up your sword. Go through the camp from one end to the other, and kill your own flesh and blood, your friends, and your neighbors."

²⁸ The Levites did as Moses commanded, and on that day about 3,000 Israelites died.

²⁹ Then Moses said to the Levites, "Today you have set yourselves apart as priests for Our God. Though every one of you has paid the price of someone closest to you, God blesses you today for what you did."

³⁰ The next day, Moses said to the people, "You have committed a terrible sin. I will go up to speak with Our God. Perhaps I can purge your sin."

³¹ So Moses went back to Our God and said, "Oh, what a grave sin these people have committed in making a god of gold for themselves! ³² Now, if you only would forgive their sin!—and if you will not, then erase me from the book that you have written!"

³³ Our God answered Moses, "It is only those who have sinned against me that I will erase from my book. ³⁴ Go now, and lead the people to the place I told you about, with my angel going before you. Nevertheless, on the day I call everyone to account, I will call them to account for their sin."

³⁵ Then Our God struck the people with a plague because of what they had done with the calf that Aaron had made.

⁓ ⁓ ⁓

33:1 Our God said to Moses, "Leave this place, and go with the people whom you brought up out of Egypt, to the land which I promised on oath to Sarah and Abraham, to Rebecca and Isaac, and to Leah and Rachel and Jacob, when I told them, 'I will give it to your descendants.' ² I will send an angel to guide you, and I will drive out the Canaanites, Amorites, Hittites, Perizzites, Hivites and Jebusites. ³ Go to the land there that flows with milk and honey. But I will not go in your midst, for you are a stubborn people and if I were to go with you along the way, I would destroy you."

⁴ The people heard this bitter judgment, they went into mourning, and none of them put on their jewelry. ⁵ Our God then said to Moses, "Tell the Israelites, 'You are a stubborn people, and if I were with you for even a moment, I would destroy you. Now take off your jewels and finery while I consider what I should do with you."

⁶ The Israelites stripped themselves of their jewels and finery there at Mount Sinai, from that time on.

⁷ During this time, Moses would take a tent and pitch it himself outside the camp, some distance away from the camp, and this he called the Tent of Meeting. Those who wished to consult with Our God would go out to that Tent of Meeting, outside the camp.

⁸ When Moses would go out to the tent, all the people would rise, and stand at the doors of their own tents and follow him with their eyes until Moses had entered the Tent of Meeting. ⁹ Whenever he entered the Tent of Meeting, the pillar of cloud would come down and stand before the entrance, and Our God would speak with Moses. ¹⁰ When they would see the pillar of cloud at the entrance of the tent, all the people would rise and bow

down at the entrance of their own tents. ¹¹ In this way Our God would speak to Moses face to face, as friends would speak to one another.

Then Moses would come back to the camp, but Moses' aide, young Joshua, would stay in the tent.

¹² Moses said to Our God, "Look, you have told me to lead this people, but you have never told me who you will send with me. You have said to me, 'I know you by name,' and 'You have found favor with me.' ¹³ So if I have found favor with you, teach me your ways so that I might truly know you, and that I might find favor in your eyes. Remember that these people are the nation you have chosen as your own."

¹⁴ Our God replied, "My Presence will go with you.* Let this set your mind at ease."

¹⁵ Moses continued, "If your Presence does not come with us, do not send us from this place. ¹⁶ How can it ever be known that we have found favor in your eyes—I, and your people—if you do not accompany us? It is your Presence alone that will mark us—I, and your people—from all others of the people on the earth."

¹⁷ And Our God said to Moses, "As you have asked, I will do, for you have found favor in my eyes, and I have known you by name."**

¹⁸ Then Moses said, "Please, show me your glory!"

¹⁹ Our God said, "I will make all of my goodness pass before your eyes, and I will pronounce my Name, I AM, in your presence: I will show my grace to whom I will show my grace, and I will show my compassion to whom I will show my compassion.† ²⁰ But you cannot see my face," God continued. "No human can see my face and live."

²¹ Then Our God said, "Look—here is a place beside me, where you can stand on a rock. ²² When my glory passes you, I will place you in a cleft in the rock, and I will cover you with my hand until I have passed by. ²³ When I remove my hand you will see my back; but my face, you must not see."

34₁ Our God said to Moses, "Carve two tablets of stone like the first ones I gave you. I will write on them again the writing that was on the first set, the ones you smashed. ² Prepare yourself for the morning. Come up onto

---

* "You" is singular here.

**"I have known you by name" indicates great intimacy, similar to the closeness in which God and Moses speak face to face as friends. While God is certainly omnicient, this speaks more to the special relationship Moses had with God.

† This recalls God's statement, "I will be however I will be," at the initial revelation at the burning thornbush.

Mount Sinai at dawn, and wait for me there on the top of the mountain. ³ Bring no one with you. No one is to be anywhere on the mountain, and not even the flocks or herds are to graze near the mountain."

⁴ So Moses chiseled out two stone tablets similar to the first two, and early in the morning, he climbed Mount Sinai carrying the two stone tablets as Our God had commanded.

⁵ Then Our God came down in a cloud and stood before Moses to proclaim the divine name, I AM. ⁶ And Our God passed before Moses, proclaiming, "I AM! I am God, Your God, compassionate and gracious, slow to anger, abundant in kindness and faithfulness; ⁷ faithful to the thousandth generation, forgiving injustice, rebellion and sin; yet not leaving the guilty unpunished, calling the children and grandchildren to account for the sins of their ancestors, to the third and fourth generation!"

⁸ Immediately Moses fell to the ground in worship, ⁹ and said, "Now, if it is true that I have won your favor, O God, then I beseech you: may God travel with us! We are indeed a stubborn people—but forgive our sin and our wickedness! Adopt us as your heritage!"

¹⁰ God said, "I make a covenant with you, here and now. In the presence of all your people I will work such wonders as have never before been seen by any people or any nation. The people whom you live among will witness what Your God can do, for what I will accomplish through you will be awe-inspring. ¹¹ Keep faith with what I command you today.

"I will drive out before you the Amorites, Canaanites, Hittites, Perizzites, Hivites and Jebusites. ¹² Take caution, and make no treaties with those who live in the lands where you are going, for such treaties will trap you. ¹³ Destroy their altars, smash their sacred pillars, cut down their Asherah poles. ¹⁴ Worship no gods but Your God, for my name is Jealous, and I am a jealous God.

¹⁵ "Make no treaties with those who live in the land, for when they consort with their gods in profligacy, and sacrifice to them, they will invite you to partake of their sacrifices. ¹⁶ Your daughters and your sons will marry theirs, and when their daughters and sons go after their gods they will induce your daughters and sons to do the same.

¹⁷ "Make no idols for yourselves.

¹⁸ "Celebrate the Feast of the Unleavened Bread. Eat unleavened bread for seven days, at the time I appointed for you in the month of Aviv, for it was in the month of Aviv when you came out of Egypt.

¹⁹ "The firstborn of every womb is mine, including the firstborn of the

flocks and the herds. ²⁰ You may redeem the firstborn of a donkey with a lamb; but if you do not redeem it, you must break its neck. Redeem all the firstborn among the people.

"No one is to come into my presence empty-handed.

²¹ "Work for six days, and rest on the seventh—even during plowing and harvest times.

²² "Celebrate these festivals as well: the Feast of Weeks; the Feast of the Firstfruits of the wheat harvest; and the Feast of Ingathering at the close of the year. ²³ Three times a year you all will come into the presence of your Sovereign God, the God of Israel. ²⁴ For I will dispossess the nations for you and expand your frontiers, and ensure that no one will try to take your land, provided you come into my presence three times a year.

²⁵ "Do not offer me the blood of a sacrifice along with anything made with yeast.

"Let nothing of the Passover feast remain until the next morning.

²⁶ "Bring the best of your firstfruits of the earth to the house of the Most High, your God.

"Do not boil a young goat in its mother's milk."

²⁷ Then Our God said to Moses, "Put these rules in writing, for they are the terms of the covenant I hereby make with you and with Israel."

²⁸ Moses stayed there with Our God for forty days and forty nights, with neither food nor water, and wrote on the tablets the words of the Covenant, the Ten Commandments.

ি়   ি়   ি়

²⁹ As Moses came down from Mount Sinai carrying the two tablets of the Covenant, he was not aware that the skin on his face was radiant from speaking with God. ³⁰ When Aaron and the other Israelites saw Moses, they were afraid to approach him because of the radiance of the skin of his face. ³¹ Only when Moses called to them did Aaron and the leaders of the community come near, and then Moses spoke to them.

³² Later, all the Israelites gathered around, and Moses gave them the instructions he had received from Our God on Mount Sinai. ³³ When he finished speaking to them, Moses put a veil over his face. Whenever Moses entered the presence of Our God, he would remove the veil until he came out again, ³⁴ and when he would come out and tell the Israelites what had been commanded, ³⁵ they would see that the skin on his face was

radiant. Then he would put the veil over his face again until he went in to speak with God.

moses called together the whole community of the Israelites and said to them, "This is what Our God has commanded you to do: ² work is to be done for six days, but the seventh day is your holy day, a Sabbath day of rest dedicated to Your God. Anyone who works on that day will be punished by death. ³ You will not even light a fire in your dwellings on that day."

⁴ To the gathered Israelites, Moses continued, "Here is what the Most High has commanded: ⁵ Raise a contribution for Our God. Whoever is willing and generous is to bring a gift for the Holy One: gold, silver and bronze; ⁶ indigo, purple and scarlet yarn, and fine linen; goat's hair, ⁷ tanned sheep's skin, and fine leather; acacia wood; ⁸ lamp oil; spices for the anointing oil and for the fragrant incense; ⁹ and onyx stones and other gems to be set in the ephod and the breastpiece.

¹⁰ "All the skilled artisans among us are to make what Our God has commanded: ¹¹ the Tabernacle with its tent and covering, clasps, frames, crossbars, posts and bases; ¹² the Ark with its poles, the Covering, and the screen curtain; ¹³ the table with its poles and all the vessels, and the Bread of the Presence; ¹⁴ the lampstand for the light and its accessories—the lamps and the oil for the lampstand; ¹⁵ the incense altar with its poles, the anointing oil, the fragrant incense and the hangings for the entryway to the Tabernacle; ¹⁶ the altar for burnt offerings, its bronze grating, its poles and its utensils; the bronze basin and its stand; ¹⁷ the courtyard with its posts and bases, and the curtain for the courtyard entrance; ¹⁸ the pegs for the Tabernacle and for the courtyard and their cords; ¹⁹ and the finely-worked vestments for ministering in the sanctuary—both the sacred vestments for Aaron the priest, and the vestments for Aaron's heirs when they serve as priests."

²⁰ All the gathered Israelites left Moses' presence, ²¹ and those who were inspired in their minds and moved in their spirits returned with freewill offerings to Our God for the work on the Tent of Meeting, for all its services and for the sacred garments. ²² Women and men alike gave freely, bringing gold jewelry: brooches, earrings, finger rings, bracelets, necklac-

es, various gold objects—every one of them presented a donation to Our God. ²³ Those who had indigo, purple or scarlet yarn, or fine linen or goats' hair, or tanned rams' skins or fine leather, brought it. ²⁴ Those who were able brought silver or bronze as offerings to Our God, and those who had acacia wood suitable for this work brought it.

²⁵ Skilled women set to spinning with their hands the indigo, purple and scarlet yarn, and the fine linen, and brought it, ²⁶ while other inspired women with practical knowledge spun the goats' hair. ²⁷ The clan leaders brought onyx stones and other gems for mounting on the ephod and the breastpiece, ²⁸ and spices and oil for the lamps, and for the anointing oil and the fragrant incense. ²⁹ Every Israelite, woman or man, whose heart was moved to contribute to this work that Our God had commanded of Moses, brought items necessary for the work, and did so freely.

³⁰ Moses said to the Israelites, "Listen: Our God has specially chosen Bezalel, begot of Uri of the tribe of Judah. ³¹ Bezalel has been filled with the Spirit of God, and has been given skills and knowledge of every craft— ³² in design work, in the working of gold and silver and copper, ³³ in the cutting and setting of precious stones, and in carving wood—indeed, in every skill. ³⁴ God has enabled both Bezalel and Oholiab, begot of Ahisamach of the tribe of Dan, to teach others, ³⁵ and to design every kind of work that needs to be done by the carvers, the artisans, the embroiderers of indigo, purple and scarlet yarn and fine linen, and the weavers—all sorts of skilled craft work and design work. 36:1 Bezalel and Oholiab, and every woman and man whom Our God has blessed with skill and understanding, will do the work of building the sanctuary, according to the instructions that Our God has given."

² Moses called together Bezalel, Oholiab, and the workers to whom God had given skills and understanding, and all who felt inspired to volunteer for the construction, and set them to work. ³ Moses gave over to them all the offerings that the Israelites had donated for the construction of the sanctuary. The people continued to give freewill offerings, morning after morning, ⁴ until in time the artisans who were doing the various jobs in the building of the sanctuary ⁵ came to Moses, saying, "The people bring far more than we need to complete the work which Our God has commanded." ⁶ So Moses sent word throughout the camp that neither woman nor man was to make any further offerings for the sanctuary. So the people no longer brought gifts, ⁷ for what was given already was more than enough for the work to be done.

⁸ The most skilled among the workers made the Tabernacle, with its ten tapestries of finely woven linen, and indigo, purple and scarlet yarn, with winged sphinxes artfully embroidered on them. ⁹ The length of each of the tapestries was 42 feet long and 6 feet wide; each was this same size. ¹⁰ Five of the tapestries were sewn together for one side of the Tabernacle and five were sewn together for the other side of the Tabernacle. ¹¹ The outermost set of tapestries on one side had indigo loops stitched to its edge, and the same was done to the edge of the tapestry on the other side. ¹² Fifty loops were attached to the edge of the one tapestry, and fifty loops for the edge of the other, so that the loops were opposite each other.¹³ Fifty gold fasteners were made to join the tapestries of one to the other, and thus the Tabernacle became a single whole.

¹⁴ They made eleven hangings of goats' hair to form a tent over the Tabernacle. ¹⁵ Each of the hangings was of the same size: 45 feet long and 6 feet wide. ¹⁶ Five of the hangings were joined together into one set, and six into a second set. ¹⁷ Fifty loops were stitched to the edge of the end curtain in one set and fifty loops along the edge of the end curtain of the second set. ¹⁸ Fifty bronze clasps were made to fasten the tent together as a unit. ¹⁹ Then they made for the tent a covering of sheep's skin, dyed red, and an outer covering of fine leather.

²⁰ From acacia wood they made the upright frames for the Tabernacle. ²¹ Each frame was 15 feet long and 27 inches wide, ²² and had a pair of tenons parallel to each other on each frame. They made all the frames of the Tabernacle in this manner. ²³ They made twenty frames for the south side of the Tabernacle, the side facing the Negev, ²⁴ with forty silver bases to go under them—two bases for one frame, and so on for all the frames. ²⁵ For the other side—the north side—of the Tabernacle, they built another twenty frames, ²⁶ with forty silver bases, two under each frame. ²⁷ Six frames were built for the rear of the Tabernacle—the west end, toward the Sea. ²⁸ Two frames were built for the rear corners of the Tabernacle, ²⁹ separate on the bottom but joined at the top, at the first ring. Two frames were made this way, for the two corners. ³⁰ So there were eight frames with their sixteen silver bases, with two bases under each frame.

³¹ They made horizontal bars of acacia wood, five for each frame on one side ³² and five for each frame on the other side, and five bars on the back side of the Tabernacle—westward, toward the Sea. ³³ The middle bar, halfway up the frame, passed through the other boards from end to end. ³⁴ The frames were overlaid with gold, and the rings that held the crossbars were made of gold, and the bars were overlaid with gold.

³⁵ Then they made the curtain of indigo, purple and scarlet yarn and

finely twisted linen, with winged sphinxes artfully embroidered on it. [36] To hang it, four posts were made of acacia wood, overlaid with gold, with gold hooks and silver bases. [37] For the entrance of the Tent they made a finely woven screen of indigo, purple and scarlet yarn with skillful embroidery on it, [38] and five posts of acacia wood, with their hooks. The tops of the posts and the bases were overlaid with gold, but the bases were cast from bronze.

37:1 Then Bezalel* made the Ark of acacia wood; it was 45 inches long, 27 inches wide, and 27 inches high. [2] It was overlaid with pure gold both inside and out, with a molding of gold around the edge. [3] Bezalel cast four gold rings for it, which were fastened to its four feet, with two on each side. [4] Poles were made of acacia wood, and these were overlaid with gold; [5] they were inserted into the rings on the side of the Ark to carry it.

[6] Bezalel made the Covering of pure gold, 45 inches long and 27 inches wide. [7] Two winged sphinxes were made out of pure hammered gold, [8] one on each end of the Covering and solidly a part of it. [9] The sphinxes' outspread wings, as they faced one other but looked down toward the Covering, pointed upward to form a canopy above the seat.

[10] He built the table of acacia wood, 3 feet long, 18 inches wide, and 27 inches high. [11] It was overlaid with pure gold, with a gold molding around it. [12] Bezalel made a rim around it as wide as a hand, a rim of gold. [13] He then cast four gold rings for the table, and these were fastened to each corner of the table, [14] close to the rim, to hold the poles that carried the table. [15] The poles were made of acacia wood and overlaid with gold. [16] And finally he made the containers, ladles, pitchers and sacrificial bowls—all out of pure gold—for the drink offerings.

[17] He made the lampstand of pure hammered gold, and it was made in a solid piece with its stem and its branches, its cups, and its buds and blossoms. [18] The lampstand had six branches, with three on each side. [19] Three cups shaped like almond blossoms, with leaves and petals, were on the first branch; three cups shaped like almond blossoms, with leaves and petals, on the second branch; three cups shaped like almond blossoms, with leaves and petals, on the third branch; and so on for each of the six branches of the lampstand. [20] Attached to the stem itself were four cups shaped like almond blossoms, with leaves and petals. [21] A bud was attached under the first pair of branches, a second bud under the second pair of branches, and a third bud under the third pair of branches. [22] The

---

* Throughout this chapter and much of the next, Bezalel is named as the one making all the items, though it is clear from the earlier context that he was the designer, and supervised a large team of artisans and workers.

buds and branches were of a solid piece with the lampstand—all a single piece of beaten gold. ²³ Bezalel made its seven lamps, as well as its wick trimmers, snuffers and pan, of pure gold. ²⁴ Seventy-five pounds of pure gold was used to make the lampstand and its accessories.

²⁵ He built the altar of incense of acacia wood, 18 inches wide and 18 inches long, perfectly square, and 3 feet high, with its horns made one with the altar. ²⁶ Bezalel overlaid the altar—the top, the sides, and the horns—with pure gold, and he put a molding of pure gold around it. ²⁷ He fastened two pairs of gold rings, two on each side, beneath the gold molding, for the poles by which it was to be carried. ²⁸ The poles were made of acacia wood and overlaid with gold.

²⁹ He also made the sacred oil for anointing and the pure, fragrant incense, blended as subtly as if by a perfumer.

38¹ Bezalel made the altar of burnt offerings from acacia wood, 7½ feet long, 7½ feet wide, perfectly square, and 4½ feet high. ² The horns at the four corners were of one piece with the altar, and all was overlaid in bronze. ³ He made all the accessories—pots, shovels, sprinkling bowls, forks and fire pans—forged from bronze. ⁴ He made a bronze grating for the altar, a mesh network to fit below the ledge of the altar so that it reached halfway down the altar. ⁵ Four bronze rings were cast, one for each corner, for the grating, to hold the poles, ⁶ which were made of acacia wood and overlaid with bronze. ⁷ The poles were inserted in the rings at the sides of the altar to carry it with. The altar was made hollow, out of boards.

⁸ The bronze basin and its stand he made from the bronze mirrors of the women who ministered at the entrance of the Tent of Meeting.

⁹ He made the courtyard thus: on the south side, facing the Negev, ¹⁰ were the hangings of finely woven linen, 150 feet long 10 with twenty posts and their twenty bases made of bronze, with bands of silver, and silver hooks. ¹¹ The north side had 150 feet of hangings, with twenty posts and their twenty bases made of bronze, and with bands and hooks made of silver. ¹² The western side of the courtyard, toward the Sea, had 75 feet of hangings, with ten posts and ten bases, with bands of silver and silver hooks. ¹³ And the eastern side, the front, facing the sunrise, was again 75 feet wide. ¹⁴ There were hangings 22½ feet in length hung on one side of the entrance, with three posts and their three bases. ¹⁵ And again, on the other side, were curtains 22½ feet in length, with three posts and their three bases. ¹⁶ All the hangings that bounded the courtyard were of finely woven linen. ¹⁷ The bases for all the posts were bronze, with the hooks and the bands on the posts made of silver; the tops of the posts, too, were

decorated in silver. All the posts of the courtyard had this silver ornamentation.

¹⁸ The embroidery on the finely woven linen screen at the courtyard's entrance was done with indigo, purple and scarlet yarns. It was 30 feet in length and—like the curtain in the courtyard—7½ feet high. ¹⁹ It had four posts and four bronze bases; their hooks and their banding were of silver, and their tops were overlaid with silver. ²⁰ All the tent pegs for the covering of the Tabernacle and of its surrounding courtyard were made of bronze.

²¹ This is the accounting of the Tabernacle, the Tabernacle of the Testimony, recorded at the command of Moses by the Levites under the direction of Ithamar, begot of Aaron the priest. ²² Bezalel begot of Uri, begot of Hur of the tribe of Judah, made everything Our God had commanded Moses to have made. ²³ Bezalel was assisted by Oholiab, begot of Ahisamach of the tribe of Dan, who was an engraver, a weaver, and an embroiderer in fine linen and indigo, purple and scarlet yarn.

²⁴ The gold of the freewill offering used for the work on the sanctuary, according to the measure of the sanctuary shekel, weighed approximately one ton. ²⁵ The silver donated by the community, measured by the sanctuary shekel, weighed approximately 3¾ tons. ²⁶ This amounted to a fifth of an ounce—half a shekel—for every person, according to the sanctuary shekel, from all who were registered in the census, twenty years of age and older—a total of 603,550 women and men. ²⁷ The 3¾ tons of silver were used for casting the bases for the sanctuary and for the curtain—one hundred bases from the 3¾ tons, or 75 pounds per base. ²⁸ Forty-five pounds were used for the hooks on the posts, and the bands, and for the overlaying of the tops of the posts. ²⁹ The bronze that was given came to 2½ tons, ³⁰ and was used for the bases for the entrance to the Tent of Meeting, and for the bronze altar with its bronze grating, and for all the utensils for the altar, ³¹ as well as the bases all around the court, the bases for the posts at its entrance, the tent pegs for the Tabernacle covering, and the pegs around the courtyard.

39:1 The indigo, purple and scarlet yarn were used to make the vestments for ministering in the sanctuary, Aaron's sacred vestments, as Our God had commanded Moses. ² The ephod was made of gold, and of indigo, purple and scarlet yarns, and finely woven linen. ³ The gold was beaten into leaf, and then sliced into fine strands so thin that a weaver could braid them into the indigo, the purple and the scarlet yarns, and weave them into the fine linen in intricate patterning. ⁴ The ephod had two shoulder pieces designed that the two upper edges were joined together. ⁵ The ornate waistband was of the same material and artisanship as the ephod, made with gold, and with indigo, purple and scarlet yarns and finely woven linen, as Our God had commanded Moses.

⁶ The onyx stones were set in gold filigree, with engraving such as one would see on a seal, giving the names of Israel's tribes. ⁷ These were mounted on the shoulder pieces of the ephod to memorialize Israel's tribes, just as Our God had commanded Moses.

⁸ The breastpiece was made like the ephod, with gold, and with indigo, purple and scarlet yarns and finely woven into linen. ⁹ When it was folded double, the breastpiece formed a square 9 inches long and 9 inches wide. ¹⁰ In it were set four rows of stones: in the first row, a ruby, a topaz and an emerald; ¹¹ in the second, a turquoise, a sapphire, and a diamond; ¹² in the third, a jacinth, an agate, and an amethyst; ¹³ and in the last, a beryl, an onyx and a jasper. All were set in gold filigree. ¹⁴ The twelve stones bore the names of the twelve heirs of Israel, engraved as if they were seals, each stone representing a tribe of Israel. ¹⁵ On the breastpiece were made fine chains of pure gold, braided like cords. ¹⁶ Two settings were made of gold filigree, and two gold rings were fixed to the upper corners of the breastpiece. ¹⁷ The two ends of the cords were fastened to two rings at these corners. ¹⁸ Two ends of the cords were fastened to the settings of gold filigree, binding them to the shoulder pieces on the front of the ephod. ¹⁹ Two gold rings were attached to the two corners of the breastpiece on the inside edge next to the ephod. ²⁰ They then made two more gold rings to be attached, low and in front, on the ephod, near to its seam above the waistband. ²¹ Then the corresponding rings on the breastpiece and the ephod were attached to each other by a blue cord, so that one would not become loosened from the other, as Our God had commanded Moses.

²² They made the finely woven robe of the ephod out of blue cloth, ²³ with an opening for the head in its middle, and a woven binding around the collar like the collar of scale armor, so that it could not tear. ²⁴ On the vestment's hem were embroidered pomegranates of indigo, purple and scarlet yarn. ²⁵ Bells were made of pure gold, and fastened between the pomegranates, ²⁶ a gold bell and a pomegranate alternating around the entire hem of the vestment to be worn when Aaron ministered, as Our God had commanded Moses.

²⁷ The tunics were made of finely woven linen for Aaron and his heirs, ²⁸ and the turban made of finely woven linen, and headdresses of fine linen, and the undergarments of finely woven linen. ²⁹ The sashes were of

finely braided linen and indigo, purple and scarlet yarn, as Our God had commanded Moses.

³⁰ They made a medal of pure gold for a sacred diadem, with "Holy to Our God" engraved on it as on a seal, ³¹ and they put a blue cord on it to attach it to the turban near its top, as commanded by Our God to Moses.

³² Thus the Israelites finished all the work on the Tabernacle and the Tent of Meeting exactly as Our God had commanded Moses. ³³ Then they brought to Moses the Tabernacle: the Tent and all its furnishings, its clasps, frames, crossbars, posts and bases; ³⁴ the covering of tanned sheep's skin and the outer covering of fine leather, and the curtain for the screen; ³⁵ the Ark of the Covenant, its poles, and its Covering; ³⁶ the table and its utensils, and the Bread of the Presence; ³⁷ the pure gold lampstand and its row of lamps with its accessories and the lamp oil; ³⁸ the gold altar, the anointing oil, the fragrant incense, the screen at the entrance of the tent; ³⁹ the bronze altar, the bronze grating which sits within the altar, the carrying poles, and the altar's utensils; the basin and its stand; ⁴⁰ the curtains of the courtyard and their posts and bases, and the curtain for the entrance of the courtyard; all the implements for assembling the Tabernacle, the Tent of Meeting; ⁴¹ and the woven vestments for ministering in the sanctuary—Aaron's sacred vestments and the vestments for Aaron's heirs, the priests. ⁴² The Israelites fulfilled completely all the commands Our God had given to Moses.

⁴³ Moses inspected the work and saw that it was done exactly as Our God had commanded. And Moses blessed them.

40:1 Our God said to Moses: 2 "On the first day of the first month,* set up the Tabernacle, the Tent of Meeting. 3 Place in it the Ark of the Covenant, and screen the Tabernacle with its curtain. 4 Set up the table and lay out its utensils on it; set up the lampstand and arrange its lamps; 5 place the gold altar of incense before the Ark of the Covenant, and hang the curtain at the entrance to the Tabernacle. 6 In front of the entrance to the Tabernacle, the Tent of Meeting, place the altar for burnt offerings, 7 and set the basin, filled with water, between the Tent of Meeting and the altar. 8 Set up the courtyard around it and hang the curtain at the entrance to the courtyard.

9 "Use the anointing oil to anoint the Tabernacle and all its furnishings to bless them and make them holy. 10 Then anoint the altar of burnt offerings and all its utensils to consecrate them and make them most holy. 11 And likewise, anoint the basin and its stand to make it holy.

---

* Two weeks shy of the one-year anniversary of the exodus from Egypt.

¹² "Bring Aaron and Aaron's heirs to the entrance of the Tent of Meeting and wash them with water. ¹³ Clothe Aaron with the holy vestments and anoint him and consecrate him to be my priest. ¹⁴ Then bring in Aaron's heirs and clothe them in the tunics. Anoint them as you anointed Aaron, so that they may serve me as my priests. ¹⁵ Their anointing will inaugurate a perpetual priesthood for all generations to come."

¹⁶ Moses did everything that Our God commanded. ¹⁷ On the first day of the first month of the second year, the Tabernacle was erected. ¹⁸ Moses set the bases for it, put up its frames, put its crossbars in position, and set up its posts. ¹⁹ He spread the tent over the Tabernacle and on top of this the covering for the tent, as Our God had directed him. ²⁰ He took the commandments and placed them inside the Ark; he attached the poles to the Ark and set the Covering upon it. ²¹ He brought the Ark into the Tabernacle and put the curtain in its place, thus screening off the Ark of the Covenant, as Our God had directed.

²² Moses put the table in the Tent of Meeting on the north side of the Tabernacle, outside the curtain, ²³ and set out the Bread of the Presence on it before Our God, as Our God had commanded. ²⁴ He set out the lampstand in the Tent of Meeting opposite the table on the south side of the Tabernacle, ²⁵ and arranged the lamps before Our God, as God had commanded. ²⁶ Next he set up the golden altar in the Tent of Meeting before the curtain, ²⁷ and offered burning fragrant incense in it, as God had commanded him. ²⁸ Moses also set up the curtain at the entrance to the Tabernacle, ²⁹ and set the altar of burnt offerings near the entrance to the Tabernacle of the Tent of Meeting, offering on it the burnt offering and grain offering, as God had commanded. ³⁰ Next he set up the basin between the Tent of Meeting and the altar, and filled it with water for washing, ³¹ and Moses and Aaron and Aaron's heirs used it to wash their hands and feet ³² when entering the Tent of Meeting or approaching the altar, as Our God had commanded Moses. ³³ Then Moses set up the courtyard around the Tabernacle and the altar, and hung the curtain at the entrance to the courtyard.

So Moses finished all the work.

³⁴ Then the cloud covered the Tent of Meeting, and the glory of Our God filled the Tabernacle. ³⁵ Moses could not enter the Tent of Meeting, because the cloud so densely covered it and because the glory of God so completely filled the Tabernacle.

³⁶ Throughout all their journeys, whenever the cloud would rise from the Tabernacle, the Israelites would set out. ³⁷ If the cloud did not rise, they waited and would not move until it did. ³⁸ The cloud rested on the Taber-

nacle in the daytime, and at night there was fire in the cloud so that the whole house of Israel could see. And so it remained for every stage of their journey.

leviticus

Our god called* to moses from the tent
of Meeting, and told him ² to tell these things to the people of Israel:

When any of you brings an offering** to Your God, bring it from the herd
or the flock.

³ If your offering is from the herd, to be sacrified as a whole burnt offering,† it is to be a whole and unblemished male,‡ and it must be presented
at the entrance to the Tent of Meeting in order to be acceptable to Your God.

---

* "Our God called" is the traditional Hebrew name for the book of *Leviticus*. It echoes the revelation at
Sinai in Exodus 24:16, where the same phrase is used. The book records how God calls the Israelites
to worship in ways different from those of other cultures in the geographical area.

** The general Hebrew word for "offering" is *korban*, which means "to bring near" or, more generally,
"gift." Later *korban* became anything given to the Temple treasury, and sometimes referred to the
treasury itself. Individuals gave offerings in accordance with their resources: the wealthiest gave
from the herd, those less well off gave from the flock, and the poorest gave an offering of birds (as in
verse 14).

† The first of the five major sacrifices described is the *olah*, or "ascent offering," referring to the smoke
as it rises to heaven; it is sometimes translated "holocaust," which means "completely burned." It
represents an individual's complete dedication and surrender to God.

‡ Female animals were too valuable to be used as regular sacrifces. There may also be a hint of the
ancient reverence of cows as symbols of the life-giving principle.

⁴ Lay your hand on the head of the animal* and it will be accepted as a ransom for you, ⁵ then slaughter it in the presence of Your God, and Aaron's heirs, the priests, are to dash the blood against all four sides of the altar at the entrance to the Tent of Meeting. ⁶ Then the offering must be skinned and cut into pieces. ⁷ The priests, the heirs of Aaron, will kindle a fire and place wood on the fire, ⁸ then arrange the pieces, including the fat and the head, on the burning wood of the altar. ⁹ The priest will then wash the entrails and the legs and add them to the altar fire. It is a burnt offering, an offering made by fire, an aroma pleasing to Your God.

¹⁰ If your offering is from the flock, from either the sheep or the goats, it is to be whole and unblemished. ¹¹ Slaughter it before Your God on the north side of the altar, and the priests, Aaron's heirs, are to dash the blood against all four sides of the altar. ¹² The offering is to be cut into pieces, including the head and the fat, and arranged by the priest on the altar on top of the burning wood. ¹³ But the entrails and the legs must be washed before the priest takes it to be burned on the altar. It is a burnt offering, an offering made by fire, an aroma pleasing to Your God.

¹⁴ If the offering is a burnt offering of birds, it is to be of turtledoves or pigeons. ¹⁵ The priest will bring the bird to the altar, wring its neck, and burn it on the altar. Its blood is to be dashed against the altar. ¹⁶ The bird's crop and its contents are to be removed and set aside to the east of the altar, on the ash heap. ¹⁷ Then the priest will tear it open at the wings, but not break it in two, and place it on the altar, atop the wood fire on the altar. It is a burnt offering, an offering made by fire, an aroma pleasing to Your God.

ରେ   ରେ   ରେ

2:1 When anyone brings a grain offering to Your God, it must be of the finest flour, and it is to be mixed with oil and frankincense. ² The worshipper will bring the grain offering to one of Aaron's heirs, the priests, who will scoop up a handful of it and burn it as a token on the altar, an offering made by fire, an aroma pleasing to Your God. ³ The rest of the offering belongs to Aaron and his heirs. It is the most holy part of the offerings made with fire to Your God.**

⁴ If you bring a grain offering baked in an oven, it is to be of the finest flour, either unleavened cakes mixed with oil, or unleavened wafers spread

---

* In this way the animal becomes the worshiper's representative: what happens to the animal physically also happens to the worshiper symbolically and spiritually.

** The grain offering, or *minchah*, was offered generally in recognition of God's blessing in the harvest, and specifically as a voluntary offering of gratitude. The token portion that is burned serves as a reminder to God of the whole offering, the rest of which is eaten by the priests.

with oil.* ⁵ If you bring a grain offering cooked on a griddle, it must be an unleavened cake made of fine flour mixed with oil. ⁶ First, crumble it, and then pour oil on it, like all grain offerings. ⁷ If you bring a grain offering cooked in crockery, it must be made of fine flour and oil.

⁸ Bring your grain offering made with these ingredients and present it to the priest to take to the altar. ⁹ The priest will take out the token portion from your grain offering and burn it on the altar, an offering made by fire, an aroma pleasing to Your God. ¹⁰ The rest of the grain offering belongs to Aaron and his heirs. It is the most holy part of the offering made with fire to Your God.

¹¹ All grain offerings made to Your God must be made without leaven. You must not put anything fermented or made with honey on the altar as an offering made with fire to Your God. ¹² You may bring them to Your God as an offering of the firstfruits, but they must not be offered on the altar as a pleasing aroma. ¹³ All grain offerings made to Your God must include salt. You must not fail to add the salt of the Covenant with Your God to your grain offering. Salt must be part of every offering.**

¹⁴ If you present a grain offering of the firstfruits to Your God, you must present crushed heads of ripened grain roasted in fire. ¹⁵ Add oil and frankincense to it to make it a grain offering. ¹⁶ The priest will take out the token portion from the grain offering—some of the crushed grain, some of the oil and all of the frankincense—as an offering made by fire to Your God.

ଔ   ଔ   ଔ

3:1 If your offering is a fellowship sacrifice† from the herd, it may be male or female, but it must be whole and unblemished. Bring it into the presence of Your God. ² Lay your hand on the head of the animal and slaughter it at the entrance to the Tent of Meeting. Then the priests, Aaron's heirs, must cast the blood against all four sides of the altar. ³ One of the priests will present a portion of the fellowship sacrifice as an offering made by fire to Your God—the fat covering the entrails and all the fat near the entrails;⁴ both

---

* Not only does unleavened bread recall the flight from Egypt, it is also symbolic: because leavening agents (and the fermenting agents mentioned in verse 11) are susceptible to rotting, only unleavened bread, like the unblemished animal sacrifices above, could honor God in an act of ritual adoration. The oil represents joy. Note also the three tiers of gifts: only the weathy could afford ovens; others used a griddle or frying pan, while poor people used some kind of crockery.

** Salt represents permanence and indestructability, and was used throughout the Middle East in the sealing of an agreement.

† Literally, "a slaughter-offering of *shalom*." Many versions translate it "peace offering," though the word *shalom* also connotes well-being, wholeness, and in particular a happy and loving relationship. This, then, is a communion offering. The fellowship sacrifice is the only place where either female or male animals are allowed to be sacrificed, testifying to the great importance of this offering.

kidneys, with the fat on them near the loins; and the fat covering the liver, which the priest will remove along with the kidneys. ⁵ Then the priests, Aaron's heirs, will place these on the altar with the burnt offering, on top of the burning wood, an offering made by fire, an aroma pleasing to Your God.

⁶ If your fellowship sacrifice to God is an animal, male or female, which comes from the flock, it may be male or female, but it must be whole and unblemished.* ⁷ If you present a ram as an offering to Your God, ⁸ lay your hand on its head and slaughter it at the entrance to the Tent of Meeting. The priests must then cast its blood on each side of the altar. ⁹ From the fellowship sacrifice you must present part of it as an offering made by fire to Your God: the fat; the entire fatty tail, to be removed near the spine; all the fat that covers the entrails or is connected to them; ¹⁰ both kidneys, with the fat on them near the loins; and the fat covering the liver, which you will remove with the kidneys. ¹¹ The priest will burn it at the altar as food offered to Your God. ¹² If you offer a goat, you must present it before Your God, ¹³ lay your hand on its head, and slaughter it before the Tent of Meeting. Aaron's heirs, the priests, must dash its blood against each side of the altar. ¹⁴ You must then present as an offering made by fire to Your God both the fat that covers or is near the entrails, ¹⁵ both of the kidneys with the fat that is on them near the loins, and the fat that covers the liver. ¹⁶ The priest will burn these on the altar as an offering made by fire, an aroma pleasing to Your God.

All fat belongs to Your God. ¹⁷ This will be a perpetual ordinance from generation to generation wherever you dwell: you must not consume fat or blood.**

 C3   C3   C3

4:1 Our God told Moses ² to give the Israelites these instructions concerning anyone who inadvertently does something forbidden by God's commandments:

³ If it is the High Priest who sins† and so brings guilt upon the people,

---

* The sort of droning repetition with subtle variations that occurs here and throughout *Leviticus* implies that this may have originally been intended as a chant for the purposes of memorization.

** While fat represented the choicest part of the animal, it also signified comfort and luxury. Some commentators feel that the prohibition against fat is a warning against a life of such ease that the people would forget God. Consuming blood, or an animal that has not been fully drained of blood, was prohibited because "the life force of every creature is in the blood" (Lev. 17:14). Blood had the power to absorb and purify all ceremonial uncleanness, and therefore was utterly sacred.

† "Sin" here literally means to miss the mark, and as used in the Torah was very close to our modern concept of failure, though it also included the sense of giving offense. The section begins with four categories of inadvertent sins, with their appropriate sacrifices: first for the High Priest, then for the entire community, then leaders, then individuals.

the priest must present to Your God a young bull without blemish as a purification offering.* ⁴ The priest must bring the young bull to the entrance to the Tent of Meeting, lay a hand on its head, and slaughter it before Your God. ⁵ The priest must then bring some of its blood to the Tent of Meeting, ⁶ dip a finger in the blood, and sprinkle it seven times before Your God, in front of the sanctuary curtain. ⁷ The priest must spread some of the blood on the horns of the altar where fragrant incense is burned before Your God, and then pour the rest of the bull's blood at the base of the altar of burnt offerings, which is at the entrance to the Tent of Meeting.**

⁸ The priest then must remove all the fat from the bull of the purification offering, and set aside the fat that covers or is near the entrails, ⁹ both kidneys with the fat on them near the loins, and the fat covering the liver. ¹⁰ It must be set aside in the same way as is the fat from the bull at the fellowship sacrifice, and the priest must burn the pieces of fat on the altar of burnt offerings. ¹¹ The hide of the bull, and all its meat, its head, the lower legs, entrails and offal— ¹² all of it must be taken outside the camp to a place that is ritually clean, to the pile of ashes, and burned on a wood fire on the ash heap.†

¹³ If the whole Israelite community sins inadvertently, doing what is forbidden by Your God's commandments, and the deed goes unnoticed by the assembly, ¹⁴ then, when the sin they committed becomes known to them, the community must present a young bull as a purification offering and bring it to the entrance of the Tent of Meeting. ¹⁵ The leaders of the community must lay their hands on the head of the bull before Your God, and it must be slaughtered before Your God. ¹⁶ The High Priest must then bring some of the bull's blood into the Tent of Meeting, ¹⁷ dip a finger into the blood, and sprinkle it in front of the curtain seven times before Your God. ¹⁸ The priest must spread some of the blood on the horns of the altar before Your God in the Tent of Meeting, and pour the remainder at the base of the altar of burnt offerings, which is at the entrance to the Tent of Meet-

---

* The traditional rendering is "sin offering," but this misses the point entirely; "decontamination offering" would be closer. As translator and biblical scholar Everett Fox has noted, ritual impurity is not uncleanness in the physical sense, but a state more akin to radioactivity, that is, a pollution that drives the divine presence away from Israel. Generally, when in a state of ceremonial uncleanness, one could still go about one's regular tasks; it only prohibited one from approaching the Tent of Meeting for worship, or entering the altar area to offer a sacrifice.

** The particularity of this ritual is significant: the curtain separates the sanctuary from the Most Holy Place, which only the High Priest could enter, so sprinkling the blood there was as close as the people and the regular priesthood could get to God; doing so seven times was symbolic of unity with God's perfection. Putting blood on the horns of the altar symbolized making one's prayers once again efficacious; and pouring the rest around the base of the sacrificial altar was the priest's rededication to God without reservation.

† Priests were not to eat of their own purification offerings the way they ate from others'.

ing. ¹⁹ Then the priest must set aside the fat from the bull and burn it on the altar. ²⁰ The priest must do the same with this bull as is done with the bull for the purification offering. In this way the priest will make atonement* for the people, and they will be forgiven. ²¹ The priest will then take the bull outside the camp and burn it as the bull for the High Priest was burned. This is the purification offering for the community.

²² When a leader inadvertently sins, doing what is forbidden by one of the commandments of Your God, and incurs guilt, ²³ when the committed sin becomes known, the leader must bring an offering of a male goat without blemish. ²⁴ The leader must lay a hand on the head of the goat and slaughter it before Your God at the place where the burnt offering is slaughtered before Your God. It is a purification offering. ²⁵ The priest must take some of the blood and spread it on the horns of the burnt offering altar. ²⁶ All of the fat must be burned on the altar the same way as the fat of the fellowship sacrifice. By doing this the priest will make atonement for the leader's sins, and the leader will be forgiven.

²⁷ When anyone among you sins inadvertently, doing something forbidden by one of Your God's commandments, and you incur guilt, ²⁸ then when the sin you committed is made known to you, you must bring a female goat without blemish for your offering for the sin you committed. ²⁹ Lay your hand on its head and slaughter it at the place where the burnt offering is slaughtered. ³⁰ The priest will take some of its blood and spread it on the horns of the burnt offering altar; the rest of the blood will be poured at the base of the altar. ³¹ The priest will remove all of its fat, in the same way the fat is removed from the fellowship sacrifice, and burn it on the altar as a sacrifice whose aroma is pleasing to God. By doing this the priest will atone for your sin, and you will be forgiven.

³² If you bring a sheep as a purification offering, it must be a ewe without blemish. ³³ Lay your hand on its head and slaughter it as a purification offering at the same place where the burnt offering is slaughtered. The priest must then take some of the blood and spread it on the horns of the burnt offering altar; the rest of the blood is to be poured at the base of the altar. ³⁵ You must remove all the fat in the same way the fat is removed from the

---

* The word translated "atonement" literally means "to cover," implying that sins are covered or sealed up, rather than simply forgiven. The same word is used to describe the Covering for the Ark of the Covenant: the cover of the box upon which the gold winged sphinxes sat, often called the Mercy Seat, where the atonement is effected. Atonement is performed not only for sins, but for a wide variety of situations after ritual purity has been restored, such as after a house has been cleaned of mildew, or after a woman's menstrual cycle.

fellowship sacrifice, and the priest will burn it on the altar, with the offering made by fire to Your God. By doing this the priest will effect purgation for the sin you committed, and you will be forgiven.

5:1 If one of you hears a public appeal for testimony, and you are a witness to the matter at hand, and yet you fail to come forward, then you have sinned and carry the burden of your error. 2 Or if you touch something that is ritually unclean, such as the carcass of a ritually forbidden animal, wild or domestic, or of a ritually forbidden insect, even though are not aware of it, you are guilty nonetheless. 3 Or if you inadvertently touch some human ritual impurity,* or come in contact with any other kind of ritual impurity, and realize later what you have done, then you are guilty. 4 Or when one of you swears an oath rashly, whether for good purpose or evil—in any situation in which a person can thoughtlessly swear—even though you did it unawares, once you realize what you have done, you are guilty.

5 When you realize your guilt in any of these situations, you must confess the sin you committed. 6 Then you are to bring your reparation offering to Your God for the sin you committed: bring a female from the flock, either a sheep or a goat, for a purification offering. The priest will atone for your sin on your behalf.

7 However, if you cannot afford even a young animal, you may bring two pigeons or two turtledoves to Your God in reparation for your sin. One is to be a purification offering and the other a burnt offering. 8 Bring them to the priest, who will first present the purification offering. The priest must wring its neck without severing it, 9 and then sprinkle some of the blood against the side of the altar. The remainder of the blood must be drained out at the base of the altar as a purification offering. 10 The priest must treat the second bird as a burnt offering according to the ritual. By doing this the priest will atone on your behalf for the sin you committed, and you will be forgiven.

11 If you cannot afford two turtledoves or two pigeons, you must bring as an offering for a purification offering two quarts of fine flour. You must not put oil or frankincense on it, for this is a purification offering. 12 You must bring it to the priest, who will scoop up a handful of it as a token and burn it on the altar atop the burnt offerings made to Your God. 13 By doing this the priest will atone on your behalf for the sin you committed, and you will be forgiven. As in the case of the grain offering, the remainder will belong to the priest.

---

* Like bodily flows or skin diseases, or dead bodies.

¹⁴ Our God spoke to Moses and said:

¹⁵ When one of you breaks faith and commits a sacrilege against anything sacred to Your God, you must bring to Your God a reparation offering of an unblemished ram from the flock, and assess its value in silver shekels according to the sanctuary standard. ¹⁶ You must make restitution for sinning against sacred things by paying with the goat and by giving one-fifth of its value in silver to the priest, who will make atonement on your behalf with the ram of reparation, and you will be forgiven.

¹⁷ If one of you sins unintentionally, and violates any of the commandments of Your God, you incur guilt, and carry the burden of your error. ¹⁸ You must bring to the priest an unblemished ram, of the appropriate value, for the reparation offering. The priest will atone on your behalf for the sin you have committed unintentionally, and you will be forgiven. ¹⁹ It is a guilt offering, for you were guilty of a sin against Your God.

6·1 Our God said this to Moses:

² If any of you sins or breaks faith with Your God by deceiving your neighbor in matters of deposits or pledges, or through robbery, or fraud, ³ or by lying about a lost item that you found, or by swearing a false oath about sins such as these, ⁴ when you have sinned and know that you have sinned, you must restore the stolen goods, repay what you defrauded, release the deposits entrusted to you, give back the lost item, ⁵ or make good on anything else about which you gave false witness; you must repay the principal and add one-fifth to that amount. The payment must be made to the person you have sinned against, as soon as you know that you are guilty.

⁶ You must also bring to the priest an unblemished ram from the flock, or its equivalent, as a reparation offering. ⁷ The priest will atone for your guilt before Your God, and you will be forgiven for the acts of which you are guilty.

℞   ℞   ℞

⁸ Our God told Moses ⁹ to give these Instructions* to Aaron and his heirs:

This is the ritual of the burnt offering. The burnt offering is to remain on the hearth of the altar all night until the morning, and the fire on the hearth is to be kept burning. ¹⁰ The priest must put on a linen robe over linen undergarments, and remove the ashes of the burnt offering that the fire

---

* The word for Instruction is *torah*; it originally referred to the rules and instructions given to the priests, but later came to describe Moses' teachings, and finally the five Books of Moses as a whole.

consumed on the altar, and place them next to the altar. ¹¹ Then the priest must change into other garments, and take the ashes outside the camp to a ritually clean place.¹² The fire on the altar must never go out; it must be kept burning constantly. Every single morning the priest must add wood and arrange the burnt offering on the fire, and burn the fat of the fellow-ship sacrifice on it. ¹³ The fire on the altar must be kept burning continually; it must never go out.

¹⁴ This is the ritual of the grain offering. The heirs of Aaron will present it before Your God in front of the altar. ¹⁵ The priest will set aside a handful of it, some of the flour with a little of the oil and the frankincense that goes on top of the offering, and burn it as a token on the altar, as a sacrifice whose aroma is pleasing to God. ¹⁶ Aaron and his heirs are to eat the remainder. This is to be consumed in the form of unleavened bread in a holy place, in the courtyard of the Tent of Meeting. ¹⁷ It must not be baked with yeast. I, Your God, have allotted it to the priests as their share of the offerings made by fire to me. It is most holy, like the purification offering and the repara-tion offering. ¹⁸ Only Aaron's heirs may eat it, their allotment through the ages, for all your generations, from the offerings made by fire to me. Any-thing that touches it must be treated as holy.

¹⁹ Our God said this to Moses:

²⁰ This is the offering Aaron and his heirs are to present to Your God on the day they are anointed for service: two quarts of flour as a regular grain offering, half of it in the morning and half of it in the evening. ²¹ It must be cooked with oil on a griddle. See that it is well-baked and crumbled into pieces, a grain offering whose aroma is pleasing to God. ²² An anointed priest in the line of Aaron must prepare the burnt offering, in perpetuity. The entire offering belongs to Your God, ²³ and must be burned completely. It must not be eaten.

²⁴ Our God told Moses ²⁵ to give this Instruction to Aaron and his heirs:

This is the ritual for the purification offering. You must slaughter the purification offering before Your God in the same place where the burnt offering is slaughtered. It is most holy. ²⁶ The priest who makes the offer-ing must eat its meat in a holy place, in the courtyard of the Tent of Meet-ing. ²⁷ Anything that touches its meat is to be considered holy, and if any of its blood splashes on your clothing, you must wash the stain in a holy place. ²⁸ You must shatter any earthenware in which the purification offering is boiled. If it is boiled in a copper container, the pot is to be scoured and rinsed with water. ²⁹ Any of Aaron's heirs may eat of this offering; it is most holy. ³⁰ However, they must not eat any purification offering whose blood is carried into the Tent of Meeting to atone for sins in the holy place; instead, the offering must be completely burned in the fire.

7:1 This is the Instruction for the reparation offering, which is most holy:

² The reparation offering is to be slaughtered at the same place where the burnt offering is slaughtered, and its blood is to be dashed against each side of the altar. ³ The priest must burn all the fat of the offering—the fatty tail, the fat covering the entrails, ⁴ both kidneys with the fat on them near the loins, and the fat that covers the liver—on the altar, as an offering made by fire. ⁵ It is a reparation offering. ⁶ It is to be eaten by the priests, in a holy place; it is most holy.

⁷ The reparation offering is like the purification offering: the ritual is to be the same, and the priest who makes atonement will keep it. ⁸ Also, the priest who makes the burnt offering has the right to its hide.

⁹ Grain offerings that are baked in an oven, and everything that is cooked in a pan or on a griddle, belong to the priest who offers them. ¹⁰ Grain offerings, dry or mixed with oil, are to be shared equally among Aaron's heirs.

¹¹ This is the Instruction for the fellowship sacrifice that is presented to Your God:

¹² If you offer it for thanksgiving, you must offer with it unleavened cakes mixed with oil, unleavened wafers spread with oil, and cakes of fine flour moistened with oil. ¹³ You must also present flat cakes of leavened bread with the fellowship sacrifice. ¹⁴ One part of every offering must be presented as a contribution to Your God, to be given to the priest who dashes the blood of the fellowship sacrifice on the altar. ¹⁵ You must eat the meat of this offering on the day you present it; none of it may be saved until the next morning.

¹⁶ On the other hand, if your sacrifice is an offering in connection with a vow, or one offered voluntarily, it should be eaten on the day it is presented, but what is left over may be eaten the next day. ¹⁷ But you must burn what is left from the meat of the sacrifice on the third day. ¹⁸ If you eat any of the meat of the fellowship sacrifice on the third day, it will not be acceptable, and it will not be credited to the person who offered it. Rather, it will be considered tainted and those who eat it will share the blame for your act.

¹⁹ Meat that touches anything ritually unclean must not be eaten, and must be burned up. All other meat may be eaten by anyone who is ritually

pure, ²⁰ but any who eat of meat from a fellowship sacrifice that is presented to Your God while they are unclean must be cut off from their people.

²¹ When any of you touches anything that is ritually unclean—whether a ritually unclean human, animal, or insect—and then eat meat from a fellowship sacrifice presented to Your God, you are to be cut off from your people.

²² Our God told Moses ²³ to tell this to the Israelites:

You are not to eat the fat of oxen, sheep or goats. ²⁴ You are not to eat the fat of any animal that dies a natural death or has been mauled by wild animals; however, you may put it to other uses. ²⁵ If you eat fat from an animal from which a food offering is presented to Your God, you are to be cut off from your people.

²⁶ You must not consume any blood from an animal or a bird throughout all your settlements. ²⁷ If you consume blood, you will be cut off from your people.*

²⁸ Our God told Moses ²⁹ to tell this to the Israelites:

When you come to present a fellowship sacrifice to Your God, you must present it yourself. ³⁰ You are to bring the fellowship sacrifice with your own hands to Your God, and you must bring the fat and the breast which is to be raised as a dedicated portion before the Almighty. ³¹ The priest will burn the fat on the altar, but the breast belongs to Aaron and his heirs. ³² Give the right thigh** of the fellowship sacrifice as your contribution to the priest. ³³ Whichever priest offers the blood and the fat of the fellowship sacrifice will receive the right thigh for a contribution. ³⁴ The breast that forms the dedicated portion of the fellowship sacrifice, and the thigh that is given as a contribution, I take from the Israelites and give to Aaron the priest and to Aaron's descendants, as perpetual allotments from the Israelites. ³⁵ This is the portion allotted to Aaron and Aaron's descendants out of God's burnt offerings when they were presented as priests to Your God. ³⁶ On the day they were anointed priests, Your God commanded that these portions be given to them as their regular share by the Israelites.

---

* "Cut off" indicates permanent excommunication, and often meant the death of the violator. In this way the sacred whole of the community was preserved from contamination. Drinking or bathing in the warm fresh blood of a sacrifice, whether human or animal, was a common practice in many Near Eastern religions. While *Leviticus* echoes the belief that the blood carries the life force of the person or animal, God makes it clear that the blood is to be poured at the base of the altar—indicating that all life belongs to God alone. In this way, the Israelites are made distinct in their ceremonial practices from the surrounding cultures.

** The right thigh symbolizes sacred intimacy, thus a fitting contribution to the priest who performs the ceremony.

[37] This, then, is the Instruction for the burnt offering, the grain offering, the purification offering, the reparation offering, the ordination offering, and the fellowship sacrifice, which Our God commanded Moses on Mount Sinai, when the people of Israel were commanded to bring their offerings to Our God in the wilderness of Sinai.

8:1–10:20

OUR God said to Moses, [2] "Bring Aaron and his heirs, together with their vestments, the anointing oil, a bull for the purification offering, two rams, and the basket of unleavened bread, [3] together with the entire community, and assemble at the entrance to the Tent of Meeting."*

[4] Moses did as God commanded, and when the community had gathered at the entrance to the Tent of Meeting, [5] Moses told them, "This is what God has ordered be done."

[6] Moses called Aaron and his heirs to come forward, and washed them with water. [7] Moses then vested Aaron the high priest in the tunic, the sash, the mantle, the ephod and the waistband. He then fastened the ephod to Aaron with the decorated waistband, [8] and vested him with the breastpiece, with the Urim and Thummim** in it. [9] Finally, Moses placed the turban on the high priest's head, and on the front he fastened the gold medallion, the symbol of holy dedication, just as God had commanded Moses.

[10] Then Moses took the anointing oil and anointed the tabernacle and all its contents, and consecrated them. [11] Moses sprinkled the altar with the oil seven times, anointing the altar, its utensils, basin and basin stand, to consecrate them, [12] and poured oil on Aaron's head to consecrate him. [13] Moses then brought Aaron's heirs forward, clothed them with tunics, tied sashes around them and placed headdresses on them, as God had commanded.

[14] Moses then presented the bull for the purification offering, and Aaron and his heirs laid their hands on its head. [15] Moses slaughtered it and took some of its blood to smear on the horns of the altar to purify it, and dashed the remainder at its base, consecrating it and making atonement for it. [16] Then Moses took all the fat covering the entrails and the liver, and the

---

* This chapter details the ceremony for ordaining Aaron and his descendants to the priesthood.

** As noted in Exodus 28, these objects for divining the will of God were likely kept in a pocket in the breastpiece, though their appearance and use are a great mystery—perhaps deliberately so. *Urim* means "lights" or "manifestations," and *Thummim* means "perfections" or "the truth." Most scholars feel they were stones for casting lots.

two kidneys with their fat, and burned them on the altar. ¹⁷ But he burned the bull's hide, flesh and offal on a fire outside the camp, as God had commanded Moses.

¹⁸ Then Moses brought in the ram for the burnt offering. Aaron and his heirs laid their hands on the ram's head. ¹⁹ Moses slaughtered it and dashed its blood on the side of the altar, ²⁰ cut it into pieces and burned the head, the pieces and the fat. ²¹ And once the entrails and the legs were washed with water, Moses burned the whole ram on the altar; it was a burnt offering with an aroma pleasing to Our God.

²² Then he brought forward the second ram, the ram for the ordination of the priests. Aaron and his heirs laid their hands on its head. ²³ Moses slaughtered it, and took some of its blood and daubed it on the ridge of Aaron's right ear, his right thumb, and on the big toe of his right foot.* ²⁴ Then Moses brought forward Aaron's heirs and put some of the blood on their right earlobes, their right thumbs, and the big toes of their right feet. The remainder of the blood was dashed against all four sides of the altar.

²⁵ Moses took the fat—the fatty tail, all the fat from around the entrails and the liver, and the two kidneys with their fat—and the right thigh. ²⁶ Then Moses took one unleavened cake, one cake of bread made with oil, and one wafer from the basket of unleavened bread that was before Our God, and laid them on the fatty parts and on the right thigh. ²⁷ He put all of these into the hands of Aaron and his heirs, who elevated them as dedicated portions before Our God. ²⁸ Then Moses took them back from their hands and burned them on the altar atop the ram offered in the purification offering. This was an ordination offering, an offering made by fire, an aroma pleasing to Our God. ²⁹ Moses took the breast and elevated it as a dedicated portion before Our God; this was Moses' portion of the ram of ordination, as God had commanded.

³⁰ Then Moses took some of the anointing oil and some of the blood from the altar, and sprinkled them on Aaron and on his vestments, and also on Aaron's heirs and on their vestments. In this way Moses consecrated Aaron and his vestments, and also Aaron's heirs and their vestments.

³¹ Moses said to Aaron and his heirs, "Boil the meat at the entrance to the Tent of Meeting and eat it there, with the bread in the ordination basket offering, as I was commanded—'Aaron and Aaron's heirs are to eat it.' ³² Destroy by fire what remains of the meat and bread. ³³ Do not

---

* The right side symbolized the sun, and sacredness. The ear was marked to signify that the priest was to hear only God's words; the thumb, that only God's work was to be done; and the toe, that only God's path was to be followed.

leave the entrance to the Tent of Meeting for seven days, for the period of ordination is seven days. ³⁴ What happened today was commanded by Our God to atone for you. ³⁵ You must stay at the entrance to the Tent of Meeting day and night for seven days, doing as God commands, so that you do not die—for this is what I have been commanded." ³⁶ So Aaron and his heirs did everything that God had commanded through Moses.

⁹:¹ On the eighth day, Moses summoned Aaron and his heirs and the clan leaders of Israel, ² and said, "Take a young, unblemished calf as a purification offering, and an unblemished ram for a burnt offering, and present them to Our God. ³ Then tell the Israelites to take a male goat for a purification offering, and a yearling calf and a yearling lamb, both unblemished, for a burnt offering, ⁴ and an ox and a ram for a fellowship sacrifice to be offered to Our God, together with a grain offering mixed with oil. For today Our God will appear to you!"

⁵ They brought what Moses had commanded to the front of the Tent of Meeting, and the whole community gathered and stood before Your God. ⁶ Moses said, "Our God commanded these things so that God's glory might appear to you."

⁷ Then Moses said to Aaron, "Approach the altar and sacrifice your purification offering and your burnt offering, to make atonement for yourself and for the people. Then sacrifice the offerings of the people, to make atonement for them, as Our God commands."

⁸ Aaron approached the altar and slaughtered the calf as the purification offering of the high priest. ⁹ Aaron's heirs presented the blood to Aaron, who dipped a finger in the blood and put it on the horns of the altar; the remainder he poured out at the base of the altar. ¹⁰ Aaron burned on the altar the fat, the kidneys, and the covering of the liver from the purification offering, as God had commanded Moses. ¹¹ But he burned the meat and the skin outside the camp.

¹² Then Aaron slaughtered the burnt offering. Aaron's heirs brought the high priest the blood, which was then dashed against all four sides of the altar. ¹³ Then they brought the burnt offering piece by piece, and the head, which Aaron put on the fire. ¹⁴ He washed the entrails and the legs, and burned them with the burnt offering on the altar.

¹⁵ Next came the offering of the people. Aaron took the goat, the purification offering of the people, and presented it as a purification offering, slaughtering it like the first one. ¹⁶ The high priest presented the burnt offering and sacrificed it according to the regulation. ¹⁷ Aaron presented the

grain offering and took a handful of it and burned it on the altar, adding it to the morning's burnt offering.

¹⁸ He slaughtered the fellowship sacrifice of the people, the bull and the ram. Aaron's heirs brought the blood to him, to be dashed on the sides of the altar. ¹⁹ They took the fat portions of the bull and the ram—the fatty tail, the fat covering the entrails, the two kidneys and their fat, and the covering of the liver—²⁰ touched them to the breasts, then Aaron burned the fat on the altar. ²¹ Aaron elevated the breasts and the right thigh as a dedicated portion before Our God, as Moses commanded.

²² Aaron raised his hands toward the people to bless them, and when the purification offering, the burnt offering and the communal offering had been sacrificed, he stepped down ²³ and entered the Tent of Meeting with Moses. When they came out, they blessed the congregation, and the glory of Our God appeared before all the people. ²⁴ A tongue of flame shot out from the presence of God and consumed the burnt offering and the fat on the altar. And when all the people witnessed this, they shouted for joy and fell on their faces.

℞ ℞ ℞

10:1 Then Aaron's heirs Nadab and Abihu took the censers, put incense on the fire, and presented to Our God unsanctified fire,* fire that God had not commanded. ² Then a tongue of flame shot out from the presence of Our God and consumed them, and they perished in God's presence.

³ Moses said to Aaron, "This is what Our God meant by saying,

'To those permitted to be near me,
   I will be proven holy;
in the presence of all,
   I will be honored.'"

Aaron, however, was silent.

⁴ Moses sent for Mishael and Elzaphan, heirs of Aaron's uncle Uzziel, and said to them, "Come and take your cousins away from the camp and away from the sanctuary." ⁵ They came and removed their cousins' bodies, as Moses instructed, carrying them by their tunics.

---

* That is, coals from outside the sanctity of the altar area. Medieval commentators saw the sudden prohibition in verse 9 against priestly intoxication as an indication of Nadab and Abihu's real crime here: that they were drunk while carrying out their duties. Biblical scholar Raymond Brown suggests that this episode underscores the importance of following the prescribed ceremonies in exacting detail, and says that the cultic rituals of the Israelites are important in their identification as separate from the surrounding peoples. "Holy" or "sanctified" literally means "separate."

⁶ Then Moses said to Aaron and his heirs Eleazar and Ithamar, "Do not to let your hair become unkempt or rip your clothes in mourning; do not grieve for them, or you will die and God will be angry with the entire community. However, your sisters and brothers, the entire house of Israel, may mourn that the fiery destruction from Our God was necessary. ⁷ You must not leave the entrance to the Tent of Meeting, or you will die, for God's anointing oil is on you." And they did as Moses told them.

⁸ Then Our God spoke to Aaron and said, ⁹ "When you and your heirs enter the Tent of Meeting, do not have wine or strong drink, or you will die, for God's anointing oil is on you. This is a perpetual statute binding your descendants for all time. ¹⁰ You are to distinguish between the holy and the profane, between the ritually unclean and the ceremonially pure. ¹¹ And you are to teach the Israelites all the statutes which Your God has given them through Moses."

¹² Moses said to Aaron and his surviving heirs, Eleazar and Ithamar, "Take what remains of the grain offering out of the food offering made to Our God by fire, and eat it unleavened beside the altar; it is most holy. ¹³ Eat it in a sacred place, for it is your allotment and that of your offspring from Our God's offering by fire. This I have been commanded to tell you. ¹⁴ You and your daughters and your sons may eat, any place that is ritually pure, the breast and the thigh of the dedicated portion, which are allotted to you from the fellowship sacrifices of the Israelites. ¹⁵ The thigh that was contributed, and the breast that was elevated, along with the gifts of the fatty parts, must be brought and elevated as a dedicated offering before Our God. They belong to you and your children forever, as Our God commanded."

¹⁶ Moses made inquiries about the goat offered as a sacrifice for the purification offering. When he learned that it had already been burned, he was angry with Aaron's surviving heirs, Eleazar and Ithamar, and asked them, ¹⁷ "Why didn't you eat the purification offering in the sanctuary? It is most holy, for it was given to you to remove the guilt of the community by atoning for them before Our God! ¹⁸ Since its blood was not taken into the sanctuary, you should have eaten its flesh there, as I commanded you."

¹⁹ Aaron replied to Moses, "Today they offered their purification offering and their burnt offering before Our God, and yet tragedies like this have happened to me! If I had eaten the purification offering on a day such as

this, would that have pleased Our God?"* ²⁰ Moses listened, and saw that Aaron was right.

11:1–17:16

Oᴜʀ God spoke to Moses and Aaron, and said to ² tell the Israelites these things:**

³ These are the living creatures you may eat:

Among all the domesticated animals on the earth, you may eat any that has cloven hooves and chews its cud. ⁴ However, these animals which only have cloven hooves or only chew the cud you must not eat: camels, which chew the cud but don't have cloven hooves; ⁵ rock badgers, which chew the cud but don't have cloven hooves; ⁶ hares, which chew the cud but don't have cloven hooves; ⁷ and pigs, which don't chew the cud but do have cloven hooves. ⁸ You are not to eat their flesh or touch their dead bodies. They are ritually unclean to you.

⁹ Of all the creatures that live in water, you may eat anything with fins and scales, whether it lives in seas or streams. ¹⁰ But anything in the seas or streams, fresh water or salt, that does not have fins or scales, small creatures or large, you are to treat as detestable.† ¹¹ And because they are detestable to you, you are to not eat their flesh or touch their dead bodies. ¹² Every creature in the water that has neither fins nor scales is detestable to you.

¹³ Among creatures that fly, you must treat the following as detestable—you must not eat them, for they are detestable to you: the eagle, the vulture, the osprey, ¹⁴ any kind of kite and falcon, ¹⁵ any kind of raven, ¹⁶ the ostrich, the screech owl, the seagull, any kind of hawk, ¹⁷ the little owl, the cormorant, the great owl, ¹⁸ the barn owl, the pelican, the horned owl, ¹⁹ the stork, any kind of heron, the hoopoe, and the bat.

²⁰ All winged insects that swarm and crawl on the ground‡ are detestable to you, ²¹ except those winged insects that crawl on the ground and

---

* Aaron is not saying that it is inappropriate to participate in the ceremony because he is grieving for his sons; rather, he is pointing out to Moses that he shares in his sons' guilt and is therefore not in the state of holiness required to eat the meat of the purification offering. This passage illustrates the belief that the guilt for the deeds of one family member rests on the heads of the entire family.

** This section of *Leviticus* is generally known as "the Purity Code," and is concerned with the causes of ritual impurity or uncleanness, and what is needs to be done to return to a state of purity. The section discusses four major categories: clean and unclean animals, childbirth, skin disorders, and uncleanness associated wtih sexuality.

† "Destestable" things, while forbidden to eat, do not convey ritual impurity.

‡ Literally, "go about on all fours," although winged insects always have six legs.

leviticus 10

have jointed legs above their feet, with which they hop on the ground. ²² You may eat any kind of locust, katydid, cricket, or grasshopper. ²³ But all other winged insects that have four legs you must treat as detestable.

²⁴ Now, these things will make you ritually impure; whoever touches the carcass of any of them will be unclean until evening— ²⁵ if you pick up any part of one of them, you must wash your clothes, and you will be ritually unclean until evening: ²⁶ Any animal with divided hooves, but where the cleft doesn't go all the way through; or any animal that does not chew its cud—they are unclean to you, and if you touch them you are ritually unclean. ²⁷ You are to consider all four-footed animals that walk on their paws as unclean. Whoever touches one of their carcasses is unclean until evening, ²⁸ and if you pick up their carcasses you must wash your clothes and you will remain ritually unclean until evening.

²⁹ The following creatures that swarm on the ground are unclean to you: the weasel, the rat, any kind of crocodile, ³⁰ the gecko, the monitor lizard, the wall lizard, the skink, and the chameleon. ³¹ These swarming creatures are unclean to you. If you touch their dead bodies you are unclean until evening. ³² Anything that falls on one of them once it has died becomes ritually unclean. Any such article—wood, cloth, hide, sackcloth—must be put in water, and it will be ritually unclean until evening. After that it will be clean. ³³ If one of these creatures falls into a clay vessel, the contents are unclean and you must destroy the vessel. ³⁴ Any edible food that comes into contact with water from such a vessel is unclean and any potable liquid from these vessels is unclean. ³⁵ Anything on which the dead carcass of one of these falls is unclean. A cooking pot or oven must be shattered. They are unclean and cannot be made clean. ³⁶ A spring or a cistern for collecting water remains clean; but anything that touches a carcass within it is unclean. ³⁷ If one of their carcasses falls on seed that is to be planted, the seed remains clean, ³⁸ but if the seed is watered and then a carcass falls on it, the seed is unclean for you.

³⁹ If an animal that you are allowed to eat dies a natural death, anyone who touches the carcass is ritually unclean until evening. ⁴⁰ If you eat any part of the carcass you must wash your clothes and you are unclean until evening. If you pick up the carcass you must wash your clothes and you are ritually unclean until evening.

⁴¹ Creatures that swarm on the ground are detestable and must not be eaten. ⁴² And you are not to eat any other creature that moves about on the ground, whether it moves on its belly or moves on all fours or uses any number of legs, for it is detestable.

⁴³ Do not defile yourselves or make yourselves ritually unclean with any

of these. ⁴⁴ I am the Most High, Your God; consecrate yourselves and be holy, for I am holy. Do not defile yourselves with any creature that swarms on the ground. ⁴⁵ I am Your God, who brought you up out of Egypt to be your Holy One. Therefore, be holy, for I am holy!

⁴⁶ This, then, is the Instruction concerning animals, birds, every living creature moving through the water and every creature that swarms on the ground. ⁴⁷ You must make a distinction between the ritually clean and the ritually unclean, between living creatures that may be eaten and those that must not be eaten.

Ↄ Ↄ Ↄ

12₁ Our God told Moses ² to tell the Israelites these things:

When a women conceives and bears a male child, she is ceremonially unclean, as she is during her time of menstruation, for seven days.* ³ On the eighth day the child is to be circumcised. ⁴ It takes thirty-three days for the mother's blood to be purified; she must not touch sacred objects or enter the sanctuary until after the thirty-third day.

⁵ When she gives birth to a daughter, she will be ceremonially unclean, as during her time of menstruation, for two weeks. Then it takes sixty-six days for her blood to be purified.

⁶ When she has finished her purification period, whether she had a son or a daughter, she must bring a yearling lamb for a burnt offering and a pigeon or a turtledove for a purification offering, and give them to the priest at the entrance to the Tent of Meeting. ⁷ The priest will present these before Your God to atone for her; then she will be purified from having given birth. This is the Instruction for a woman who gives birth, whether to a female or a male. ⁸ If the family cannot afford a lamb, they may bring two pigeons or turtledoves, one for the burnt offering and one for the purification offering. The priest must then make atonement for her and she will be purified.

Ↄ Ↄ Ↄ

---

* The loss of blood, according to Raymond Brown, meant the loss of life force and thus the loss of closeness to God. In this instance, the loss of blood in childbirth diminishes vitality and connection to God—and the result is ritual uncleanness. Males, in this patriarchal society, were associated wtih greater vitality, so lesser weakness resulted after the birth of a male than a female child. Along the same lines as Brown, commentator Everett Fox says that the mother's ritual impurity comes from her intimate contact with both life and death during childbirth. Giving birth to a girl "potentially doubles the 'life-leak' that has taken place, since she will one day be a childbearing woman who will herself confront the life-death continuum."

13:1 Our God told Moses and Aaron these things:

2 When one of you has a swelling, an inflammation, or a shiny spot on your skin that could develop into an infectious skin disease,* you must go to a priest, either to Aaron or one of Aaron's heirs. 3 The priest will examine the afflicted area, and if the hair in or around the infected spot is white and appears to be more than skin deep, you have an infectious skin disease; the priest, after the examination, will pronounce you ceremonially unclean. 4 But if on the other hand the inflammation is white and does not appear to be more than skin deep and the hair in it is not white, the priest will isolate you for seven days. 5 On the seventh day the priest will reexamine you, and if the sore remains as it was and has not spread on the skin, you will be isolated for another seven days. 6 On the seventh day the priest must examine you once again, and if the sore has faded and not spread on the skin, the priest will pronounce you ceremonially clean—it is only a rash. You must wash your clothes, then you will be clean. 7 But if the inflammation spreads on the skin after you have shown yourself to the priest and were pronounced ritually clean, you must return to the priest. 8 If it has spread on the skin, the priest will pronounce you ritually unclean; for it is infectious.

9 When you have sores from an infectious skin disease, you must go to the priest, 10 who will examine you. If there is a white swelling on the skin that turns the hair white with an ulceration appearing in the swelling, 11 you have a chronic skin disease on your body and the priest must pronounce you ceremonially unclean. There is no need to isolate you to determine the disease's spread—you are unclean already. 12 If the disease covers your body as far as the priest can see, from your head to your feet, 13 the priest will examine you, and if the disease covers your whole body, you will be declared ceremonially clean; since the disease has turned white, you are clean.** 14 But as soon as eruptions break out, you must be considered unclean. 15 Once the priest sees them, you will be pronounced unclean. Raw flesh is unclean, since it is a sign of an infectious disease. 16 But if the raw flesh turns white again, return to the priest, 17 who will examine you. If the sores are indeed white, the priest will pronounce you ceremonially clean.

18 When a boil appears on the skin and then heals, 19 but is followed by a

---

* Not, as has been translated most frequently, leprosy (Hansen's Disease), but *tzara'at,* any one of several skin diseases that involve scaling or flaking. It was the object of so much concen not out of fear of contagion, but because it was felt to resemble death and decay. Indeed, the same word is used to describe mildew on clothing (verse 47) and dry rot in houses, even though there is no indication that a mildewed garment was considered "leprous."

** The implication here is that it is the *contrast* between normal skin and diseased skin (or between uniformly diseased skin and new eruptions) that is the concern, not the disease itself. The "two different kinds" prohibition in 19:19 expresses a similar tension.

whitish inflammation where the boil was, you must show yourself to the priest. ²⁰ If the priest examines you and finds that it appears to be beneath the skin and the hair has turned white, the priest must pronounce you ceremonially unclean, since it is an infectious skin disease which has broken out on the site of the boil. ²¹ But if the priest examines you and finds no white hairs on it, and it is not beneath the skin but has faded, you must be isolated for seven days. ²² If the disease spreads on the skin the priest must pronounce you unclean, since it is an infectious skin disease. ²³ But if the inflammation has not worsened and has not spread, and there is only the scar of the boil, the priest will pronounce you ritually clean.

²⁴ When you suffer a burn on the skin, and the area of the burn becomes a white or reddish-white inflammation, ²⁵ the priest is to examine it. If the hair in the inflammation has turned white or it appears to be beneath the skin, an infectious disease has broken out in the burn. The priest must pronounce you ceremonially unclean, since it is an infectious disease. ²⁶ If the priest examines you and finds that there are no white hairs on the inflammation and that it is not beneath the skin, you must be isolated for seven days. ²⁷ You will be examined on the seventh day—if it is spreading on the skin, you will be pronounced unclean, since it is an infectious disease. ²⁸ But if the inflammation is the same and has not spread and has faded, the priest will pronounce you ceremonially clean, for it is only a scar from the burn.

²⁹ When you—woman or man—have a sore on your head or, in the case of a man, in your beard, ³⁰ go to the priest for an examination. If it appears to be deeper than the skin and the hair is yellow and thinned out, the priest must pronounce you ceremonially unclean. It is ringworm of the head or the beard. ³¹ If the priest examines the ringworm and it appears to be only skin deep, and there is no yellowing of the hair, then the priest must isolate you for seven days. ³² When the priest examines you on the seventh day, if the ringworm has not spread and there is no yellowing of the hair and it appears only skin deep, ³³ you must shave, excluding the affected hair. The priest will isolate you for seven more days. ³⁴ The priest will examine you on the seventh day—if the ringworm has not spread on the skin and the disease does not appear to be more than skin deep, the priest will pronounce you ceremonially clean. You must wash your clothes and then you will be ceremonially clean. ³⁵ But if the ringworm spreads on the skin after you were pronounced clean, ³⁶ you must be reexamined by the priest. If the ringworm has spread in the skin, the priest need not check for the yellow hair; you are unclean. ³⁷ But if the ringworm remains as it was and black hair appears, you are healed. You are clean, and the priest will declare you clean.

³⁸ When you—woman or man—notice whitish shiny spots on your skin, ³⁹ you must be examined by the priest. If they are a dull white, it is vitiligo that has broken out on your skin. You are ceremonially clean.

⁴⁰ When your hair starts falling out of your head, you are bald but not ceremonially unclean. ⁴¹ If the hair falls out from the front of your scalp and temples, you are ceremonially clean. ⁴² But if, on the bald patch of your head or on your forehead, you have a reddish-white sore, you have an infectious disease breaking out on the bald part of your head or your forehead. ⁴³ You must be examined by the priest—if the swollen spot on the bald patch of your head or your forehead is reddish white and appears to be an infectious disease of the skin of the skin, ⁴⁴ then you are diseased and ceremonially unclean. ⁴⁴ The priest must pronounce you ceremonially unclean because of the sore on your head.

⁴⁵ When you have an infectious skin disease, you must wear torn clothes, let your hair become unkempt, and cover the lower half of your face and cry out, "Unclean! Unclean!" ⁴⁶ As long as you have the infection you remain ceremonially unclean. You must live alone. You must live outside the camp.

⁴⁷ When your clothing is contaminated with mildew, whether the mildew is on a woolen or linen garment, ⁴⁸ or on the yarn of a woven piece of wool or linen, or on leather or things made of leather— ⁴⁹ if the contamination in the clothing, or piece of leather, or woven or knitted article, or anything made with leather, is greenish or reddish, it is spreading mildew and you must take it to the priest. ⁵⁰ The priest must examine the mildew and isolate the affected articles for seven days. ⁵¹ On the seventh day the priest must examine the articles again, and if mildew has spread in the clothing, or the woven or knitted material of wool or linen, or the leather—regardless of what it is used for—it is a destructive mildew, and it is ceremonially unclean. ⁵² You must burn the clothing, the woven or knitted material of wool or linen, or the contaminated leather. The mildew is destructive, and so you must burn the articles.

⁵³ Once the priest has examined the clothing, the woolen or linen material, or the leather items, ⁵⁴ and confirms that the mildew has not spread, the priest must order the contaminated items to be washed and be isolated for seven days. ⁵⁵ After the affected clothes have been washed, the priest will examine them, and if the mildew has not changed its appearance, even if it has not spread, it is unclean. You must burn it in a fire, whether the mildew is on the inside or the outside. ⁵⁶ If, when the priest examines it, the mildew has faded after being washed, the priest is to tear out the contaminated part of the clothing, or the leather, or the woven or knitted ma-

terial. ⁵⁷ But if the mildew reappears in the clothing, or in the woven or knitted material, or in the leather, it is spreading and you must burn it in a fire. ⁵⁸ Any clothing, woven or knitted material, or leather item that has been washed and is free of mildew, must be washed a second time, and then it will be clean.

⁵⁹ This is the Instruction concerning contaminations by mildew in woolen or linen clothing, woven or knitted material, or any leather items, for pronouncing them ceremonially clean or unclean.

14¹ Our God said to Moses:

² This is the Instruction for the ritual of ceremonial cleansing from infectious skin diseases. ³ You must come to the priest, who will come outside of the camp to examine you. If you have been healed of your infectious skin disease, ⁴ the priest will order that two live unblemished birds, some cedar wood, scarlet yarn, and hyssop* be brought out for you who are to be purified. ⁵ The priest will have one of the birds slaughtered over an earthen bowl filled with water from a running stream, ⁶ and then will take the live bird, the cedar wood, the scarlet yarn and the hyssop, and dip them all in the blood of the bird slaughtered over the water from the running stream, ⁷ and then sprinkle it seven times on you who are to be cleansed of the infectious disease. The priest will then pronounce you clean and release the bird to fly into open country.

⁸ You must wash your clothes, shave off all your hair, and bathe in water; then you will be ceremonially clean. After this you will be allowed to return to the camp, but you must stay outside of your tent for seven days. ⁹ On the seventh day you must shave off the hair on your head, including your eyebrows and all the hair on your body. Then you must wash your clothes and bathe your body in water; and you will be ceremonially clean.

¹⁰ On the eighth day you must bring two male lambs without blemish and one female yearling lamb without blemish, a grain offering of six quarts of fine flour mixed with oil, plus one and a half measures of oil. ¹¹ The priest will present you and your offerings before Your God at the entrance to the Tent of Meeting. ¹² The priest will also take one of the lambs and the measure of oil and offer them as a reparation offering, and present all these as a dedicated portion before Your God.

---

* Cedar and hyssop are traditional tools for purification, though here, with the addition of the scarlet yarn, the emphasis is on their color: all three are red, the color of blood, the symbol of life, and the only color believed by the ancients to have the inherent power to drive away evil spirits—particularly appropriate for removing the death symbolism of the *tzara'at*. According to Brown, the release of a live bird in verse 7 symbolizes the flight of the evil spirit from the afflicted person.

¹³ The priest will slaughter the lamb at the same place where the purification offerings and the burnt offering are slaughtered—within the holy precincts, since the reparation offering, like the purification offering, belongs to the priest. It is most holy. ¹⁴ Then the priest must take some of the blood of the reparation offering and put it on the lobe of your right ear, on the thumb of your right hand, and on the big toe of your right foot.* ¹⁵ Then some of the oil from the measure will be poured into the palm of the priest's left hand, ¹⁶ and with the right finger, the priest will dip into the oil from the left hand and sprinkle some of the oil with the right finger seven times before Your God. ¹⁷ The priest will put some of the same oil on the lobe of your right ear to purify it, on the thumb of your right hand, on the big toe of your right foot and on top of the blood of the reparation offering. ¹⁸ The remainder of the oil in the priest's hand will be put on your head to purify it. ¹⁹ Then the priest will atone for your ceremonial uncleanness before Your God by sacrificing the purification offering. Later the priest will slaughter the burnt offering, ²⁰ and offer the burnt offering and the grain offering on the altar. In this way the priest will atone for you and you will be ceremonially clean.

²¹ If you are poor, however, and cannot afford this much, you may take a male lamb as a reparation offering to atone for you, together with a grain offering of two quarts of fine flour mixed with oil, a separate measure of oil, ²² and two turtledoves or two young pigeons, whichever you can afford, one for the purification offering and one for the burnt offering. ²³ On the eighth day you must bring them for your cleansing to the priest at the entrance to the Tent of Meeting, before Your God. ²⁴ The priest will take the lamb for the reparation offering, and the measure of oil, and present them as a dedicated portion before Your God. The priest will slaughter the lamb for the reparation offering and take some of its blood and put it on the lobe of your right ear, on the thumb of your right hand and on the toe of your right foot. ²⁴ Some of the oil from the measure will be poured into the palm of the priest's left hand, ²⁷ and with the right finger, the priest will dip into the oil from the left hand and sprinkle some of the oil with the right finger seven times before Your God. ²⁸ The priest must put some of the oil in the left hand on the each of the places as the blood of the reparation offering—on the lobe of your right ear, on the thumb of your right hand, and on the big toe of your right foot. ²⁹ The rest of the oil in the priest's left hand is to be put on your head, to atone for you before Your God. ³⁰ Then the priest will sacrifice the doves or young pigeons, whichever you can afford, ³¹ one as a purification offering and one as a burnt offering. In

---

* The same marking that is done for the ordination of priests. This anointing both returns the person to a state of ritual purity, and represents a new life of service given in gratitude for being healed.

this way the priest will perform the rite of atonement before Your God on your behalf.

[32] This is the Instruction for you, if you suffer from infectious skin diseases, and you cannot afford the regular offering for your purification.

[33] Our God told Moses and Aaron to tell the Israelites these things:

[34] When you enter the land of Canaan, which I give to you for your possession, and I put a live mildew on a house in that land,* [35] as the owner of the house you must go to the priest and say, "I notice something looking like mildew in my house." [36] The priest will order your house to be emptied before entering it to examine the infection—otherwise, everything in it will be judged unclean. [37] If on inspection the priest finds patches on the walls consisting of greenish or reddish spots that appear to be deeper than the surface of the wall, [38] the house must be sealed for seven days. [39] On the seventh day the priest will return and inspect your house, and if the patch has spread into the walls, [40] the order will be given to have the infected stones pulled out of the wall and disposed of outside the town in an unclean place. [41] Then the walls must be scraped throughout the inside. All the scraped-off plaster must be taken out of the town to a ceremonially unclean place. [42] Then you are to use new stones to replace the affected stones and use new plaster to replaster the house.

[43] If the infection reappears after the affected stones have been replaced and the house has been replastered, [44] the priest must come and inspect it. If the infection has spread in the house, it means that there is a live mildew, and your house is unclean. [45] It must be demolished—stones, timber, plaster, everything—and must be taken out of the town to an unclean place. [46] Anyone entering the house during its time of quarantine is unclean until evening. [47] All who ate or slept in the house must wash their clothes.

[48] If the priest inspects your house and finds that the infection has not spread after the replastering, then it will be pronounced that the house is ceremonially clean, for the mildew is gone. [49] To purify the house, the priest must take two small birds, cedar wood, scarlet yarn and hyssop. [50] The priest will kill one of the birds over an earthenware bowl filled with water from a running stream. [51] Your house must be purified using the cedar wood, hyssop, scarlet yarn, and the live bird, by dipping them in the blood of the bird that was killed, and in the water from a running stream, and then sprinkling the house seven times. [52] The priest will purify your house with the blood of the bird, the water from a running stream, the live bird, the cedar wood, the hyssop and the scarlet yarn. [53] Then the priest will re-

---

* God is assumed to be the cause of everything, clean and unclean (Brown).

lease the live bird out of town in an open place. This is how you will make atonement for your house.*

⁵⁴ This, then, is the Instruction concerning infectious skin diseases, for ringworm, ⁵⁵ clothing and household mildew, ⁵⁶ and any swellings, inflammations or shiny spots, ⁵⁷ to determine what is ritually clean or unclean. This is the Instruction for these diseases.

ରେ ରେ ରେ

15:1 Our God told Moses and Aaron ² to tell the Israelites these things:

If any of you have a discharge from your genitals, you are ceremonially unclean. ³ Whether it is a flowing discharge or it is stopped up, it is unclean.**

⁴ If you have a discharge, the bedding on which you lie is ceremonially unclean, and so is anything you sit on. ⁵ All who touch your bedding must wash their clothes and bathe with water, and they will be unclean until evening. ⁶ All who sit on anything you sat on must wash their clothes and bathe with water, and they will be unclean until evening. ⁷ All who touch your body must wash their clothes and bathe with water, and they will be unclean until evening. ⁸ If you have such a discharge, and you spit on someone who is clean, that person must wash their clothes and bathe with water and will be unclean until evening. ⁹ A saddle that you ride on will be unclean, ¹⁰ and anyone who touches anything you have sat upon is unclean until evening; anyone who picks up such things must wash their clothes and bathe with water and is unclean until evening. ¹¹ If you have such a discharge, unless you have washed your hands first, everyone you touch must wash their clothes and bathe with water and they will be unclean until evening. ¹² Any clay pot that you touch must be broken, and any wooden vessel that you touch must be rinsed with water.

¹³ When you are healed from such a discharge, seven days must be allowed for your purification; then you must wash your clothes and bathe

---

* The notion that disease can infect not only clothing but even stones—while it denotes a certain practical savvy in terms of germs—also carries the assumption that the stones of the house not only *carry* the disease, but also that they *are* diseased. The concept is remarkably animistic—that is, the belief that even inanimate objects are alive and have souls. Even more fascinating is that it is dealt with on a stone-by-stone basis, rather than treating the house as a single entity—although the house must be atoned for in its entirety, rather like the entire people atoning for certain sins *en masse.*

** This ritual impurity occcurs whether the discharges are from disease, or whether they are normal but involuntary. All individuals who approached the sanctuary were to be unassailably pure sexually, in contrast to other ancient cultures where sexuality was a large part of the worship ceremony.

your body in running water. Then you will be ceremonially clean. ¹⁴ On the eighth day you must take two doves and two young pigeons and come before Your God at the entrance to the Tent of Meeting and give them to the priest. ¹⁵ The priest must sacrifice them, one as a purification offering, and one as a burnt offering. In this way the priest will make atonement for you before Your God for your discharge.

¹⁶ Any time a man has a seminal emission, he must wash his entire body with water. He will be ceremonially unclean until evening.* ¹⁷ Any clothing or leather which gets semen on it must be washed with water, and it will be ceremonially unclean until evening. ¹⁸ When he lies with a woman and there is an emission of semen, both of them must bathe with water, and both of them will be ceremonially unclean until evening.

¹⁹ When a woman among you has her menstrual cycle, she is to remain apart for seven days, and anyone who touches her will be ceremonially unclean until evening. ²⁰ Anything that she lies upon during her period will be ceremonially unclean, and anything she sits upon will be ceremonially unclean. ²¹ Any who touch her bed must wash their clothes and bathe with water. They will be unclean until evening. ²² Those who sit on anything she sits upon must wash their clothes and bathe with water, and will be unclean until evening. ²³ Whether it is the bed or anything she sits on, if others touch it, they will be unclean until evening. ²⁴ If a man lies with her and menstrual blood touches him, he will be ceremonially unclean for seven days, and any bed that he lies on will be unclean.

²⁵ If a woman has a flow of blood for many days when it is not time for her period, or when it continues to flow longer than the time of her period, she will be ceremonially unclean for as long as the flow occurs, just as during her period. ²⁶ Any bed she lies upon while this flow lasts will be unclean—just like any bed she lies on during her monthly renewal of blood—and anything she sits on will be unclean. ²⁷ Any who touch these things will be unclean. They must wash their clothes and bathe in water, and they will be unclean until evening.

²⁸ When her menstrual cycle is over, she must count seven days, and then she will be ceremonially clean. ²⁹ On the eighth day she must bring two turtledoves and two young pigeons to the priest at the entrance to the Tent of Meeting. ³⁰ The priest will sacrifice one as a purification offering and the

---

* Like the loss of blood in childbirth or menstruation, the discharge of semen indicates a lost of life force and, therefore, unworthiness before God. As shown by verse 18, semen is imbued with the extraordinary power to both sap vitality when it is lost, and make unclean whatever it touches—thus "contaminating" both men and women.

other as a burnt offering. In this way the priest will make atonement for her before Your God for her menstrual cycle.

[31] You, Moses and Aaron, are to ensure that the Israelites avoid those things that make them ceremonially impure, so that they do not die from their impurity for defiling my dwelling place among you.*

[32] This is the Instruction for you, when you have any kind of flow: for a man when he has an emission of semen; [33] for a woman when she has her menstrual cycle; for anyone, male or female, who has a discharge; and for all who lie with anyone who is ceremonially unclean.

ର   ର   ର

16[1] Our God spoke to Moses after the death of Aaron's two heirs, who had died when they approached Our God improperly, and told him [2] to tell Aaron these things:

You must not enter the sanctuary before the Covering on the Ark, behind the curtain, whenever you choose, or you will die, for I appear in a cloud over the Covering.

[3] Aaron, this is what you must do before you enter the sanctuary. First, you must bring a young bull for a purification offering and a ram for a burnt offering. [4] Then you must vest in a sacred linen tunic with the sacred linen undergarment next to your body, with a linen sash around your waist and a linen turban around your head. These are sacred garments; you must bathe in water, then put them on. [5] You are to take two male goats from the Israelite community for a purification offering and a ram for the burnt offering.

[6] You are to offer the bull for your own purification offering to atone for you and your household. [7] Then you are to take the two goats and present them before Your God at the entrance of the Meeting Gate. [8] You are to cast lots for the two goats—one lot for Your God, and the other for Azazel.** [9] You must bring the goat whose lot falls to Your God and sac-

---

* This verse makes it clear that all of the clean-and-unclean legislation has a single focus: the ceremonial and ritual life of the people. "Unclean" did not impute any moral judgment whatsoever; it merely indicated those times when an individual could not enter the holy area or participate in sacred rituals, and was only a temporary state—one that affected most people at one time or another.

** Traditionally translated as "scapegoat," from reading the Hebrew as *ez azal*, "a goat that escapes" into the wilderness. However, most scholars now feel that Azazel was the name of a wilderness demon who would devour the goat that had "escaped" into the desert, and with it, the sins of the entire people. This placing of sins on the head of a third party, in this case a goat, is present throughout the book of *Leviticus* and all the descriptions of Israel's ritual life. This was a common theme throughout the ancient world, and can still be seen today when we blame the victim for a crime instead of the perpetrator.

rifice it for a purification offering. ¹⁰ But the goat chosen by lot for Azazel will be presented live before Your God to make atonement, so that it may be sent into the wilderness to Azazel.

¹¹ Then, Aaron, you are to present the bull for your own purification offering; you must slaughter the bull to make atonement for yourself and for your family. ¹² Then you are to take a censer full of burning coals from the altar before Your God and two hands full of finely ground aromatic incense, and take them behind the curtain. ¹³ You are to put the incense on the fire before Your God, so that the smoke of the incense will conceal the Covering and you will not die.* ¹⁴ Then you must dip your finger in the bull's blood and sprinkle it on the side of the Covering; in front of the Covering you must sprinkle some of the blood with your finger seven times.

¹⁵ Then you must slaughter the goat for the people's purification offering, and take its blood behind the curtain and do with it as you did with the bull's blood: sprinkle it on the side of the Covering and in front of it. ¹⁶ In this way you will atone for the sanctuary, because of the ritual uncleanness of the Israelites, their rebellious acts, and all their sins. You must do this also for the Tent of Meeting which is among them in the midst of their ritual uncleanness. ¹⁷ No one is to be with you in the Tent of Meeting from the time you enter it to make atonement in the sanctuary until you come out. You are to make atonement for yourself, your household, and the whole assembly of Israel.

¹⁸ Then you are to come out to the altar before Your God and purify it by taking some of the bull's blood and some of the goat's blood and smearing them on each of the horns of the altar. ¹⁹ You must sprinkle some of the blood on the altar with your finger seven times. In this way, you will purify it from all the Israelites' uncleanness, and make it holy.

²⁰ When you are finished with the purification of the sanctuary, the Tent of Meeting and the altar, you are to bring in the live goat. ²¹ Lay both your hands on its head, and confess over it all the sins of the Israelites, all their acts of rebellion, and all their sins. You are to lay your hands on the head of the goat and then send it away into the wilderness by the hand of someone appointed for the task. ²² The goat will bear all the iniquities of the Israelites into a barren area,** and it will released in the wilderness.

²³ Then you must go into the Tent of Meeting and remove the linen vest-

---

* In other words, the cloud of incense conceals the cloud of God's presence; otherwise, the high priest might catch a glimpse of God and be struck dead.
** Literally, "to a land cut off," a place remote from human experience, echoing the ceremonially clean/unclean dichotomy: in the view of the Priestly tradition (see the Introduction), godliness lies in order, whereas the wilderness—chaos—is the place of evil.

ments that you put on before entering the sanctuary, and leave them there.* ²⁴ You must bathe in water in a holy place, dress yourself in your own clothes, then come out to offer your burnt offering and the burnt offering of the people to atone for yourself and for the people. ²⁵ You must burn the fat of the purification offering on the altar. ²⁶ The one appointed to release the goat to Azazel must bathe in water and put on freshly washed clothes before returning to the camp. ²⁷ The bull and the goat of the purification offering whose blood was taken into the sanctuary for the atonement ritual are to be taken outside the camp and burned—their skin, flesh and offal. ²⁸ The person who is responsible for burning them must bathe in water and put on freshly washed clothing before returning to the camp.

²⁹ This is to be a perpetual ordinance for you: on the tenth day of the seventh month, both the native Israelites and the foreigners who live among you must fast and abstain from work, ³⁰ for this day is the day when atonement will be made for you, to cleanse you of all your sins.** ³¹ This will be a Sabbath of rest, and you must fast. This is a perpetual ordinance. ³² The anointed and consecrated priest of Aaron's line must make atonement, wearing linen vestments, the holy vestments. ³³ The priest must atone for the sanctuary, for the Tent of Meeting and for the altar, as well as for the priests and for all the assembled people. ³⁴ This is a perpetual statute for you, to make atonement for the people of Israel once a year for their sins.

And Moses did as Our God commanded.

ɔ̃   ɔ̃   ɔ̃

17:1 Our God told Moses ² to tell these things to Aaron and his heirs, together with all the Israelites:

This is what Our God commands: ³ If anyone of the house of Israel slaughters an ox, a lamb, or a goat anywhere within the camp or outside of it ⁴ rather than bringing it to the entrance to the Tent of Meeting to present it as an offering to Your God, you will be considered guilty of bloodshed. You have shed blood and must be cut off from your people. ⁵ The reason for this is so that the Israelites will take the animals that would have been slaughtered in an open field and instead bring them to the priest at the entrance to the Tent of Meeting and offer them as fellowship sacrifices to

---

* In other words, the linen vestments are to be worn only in the sanctuary, the inner part of the Tent of Meeting.

** That is, Yom Kippur.

Your God. ⁶ The priest will cast the blood against the altar at the entrance to the Tent of Meeting and burn the fat as a sacrifice whose aroma is pleasing to Your God. ⁷ No longer are you to offer your slaughtered animals to the goat-demons with whom you used to disgrace yourselves in your worship of them. This will be a law binding you and your descendants for all times.

⁸ Also tell them that any Israelite or any foreigner who has settled among the Israelites who offers a burnt offering or a sacrifice ⁹ and does not bring it to the entrance to the Tent of Meeting to offer it to Your God is to be cut off from your people. ¹⁰ If any Israelites or foreigners who have settled among the Israelites consume any blood, I will set my face against them and cut them off from the people, ¹¹ because the life force of a creature is in the blood. I give that blood to you so that you can atone for your lives on the altar, for it is blood—life—that makes atonement. ¹² That is why I say to the Israelites that no one among you is to eat blood, nor is any foreigner living among you to eat blood.

¹³ Any Israelite or foreigner living among you who hunts any animal or any bird that may be eaten must drain out its blood and cover the blood with dirt; ¹⁴ for the life force of every creature is its blood. This is why I say to the Israelites that you must not eat the blood of any creature, for the life force of every creature is its blood. Anyone who eats it must be cut off.

¹⁵ Whether you are native Israelite or a foreigner, if you eat anything found dead or torn by wild animals, you must wash your clothes and bathe with water, and you will be ceremonially unclean until evening; after that you will be clean. ¹⁶ But if you do not wash your clothes and bathe yourself, you will continue to bear your guilt.

18:1–26:36

OUR God told Moses ² to tell this to the Israelites:*

I am the Most High, your God. ³ You must not do what is done in Egypt,

---

* This section begins what is known as "the Holiness Code." In it God calls the people to be "a holy nation," separate from other nations, beginning with their sexual behaviors. Many of the harsh and, to our sensibilities, repressive commandments in this section are given primarily so that the Israelites would not duplicate any of the practices of the Egyptians or Canaanites, the latter being of particular concern to the intensely patriarchal Hebrews because of the threat of the Canaanites' strong goddess-centered religious practices. Many of the prohibitions must be placed in this limited and polemical context, and must not be viewed as being on a level with, say, the Ten Commandments, or statutes that promote justice and fairness.

where you once dwelled, nor may you do what is done in Canaan, where I am leading you. You must not take up their customs. ⁴ Rather, you must observe my statutes and follow my laws faithfully: I am the Most High, your God. ⁵ Observe my statutes and my laws: if you do them, you will live because of them. I am Your God.

⁶ No one is to have sexual contact with a blood relative.* I am Your God. ⁷ Do not have sexual contact with your parents—the expression of their sexuality is reserved for one another. Do not have sexual contact with them! ⁸ Do not have sexual contact with your step-parent—the expression of their spouse's sexuality belongs to your parent. ⁹ Do not have sexual contact with your sister or your brother, whether they are your father's children or your mother's children, whether raised in your household or another household. You must not have sexual contact with them! ¹⁰ Do not have sexual contact with your grandchildren. They are your own flesh and blood.

¹¹ Do not have sexual contact with the daughter of your stepmother and your father; she is your sister. ¹² Do not have sexual contact with your father's sister, for she is related by blood to him. ¹³ Do not have sexual contact with your mother's sister, for she is related by blood to your mother. ¹⁴ Do not humiliate your father's brother by approaching his wife, for she is your aunt. ¹⁵ Do not have sexual contact with the spouse of your daughter or son, for they are your children's partners. You must not have sexual contact with them! ¹⁶ Do not have sexual contact with your brother's or sister's spouse—the expression of their sexuality is reserved for one another.

¹⁷ Do not have sexual contact with both a woman and her daughter, nor marry her son's daughter or her daughter's daughter, for they are blood relations. Such conduct is depraved. ¹⁸ Do not marry both a woman and her sister, which would create a rivalry; you must not have sexual contact with the sister as long as your first wife is alive.

¹⁹ Do not have sexual contact with a woman during her period.

²⁰ If you have sexual intercourse with your neighbor's spouse, you make yourself ceremonially unclean.

²¹ Do not give your children to be sacrificed to Molech,** for it profanes the Name of Your God. I am Your God!

---

* Literally, "to approach a blood relative to expose their nakedness." In contexts that are not directly sexual, we have translated "expose their nakedness" as "humiliate [or dishonor] them."

** Molech was a Canaanite and Assyrian fire divinity whose worshipers embraced human sacrifice, ordeals by fire, and self-mutilation, the stereotype of the volcano god to whom young women were sacrificed in propitiation. The name means "ruler," which was a particular affront to God, who was to be the Israelites' sole Ruler.

²² Do not lie with a person of the same sex in the same way as you would lie with a person of the opposite sex; this is detestable.*

²³ Do not have sexual intercourse with an animal, and in doing so become ceremonially unclean; this violates nature.

²⁴ Do not make yourself unclean in any of these ways, for it is with such practices that the nations I am driving out before you make themselves ceremonially unclean. ²⁵ Because of them the land became ceremonially unclean, and I called it to account for their wickedness, and the land vomited them out. ²⁶ Unlike them, you must observe my statutes and my laws, and you must never do any of these detestable things, whether you are native Israelite or a foreigner. ²⁷ The land became ceremonially unclean because those who inhabited the land before you committed these detestable acts. ²⁸ The land will vomit you out if you make it unclean, just as it did the nation that was before you.** ²⁹ Any who practice these detestable acts will be cut off from their people. ³⁰ Honor my commandment to abandon all of these detestable acts that were committed before your time. Do not make yourselves ceremonially unclean with them: I am Your God.

19·1 Our God told Moses ² to tell the entire Israelite community these things:

Be holy, for I, Your God, am holy.

³ Each one of you must revere your mother and father. You must keep my Sabbaths. I am Your God. ⁴ Do not turn to idols or cast metal images of gods for yourself. I am Your God.

⁵ When you offer a fellowship sacrifice to Your God, you must offer it in such a way that it is acceptable on your behalf. ⁶ You must eat it on the same day you offer it, or the next day; anything left after that must be burned. ⁷ If it is eaten on the third day, it is tainted meat, and it is not acceptable. ⁸ If you eat it on the third day you must assume guilt, for you desecrated what is holy to Your God; you must be cut off from your people.

⁹ When you reap the harvest from your fields, do not cut the grain to the very edges of the field, or gather in all the gleanings. ¹⁰ Nor are you to com-

---

* Not, as other translations render it, "abomination": the same Hebrew word is used in reference to the eating of shellfish and game birds in chapter 11. Men who allowed themselves to be penetrated by another man were felt to have made themselves like women—who were, of course, not valued in partiarchal cultures. The absence of a similar injunction against "a woman lying with a woman as with a man" indicates that this passage does not refer to homosexuality at all, but the "dishonor" that one's maleness would suffer through being penetrated.

** Despite their efforts to dissociate themselves from the surroundig goddess-worshiping cultures, the Israelites continue to identify the land with its ruler—in this case, God. The belief that the ruler and the land were one was common in all ancient cultures. In this passage, the land is reflecting God's displeasure.

pletely strip your vines or pick up the fallen fruit. Leave the extra grain and fruit for poor people and foreigners to gather for themselves. I am Your God.

[11] Do not steal. Do not lie. Do not cheat your neighbor. [12] Do not swear by my Name with the intent to deceive, for if you do, you profane my Name. I am Your God. [13] Do not oppress your neighbors or rob them. Do not hold back the hired hand's wages until the next day. [14] Do not insult deaf people, or put obstacles in the way of blind people. Revere the Most High, your God.

[15] Do not be corrupt in administering justice. Do not show partiality to the poor or give honor to the great. Judge your neighbor with fairness. [16] Do not go about slandering others.

Do not profit by the blood of your neighbor. I am Your God. [17] Do not nurse hatred for a neighbor. If you are angry with your neighbor, speak frankly about it, to avoid storing up ill feelings.* [18] Never seek revenge or hold a grudge toward your relatives. You must love your neighbor as you love yourself.** I am Your God.

[19] Keep my laws: Do not let two different kinds of animals inter-breed. Do not sow the same field with two different kinds of seed. Do not wear clothes made of two different kinds of materials.†

[20] When you have sexual intercourse with a bonded worker who has been promised to another, but is not yet freed, compensation will be demanded. You are not to be put to death, for the bonded worker is still without freedom. [21] However, you must bring a ram to the entrance to the Tent of Meeting for a reparation offering to Your God. [22] With it the priest will make atonement with the ram as a purification offering before Your God for the sin you committed, and you will be forgiven.

[23] When you enter the land and plant all kinds of fruit trees, consider its fruit to be forbidden for the first three years, and do not eat it. [24] In the fourth year the fruit is to be set aside as a praise offering to Your God. [25] In the fifth year you may eat the fruit. By doing it this way, your harvest will increase. I am Your God.

[26] Do not eat anything with blood in it.

Do not not practice divination or sorcery.

---

* Or possibly, "to avoid bearing the guilt for not having warned your neighbor about the consequences of his or her behavior."

** Another translation, following the approach taken by Martin Buber and Franz Rosenzweig, might be, "Be loving toward your neighbor as one who is like yourself."

† These "two different kinds" prohibitions are another example of the discomfort, in the Priestly tradition, with mixing disparate elements together; separateness was critical, since separateness meant holiness. Mixing signified disorder and, by extension, chaos and mystery, which they felt was God's domain exclusively. The same argument was used later, particularly during the Babylonian exile, to forbid intermarriage between the Israelites and the surrounding peoples.

²⁷ Your men must not trim the hair on their heads or the edges of their beards in mourning. ²⁸ You must not gash yourself when mourning for the dead, or tattoo yourself.* I am Your God.

²⁹ Do not debase your daughter or son by selling them into prostitution, or the land may be unfaithful and become filled with depravity.

³⁰ You must keep my Sabbaths and have reverence for my sanctuary. I am Your God.

³¹ Do not resort to mediums or visit necromancers, for you will be defiled by seeking them out. I am Your God.

³² Stand up in the presence of the aged; respect the elderly, and by this you will honor Your God. I am Your God.

³³ Do not mistreat the foreigners who reside in your land. ³⁴ The foreigner who lives among you must be treated like one of your own. Love them as you love yourself, for you too were a foreigner in the land of Egypt. I am Your God.

³⁵ Do not cheat when measuring length, weight or quantity. ³⁶ Use honest scales and honest weights, an honest dry measure and an honest liquid measure. For I, Your God, brought you out of Egypt.

³⁷ You must keep all my statutes and all my laws and carry them out. I am Your God!

20·¹ Our God told Moses to ² speak to the entire Israelite community and tell them these things:**

Any of you Israelites, or any foreigners dwelling in Israel, who sacrifice your children to Molech, will be put to death. The people of the community must stone you to death. ³ I will set my face against you and I will cut you off from my people. If you give your children to Molech you will defile my sanctuary and profane my holy Name. ⁴ If you, as Israelites, ever close your eyes when a person gives a child to Molech, and you fail to carry out this law, ⁵ I will set my face against you and your family. I will cut off from the community both the accused and all who make themselves idolaters by following Molech.

⁶ I will set my face against you if you turn to mediums and necromancers, and I will cut you off from the people. ⁷ Consecrate yourselves and become holy, for I, Your God, am holy. ⁸ Keep my decrees and observe them, for it is I, Your God, who makes you holy.

---

* These were specific Canaanite funeral practices.

** This chapter lays out the punishment for the acts described in chapter 18. Here again we see the ancient belief that only death will prevent the contamination of the whole.

⁹ If any of you curse your parents, you must be put to death. When you curse your parents, your own blood will be on your head.

¹⁰ If a married person commits adultery with another married person, both parties must be put to death.

¹¹ If you lie with the new spouse of one of your parents, you have violated your parent, and both you and your step-parent must be put to death, and your blood will be on your own heads.

¹² If you lie with your daughter- or son-in-law, what you did violates nature, and both you and your daughter- or son-in-law must be put to death. Your blood will be on your own heads.

¹³ If a man lies with a male as with a woman, both of them have done a detestable thing; they must be put to death, and their blood will be on their own heads.*

¹⁴ If a parent and a child get married to the same person at the same time, what you have done is detestable. All three of you must be burned to death in order to remove such depravity from your midst.

¹⁵ Any man among you who has sexual intercourse with an animal must be put to death, and the animal as well. ¹⁶ Any woman among you who approaches an animal to mate with it must be put to death, and so must the animal. Your blood will be on your own heads.

¹⁷ When you marry your sister or brother, the child of either of your parents, and you have sexual contact with one another, it is a disgraceful act, they are to be cut off from the sight of their people. You have violated your own sibling, and you must bear the guilt.

¹⁸ Whoever has sexual contact with a woman during her period has dishonored her time of renewal—and so has she. You must both be cut off from your people.

¹⁹ You must not have sexual contact with the sister or brother of either of your parents. You have violated a blood relationship, and both must be bear the guilt.

²⁰ If you have sexual contact with your aunt or uncle, you have violated your relatives. You must both suffer the consequences of your sin, and you will die in shame.

²¹ Do not marry the spouse of your sister or brother, for they belong to your sibling. You have dishonored your sibling, and you will die in shame.

---

* Again, it is the dishonoring of a man's maleness that is forbidden, with no discussion of love or other same-gender sexual behaviors. Female homosexuality poses little threat to patriarchal cultures primarily due to the low status of women within the culture. One might even argue that female homoexuality prior to marriage supports the patriarchal culture by providing a sexual outlet yet preserving a woman's virginity until given by her father in marriage to a man.

²² You must keep my statutes and my laws and observe them so that the land that I am giving to you to dwell in will not vomit you out. ²³ Do not take on the customs of the nations whom I am driving out before you. They practiced all these things that I detest. ²⁴ Remember that I will give you possession of their land, a land flowing with milk and honey. I, the Most High, your God, have made a clear separation between you and the other nations, ²⁵ and you also are to make a clear separation between ceremonially clean animals and ceremonially unclean animals, and between ceremonially clean birds and ceremonially unclean birds. You must not contaminate yourselves with any animals or birds or creatures that crawl on the ground, for I have made a clear separation between them and you, by declaring them ceremonially unclean. ²⁶ You must be holy to me, as I, Your God, am holy to you.

²⁷ Any person among you who is a medium or a spiritualist must be put to death. You are to pelt them with stones, and their blood is on their own heads.

ભ   ભ   ભ

21:1 Our God told Moses to tell these things to Aaron's heirs, the priests:

Do not make yourselves ceremonially unclean by coming in contact with a relative who has died, ² unless it is a close relative—your mother, father, daughter, son, brother, ³ or an unmarried sister—for them, you may make yourself unclean. ⁴ Nor are you to make yourselves unclean for people related to you by marriage, and so defile yourselves.

⁵ When in mourning, you are not to shave your heads, or trim the edges of your beards or slash any part of your bodies. ⁶ You must be holy to Your God, and you must not profane the name of Your God. For you present the offerings made to God by fire—God's food, by which you become holy.

⁷ Because you are priests you must not become married to persons who who were promiscuous or divorced, for you are holy to God. ⁸ You must keep yourselves holy, for you offer the food of Your God. Regard yourselves as holy, for I, Your God, I who sanctify you, am holy. ⁹ If one of your children becomes promiscuous, your child defiles you, a priest, and the child must be burned to death.

¹⁰ If you become high priest—if, among all the heirs of Aaron, you have been raised above the rest, anointed with oil poured over your head, and now wear the priestly vestments—you must neither let your hair hang loose nor tear your clothes when you mourn. ¹¹ You must not enter places where dead bodies lie—not even the body of your mother or your father— lest you become ceremonially unclean. ¹² You must not leave the sanctuary

while mourning, lest you desecrate the holy place of Your God—for you were consecrated by the anointing oil of Your God. I am Your God.

13 As high priest, you must marry someone who is a virgin. 14 You must not marry someone who has been widowed or divorced—only a virgin from among your parents' relatives. 15 You must not dishonor the descendants of your tribe, for it is I, Your God, who makes you holy.

16 Our God told Moses 17 to tell this to Aaron:

No one among your descendants for all time who has a physical defect may come and present the food of Your God. 18 No one who has any physical defect may come near, whether they are blind or crippled or injured or too tall, 19 or theyhave a broken leg or a broken arm, 20 or they have a twisted spine, or are too short, or have bad eyesight, festering sores, or crushed testicles.* 21 No Aaronite who has any defect may approach the altar to present an offering by fire to Your God. 22 Such a person may eat the food of Your God—the most holy as well as the holy. 23 But because of their defect they must not go near the curtain or approach the altar. To do so would desecrate my holy places—places that I, Your God, have made holy.

24 Moses related all these things to Aaron and his heirs, and to all the Israelites.

22:1 Our God told Moses to 2 tell Aaron and his heirs these things:

You must be careful in handling the sacred offerings that the Israelites consecrate to me, so that you do not profane my holy Name. I am Your God.

3 Further, if one of your descendants is ceremonially unclean and yet approaches the sacred offerings that the Israelites consecrate to Your God, you must cut off that person from my presence. I am Your God.

4 If you are ceremonially unclean with an infectious skin disease or a bodily discharge, you may not eat the sacred offerings until you are made clean. You will be ceremonially unclean if you touch what has been defiled by a corpse, or by any man who has had an emission of semen. 5 You are unclean if you touch any crawling thing; you are unclean if you touch any person who, for whatever reason, is unclean. 6 If you become ceremonially unclean for any of these reasons, you are unclean until evening, and you must not eat of the sacred offerings until you wash yourself with water. 7 When the sun sets, you will be clean, and then you may partake of the sacred offerings, for they are your food.

---

* In other words, any physical defect whether by birth or by accident, or anything that represents a deviation from "normal."

⁸ You must not eat any animal that was found dead or was killed by wild animals. You will be unclean if you do; I am Your God.

⁹ You must honor my regulations so that you do not incur guilt and die for profaning them: for it is I, Your God, who has sanctified them.

¹⁰ No one who does not belong to a priestly family may eat the sacred offerings, nor may a guest of a priest, nor a person employed by a priest. ¹¹ But if you take a bonded worker, or if a bonded worker is born in your household, the bonded worker may eat the sacred offerings.

¹² If a priest's daughter marries a lay person, she may not eat of the sacred offerings. ¹³ However, if a priest's daughter is widowed or divorced, and childless, and she returns to live in her parents' house, she may eat the sacred offerings. But no lay person may partake of it.

¹⁴ If anyone eats the sacred offering in error, that person must make full restitution to the priest for the offering, plus an additional one-fifth of its value. ¹⁵ Lay people must not desecrate the sacred offerings of the Israelites presented to Your God ¹⁶ by eating the sacred offerings themselves, thus causing the priest to bear the guilt. For it is I, Your God, have made these offerings holy.

¹⁷ Our God instructed Moses ¹⁸ to tell these things to Aaron and his heirs, and the Israelites:

If any among you, Israelite or foreigner, presents a gift of a burnt offering, either to fulfill a vow or as a voluntary offering, ¹⁹ you must present a male without defect from among the cattle, sheep or goats, so that it may be accepted on your behalf. ²⁰ Bring only what is unblemished, or it will not be accepted on your behalf.

²¹ When you bring from the herd a fellowship sacrifice, it must be without blemish or defect in order to be accepted. ²² If the animal is blind, injured or maimed, or has running sores or scabs, you are not to bring any such creature to the altar as an offering made by fire to Your God.

²³ If a bull or a sheep has a leg that is too long or too short, you may offer it as voluntary offering, but it will not be accepted in fulfillment of a vow. ²⁴ You must not offer to Your God an animal with testicles that are bruised, cut, crushed or torn. You must not do this in your own land, ²⁵ and you must not accept such an animal from a foreigner to be presented as an offering made by fire to Your God. Since they are deformed and defective, they will not be accepted on your behalf.*

---

* Note that the list of "defects" for exempting a sacrificial animal is virtually identical to the list for excluding a priest from service.

²⁶ Our God said this to Moses:

²⁷ When a calf, a lamb or a goat is born, it is to remain with its mother for seven days. From the eighth day on it will be acceptable as an offering made to Your God by fire.

²⁸ You must not slaughter a cow or a sheep on the same day as its young.

²⁹ When you give an offering in thanksgiving to Your God, sacrifice it in such a way that it will be acceptable on your behalf. ³⁰ It must be eaten that same day; leave nothing of it to the next day.* I am Your God. ³¹ Keep my laws and follow them: I am Your God. ³² Do not profane my holy Name, but let Israel acknowledge me as holy. I am Your God, who makes you holy, and who brought you out of Egypt to be Your God. I am Your God!

ରେ   ରେ   ରେ

23:1 Our God told Moses to ² tell the Israelites these things:

These are the festivals of Your God. You are to celebrate them at the proper time with a sacred assembly.**

³ For six days, work may be done, but the seventh day is a Sabbath of rest, a day of sacred assembly. You are not to do any work wherever you are; it is a Sabbath of Your God.

⁴ These, then, are the appointed feasts of Your God, sacred assemblies which you are to proclaim at their appointed times:

⁵ Your God's Passover begins at twilight on the fourteenth day of the first month. ⁶ On the fifteenth day of the first month begins the Feast of Unleavened Bread. For seven days you must eat bread made without yeast. ⁷ On the first day you will hold a sacred assembly; you are not to do any heavy labor. ⁸ For seven days, you are to present an offering made to Your God by fire, and on the seventh day hold a sacred assembly and do no heavy labor.

---

* Leviticus 19:6 says that fellowship sacrifices can be eaten over two days, whereas the thanksgiving offering mentioned here must be eaten in a single day. The difference seems to be one of gravity and formality: fellowship sacrifices are the great communion feasts, whereas thanksgiving offerings are voluntary and more spur-of-the-moment.

** This chapter describes each of the seven sacred festivals in turn: the Sabbath; the feasts of Passover and Unleavened Bread; the feast of the Firstfruits; the feast of Weeks, also called Shavuot or Pentecost; the feast of Trumpets, which became Rosh Hashanah, the civil new year, and is celebrated even today with the blowing of the shofar, or ram's horn; Yom Kippur, the Day of Atonement; and the feast of Tabernacles, or Sukkot.

⁹ Our God told Moses to ¹⁰ speak to the Israelites and tell them this:

When you come into the land that I will give you, and reap your harvest, you must bring the first sheaf of your harvest to the priest, ¹¹ who will elevate the sheaf before Your God so that it may be accepted on your behalf. ¹² On the day you elevate the sheaf, you must sacrifice as a burnt offering to Your God a yearling lamb without defect, ¹³ and present a grain offering of four quarts of fine flour mixed with oil—an offering made to Your God by fire, a pleasing aroma—and a drink offering of a quart of wine. ¹⁴ You must not eat any bread or any roasted or fully ripened grain until that day, the day you bring this offering to Your God. This is to be a lasting ordinance for all generations to come, wherever you live.

¹⁵ Beginning with the day after the Sabbath, the day on which you bring the firstfruits, you must count seven full weeks, ¹⁶ and then on the day after the seventh week, the fiftieth day, you will present the new grain offering to Your God. ¹⁷ Bring from your homes two loaves made of four quarts of fine flour, baked with yeast, as a dedicated portion. ¹⁸ You must present with your bread seven yearling lambs without blemish, one young bull and two rams. They will be a burnt offering to Your God, together with the grain offerings and the drink offerings, an offering by fire, a pleasing aroma to Your God. ¹⁹ You must offer one male goat for a purification offering and two yearling lambs as a fellowship sacrifice. ²⁰ The priest will present the two lambs in addition to the bread of the firstfruits as a dedicated portion before Your God. They will be holy to Your God and will be returned to the priest. ²¹ On this day you must proclaim a sacred assembly for yourselves and refrain from work. This regulation is binding on your descendants for all time regardless of where you dwell.

²² When you harvest the grain in your fields, do not cut right up to the edges of your field or gather the gleanings of your crop. Leave that for the poor and for the foreigners: I am the Most High, your God.

²³ Then Our God spoke to Moses and said ²⁴ to tell the Israelites this:

In the seventh month you are to keep the first day as a day of solemn abstinence from work, a holy day of assembly commemorated with trumpet blasts. ²⁵ You must not do any regular work, and must present an offering made by fire to Your God.

²⁶ Then Our God spoke to Moses and said this:

²⁷ The tenth day of the seventh month will be the Day of Atonement. You are to hold a sacred assembly; you must fast, and present an offering by

fire to Your God. ²⁸ On that day you are to do no work, for it is the day when atonement is to be made for you before the Most High, your God. ²⁹ Any who do not fast on that day must be cut off from the people. ³⁰ Anyone who does work on this day I will root out from among the people. ³¹ You are to do no work at all. This is a lasting ordinance for all generations to come, wherever you dwell. ³² It is to be a Sabbath of complete rest for you, and you must fast. From the evening of the ninth day of the month to the evening of the tenth day you are to observe this Sabbath.

³³ Our God instructed Moses to ³⁴ tell the Israelites these things:

On the fifteenth day of the seventh month, the Feast of Tabernacles will begin, and it will last for seven days. ³⁵ On the first day of the feast there will be a sacred assembly before Your God, and you will do no work. ³⁶ For seven days you will present an offering by fire to Your God, and on the eighth day you will again hold a sacred assembly and present an offering by fire to Your God. On that solemn day of meeting you must do no work.

³⁷ These are the festivals of Your God, on which you will proclaim a sacred assembly and bring offerings by fire to Your God: burnt offerings and grain offerings, sacrifices and libations, as prescribed for each day. ³⁸ These offerings are in addition to Your God's Sabbaths, in addition to whatever gifts you make, and in addition to all the voluntary offerings you present to Your God.

³⁹ Beginning on the fifteenth day of the seventh month, after gathering the crops from the land, you will celebrate a great pilgrimage festival to Your God for seven days. The first day is a day of rest, and the eighth day also is a day of rest. ⁴⁰ On the first you are to take choice fruit from the trees, palm fronds, leafy branches and willows from the waterside, and rejoice in the presence of the Most High, your God, for seven days. ⁴¹ You are to celebrate this as a pilgrim festival in honor of Your God. This is an ordinance binding your descendants for all time. You are to celebrate the pilgrim festival in the seventh month. ⁴² All native Israelites are to live in shelters for seven days ⁴³ so that your descendants will be reminded how I made you live in shelters when I brought you out of Egypt. I am the Most High, your God.

⁴⁴ And in this way, Moses appointed for the Israelites the feasts of Our God.

രു   രു   രു

24:1 Our God said to Moses, ² "Order the Israelites to provide you with clear oil of pressed olives for the lamp to be kept continually burning. ³ Aaron is to set it up in the Tent of Meeting, outside the curtain of the Testimony, and to burn the lamp in the presence of Our God from sunset until sunrise. This is a lasting ordinance for your descendants, for all time. ⁴ The lamps, in their stand of pure gold before Your God, must be tended continually.

⁵ "You are to take flour and bake it into twelve loaves of bread, four quarts for each loaf. ⁶ These are to be arranged in two rows, six to a row, on the pure gold table that stands before Your God. Sprinkle pure frankincense on each row, as a token offering for the bread, as an offering by fire to Your God. ⁸ The bread is to be set out before Your God on every Sabbath, as a symbol of the dedication of the people of Israel. This is an everlasting covenant. ⁹ These loaves will belong to Aaron and his heirs, who will eat them in a holy place, for it is the holiest part of their regular share of the offerings made to Our God by fire."

¹⁰ Two individuals—one was the offspring of an Israelite mother and an Egyptian father, and the other was a full-blooded Israelite—began fighting in the camp. ¹¹ The son of the Israelite woman, Shelomit daughter of Divri, of the tribe of Dan, blasphemed the Name with a curse, so they brought him to Moses. ¹² They confined the youth until the will of God should be made clear to them.

¹³ Our God said to Moses, ¹⁴ "Take the blasphemer outside the camp. All those who heard the blasphemy are to lay their hands on the head of the accused, and then the entire community is to stone the youth to death.

"Then tell the Israelites, 'When you curse Your God, you must suffer the consequences of the sin. ¹⁶ Any who curse the Name of Your God must die; the whole community must stone you. Whether native Israelite or a foreigner, if you blaspheme the Name you must be put to death.

¹⁷ "'If you strike another and that person dies, you must be put to death. ¹⁸ If you strike an animal and it dies, you must make restitution: a life for a life. ¹⁹ If you disfigure another, you are to be disfigured— ²⁰ fracture in place of fracture, eye in place of eye, tooth in place of tooth: you are to be injured in the same way that you have injured another. ²¹ If you kill an animal, you must make restitution for it, but if you kill a person, you must be put to death. ²² You are to have the same laws for native Israelites and foreigners: I am Your God.'"

²³ So Moses told the Israelites these things, and they took the blasphemer outside the camp and stoned him to death. The Israelites did as Our God had commanded Moses.

ᘐ   ᘐ   ᘐ

25¹ At Mount Sinai, Our God instructed Moses ² to tell the Israelites these things:

When you enter the land I am giving you, the land itself must observe a Sabbath for Your God. ³ For six years you may sow your fields and prune your vineyards and gather their crops. ⁴ But in the seventh year the land is to have a Sabbath of rest, a Sabbath for Your God. Do not sow your fields and do not prune your vineyards. ⁵ Do not harvest what grows of itself, or store the grapes of your untended vines. It will be a year of complete rest for the land. ⁶ On the other hand, what the land produces on its own will be food for you, for your female and male bonded workers, for your hired hands, for the strangers living among you, ⁷ for your livestock and for the wild animals in your land. You may eat whatever the land yields.*

⁸ Count off seven "weeks" of years—seven times seven years—so that the seven Sabbaths of years come to a period of forty-nine years. ⁹ Then, on the tenth day of the seventh month—the Day of Atonement—sound the trumpet throughout all your land. ¹⁰ Consecrate the fiftieth year and proclaim freedom in the land for all its inhabitants. It is your year of Jubilee:** each of you is to return to your ancestral land, to your own family. ¹¹ The fiftieth year is a Jubilee for you; do not sow and do not reap what grows of itself or harvest the untended vines. ¹² For it is a Jubilee and it is to be holy for you. Eat only what comes directly from the fields.

¹³ In this year of Jubilee all of you are to return to your ancestral land. ¹⁴ If you sell or buy land among yourselves, neither of you may use the calculation of the Jubilee year to cheat one another. ¹⁵ You must determine the price according to the number of years of produce that are left until the next Jubilee. ¹⁶ The greater the number of years left until the next Jubilee, the higher the price; the fewer the number of years left, the lower the price: for the seller is selling you a particular number of harvests.† ¹⁷ You must not cheat one another, but revere Your God: I am the Most High, your God.

¹⁸ Keep my statutes, obey my laws, and you will live securely on the land.

---

* In other words, what grows on its own may be gathered and eaten as gleanings, but not stored up, as one would a grain or grape harvest.

** This is a transliteration of the Hebrew word; it may be translated as "homecoming" or perhaps "homebringing," with the image of a ram's horn being blown to bring in the sheep; or, as several medieval commentators interpreted it, it may mean "release."

† In the Jubilee year, all property reverts to the family who owned it originally, who then redeem it, and may, if they choose, sell it to a new buyer. So in essence, one is not selling the land itself, but selling the rights to all the harvests that are left until the next Jubilee year.

¹⁹ The land will yield its bounty, and you will eat your fill and dwell there in safety. ²⁰ Now, if you say to yourselves, "What will we eat in the seventh year, seeing that we will neither sow nor reap a harvest?", ²¹ I will send you such a bountiful blessing in the sixth year that the land will yield enough for three years. ²² While you plant in the eighth year, you will still be eating from the earlier crop, and you will eat from it until the harvest of the ninth year is gathered.

²³ You must not sell land in perpetuity, for the land belongs to me, and you are only foreigners and tenants. ²⁴ Throughout all the land that you hold, you will allow the right of redemption.*

²⁵ If any of you are reduced to poverty and sell off some of your property, your next of kin, who holds the duty of redemption, must come and redeem what the relative sold. ²⁶ If you have no next of kin, but later do well and are able to afford the right of redemption, ²⁷ you must take into account the years since the sale and repay the purchaser the balance due up to the next Jubilee year. ²⁸ But if you cannot afford to redeem the property, it will remain in the hands of the purchaser until the Jubilee year. It will then revert to you, and you may return to your property.

²⁹ If you sell a house in a walled city, you will have the right of redemption until a full year after its sale. During that time you may redeem it. ³⁰ If it is not redeemed within that year, the house in the walled city will belong permanently to the buyer and the buyer's descendants, forever. It will not revert to its original owner at the Jubilee. ³¹ But houses that are not built in walled cities are to be considered as if they were in open country. They can be redeemed, and they are to be relinquished at the Jubilee.

³² The Levites will always retain the right to redeem their houses which they possess in the Levitical cities. ³³ So the property of the Levites is redeemable in Jubilee year, for the houses of the Levites in the Levitical cities belong to them in perpetuity. ³⁴ The common land around their cities cannot be sold, for it, too, is their property in perpetuity.

³⁵ If Israelites who are your relatives become impoverished so that they cannot support themselves in the community, they must be given assistance as if they were aliens or strangers, and they will live with you. ³⁶ You must not charge interest on a loan, either by demanding it in advance or otherwise by adding it to the principal. Revere Your God, and let your neighbor live with you. ³⁷ Never charge interest when advancing money, or profit from food advanced on credit. ³⁸ I am the Most High, your God,

---

* That is, allow it to revert to the family who owned it originally every fiftieth year.

who brought you out of the land of Egypt to give you the land of Canaan and to be Your God.

[39] If any of your neighbors are reduced to such poverty that they sell themselves to you, you must not treat them as bonded workers. [40] Their status is to be that of hired hands or resident laborers with you, and will be subject to you only until the Jubilee year. [41] They may then leave your service with their children and return to their own ancestral property. [42] You were all bonded workers in Egypt, and I freed you from your bondage. They must not be sold as bonded workers are sold. [43] You are not to work them ruthlessly; you are to revere Your God.

[44] Any bonded household workers who live with you, whether female or male, must come only from neighboring countries; acquire bonded workers from there, [45] or from the clans of foreigners who live beside you and have children in your land. You may have them become permanently attached to you, [46] and you may pass them on as an inheritance to your children, in perpetuity. But you are not to have dominion over your sisters and brothers, and you must not be ruthless toward Israelite workers and their families.

[47] If foreigners living among you become wealthy, and if any of your kin fall into debt with one of them, and sell themselves to the foreigner, or some part of the foreigner's family— [48] after they have sold themselves they will have the right of redemption, and one of their own may redeem them. [49] Their in-laws, or the children of their in-laws, may redeem them; or anyone in the family who is a blood relative may redeem them; or if they become prosperous again they may redeem themselves. [50] They and the purchaser will count the number of years from the date they sold themselves to the foreigner until the Jubilee year, and the price of the sale will be calculated accordingly.* The time they were with the owner will be accounted as if they had been hired laborers. [51] If many years remain, they will pay for their redemption in proportion to the purchase price. [52] And if a few years remain until the Jubilee year, they will compute and repay an amount proportionate to the time remaining in bondage. [53] They will have the status of seasonal laborers, and you will not allow the foreigner to mistreat them. [54] If they are not redeemed in the intervening years, they and their children must be released in the Jubilee year, [55] for the Israelites belong to me. They are my bonded workers, whom I brought out of Egypt. I am the Most High, your God.

---

* In other words, because all bonded laborers are freed at the Jubilee year anyway, the redemption price of the laborer ("the sale") is dependant upon the total number of years of service the owner would have received had the laborer remained in service until the Jubilee.

26:1 Do not make idols or set up carved images or stone pillars for yourselves, and do not place decorated stones in your land to bow down to: I am the Most High, your God.

2 Keep my Sabbaths and revere my sanctuary. I am Your God.

3 If you follow my decrees and keep my commandments and faithfully observe them, 4 I will give you the rain you need in due season, your crops will flourish in your fields, and your trees will bear fruit. 5 Your threshing will keep you busy until the grape harvest; and the grape harvest will keep you busy until planting time. You will have all the food you need, and live safely in the land.

6 I will make peace throughout the land, and you will lie down to sleep with no worries to keep you awake. I will remove from the land the beasts of prey, and the sword will not cross through your land. 7 You will put your enemies to flight, and they will fall before the sword. 8 Five of you will rout one hundred, and one hundred of you will pursue ten thousand, and your enemies will fall by the sword before you.

9 I will look on you with favor, and make you fruitful and increase your numbers, and I will keep my covenant with you. 10 You will still be eating last year's harvest when you will need to make room for the new. 11 I will establish my dwelling place among you and will not abandon you. 12 I will walk among you and be Your God, and you will be my people. 13 I am the Most High, your God, who brought you up out of Egypt and freed you from your bondage to them. I broke the yoke that bound you and enabled you to walk with your heads held high.

14 But if you do not listen to me, if you fail to keep my commandments, 15 if you reject my statutes, spurn my laws and violate my Covenant, 16 this is what I will do: I will bring upon you sudden terror, wasting diseases, and fevers, wearing out the eyes and exhausting the breath. You will plant your crops in vain, for your enemies will feast on them. 17 I will set my face against you, and you will be routed before your enemies. Those who hate you will hound you, and you will flee even when no one pursues you.

18 And if, after this, you still refuse to listen to me, I will heap punishment upon you seven times over for your sins. 19 I will break your hard hearts. I will make the sky above you like iron and the earth under you like bronze. 20 Your strength will be spent to no avail; for your land will not yield its crops nor will the trees of the land bear fruit.

²¹ If you continue to defy me and refuse to listen, I will plague you sevenfold more for your sins. ²² I will release wild animals against you; they will snatch your children from you and destroy your livestock. They will diminish your numbers and your roads will be deserted.

²³ If after all this you do not accept discipline from me but continue to oppose me, ²⁴ I will oppose you as well, and scourge you seven times over for your sins. ²⁵ I will bring the sword against you to avenge the covenant. If you hide in your cities, I will send pestilence among you, and you will be given to the treachery of the enemy. ²⁶ I will cut short your daily rations until ten people can bake your bread in one oven. It will be doled out by weight, and even after you eat it, you will still be hungry.

²⁷ If, in spite of all this, you still do not listen to me and continue to oppose me, ²⁸ I will oppose you with anger, and I will punish you seven times over for your sins. ²⁹ Instead of meat you will eat the flesh of your own daughters and sons. ³⁰ I will destroy your sacred high places and your pagan shrines. I will pile up your corpses on top of your lifeless idols, and I will hate you. ³¹ I will empty out your cities and I will lay waste to your sanctuaries. I will not accept the soothing aromas of your offerings. ³² I will so destroy your land that your enemies, coming to occupy it, will be appalled. ³³ I will scatter you among the nations, and draw my sword in pursuit of you. Your land will be laid waste, and your cities will end up as rubble.

³⁴ Then, while the land lies desolate, and you are in exile among your enemies, your land will enjoy its Sabbath years. ³⁵ For all the years it lies desolate, the land will have its rest, the rest it did not get when you worked it. ³⁶ I will make those of you still alive in the land of your enemies so full of fear that the sound of a falling leaf will put you to flight, as if one with a sword pursued you; and you will collapse from running when no one is following you. ³⁷ Even when no one pursues you, you will stumble over each other, as if a sword hung over you, and you will be helpless to make a stand against your enemies. ³⁸ You will meet your end among the nations, and their land will swallow you up. ³⁹ Those of you who survive will waste away in the foreign land of your enemies because of your sins, and because of the sins of your ancestors, you will waste away.

⁴⁰ But if you confess your sins and the sins of your ancestors—that they committed treachery against me, and that they continued to be hostile to me, ⁴¹ so that I, in turn, opposed them and carried them off into their enemies' territory—if, then, your obstinate spirit is broken, and you accept your punishment fully, ⁴² I will remember my covenant with Leah and Rachel and Jacob, my covenant with Rebecca and Isaac, and my covenant with Sarah and Abraham, and I will remember the land. ⁴³ The land, deserted and without people, will enjoy the full Sabbaths while it lies dor-

mant. You will pay the penalty because you rejected my laws and abhorred my decrees. ⁴⁴ Yet, in spite of this, when you are in the land of your enemies, I will not reject you or disdain you in a way that would destroy you completely, for that would break our covenant. I am the Most High, your God. ⁴⁵ But for your sake I will remember the covenant with your ancestors, whom I brought out of Egypt in full sight of the nations, so that I would be Your God. I am Your God.

⁴⁶ These are the decrees, the statutes and the ordinances that Our God established on Mount Sinai with the Israelites through Moses.

27:1-34

Our God told Moses to tell ² the Israelites these things:*

When anyone would make a singular vow to Your God, the redemption fee is based on the equivalent value of the person.** ³ If the person is a male between the ages of twenty years and sixty years old, the payment will be twenty ounces of silver, according to the sanctuary shekel standard; ⁴ if the person is female, then the payment will be twelve ounces of silver. ⁵ If the person is between the ages of five years and twenty years old, then the payment will be eight ounces of silver for a male and four ounces for a female. ⁶ If the person is between one month and five years old, then the payment will be two ounces for a male and one ounce for a female. ⁷ If the person is sixty years old or older, the payment will be six ounces for a male and four ounces for a female. ⁸ But if the person is too poor to pay the regular amount then that person may appeal to the priest, and the priest will judge an appropriate amount according to the person's ability to pay.

⁹ If you are offering an animal to Your God as part of your vow, everything that is given is a holy portion. ¹⁰ You must not substitute it or exchange it in any way, regardless of whether you would exchange a good animal for a bad one, or a bad animal for a good one. If the animal is exchanged for another, then both animals will be considered holy. ¹¹ If the

---

* This chapter is a later addition.

** When individuals wished to make a difficult or extraordinary vow, particularly in times of extreme gratitude, they gave themselves (or anything else under their control) to God. Any object or person lawfully consecrated to God might be purchased back again upon payment of a sum to be fixed according to the "valuation schedule" described in the next few verses. The money paid was accounted to the individual as the equivalent of whatever had been consecrated. This was a convenient arrangement both for the one making the vow, and for the priests who needed funds for the upkeep of the sanctuary.

animal is unclean, the kind of which is not to be offered as a sacrifice to Your God, then it will be presented before the priest, ¹² who will judge its value. Whatever value the priest gives it will be its value. ¹³ If you want to buy back the animal, you must pay an additional one-fifth of its value.

¹⁴ If you want to dedicate your house as holy to Your God, then the priest will determine its value, great or small. Whatever value the priest gives it will be its value. ¹⁵ If any of you who dedicate your house wishes to buy it back, you must pay an additional one-fifth of its value.

¹⁶ If any of you dedicates part of your field to Your God, the estimated value will be determined by how much seed is required for it—twenty ounces of silver for six bushels of barley seed. ¹⁷ If the field is dedicated during the year of Jubilee, the set value will remain. ¹⁸ But if the field is dedicated after the Jubilee, then the priest will determine the value by the number of years that remain until the next Jubilee, and the value will be reduced in accordance with this. If you wish to buy back the field, one-fifth of its value will be added, and then you will again own the field. ¹⁹ If you do not buy back the field, or if you sell it to another, you will forever give up the right to buy it back. ²¹ When a field is released during the Jubilee year, it will be considered holy to Your God, the same as a dedicated field, and will become the possession of the priests.

²² If any of you dedicate to Your God a field you have bought, one that is not part of your family property, ²³ the priest will determine its value up to the year of the Jubilee and you must pay its determined value as a thing holy to Your God. ²⁴ In the year of the Jubilee the field will return to the person from whom it was bought, whose land it was. ²⁵ All values will be set according to the sanctuary shekel: twenty gerahs to the shekel.*

²⁶ You may not dedicate a firstborn animal—whether it is a cow or a sheep—because it already belongs to Your God. ²⁷ If the animal is a ceremonially unclean beast, it can be bought back at its set value plus one-fifth. If it is not bought back, it will be sold at its set value.

²⁸ Nothing that you own and devote utterly to Your God** may be redeemed—whether it is a person, an animal, or land. Everything so dedicated is the holiest of holy portions to Your God. ²⁹ No one who has been dedicated as an oblation may be bought back—he or she must be put to death.

---

* A shekel of silver weighed about two-fifths of an ounce.

** This is the concept of *cherem*, the complete and irrevocable giving of something to God. It usually entailed the annihilation of whatever (or whomever) was thus devoted—theoretically to be consumed by God's glory, though in the later conquests of Canaan, entire peoples were declared *cherem* and were completely wiped out. The notion of declaring a person *cherem* speaks very strongly of a form of human sacrifice, which contradicts the command in Lev. 18:21 to not sacrifice one's children to Molech, and of the attempts by Judeo-Christians throughout the ages to set themselves above cultures that practice human sacrifice.

[30] One-tenth of everything from the land, whether grain or fruit, belongs to Your God and is holy. [31] If you wish to buy back any part of this tithe, you must add one-fifth of the value to the cost. [32] The entire tithe of your herd or flock—every tenth animal that passes under the shepherd's staff—will be holy to Your God. [33] The shepherd must not separate out the good ones from the bad ones or substitute one for another. If a substitution is made, both animals become holy and cannot be bought back.

[34] These are the commandments that Our God gave to Moses on Mount Sinai for the Israelites.

numbers

In the wilderness* of sinai, on the first day
of the second month, in the second year after the Israelites left Egypt, Our God spoke to Moses in the Tent of Meeting, and said, ² "Take a census of the whole Israelite community by clans and families. Count every person by name, one by one. ³ You and Aaron are to enroll every person of twenty years or older, company by company, who is fit for military service.

⁴ "One person from each tribe, the head of a family, is to assist you. ⁵ Here are the names of those who will assist you: from Reuben, Elizur begot of Shedeur; ⁶ from Simeon, Shelumiel begot of Zurishaddai; ⁷ from Judah, Nahshon begot of Amminadab; ⁹ from Issachar, Nethanel begot of Zuar; ⁹ from Zebulun, Eliab begot of Helon; ¹⁰ from the heirs of Joseph: from Ephraim, Elishama begot of Ammihud, and from Manasseh, Gamaliel begot of Pedahzur; ¹¹ from Benjamin, Abidan begot of Gidoni; ¹² from Dan, Ahiezer begot of Ammishaddai; ¹³ from Asher, Pagiel begot of Ochran; ¹⁴ from Gad, Eliasaph begot of Reuel; ¹⁵ and from Naphtali, Ahira begot of Enan."

¹⁶ These were the Israelites, appointed by the community, the leaders of their ancestors' tribes and the heads of the Israelite clans.

---

* "In the Wilderness" is the Hebrew name for the book of *Numbers*.

¹⁷ Moses and Aaron took these leaders, chosen by name, ¹⁹ and called together all the Israelites on the first day of the second month. They registered everyone twenty years and older by name, individually, ¹⁹ as God had commanded. This was how Moses counted them in the desert of Sinai.

²⁰ From the descendants of Reuben, the firstborn of Israel: all the Israelites twenty years or older who were fit for military service were listed by name, individually, according to the records of their clans and families. ²¹ All those enrolled from the tribe of Reuben numbered 46,500.

²² From the descendants of Simeon: all the Israelites twenty years old or older who were fit to serve were listed by name, individually, according to the records of their clans and families. ²³ Those enrolled from the tribe of Simeon numbered 59,300.

²⁴ From the descendants of Gad: all the Israelites twenty years old or older who were fit to serve were listed by name, individually, according to the records of their clans and families. ²⁵ Those enrolled from the tribe of Gad numbered 45,650.

²⁶ From the descendants of Judah: all the Israelites twenty years old or older who were fit to serve were listed by name, individually, according to the records of their clans and families. ²⁷ Those enrolled from the tribe of Judah numbered 74,600.

²⁹ From the descendants of Issachar: all the Israelites twenty years or older who were fit to serve were listed by name, individually, according to the records of their clans and families. ²⁹ Those enrolled from the tribe of Issachar numbered 54,400.

³⁰ From the descendants of Zebulun: all the Israelites twenty years or older who were fit to serve were listed by name, individually, according to the records of their clans and families. ³¹ Those enrolled from the tribe of Zebulun numbered 57,400.

³² From the heirs of Joseph—

From the descendants of Ephraim: all the Israelites twenty years old or older who were fit to serve were listed by name, individually, according to the records of their clans and families. ³³ Those enrolled from the tribe of Ephraim numbered 40,500.

³⁴ From the descendants of Manasseh: all the descendants twenty years old or older who were fit to serve were listed by name, individually, according to the records of their clans and families. ³⁵ Those enrolled from the tribe of Manasseh numbered 32,200.

³⁶ From the descendants of Benjamin: all the descendants twenty years old or older who were fit to serve were listed by name, individually, ac-

cording to the records of their clans and families. ³⁷ Those enrolled from the tribe of Benjamin numbered 35,400.

³⁹ From the descendants of Dan: all the descendants twenty years old or older who were fit to serve were listed by name, individually, according to the records of their clans and families. ³⁹ Those enrolled from the tribe of Dan numbered 62,700.

⁴⁰ From the descendants of Asher: all the descendants twenty years old or older who were fit to serve were listed by name, individually, according to the records of their clans and families. ⁴¹ Those enrolled from the tribe of Asher numbered 41,500.

⁴² From the descendants of Naphtali: all the descendants twenty years old or older who were fit to serve were listed by name, individually, according to the records of their clans and families. ⁴³ Those enrolled from the tribe of Naphtali numbered 53,400.

⁴⁴ These were the able-bodied Israelites counted by Moses and Aaron, and the twelve leaders of Israel—each representing an ancestral family. ⁴⁵ All the able-bodied Israelites twenty years or older were counted according to their families' records. ⁴⁶ The number of all those counted was 603,550.

⁴⁷ The families of the tribe of Levi, however, were not counted with the other tribes. ⁴⁹ Our God said to Moses, ⁴⁹ "You must not count the tribe of Levi or include them in the census of the other tribes. ⁵⁰ Instead, you are to place them in charge of the Tabernacle of the Testimony. They are to look after its furnishings and everything that is with it. They alone are to carry the Tabernacle, with its furnishings and everything belonging to me, and they are to pitch their tents around it. ⁵¹ The Levites will take it down when it is time to move, and when it is to be erected, the Levites will do it. Anyone else who comes near it will die. ⁵² All the other Israelites are to set up their tents by their companies, ⁵³ but the Levites will set up camp around the Tabernacle of the Testimony. In this way the divine wrath will not fall on the community of Israel. The Levites are responsible for the care of the Tabernacle of the Testimony."

⁵⁴ The Israelites did everything exactly as Our God had commanded Moses.

☙   ☙   ☙

2:1 Our God said to Moses and Aaron, ² "The families of the Israelites are to camp around the Tent of Meeting, each in their own camp under their own banner and clan standard, some distance from it, with their tents facing it.

³ "On the east side of the Tent of Meeting, toward the sunrise, the people of Judah will set up their camp under their standard. Nahshon, begot of Amminadab, ⁴ will lead a company of 74,600. ⁵ Beside them, Nethanel, begot of Zuar, will lead the tribe of Issachar, ⁶ with their company of 54,400. ⁷ Next to them, Eliab, begot of Helon of the tribe of Zebulun, ⁹ will lead their company of 57,400. ⁹ The number of troops assigned to Judah, company by company, will total 196,400. They will lead the march.

¹⁰ "On the south side, the people of Reuben will set up their camp under their standard. Elizur, begot of Shedeur, of the tribe of Reuben, ¹¹ will lead their company of 46,500. ¹² Beside them, Shelumiel, begot of Zurishaddai of the tribe of Simeon, ¹³ will lead a company of 59,300. ¹⁴ Next to them, Eliasaph, begot of Reuel, of the tribe of Gad, ¹⁵ will lead a company of 45,650. ¹⁶ The total number of troops assigned to Reuben, company by company, will total 151,450. They will follow, second in the march.

¹⁷ "Then the Levites will bring the Tent of Meeting, maintaining their place in the middle of the camps; all will move in the order in which they encamp, all in their proper places under their standards.

¹⁹ "On the west side, toward the sea, the people of Ephraim will set up their camp under their standard. Their leader, Elishama, begot of Ammihud, ¹⁹ will lead a company of 40,500. ²⁰ Beside them will be Gamaliel, begot of Pedahzur, of the tribe of Manasseh, ²¹ with a company of 32,200. ²² Next to them will be Abidan, begot of Gideoni, of the tribe of Benjamin, ²³ with a company of 35,400. ²⁴ All the troops assigned to the camp of Ephraim, by companies, will amount to 109,100. They will set out third.

²⁵ "On the north side, the people of Dan will set up their camp under their standard. Their leader will be Ahiezer, begot of Ammishaddai, ²⁶ with a company of 62,700. ²⁷ Beside them will be Pagiel, begot of Ochran, of the tribe of Asher, ²⁹ with a company of 41,500. ²⁹ Next to them will be Ahira, begot of Enan of the tribe of Naphtali, ³⁰ with a company of 53,400. ³¹ All the troops assigned to the camp of Dan, by companies, will number 157,600. These are to set out last, by companies."

³² So the Israelites were counted, in the orders of their ancestral families. The total in their camps, by companies, numbered 603,550. ³³ The Levites, however, were not counted with the other Israelites, as Our God commanded Moses.

³⁴ The Israelites did as the Most High commanded Moses. They encamped and decamped by companies under their banners, each according to their ancestral line.

ભ   ભ   ભ

3:1 This is the account of the family of Aaron and Moses at the time Our God talked with Moses on Mount Sinai. 2 The names of Aaron's children were Nadab, the firstborn, then Abihu, Eleazar, and Ithamar. 3 These were Aaron's heirs, anointed priests who were installed in the office of priesthood. 4 However, Nadab and Abihu died in the presence of Our God when they made an offering with unsanctified fire* in the desert of Sinai. They left no offspring, but Eleazar and Ithamar served as priests during the lifetime of Aaron.

5 Our God spoke to Moses and said, 6 "Call together the tribe of Levi and place it at Aaron's disposal. Tell them, 'You are to attend the high priest. 7 You will attend to Aaron and to the whole community at the Tent of Meeting by celebrating the ceremonies of the Tabernacle. 9 You are to care for the Tabernacle's furnishings and carry out the duties of Israel in matters of the Tabernacle. 9 Commit yourselves to the high priest; you among all the Israelites are to be committed entirely to the service of the high priest. 10 But a record must be made of Aaron and his descendents; they alone are to fulfill the priestly office and its duties. Anyone else who approaches** the sanctuary will be put to death.' "

11 Then Our God said to Moses, 12 "I have taken the Levites from among the Israelites, just as the firstborn of every Israelite is mine. 13 Every firstborn became mine when I struck the firstborn of Egypt. So I consecrated for myself all the firstborn of Israel, both human and animal. They are mine—I am Your God!"

14 Our God said to Moses in the desert of Sinai, 15 "Make a list of all the Levites by their families in the family line, every child aged one month or more." 16 Moses made this list according to the command of the Most High. 17 Here are the names of Levi's heirs: Gershon, Kohath, and Merari.

19 Descendants of Gershon, by clans: Libni and Shimei.

19 Descendants of Kohath, by clans: Amram, Izhar, Hebron and Uzziel.

20 Descendants of Merari, by clans: Mahli and Mushi.

These were the clans of Levi according to their families.

---

* Or "outside fire." This refers to the incident in *Leviticus* in which they brought coals from a fire from the camp, outside the sanctity of the altar area.

** The word for "approach" is a specialized term for entering sacred space or dealing with holy things—not merely getting close in proximity. To "approach" God or the Tabernacle is to encounter the realm of the Holy, and much of the Hebrew scriptures takes great pains to show that to touch the Holy is to risk annihilation from the encounter. Only those ceremonially pure, or specially designated as mediators, could approach God and live.

²¹ Gershon: the clan of Libni and the clan of Shemei. These were the clans of Gershon. ²² The number of those one month and older was 7,500. ²³ The clans of Gershon were assigned to camp behind the Tabernacle on the west, toward the sea. ²⁴ The leader of their clans was Eliasaph begot of Lael. ²⁵ In the service of the Tent of Meeting they were in charge of the Tabernacle and the Tent, its covering, the curtain at the entrance of the Tent of Meeting, ²⁶ the curtains of the courtyard, the curtain at the entrance of the courtyard surrounding the Tabernacle and the altar, the rope, and all that is related to their use.

²⁷ Kohath: the clan of Amram, the clan of Izhar, the clan of Hebron and the clan of Uzziel. ²⁹ The number of those one month or older was 9,600. The clans of Kohath were responsible for the care of the sanctuary. ²⁹ They camped on the south side of the Tabernacle. ³⁰ The leader of the Kohath clans was Elizaphan begot of Uzziel. ³¹ They were responsible for the Ark, the table, the lampstands, the altars, the sacred vessels used in the service, the curtain, and everything related to their use. ³² Eleazar, begot of Aaron the priest, was appointed supervisor of all those Levites who were in the service of the sanctuary.

³³ Merari: the clan of Mahli and the clan of Mushi; these were the clans of Merari. ³⁴ The number of those one month or older was 6,200. ³⁵ The leader of the Merari clans was Zuriel begot of Abihail. They camped on the north side of the Tabernacle. ³⁶ The clans of Merari were responsible for the frames of the Tabernacle, its crossbars, posts, bases, all its equipment, and everything related to their use, ³⁷ as well as the posts of the surrounding courtyard with their bases, tent pegs and ropes.

³⁹ Moses, Aaron, and Aaron's heirs camped to the east of the Tabernacle, the side facing the sunrise, in front of the Tent of Meeting. They were responsible for the protection of the sanctuary on behalf of the Israelites. Any other person who approached it was to be put to death.

³⁹ The number of Levites counted by Moses and Aaron at God's command, clan by clan, including the able-bodied one month or older, came to 22,000.

⁴⁰ Our God said to Moses, "Count all the Israelites one month or older and list them by names, ⁴¹ but all the Levites you will present to me—I am Your God—to stand in place of all the firstborn of Israel. In the same way, the Levites' cattle will stand in place of the firstborn cattle of all the Israelites." ⁴² As God commanded, Moses made a list of all the firstborn of the Israelites, ⁴³ and the total number of the firstborn recorded by name in the register, aged one month or older, came to 22,273.

⁴⁴ The Most High also said to Moses, ⁴⁵ "Take the Levites in place of the

firstborn of the Israelites, all one month or older, and the cattle of the Levites in place of the cattle of the Israelites. For the Levites will be my own. I am Your God. ⁴⁶ To redeem the 273 firstborn of the Israelites who exceed the number of the Levites, ⁴⁷ collect one ounce of silver from each one, weighed according the sanctuary shekel that weighs twenty *gerahs*. ⁴⁸ Give this money for the redemption of the additional Israelites to Aaron and his heirs."

⁴⁹ So Moses collected the redemption money from those who exceeded the number redeemed by the Levites. ⁵⁰ He garnered from the firstborn Israelites over eighty-five pounds of silver, weighed according to the sanctuary shekel. ⁵¹ Then Moses gave the redemption money to Aaron and Aaron's heirs, as God had commanded.

CR   CR   CR

4¹ Our God said to Moses and Aaron, ² "Take a census of Kohath's branch of the Levites, by their clans and families. ³ Include all the able-bodied from thirty to fifty years of age who are qualified to work on the Tent of Meeting.

⁴ "The service which Kohath's clan will provide is to care for the most holy things. ⁵ When it is time to move the camp, Aaron and his heirs will go in and take down the screening curtain and cover the Ark of the Covenant with it. ⁶ They will wrap this with a fine leather covering, and then a solid indigo cloth over that, and then put its poles in place. ⁷ Over the Table of the Bread of Presence and its articles—the plates, dishes, and bowls, the bowls for drink offerings, and the bread that is kept there—they are to spread an indigo cloth. ⁸ Over this, they must place a purple cloth, and then everything must be covered with a fine leather covering, and the poles put in place. ⁹ They are to take an indigo cloth and cover the lampstands, the lamps, tongs, firepans, and the containers for the oil used for the service. ¹⁰ These, with all their accessories, are to be wrapped in a fine leather covering, and placed on a carrying frame. ¹¹ Cover the gold altar with an indigo cloth, then with a fine leather covering, and put its poles in place. ¹² They are to take all the articles used for the sanctuary services, wrap them with an indigo cloth, and then cover them with a fine leather covering and put them on a carrying frame. ¹³ The ashes are to be removed from the bronze altar, and then an indigo cloth spread over it. ¹⁴ They are to lay on it all the articles used at the altar: the fire pan, forks, shovels, and the tossing bowls. Then a fine leather covering will be spread over it, and its poles put in place.

¹⁵ "When Aaron and his heirs complete the packing of the holy furnishings and the holy articles, and the camp is prepared to move, the Kohathites

will come forward to carry them. But no one of them is to touch the holy articles of the Tent of Meeting or they will die. ¹⁶ Eleazar begot of Aaron will be in charge of the lamp oil, the fragrant incense, the regular grain offering, the anointing oil, and oversight of the Tabernacle and all its contents, the sanctuary and its accouterments."

¹⁷ Our God said to Moses and Aaron, ¹⁹ "You must not let the tribe of the Kohathites be wiped out and lost to the Levites. ¹⁹ This is what you must do to prevent them from dying by approaching the holy things: Aaron and his heirs are to enter the sanctuary and assign to each a specific task, what they must carry. ²⁰ But the Kohathites must not enter the sanctuary and look at the holy things, even momentarily, or they will die."

²¹ Our God said to Moses, ²² "Take a census of the clans of Gershon by their families, ²³ counting those between thirty and fifty years of age; these will be qualified to work in the Tent of Meeting. ²⁴ Here are the duties they are to carry out, in serving and in carrying: ²⁵ They are to carry the curtains of the Tabernacle—the Tent of Meeting—with its coverings and the outer covering of fine leather; the curtains for the Tent of Meeting entrance; ²⁶ the courtyard curtains surrounding the Tabernacle and the altar; the curtain for the entrance; the ropes; and all the equipment used in the services. The Gershonites will be responsible for carrying out all tasks pertaining to these things. ²⁷All of the work of the Gershonites, both in what they do and in what they carry, are to be under the supervision of Aaron and his heirs. ²⁹ Such are the duties of the Gershonites concerning the Tent of Meeting; Ithamar, begot of the priest Aaron, is to supervise them in these duties.

²⁹ "Make a list of the clans of the Merarites by their families, ³⁰ counting those between thirty and fifty years of age; these will be qualified to perform duties at the Tent of Meeting. ³¹ Their duties at the Tent of Meeting will be to carry the Tabernacle's frame, with its crossbars, posts and bases, ³² and the posts of the surrounding courtyard with their bases, tent pegs, ropes, and all their equipment. ³³ These are the duties of the Merarite clans concerning the Tent of Meeting. They are to be supervised by Ithamar, begot of Aaron, the priest."

³⁴ Moses, Aaron and the community leaders counted the Kohathites by their clans and families. ³⁵ All the able-bodied between the ages of thirty and fifty who were to serve in the Tent of Meeting, ³⁶ counted by clan, came to 2,750. ³⁷ This was the total counted of the clan of Kohath who served in the Tent of Meeting. Moses and Aaron counted them as commanded by Our God through Moses.

⁣³⁹ The Gershonites were counted by their clans and families— ³⁹ all those between thirty years old to fifty years old who were to serve at the Tent of Meeting. ⁴⁰ The count, by clans and families, came to 2,630. ⁴¹ This was the total number of the clans of Gershon who served at the Tent of Meeting. Moses and Aaron counted them as commanded by Our God through Moses.

⁴² The Meraites were counted by their clans and families, ⁴³ all those between thirty years old to fifty years old who were to serve at the Tent of Meeting. ⁴⁴ The count, by clans and families, came to 3,200. ⁴⁵ This was the total counted of those in the Merarites clans. Moses and Aaron counted them as commanded by Our God through Moses.

⁴⁶ So Moses, Aaron and the Israelite leaders counted all the Levites by their clans and families. ⁴⁷ All the able-bodied between thirty and fifty years of age who were qualified to serve or carry the Tent of Meeting ⁴⁹ numbered 9,590. ⁴⁹ At God's command through Moses, each Levite was assigned to work or to carry. So they were enlisted by Moses, according to Our God's command.

ଛ ଛ ଛ

5:1 Our God said to Moses, ² "Command the Israelites to expel from the camp anyone suffering from an infectious skin disease or a discharge, or who has become ceremonially unclean by touching a corpse. ³ Male or female, they must be expelled from the camp. Otherwise, they will defile the camp, where I dwell among you." ⁴ The Israelites did as they were told; they expelled them from the camp.* They did exactly what Our God told Moses to do.

⁵ Our God said to Moses, ⁶ "Say to the Israelites: If one of you wrongs another in any way whatsoever—and thus becomes unfaithful to me—that person is guilty ⁷ and must confess it. The wrongdoer must, for their guilt, pay full restitution plus one-fifth, and give it to the person who was wronged. ⁹ If the injured person has no close relative to whom the restitution can be paid, the restitution belongs to Your God and must be given to the priest, along with a ram with which atonement can be made for the guilty person. ⁹ All sacred contributions that the Israelites give to the priest will belong to the priest. ¹⁰ Your personal sacred gifts belong to you, but what you give to the priest belongs to the priest."

---

* As noted in *Leviticus,* being "ceremonially unclean" was a temporary condition; it meant that one could not approach the sanctuary area until one has either been pronounced "clean" or has sacrificed a purification offering.

¹¹ Then Our God said to Moses, ¹² "Speak to the Israelites and tell them: If your spouse goes astray ¹³ and commits adultery with another, and if it is kept from you and continues to go on undetected—without witnesses and without anyone catching them—¹⁴ or if you begin to grow jealous of your spouse and suspect unfaithfulness even when there is none, ¹⁵ then you must bring your spouse to the priest. You must also bring an offering of two quarts of barley flour* on your spouse's behalf. You are not to pour oil on it or put frankincense on it, for it is a grain offering of jealousy, a grain offering as a memorial of guilt.

¹⁶ "The priest will bring the suspected spouse forward to stand before Your God. ¹⁷ Then the priest will take holy water in an earthen bowl, and add dust from the Tabernacle floor to it. ¹⁸ After placing the accused before the Most High, the priest will loosen the hair of the suspected spouse and—while holding the Water of Bitterness and Curses**—will place the memorial offering, that is, the jealousy offering, into that person's hands. ¹⁹ Then the priest will accuse the spouse under oath and say, 'If no other person has lain with you and you have not strayed or defiled yourself while married, let this "bitter water that carries a curse" bring you no harm. ²⁰ But if you have gone astray while married and you have defiled yourself by lying with someone other than your spouse'— ²¹ here the priest is to place the accused spouse under oath—'may Your God cause you to become filth in the eyes of your people, and a curse in their mouths, and cause your sexual organs to cease functioning. ²² May this bitter water enter your body and cause your sexual organs to cease functioning.' Then the accused is to say, 'Amen. So be it!'

²³ "The priest is to write these curses on a scroll and wash them off in the bitter water. ²⁴ Then the priest must make the accused drink 'the bitter water that carries a curse,' and the water will enter the body of the accused, which will either cause the curse to take place or to pass through without harm. ²⁵ The priest must take the grain offering for jealousy, raise it before the Most High, and place it on the altar. ²⁶ Then the priest must take a handful of the grain as a memorial offering and burn it on the altar, after which the accused must drink the water. ²⁷ If the accused is defiled and has been unfaithful, the sexual organs will fill with pain and cause bitter suffering, and they will cease to function. The spouse will become filth in the eyes of the community. ²⁸ But if the accused is not

---

* The least expensive grain, and so available even to the poorest people.

** This is Judith Antonelli's rendering, from *In the Image of God: A Feminist Commentary on the Torah*. The Hebrew is here strongly alliterative and has a ritual sound to it, reminiscent of a magical incantation. Jewish feminist scholar Tikva Frymer-Kensky renders the phrase, "Waters of Instruction, of Spell-Induction."

defiled but is pure and innocent, then that person will be free of this curse, and be fertile.

²⁹ "This, then, is the law for cases of jealousy, where a spouse goes astray and breaks the vow to be faithful, ³⁰ or when a flush of jealousy overcomes a spouse. The priest is to have the accused spouse stand before the Most High and apply this entire ritual of law to the person. ³¹ A faithful spouse will be proven innocent, but an unfaithful spouse will bear the punishment for sin."

6:1 Our God said to Moses, ² "Speak to the Israelites and tell them: If you are a woman or man who wishes to become a Nazirite,* and you want to set yourself apart by consecrating yourself to Your God, ³ you are to abstain from wine and strong drink. You must not drink wine vinegar or any other kind of fermented liquid, or even eat grapes or raisins. ⁴ While a Nazirite you must not eat anything grown on a vine, not even the seeds or skin. ⁵ While a Nazirite you must not touch a razor to your head—let your hair grow for as long as you are consecrated and holy to Your God.

⁶ "Throughout the time of your vow you must not go near a dead body. ⁷ Even if it is your mother, father, sister or brother, you must not make yourself ritually unclean because of them, for the Nazirite consecration to Your God is on your head. ⁹ Throughout the time of your separation, you are consecrated to Your God. ⁹ If a person dies suddenly in your presence, thereby defiling your consecrated hair, you must shave your head on the day you become clean again—the seventh day. ¹⁰ On the eighth day** you must take two turtle doves or two young pigeons to the priest at the entrance to the Tent of Meeting. ¹¹ The priest will offer one as a decontamination offering and the other as a burnt offering to atone for you, since you were contaminated by being in the presence of a dead person. You must consecrate your head anew on that same day, ¹² and consecrate yourself to Your God for the duration of your vow, bringing a yearling lamb as a compensation offering. The former days are null and void, since your consecration became ritually impure.

¹³ "This is the ritual for a Nazirite whose days of consecration are fulfilled: You are to be led to the entrance of the Tent of Meeting ¹⁴ and there you will present your offering to God: a yearling ram without blemish as a burnt offering, a yearling ewe lamb without blemish as a sin offering, and a ram without defect as a fellowship offering. ¹⁵ Then you must present a grain

---

* Literally, a consecrated or "separate" person.
** Symbolic of a new beginning.

offering and a drink offering, a basket of unleavened bread, cakes made with fine flour mixed with oil, and wafers spread with oil.

¹⁶ "The priest will present these to Your God and offer your sin offering and your burnt offering. ¹⁷ The priest will then present the basket of unleavened bread, and sacrifice the ram as a fellowship offering to Your God, together with the grain offering and the drink offering.

¹⁸ "Then you will shave your consecrated hair at the entrance of the Tent of Meeting, and put it in the fire under the fellowship offering. ¹⁹ After you have shaved off your consecrated hair, the priest will hand you a boiled shoulder of the ram and an unleavened cake and an unleavened wafer from the basket. ²⁰ Then the priest will elevate them before Your God as a raised offering. This becomes a holy portion for the priest, along with the breast that is elevated and the thigh that was presented. When this is accomplished, you are again free to drink wine.

²¹ "This is the law for those of you who take the Nazirite vow. This offering you must make to Your God for your dedication, beyond what you can comfortably afford to give. You must carry out your vow to the full, according to this law that governs your dedication."

²² The Most High God said to Moses, ²³ "Tell Aaron and his heirs: This is how you will bless the Israelites. Say to them,

> 'May Our God bless you and keep you!
> May Our God's face shine upon you, and be gracious to you!
> ²⁶ May Our God look kindly upon you, and give you peace!'

²⁷ "Thus will they invoke my Name over the Israelites, and then I myself will bless them!"

ও   ও   ও

7:1 When Moses had finished setting up the Tabernacle, he anointed and consecrated it and all its furnishings. He also anointed and consecrated the altar and all its accessories. ² Then the leaders of Israel—the heads of the ancestral families that had been included in the census—came forward ³ and presented their gifts: six covered wagons and twelve oxen, that is, an ox from each leader and a wagon from every two. They presented these gifts in front of the Tabernacle.

⁴ Our God said to Moses, ⁵ "Accept these from your leaders, that they may be used in the service of the Tent of Meeting. Give them to the Levites as their service requires."

⁶ So Moses accepted the carts and oxen and distributed them to the Levites. ⁷ Two carts and four oxen went to the Gershonites for the duties they were to carry out; ⁹ and four carts and eight oxen went to the Merarites for the duties they were to carry out ⁹ under the supervision of Ithamar, begot of Aaron the priest. ⁹ Moses did not assign any to the Kohathites, for it was their duty to carry the holy things on their shoulders.

¹⁰ Once the altar was anointed, the leaders brought their offerings for its dedication and presented them before it. ¹¹ For God had said to Moses, "Have the leaders bring an offering for the dedication of the altar one by one, on consecutive days."

¹² On the first day, the offering was presented by Nahshon, begot of Amminadab, the leader of the descendants of Judah: ¹³ a silver dish* weighing over three pounds, and a silver bowl weighing nearly two pounds, as measured by the standard of the sanctuary shekel—each filled with fine flour mixed with oil as a grain offering; ¹⁴ a gold dish weighing four ounces, filled with incense; ¹⁵ a young bull, a ram, and a male yearling lamb, for burnt offerings; ¹⁶ a male goat for a sin offering; ¹⁷ and two oxen, five rams, five male goats and five male yearling lambs as a fellowship offering. This was the offering of Nahshon begot of Amminadab.

¹⁹ On the second day, the offering was presented by Nethanel, begot of Zuar, the leader of the descendants of Issachar: ¹⁹ a silver dish weighing over three pounds, and a silver bowl weighing nearly two pounds, as measured by the standard of the sanctuary shekel—each filled with fine flour mixed with oil as a grain offering; ²⁰ a gold dish weighing four ounces, filled with incense; ²¹ a young bull, a ram, and a male yearling lamb, for burnt offerings; ²² a male goat for a sin offering; ²³ and two oxen, five rams, five male goats and five male yearling lambs as a fellowship offering. This was the offering of Nethanel, begot of Zuar.

²⁴ On the third day, the offering was presented by Eliab, begot of Helon, the leader of the descendants of Zebulun: ²⁵ a silver dish weighing over three pounds, and a silver bowl weighing nearly two pounds, as measured by the standard of the sanctuary shekel—each filled with fine flour mixed with oil as a grain offering; ²⁶ a gold dish weighing four ounces, filled with incense; ²⁷ a young bull, a ram, and a male yearling lamb, for burnt offerings; ²⁹ a male goat for a sin offering; ²⁹ and two oxen, five rams, five male goats and five male yearling lambs as a fellowship offering. This was the offering of Eliab, begot of Helon.

---

* In the following list, the bowls and dishes were not made of clay or other materials and simply gilded, but were made completely of hammered gold or silver—hence the importance of their weight.

³⁰ On the fourth day, the offering was presented by Elizur begot of Shedeur, the leader of the descendants of Reuben: ³¹ a silver dish weighing over three pounds, and a silver bowl weighing nearly two pounds, as measured by the standard of the sanctuary shekel—each filled with fine flour mixed with oil as a grain offering; ³² a gold dish weighing four ounces, filled with incense; ³³ a young bull, a ram, and a male yearling lamb, for burnt offerings; ³⁴ a male goat for a sin offering; ³⁵ and two oxen, five rams, five male goats and five male yearling lambs as a fellowship offering. This was the offering of Elizur begot of Shedeur.

³⁶ On the fifth day, the offering was presented by Shelumiel begot of Zurishaddai, leader of the descendants of Simeon: ³⁷ a silver dish weighing over three pounds, and a silver bowl weighing nearly two pounds, as measured by the standard of the sanctuary shekel—each filled with fine flour mixed with oil as a grain offering; ³⁹ a gold dish weighing four ounces, filled with incense; ³⁹ a young bull, a ram, and a male yearling lamb, for burnt offerings; ⁴⁰ a male goat for a sin offering; ⁴¹ and two oxen, five rams, five male goats and five male yearling lambs as a fellowship offering. This was the offering of Shelumiel, begot of Zurishaddai.

⁴² On the sixth day, the offering was presented by Eliasaph begot of Reuel, the leader of the descendants of Gad: ⁴³ a silver dish weighing over three pounds, and a silver bowl weighing nearly two pounds, as measured by the standard of the sanctuary shekel—each filled with fine flour mixed with oil as a grain offering; ⁴⁴ a gold dish weighing four ounces, filled with incense; ⁴⁵ a young bull, a ram, and a male yearling lamb, for burnt offerings; ⁴⁶ a male goat for a sin offering; ⁴⁷ and two oxen, five rams, five male goats and five male yearling lambs as a fellowship offering. This was the offering of Eliasaph begot of Reuel.

⁴⁹ On the seventh day, the offering was presented by Elishama begot of Ammihud, the leader of the descendants of Ephraim: ⁴⁹ a silver dish weighing over three pounds, and a silver bowl weighing nearly two pounds, as measured by the standard of the sanctuary shekel—each filled with fine flour mixed with oil as a grain offering; ⁵⁰ a gold dish weighing four ounces, filled with incense; ⁵¹ a young bull, a ram, and a male yearling lamb, for burnt offerings; ⁵² a male goat for a sin offering; ⁵³ and two oxen, five rams, five male goats and five male yearling lambs as a fellowship offering. This was the offering of Elishama begot of Ammihud.

⁵⁴ On the eighth day, the offering was presented by Gamaliel begot of Pedahzur, the leader of the descendants of Manasseh: ⁵⁵ a silver dish weighing over three pounds, and a silver bowl weighing nearly two pounds, as measured by the standard of the sanctuary shekel—each filled with fine flour mixed with oil as a grain offering; ⁵⁶ a gold dish weighing four ounces,

filled with incense; ⁵⁷ a young bull, a ram, and a male yearling lamb, for burnt offerings; ⁵⁹ a male goat for a sin offering; ⁵⁹ and two oxen, five rams, five male goats and five male yearling lambs as a fellowship offering. This was the offering of Gamaliel begot of Pedahzur.

⁶⁰ On the ninth day, the offering was presented by Abidan begot of Gideoni, the leader of the descendants of Benjamin: ⁶¹ a silver dish weighing over three pounds, and a silver bowl weighing nearly two pounds, as measured by the standard of the sanctuary shekel—each filled with fine flour mixed with oil as a grain offering; ⁶² a gold dish weighing four ounces, filled with incense; ⁶³ a young bull, a ram, and a male yearling lamb, for burnt offerings; ⁶⁴ a male goat for a sin offering; ⁶⁵ and two oxen, five rams, five male goats and five male yearling lambs as a fellowship offering. This was the offering of Abidan begot of Gideoni.

⁶⁶ On the tenth day, the offering was presented by Ahiezer begot of Ammishaddai, the leader of the descendants of Dan: ⁶⁷ a silver dish weighing over three pounds, and a silver bowl weighing nearly two pounds, as measured by the standard of the sanctuary shekel—each filled with fine flour mixed with oil as a grain offering; ⁶⁹ a gold dish weighing four ounces, filled with incense; ⁶⁹ a young bull, a ram, and a male yearling lamb, for burnt offerings; ⁷⁰ a male goat for a sin offering; ⁷¹ and two oxen, five rams, five male goats and five male yearling lambs as a fellowship offering. This was the offering of Ahiezer begot of Ammishaddai.

⁷² On the eleventh day, the offering was presented by Pagiel begot of Ochran, the leader of the descendants of Asher: ⁷³ a silver dish weighing over three pounds, and a silver bowl weighing nearly two pounds, as measured by the standard of the sanctuary shekel—each filled with fine flour mixed with oil as a grain offering; ⁷⁴ a gold dish weighing four ounces, filled with incense; ⁷⁵ a young bull, a ram, and a male yearling lamb, for burnt offerings; ⁷⁶ a male goat for a sin offering; ⁷⁷ and two oxen, five rams, five male goats and five male yearling lambs as a fellowship offering. This was the offering of Pagiel begot of Ocran.

⁷⁹ On the twelfth day, the offering was presented by Ahira begot of Enan, the leader of the descendants of Naphtali: ⁷⁹ a silver dish weighing over three pounds, and a silver bowl weighing nearly two pounds, as measured by the standard of the sanctuary shekel—each filled with fine flour mixed with oil as a grain offering; ⁹⁰ a gold dish weighing four ounces, filled with incense; ⁹¹ a young bull, a ram, and a male yearling lamb, for burnt offerings; ⁹² a male goat for a sin offering; ⁹³ and two oxen, five rams, five male goats and five male yearling lambs as a fellowship offering. This was the offering of Ahira begot of Enan.

⁹⁴ These were the offerings of the Israelite leaders for the dedication of the altar when it was anointed: twelve silver dishes, twelve silver bowls and twelve gold dishes. ⁹⁵ Each silver dish, measured by the standard of the shekel of the sanctuary, weighed over three pounds, and each silver bowl weighed nearly two pounds, for a total of sixty pounds of silver, by the sanctuary standard. ⁹⁶ The twelve gold dishes filled with fragrant incense weighed four ounces each by the sanctuary standard. The total weight of gold dishes was three pounds. ⁹⁷ All the animals for the burnt offering added up to twelve young bulls, twelve rams and twelve male yearling lambs, together with a grain offering. Twelve male goats were offered for the sin offering. ⁹⁹ All the animals for the fellowship offering added up to twenty-four oxen, sixty rams, sixty male goats and sixty male yearling lambs. These were the offerings for the dedication of the altar when it was anointed.

⁹⁹ When Moses would enter the Tent of Meeting to speak with God, he would hear a voice from the space where the two winged sphinxes met above the Covering of the Ark of the Covenant. In this way God would speak with Moses.

8:1 Our God spoke to Moses, ² saying, "Tell Aaron, 'When you set up the seven lamps, they must illumine the area in front of the lampstand.' "

³ Aaron did this, setting up the lamps so that they faced the front of the lampstand, as Our God had commanded Moses. ⁴ The lampstands were made of hammered gold, from its base to its flowers. The lampstand was made to the exact specifications God had given to Moses.

⁵ Our God said to Moses, ⁶ "Separate the Levites from all the other Israelites to make them ceremonially clean. ⁷ Purify them by sprinkling them with ceremonial water, after which they must shave all the hair from their bodies and wash their clothes, so that they will be ceremonially clean. ⁹ Tell them to take a young bull with a grain offering of fine flour mixed with oil. Then take a second bull for a sin offering. ¹⁰ Place the Levites before the Tent of Meeting and assemble the Israelites, and have them all lay hands on them. ¹¹ Then Aaron will present the Levites to God as an elevation offering from the Israelites, so that they will be dedicated to the service of Your God. ¹² Then have the Levites lay their hands on the heads of the bulls and offer one for a sin offering and the other for a burnt offering to atone for the Levites. ¹³ Let the Levites stand before Aaron and Aaron's heirs, while you present them to God as a special gift. ¹⁴ By doing this you set the Levites apart from all the other Israelites, for the Levites belong to me.

[15] "When you have purified the Levites and presented them as a special offering, they may enter the Tent of Meeting to serve in it; [16] for out of all the Israelites, they are dedicated to me. I have accepted them as mine in place of the firstborn, every firstborn of Israel. [17] For every firstborn among the Israelites, whether human or animal, belongs to me. On the day I struck down every firstborn creature in Egypt, I consecrated all the firstborn of the Israelites to myself, [19] and I have accepted the Levites in their place. [19] I have assigned the Levites to Aaron and his heirs to carry out the Tent of Meeting services on behalf of the Israelites, and to atone for them so that no plague will strike them should they approach the sanctuary."

[20] Moses, Aaron and the entire Israelite community consecrated the Levites as Our God had said. [21] The Levites purified themselves and washed their clothes. Then Aaron presented them as a dedicated offering before the Most High God and atoned for them so that they would be purified. [22] Only then did the Levites take up their duties at the Tent of Meeting under the supervision of Aaron and his heirs. They commissioned the Levites exactly as God had commanded Moses.

[23] Our God said to Moses, "Take care to follow these instructions: Levites over twenty-five years of age will take on the service of the Tent of Meeting. [25] At the age of fifty they will have fulfilled their service and serve no more. [26] They may assist other Levites in the Tent of Meeting duties, but they will not preside. Follow these instructions when assigning the Levites their duties."

෬   ෬   ෬

[9:1] In the first month of the second year after the Israelites came up out of Egypt, Our God spoke to Moses in the desert of Sinai and said, [2] "Have the Israelites prepare the Passover at the appointed time: [3] on the fourteenth day of this month, between sunset and total darkness, at twilight, following all its rules and regulations."

[4] So Moses told the Israelites to prepare the Passover, [5] and they prepared it on the fourteenth day of the first month, at twilight, in the desert of Sinai. The Israelites did everything exactly as God had instructed Moses.

[6] It happened that some workers became ceremonially unclean by having come into contact with a corpse and could not keep the Passover as prescribed. Therefore, they came to Moses and Aaron, [7] saying, "We have become ceremonially unclean through contact with a corpse. Why are we

banned from presenting Our God's offering at the prescribed time with all the other Israelites?"

⁹ Moses replied, "Wait a bit, while I listen for Our God's counsel on this matter."

⁹ Then the Most High told Moses ¹⁰ to say to the Israelites, "If any of you or your descendants becomes ceremonially unclean because of contact with a corpse, or is away on a long journey, you may still celebrate Your God's Passover. ¹¹ Celebrate it on the fourteenth day of the second month, at twilight. Sacrifice the lamb, and eat it with unleavened bread and bitter herbs. ¹² Do not leave any of it until morning or break any of its bones. When you celebrate the Passover, you must follow all the regulations. ¹³ But if a person who is ceremonially clean and not on a journey fails to celebrate the Passover, that person is to be cut off from my people for not presenting Our God's offering at the appropriate time. That person must bear the responsibility for their own sin.

¹⁴ "When foreigners live among you, they, too, must keep the Passover to Your God, observing all the rules and regulations. You must have the same rules and regulations for foreigners as for native-born."

෫   ෫   ෫

¹⁵ On the day the Israelites set up the Tabernacle, that is, the Tent of the Testimony, a cloud covered it, and in the evening a fire-like brightness stood over it until morning. ¹⁶ It was always this way: the cloud covered it by day and the appearance of fire covered it by night. ¹⁷ Whenever the cloud lifted from over the Tent, the Israelites broke camp; whenever the cloud settled, the Israelites set up camp. ¹⁸ At God's command the Israelites would march, and at God's command the Israelites would set up camp. For however many days the cloud covered the Tent, they would stay encamped. ¹⁹ When the cloud would hang over the Tabernacle for many days, the Israelites obeyed God's command and did not march on. ²⁰ It was the same when the cloud hovered over the Tabernacle only for a few days: at God's command they remained in camp; and at God's command they broke camp. ²¹ And there were times when the cloud remained only from evening till morning, and, in the morning, when the cloud lifted, they broke camp. Whether it was day or night, they moved when the cloud lifted. ²³ They broke camp when Our God gave the command, and at Our God's command, they set up camp. They were faithful to Our God's command, through the direction of Moses.

10:1 Our God said to Moses, 2 "Make two trumpets of hammered silver, and use them to summon the Israelites and to signal the time to break camp. 3 When both trumpets sound, the whole community is to gather before you at the entrance of the Tent of Meeting. 4 When only one trumpet sounds, the leaders—the heads of the Israelite clans—are to gather before you.

5 "When a long trumpet blast is sounded, the tribes camping on the east side are to leave. 6 At the second long blast the tribes camping on the south are to leave. Long trumpet blasts are the signal for setting out. 7 To gather the assembly blow the trumpet, but use short blasts instead of long ones.

9 "Aaron's heirs, the priests, will blow the trumpets. This is to be an ordinance for you always, for the generations to come.

9 "When you go into battle in your territory against a foe oppressing you, sound a blast on the trumpet. Then you will be remembered by the Most High, Your God, and rescued from your enemies.

10 "When you are celebrating your appointed feasts and your new moon festivals, you are to blow the trumpets over the burnt offerings and over your shared offerings. The trumpets will be a reminder for you before your God. I am the Most High, Your God."

11 On the twentieth day of the second month of the second year, the cloud lifted from above the Tabernacle of the Covenant, 12 and the Israelites moved by stages from the Sinai desert until the cloud came to rest in the Paran desert. 13 Here for the first time they set out at the command of Our God through Moses.

14 The tribe of Judah, company by company, was the first to leave, under their banner, with Nahshon begot of Amminadab in command. 15 Nethanel begot of Zuar led the tribe of Issachar under its banner. 16 Eliab begot of Helon led the tribe of Zebulun under its banner. 17 Then the Tabernacle was dismantled and the Gershonites and Merarites set out carrying it.

19 Elizur begot of Shedeur led the tribe of Reuben under its banner. 19 Shelumiel begot of Zurishaddai led the tribe of Simeon under its banner. 20 Eliasaph begot of Reuel led the tribe of Gad under its banner. 21 Then the Kohathites set out carrying the holy things, so that by the time the others arrived, the Tabernacle would already be set up.

22 Elishama begot of Hammihud led the tribe of Ephraim under its banner. 23 Gamaliel begot of Pedahzur led the tribe of Manasseh under its banner. 24 Abidan begot of Gideoni led the tribe of Benjamin under its banner.

25 Finally, as the rearguard of all the others, Ahiezer begot of Ammishaddai led the tribe of Dan under its banner, 26 Pagiel begot of Ochran let the tribe of Asher under its banner, 27 and Ahira begot of Enan led the tribe

of Naphtali under its banner. ²⁹ This was the order of march for the Israelites as they set out.

²⁹ Moses met with his brother-in-law Hobab, begot of Reuel the Midianite, and said, "We are setting out for the place which Our God has promised to us. Come with us; it will go well for you, for Our God promised many blessings to Israel."

³⁰ Hobab replied, "I will not be going with you; I will return to my own land and my own people."

³¹ But Moses said to him, "Do not leave us! You know the best places to camp in the desert. You will be our eyes for us, ³² and then you can share in all the good things Our God has promised us. Come with us, and we will do this for you."

³³ So they set out from the mountain of Our God, and traveled for three days. The Ark of the Covenant of Our God went before them during those three days to locate a place to rest. ³⁴ The cloud of the Most High hovered over them by day once they set out from camp.

³⁵ Every time the Ark set out, Moses would say,

> "Rise up, O God!
>   May your enemies be scattered!
> Let your foes flee before you,
>   may those who hate you flee as you approach!"

³⁶ And when it came to rest, Moses would say,

> "Return, O God,
>   to the thousand thousands of Israel!"

11:1–25:19

now the people complained bitterly about their hardship; the Most High heard them, and God's anger blazed up. Fire broke out and burned down some of the outlying parts of the camp. ² When the people asked Moses to intercede with God, the fire died down. ³ They named that place Taberah, or "Blaze," for God's fire blazed against them.

⁴ Soon the riffraff among them started complaining and whining, and Israelites said, "Who will give us meat to eat? ⁵ We remember the fish we used to eat freely in Egypt, and the cucumbers, melons, leeks, onions and garlic! ⁶ But out here we're wasting away; there is nothing here but manna for us to look at!"

⁷ The manna was like coriander seed, and looked like droplets of gum from the bark of a tree. ⁹ The people would go about gathering it, then grind it in a mill or crush it with a pestle. Then they would cook it in a pot and make it into dumplings. It had a rich taste, as if it had been made with oil. ⁹ When the dew fell on the camp at nighttime, the manna fell with it.

¹⁰ Moses heard the people, family after family, wailing at the entrances of their tents, so much so that Our God's anger flared up again. Moses was aggrieved, ¹¹ and said to God, "Why do you treat me this way? Are you so displeased with me that you must burden me with this whole nation? ¹² Was it I who conceived these people, was it I who gave birth to them, that you should say to me, 'Carry them at your bosom, like a nurse with a baby at the breast, to the land that I swore to give to their ancestors?' ¹³ Where am I to find meat to give to these people, when they come to me weeping and saying, 'Give us meat to eat'? ¹⁴ I cannot carry this nation alone! The weight is too much for me. ¹⁵ If this is how you will deal with me, just allow me this one favor and kill me now! Spare me from seeing such misery as this!"

¹⁶ The Most High said to Moses, "Gather together seventy of your elders, those you know to be leaders and officials among the people. Have them come to the Tent of Meeting and take their place there with you. ¹⁷ I will come down and speak to you there. I will take some of the Spirit that lives in you and give it to them. They will share the burden of your people, so that you do not carry all of it by yourself. ¹⁹ Say to the people: Consecrate yourselves for tomorrow, for then you will eat meat. Your God heard you when you cried out, 'If only we had meat to eat! Why did we ever leave Egypt?' ¹⁹ Now Your God will give you meat to eat, not for just one day, or two, or five, ten or twenty, ²⁰ but for a whole month—until it comes out of your nostrils and you loathe it—because you rejected the Most High God who dwells among you with your endless complaining, with your constant refrain of 'Why did we ever leave Egypt?'"

²¹ But Moses objected: "Here I am with 600,000 people on foot, and you say, 'I will give you meat to eat for a whole month'! ²² If all our flocks and herds were slaughtered, would that be enough? If all the fish in the sea were gathered, would that be enough?"

²³ Our God answered Moses, "Is Your God's arm too short? You will see whether or not what I say will come to be!"

²⁴ So Moses went and told the people what God had said. He gathered seventy elders and had them surround the Tent. ²⁵ Our God came down in a cloud and spoke to Moses. Taking some of the Spirit that was in Moses, God bestowed it on the seventy elders whom Moses had gathered there;

and as the Spirit came to rest on them, they were seized with prophesying, and did not stop.*

²⁶ Now two other elders, one named Eldad and the other Medad, were not in the gathering but had stayed behind in the camp. They had been summoned to the tent, but had not gone; yet the Spirit came to rest on them also, and they prophesied in the camp. ²⁷ When a youth came running to tell Moses, "Eldad and Medad are prophesying in the camp," ²⁸ Joshua, begot of Nun, who from youth had been Moses' aide, cried, "Moses, stop them!"

²⁹ But Moses answered, "Are you jealous for my sake? If only all of God's people were prophets! If only Our God would bestow the Spirit on them all!" ³⁰ Then Moses returned to the camp with the elders.

³¹ Now the Spirit** went out from God and drove quail in from the west, and they alighted all over the camp as far as a day's walk in any direction, in piles three feet thick. ³² All that day and night and all the next day the people went out and gathered quail. No one gathered less than about sixty bushels.

³³ The meat was still between their teeth—they had not yet exhausted their supply—when Our God's anger rose up against the people and struck them with a severe plague. ³⁴ That place was called Kibroth Ha-Taavah, or "Graveyard of Those Who Craved," because there they buried those who had craved other food.

³⁵ From Kibroth Ha-Taavah they moved on to Hazeroth.

ભ   ભ   ભ

12:1 Miriam and Aaron created a public outcry against Moses over his marriage to a Cushite woman.† ² But privately they complained, "Is it only through Moses that Our God speaks? Doesn't the Most High speak through us also?" And Our God heard this.

---

* The form of the Hebrew verb suggests ecstatic or trance-like prophecy, rather than the kind of prophecy in which one speaks in God's name. Our rendering, "and did not stop," is supported by a different vowel pointing, and is preferred to the more common translation, "but they did not continue."

** Or "a wind."

† Cush is the ancient name of Ethiopia; the controversy here may have been because of her race (*Exodus* reveals that his wife, Zipporah, was from Midian, a region near Cush) or simply because she was a Gentile. Most commentators feel that the outcry was a smokescreen for Aaron and Miriam's real motivation, jealousy, as revealed in the next verse. On the other hand, feminist scholar Judith Antonelli proposes that since Moses was "on call" to approach God at any moment, he had to stay in a state of ritual purity and thus no longer had marital relations with his wife—so Miriam was merely speaking out of sympathy for Zipporah: "She wanted to know why she could be a prophet and stay married to Caleb, and Aaron could be a prophet and stay married to Elisheva, but Moses had to leave Zipporah in order to prophesy."

³ Now Moses was the humblest person on the face of the earth. ⁴ So immediately God said to Moses and Miriam and Aaron, "Come, you three, to the Tent of Meeting." ⁵ They went, all three of them, and Our God came down in a pillar of cloud and stood at the entrance of the Tent. God called Miriam and Aaron, and they both came forward.

⁶ Our God said, "Listen, now, to my words:

> Those of you who are called to be a prophet know that
> I make myself known to you in a vision;
> I speak to you in a dream.
> ⁷ Not so with Moses,
> who is at home in my house:
> ⁸ I speak with Moses face to face,
> plainly, and not in riddles,
> and he sees the form of Your God.

"Why, then, were you not too awestruck to speak against my faithful one, my Moses?"

⁹ So angry was the Most High against them that when God departed, ¹⁰ and the cloud withdrew from the Tent, Miriam* had turned white as snow with an infectious skin disease.

When Aaron saw that Miriam had a skin disease, ¹¹ he said to Moses, "Please do not charge us with the sin that we have foolishly committed! ¹² Do not let her be like the stillborn baby that comes forth from its mother's womb with its flesh half consumed!"

¹³ Then Moses cried to God, "Please, not this! Please, heal her!"

¹⁴ But God said to Moses, "If her parents had but spit in her face, she would carry her shame for seven days. Let her be shut out of the camp for seven days, then she may return."

¹⁵ So Miriam was shut out of the camp for seven days, and the people did not set out on the march until Miriam had been returned to the camp. ¹⁶ After that the people set out from Hazeroth, and camped in the desert of Paran.

ଓ   ଓ   ଓ

---

* The reason Miriam was afflicted and not Aaron isis likely because she had been the leader of the outcry against Moses. According to medieval Jewish scholar Rashi, the text in 12:1 places Miriam's name first and uses the feminine singular form of the verb in the Hebrew to indicate that she instigated the discussion. There may also be a play on words: the name Miriam means both "bitter sea" and "rebellious." At the same time, Rashi says that the people remained encamped there an additional week out of the great respect they had for her—both for her stature as a prophet, and for her having raised Moses from infancy—refusing to move on until she was healed.

13:1 Our God said to Moses, 2 "Send out scouts to survey the land of Canaan, which I give to Israel. Send one person representing each of the ancestral tribes, but each must be a leader."

3 So, at God's command, Moses sent out scouts selected from each ancestral tribe. 4 They were: from the tribe of Reuben, Shammua begot of Zaccur; 5 from the tribe of Simeon, Shaphat begot of Hori; 6 from the tribe of Judah, Caleb begot of Jephunneh, 7 from the tribe of Issachar, Igal begot of Joseph; 9 from the tribe of Ephraim, Hoshea begot of Nun; 9 from the tribe of Benjamin, Palti begot of Raphu; 10 from the tribe of Zebulun, Gaddiel begot of Sodi; 11 from the tribe of Manasseh—that is, a tribe of Joseph—Gaddi begot of Susi; 12 from the tribe of Dan, Ammiel begot of Gemalli; 13 from the tribe of Asher, Sethur begot of Michael; 14 from the tribe of Naphtali, Nahbi begot of Vophsi; 15 and from the tribe of Gad, Geuel begot of Machi.

16 These are the names of the scouts Moses sent to explore the land. And Moses changed the name of Hoshea, begot of Nun, to Joshua.*

17 Moses sent them to explore the land of Canaan, and said, "Go through the Negev and up into the hill country. 19 See what the land is like, whether those dwelling there are strong or weak, few or many. 19 Is the land there good or bad? What kind of towns do they live in—unwalled, or fortified? 20 What about the soil—is it fertile or poor? Are there trees on it or not? Do your best, and bring back some of the fruit of this land." 21 This was in the earliest part of the season for grapes.

So they went up to scout the land from the Zin desert to as far as Rehob, near Lebo-hamath. 22 Coming by way of the Negev they came to Hebron, where Ahiman, Sheshai and Talmai, descendants of the Anakim, lived. Hebron was built seven years before Zoan, in Egypt.** 23 When they arrived at the Valley of Eshcol they cut down a cluster of grapes. It was so huge two of the scouts had to carry it between them on a pole. They also picked pomegranates and figs. 24 They called that place the Valley of Eshcol, or "Clusters," because of the cluster of grapes they cut down there.

25 After surveying the land for forty days, they returned, 26 meeting Moses and Aaron and the whole Israelite community in the desert of Paran at Kadesh. 27 There they made report to them all, showing them the fruit of the country. They told Moses, "We went into the land where you sent us. It does indeed 'flow with milk and honey,' and here is its fruit. 29 But the

---

* Hoshea means simply "deliverer," whereas Joshua means "Our God, the deliverer"—indicating by the change of name that Joshua was to rely less on his own power and more on God's.

** The Anakim were mythic giants; the Canaanites, who were tall of stature, were reputed to have descended from them. Zoan was another name for Tanis, the capital of Egypt in that era.

people who live there are fierce, with large towns that are well fortified. We saw descendants of the Anakim there. ²⁹ Amalekites live in the region of the Negev; Hittites, Jebusites and Amorites live in the highlands; and Canaanites live along the seacoast and the banks of the Jordan."

³⁰ Caleb urged the people as they stood before Moses: "Let us go up at once and take possession of it," he said, "for we are well able to do it."

³¹ But the others who had scouted with him protested, "We cannot attack these people! They're too strong for us!" ³² So out of fear, they spread false reports about the land they had explored and said, "The land that we scouted is a country that consumes its inhabitants. And all the people we saw there were huge! ³³ We saw giants there—the descendants of the Anakim, a whole *race* of giants—and we felt like mere grasshoppers, and so we must have seemed to them!"

14·¹ At this, the whole community broke out with loud cries, and even in the night the people wailed. ² The Israelites grumbled against Moses and Aaron and said to them, "If only we had died in Egypt! Or in the desert! ³ Why should Our God bring us into this land only to fall dead in battle and leave our spouses and children to become spoils of war? ⁴ The best thing we can do is return to Egypt!" And they talked among themselves of choosing a leader to take them back to Egypt.

⁵ Then Moses and Aaron threw themselves face down on the ground before the whole Israelite community gathered there. ⁶ Joshua begot of Nun, and Caleb begot of Jephunneh, members of the scouting team, tore their clothes ⁷ and told the whole Israelite community gathered there, "The land we passed through and scouted is extremely good land. ⁹ If Our God is pleased with us, we will be led into it and it will be given to us, a land flowing with milk and honey. ⁹ But do not rebel against Our God, and have no fear of the people of that land, for we will swallow them up. They are no longer protected, for God is with us! Don't be afraid of them!"

¹⁰ The whole community was thinking about stoning them, when the glory of the Most High appeared in the Tent of Meeting to all the Israelites. ¹¹ Our God said to Moses, "How long will these people show only contempt toward me? How long will they fail to believe in me, despite all the miraculous signs I give them? ¹² I will destroy them by striking them down with a plague—but I will make you into a nation stronger and greater than they."

¹³ Moses responded to God: "But then the Egyptians will hear of it. By your power you brought these people up from them. ¹⁴ The Egyptians will spread news of this plague throughout the people of this land. They already know, O God, that you dwell among your people and that you, O

God, are seen face to face; that your pillar of cloud stays over them, and that you precede them by a pillar of cloud by day and a pillar of fire by night. ¹⁵ If you do destroy your people with a single blow, the nations that hear of this will say, ¹⁶ 'This God couldn't bring these people into the land that was promised upon oath, and so instead, God destroyed them in the desert.' ¹⁷ Now is the time to show how great your power is, as you proclaimed of yourself when you declared,

> ¹⁹ 'I, your God, am slow to anger,
>   and I overflow with constant love.
> I forgive your abominations, your atrocities,
>   yet I punish your children for your iniquity,
> but only to the third and fourth generation,
>   because I dare not sweep them clean away.'

¹⁹ "You have been constant with us in your love. Once more forgive us our sins, as you have forgiven us so many times since we left Egypt."

²⁰ God replied, "I grant pardon, as you have asked. ²¹ But as surely as I live and as surely as the earth will be filled with my glory, ²² none of you who saw my glory and the signs I did in Egypt and in the desert—and still tested me these ten times— ²³ none of you will ever see the land I promised by oath to your ancestors! Not one who ever treated me with contempt will ever see it. ²⁴ But because Caleb is of a different spirit and has followed me wholeheartedly, I will bring him into the land to which he went, and his descendants will possess it.

²⁵ "Now, because the Amalekites and the Canaanites dwell in the valleys, turn back tomorrow and set out toward the desert along the route to the Sea of Reeds."

²⁶ Our God then spoke to both Moses and Aaron: ²⁷ "How long will this wicked community grumble against me? I have heard their complaints against me. ²⁸ Tell them, 'As I live—it is Your God who speaks—I will deal with you exactly according to the words I have heard from you. ²⁹ In the desert your dead bodies will fall—every one of you twenty years or older at the time of the census who grumbled against me! ³⁰ Not one of you will enter the land which I swore to make your home, except Caleb begot of Jephunneh and Joshua begot of Nun. ³¹ Your little ones, whom you predicted would become spoils of war, I will bring into the land which you rejected, and they will enjoy it. ³² But the rest of you, your bones will lie on the floor of the desert. ³³ Your children will graze* in the wilderness for forty years, paying the penalty for your faithlessness, until the last of your dead

---

* The implication is that if the people act like sheep, God will treat them like sheep.

bodies lies in the desert. ³⁴ Forty days you scouted the land, and forty years will you suffer for your crimes—one year for each day. Then you will know the extent of my hostility! ³⁵ I am Your God, and I have sworn to do this to this entire evil community that has conspired against me. Here in this desert, they will come to an end; here they will die!' "

³⁶ The scouts whom Moses sent to explore the land, who returned and who by their report turned the whole community into complaining against him, ³⁷ died of the plague in the presence of the Most High God. ³⁹ Of the scouts who went to explore that land, only Joshua begot of Nun and Caleb begot of Jephunneh survived.

³⁹ When Moses told God's words to the Israelites, they mourned bitterly. ⁴⁰ Early the next morning they set out for the high hill country and said, "Here we are. Let us go up to the place Our God promised, for we have sinned."

⁴¹ But Moses exclaimed, "Why do you continue to disobey Our God's command? This will not succeed! ⁴² Do not go up, for the Most High is not with you! Your enemies will defeat you. ⁴³ The Amalekites and Canaanites are waiting for you, and you will die by the sword, for you have ceased following Our God. God will not be there with you!"

⁴⁴ But they went on anyway, recklessly ascending the heights of the hill country, though neither the Ark of the Covenant of Our God nor Moses moved from the camp. ⁴⁵ Then the Amalekites and the Canaanites who lived in the hills descended on them and crushed them, and chased them as far as Hormah.

ભ   ભ   ભ

15·¹ Our God said to Moses, ² "Speak to the Israelites; tell them, 'After you enter the land I will give you as a homeland, ³ and you present a burnt offering from the flock or from the herd—whether a burnt offering or a sacrifice, to fulfill a vow or as a freewill offering or at your appointed festivals—to make a pleasing odor for Your God, ⁴ you must also present a grain offering of two quarts of fine flour mixed with one quart of oil. ⁵ With each lamb for the burnt offering or the sacrifice, pour out a quart of wine as a drink offering.

⁶ "With the ram, prepare a grain offering of a gallon of fine flour mixed with one-and-a-quarter quarts of oil, ⁷ and one-and-a-quarter of wine as a drink offering. Offer it as a pleasing odor to Your God.

⁹ "When you present a young bull as a burnt offering or a sacrifice, for a special vow or a fellowship offering to Your God, ⁹ bring with the bull a

grain offering of six quarts of fine flour mixed with two quarts of oil. ¹⁰ Bring also two quarts of wine as a drink offering. It will be an offering made by fire, an aroma pleasing to Your God. ¹¹ Each bull or ram, each lamb or young goat is to be prepared this way. ¹² Do this for each offering, regardless of the number offered.

¹³ "If you are native-born, you are to do these things this way when you present an offering made with fire as an aroma pleasing to Your God. ¹⁴ For all generations to come, foreigners living among you or anyone else living among you must present an offering made by fire as an aroma pleasing to Your God. They must do it exactly as you do. ¹⁵ The community is to have the same rules for you as for the foreigner living among you. This ordinance is to last for all generations to come. Both you and the foreigner will be seen as the same before Your God. ¹⁶ The same laws and regulations apply both to you and to foreigners living among you."

¹⁷ Our God said to Moses, ¹⁹ "Speak to the Israelites and tell them this: Once you enter the land to which I am taking you ¹⁹ and you eat the food of that land, present a portion as an offering to Your God. ²⁰ Prepare a cake from the first of your ground meal and present it as an offering from the threshing floor. ²¹ For all generations to come you are to make this offering to Your God from the first of your ground meal.

²² "Now, if you unintentionally fail to keep any of these commands which Your God has given to Moses— ²³ any one of Your God's commands given to you through Moses, from the day Your God gave them through all the generations to come— ²⁴ and if this is done unintentionally without the community aware of it, then the whole community must offer a young bull for a burnt offering as an aroma pleasing to Your God, along with its prescribed grain offering and drink offering, and a male goat as a sin offering. ²⁵ The priest will atone for the whole Israelite community, and they will be forgiven, for it was not intentional and the community brought to God an offering made by fire as a sin offering for their wrong. ²⁶ The whole Israelite community and the foreigners living among you will be forgiven, because the people who did wrong did so unintentionally.

²⁷ "An individual who sins unintentionally must bring a female yearling goat for a sin offering. ²⁹ The priest will atone before God for the person who erred by sinning unintentionally, and when atonement has been made, the sin will be forgiven. ²⁹ The same law will apply to all unintentional sins, whether you are native-born or a foreigner.

³⁰ "But anyone who sins defiantly, whether native-born or a foreigner, blasphemes Your God. That person must be cut off from the community. ³¹ The

blasphemer despises Our God's word and breaks God's commands. That person must be completely cut off, and must bear the guilt perpetually."

³² While the Israelites were still dwelling in the desert, a person was found gathering wood on the Sabbath. ³³ Those who discovered it went to Moses, Aaron and the whole community, ³⁴ and put the offender in custody, for no one knew what to do about it.

³⁵ Then God said to Moses, "The offender must die. The whole assembly must stone the offender to death outside the camp." ³⁶ So the assembly took the wood gatherer outside the camp, and there stoned the offender to death, as Our God had commanded Moses.

³⁷ Our God said to Moses, ³⁸ "Tell this to the Israelites, and say to them: For all generations to come, you are to make tassels on the corners of your garments, with an indigo cord on each tassel. ³⁹ You will have these tassels to look at to remind you of all of Your God's commands, that you may obey them and not prostitute yourselves by going after the lusts of your hearts and eyes. ⁴⁰ Then you will remember to obey my commands and will be consecrated to Your God. ⁴¹ I am the Most High, your God, who brought you out of Egypt to be your God: I am the Most High, your God!"

❦   ❦   ❦

16:1 Now Korah begot of Izhar, begot of Kohath, begot of Levi, along with the descendents of Reuben, Dathan and Abiram begot of Eliab, and On begot of Peleth, rebelled against Moses. ² They brought with them 250 Israelites, respected leaders and members of the council, ³ and approached Moses and Aaron as a group. They said, "You make too much of yourselves! The whole community is holy, every one of us, and Our God is in our midst. Why then do you set yourselves above God's assembly?"

⁴ When Moses heard this, he fell on his face ⁵ and said to Korah and the others, "Tomorrow morning Our God will be revealed, and will reveal who is holy, and declare that person near to God's heart. The one who is chosen is consecrated to approach the Most High.* ⁶ You, Korah, and your followers—take censers, ⁷ and tomorrow put fire and incense in them before Our God. The person God chooses is the one who is holy. It is you Levites who make too much of yourselves!"

⁸ Moses said also to Korah, "Listen, descendants of Levi! ⁹ Is it not enough

---

* A person who is "consecrated to approach" God is anointed to make atonement for the community.

for all of you that the God of Israel set you apart from the rest of the Israelite community, and that you are allowed to approach the Most High, do the work of God's Tabernacle, and stand before the community and serve them? ¹⁰ The Most High God brings you and all the other Levites the closest to God—yet now you seek the priesthood as well? ¹¹ You and your followers have banded together against Your God. Who is Aaron that you should grumble against him?"

¹² Then Moses summoned Dathan and Abiram, both begot of Eliab. But they said, "No! We will not come! ¹³ Isn't it enough that you brought us up out of a land flowing with milk and honey to kill us in the desert? Now you want to act as ruler over us? ¹⁴ But now you have brought us here, not to a land flowing with milk and honey; you have not given us our promised inheritance of fields and vineyards. Will you gouge out their eyes because they dare to protest? No, we will not come!"

¹⁵ Then Moses was enraged, and said to God, "Reject their grain offerings! I have not taken so much as a donkey from these people, nor have I wronged a single one of them!"

¹⁶ Moses said to Korah, "You and your entire community are to appear before Our God tomorrow—you and your followers, and Aaron. ¹⁷ Each of you is to take a censer and fill it with incense—250 censers in all—and present them before Our God. You and Aaron are to present censers also."

¹⁹ So each of them put fire and incense in a censer, and stood with Moses and Aaron at the entrance of the Tent of Meeting. ¹⁹ When Korah and the rest gathered at the entrance of the Tent of Meeting, the glory of the Most High appeared to the entire assembly.

²⁰ Our God then told Moses and Aaron, ²¹ "Separate yourselves from this assembly so I may annihilate them in an instant!"

²² But Moses and Aaron fell face down to the ground and pleaded, "O God, God of the spirits of all humankind, will you turn your anger on an entire assembly when only one of them sins?"

²³ Then the Most High instructed Moses, ²⁴ "Tell the assembly to move away from the tents of Korah, Dathan and Abiram."

²⁵ Moses arose and approached Dathan and Abiram, and the Israelite elders followed. ²⁶ Moses warned the assembly, "Move away from the tents of these wicked dissidents. Don't touch anything that is theirs, or you will be swept away because of their sins." ²⁷ So they moved away from the tents of Korah, Dathan and Abiram. Dathan and Abiram had come out and were standing at the entrance of their tents with their spouses, their children and their dependents.

²⁹ Moses said, "By this you will understand that it is Our God who sent

me to do all I have done; I have done nothing of my own accord. ²⁹ If these dissenters die a natural death, merely sharing the common fate of all peoples, then God did not send me. ³⁰ But if Our God works a miracle and the earth opens up its mouth and swallows them and all that is theirs, and they go alive down to Sheol, then you will know that these dissenters have rejected Our God."

³¹ No sooner had Moses said these words ³² than the ground opened up, swallowing them and their households—all of Korah's dissenters and all their possessions. ³³ They and all that was theirs went down alive into Sheol. Then the earth closed over them, and they vanished from the assembly. ³⁴ At their cries, all the Israelites around them fled, shouting, "The earth will swallow us too!" ³⁵ And fire came out from Our God and consumed the 250 dissenters who were offering the incense.

³⁶ Our God said to Moses, ³⁷ "Tell Eleazar begot of Aaron the priest to remove the censers from the flames and scatter the coals everywhere— ³⁹ for the censers have been made holy, at the price of the lives of these dissenters who sinned. You are to beat them into plates to overlay the altar. For they were presented before Your God and they became holy. Let them be a sign to all the Israelites."

³⁹ So Eleazar the priest collected the bronze censers which had been borne by those now consumed in the fire, and they were hammered out to overlay the altar— ⁴⁰ a reminder to the Israelites that no outsider who is not one of Aaron's descendants may approach to offer incense before the presence of Our God, so as not to become like Korah and his community—as Our God, through Moses, had directed Eleazar to do.

⁴¹ The next day, the whole Israelite community was grumbling against Moses and Aaron. "You have killed God's people!" they said.

⁴² As the assembly gathered in opposition, Moses and Aaron turned toward the Tent of Meeting and saw that the cloud covered it, and the glory of the Most High appeared. ⁴³ When Moses and Aaron came to the front of the Tent of Meeting, ⁴⁴ Our God said to Moses, ⁴⁵ "Stand well clear of the community, so that I may annihilate them in an instant!"

They fell face down to the ground, ⁴⁶ and then Moses said to Aaron, "Take your censer and put incense in it, along with fire from the altar, and hurry to the assembly to atone for them. God's wrath is upon us! The plague is here!" ⁴⁷ So Aaron did as Moses ordered, and ran into the midst of the assembly. The plague had started among the gathered people, but Aaron put incense into the censer and made atonement for the people. ⁴⁹ Aaron stood between the living and the dead, and the plague was held back. ⁴⁹ But those who died from the plague numbered 14,700, in addition to those who had died because of Korah. When the plague was halted, Aaron returned to Moses at the entrance to the Tent of Meeting.

CR   CR   CR

17:1 Our God said to Moses, 2 "Speak to the Israelites and get twelve staffs from them, one from the leader of each ancestral tribe. Write the name of each leader on each staff. 3 On the staff of Levi write Aaron's name, for there must be one staff for the head of each ancestral tribe. 4 Place them in the Tent of Meeting in front of the Covenant, where I meet with you. 5 The staff belonging to the person I choose will sprout, for I will rid myself of this constant grumbling against you by the Israelites."

6 So Moses told this to the Israelites, and the leaders gave him their twelve staffs, with Aaron's staff among them, 7 and Moses placed them before Our God in the Tent of the Testimony. 9 The next day Moses entered the Tent of the Covenant and found that Aaron's staff, the staff of the tribe of Levi, had not only sprouted, but had budded, blossomed, and borne ripened almonds! 9 Moses brought all the staffs out from God's presence to all the Israelites. The leaders saw what had happened, and took back their own ancestral staffs.

10 The Most High said to Moses, "Keep Aaron's staff in front of the Testimony, as a sign to the rebellious. Let them put an end to their grumbling against me, or they will die." 11 Moses did as God commanded.

12 Then the Israelites cried to Moses, "We will die! We are lost! We are all lost! 13 Anyone who ever approaches the Tabernacle of Our God will die! Will there ever be an end to all our dying?"

18:1 Our God said to Aaron, "You, your descendants, and your ancestral tribe are completely responsible for any impurity in the sanctuary. You and your descendants alone will be answerable for your priestly office. 2 All those from the ancestral tribe of Levi are to join you, assisting you and your descendants when you minister before the Tent of the Testimony, where I will meet you. 3 They are to serve you and perform all the duties pertaining to the Tent of the Testimony. But they must not approach the furnishings of the sanctuary or the altar; otherwise, both they and you will die. 4 They are to be attached to you and responsible for the maintenance of every detail of the Tent of Meeting. No others are to approach with you.

5 "You alone will be responsible for the duties of the sanctuary and the altar, to assure that the wrath will not strike the Israelites again. 6 I have chosen the Levites from among the Israelites as my gift to you, given over

utterly to the Most High. ⁷ But only you and your descendants may fulfill the duties of your priestly office that pertain to the area surrounding the altar or within the Tent. I give you the service of the priesthood as a gift. All others who approach the sanctuary will die."

⁸ Then Our God said to Aaron, "I give into your charge the responsibility for all the offerings presented to me; the holy contributions which the Israelites give to me, I give to your descendants as your share, now and for all time. ⁹ Of these most holy offerings from the fire, these are to be yours: every offering, including every gift of grain, every offering for purification or as payment for guilt that they give me, is a most holy share for you and your descendants. ¹⁰ Eat it as something most holy. Every Aaronite may eat it; it is sanctified to you.

¹¹ "This also I give you, to your daughters and sons as your regular share, forever: everything which is set aside from the gifts of all Israelites for the elevation offerings. Everyone in your household who is ceremonially clean may eat of them.¹² All the finest olive oil, the finest new wine and all the grain the Israelites present to me as the choicest part of what they give to the Most High, I give to you. ¹³ All the firstfruits of the land that they bring to Their God is yours, and every person in your household who is ceremonially clean may eat them.

¹⁴ "Everything in Israel that is dedicated to God is yours. ¹⁵ The first offspring of every womb—human or animal—that is offered to God is yours. But you must redeem every firstborn, both humans and non-kosher animals. ¹⁶ When they are one month old, you must redeem them. The redemption price is two ounces of silver, according to the standard sanctuary shekel that weighs twenty *gerahs*. ¹⁷ However, you must not redeem the firstborn of oxen, sheep or the goats. These are already holy. Sprinkle their blood on the altar and burn their fat as an offering made by fire, an odor pleasing to Your God. ¹⁸ Their meat belongs to you, just as the breast of the elevation offering and the right thigh belong to you.

¹⁹ "Everything set aside from the holy offering, the dedicated portion, I present to you and your daughters and sons as what is due to you for all time. It is an everlasting covenant of salt before God for both you and your descendants."

²⁰ Our God said to Aaron, "You will hold no property in Israel, nor will you share in the inheritance. I myself am your property and your inherit-

---

* The tithe was one-tenth of all increase, whether of money, of flocks or herds, or of the land's produce.

ance. ²¹ I give to the Levites all tithes* in Israel as their share, in return for their service in maintaining the Tent of Meeting. ²² From this day forward no Israelite may approach the Tent of Meeting. To do so is to die. ²³ Levites alone will perform the rituals pertaining to the Tent of Meeting, and they will be responsible for their own offenses against it. This is perpetual ordinance for all generations to come. ²⁴ All tithes that the Israelites set aside for God as an offering, I give to the Levites as their inheritance. This is why I said, 'They will have no inheritance among the Israelites.'"

²⁵ Our God said to Moses, ²⁶ "Speak to the Levites, and tell them, 'When you receive from the Israelites the tithe I give you as your share, you must present a tithe of that tithe as an offering to Your God. ²⁷ This is to be your contribution, like the corn from the threshing floor or new wine from the press. ²⁸ In this way you, too, will present an offering to Our God from all the tithes that you receive from the Israelites. ²⁹ Out of all the contributions you receive, you are to set aside the gifts due to Your God, and the contribution you consecrate must be taken from the choicest of them.'

³⁰ "Also tell the Levites, 'When you present the best parts, the rest will be reckoned to you as if taken from the threshing floor or the wine press. ³¹ You and your household may eat of it anywhere. It is your reimbursement for your service at the Tent of Meeting. ³² So long as you set aside the choicest part, you will suffer no recriminations for it. But you must not profane the holy gifts of the Israelites, or the consequence will be death."

ભ   ભ   ભ

19:¹ Our God said to Moses and Aaron, ² "This is a statute of the law Your God has commanded. Tell the Israelites to bring you a red heifer without defect or blemish that has never been harnessed. ³ Give it to Eleazar the priest. It is to be taken outside the camp and slaughtered outside the camp. ⁴ Eleazar is take some of its blood with his finger, and sprinkle it seven times toward the front of the Tent of Meeting. ⁵ Then, in the presence of Eleazar, the heifer is to be consumed on the fire—its hide, flesh, blood and viscera. ⁶ Then the priest must take some cedar wood, hyssop and scarlet wool and throw it into the fire with the burning heifer.

⁷ "Then the priest's clothes must be washed and the priest must bathe in water before returning to the camp; even so, the priest will remain ceremonially unclean until sunset. ⁸ The person who burned the sacrifice must also wash both clothing and body, and will remain ceremonially unclean until sunset. ⁹ Then someone who is ceremonially clean must gather up the ashes of the heifer and put them in a ceremonially clean place outside the camp.

"The ashes will be kept by the Israelite community for use in the holy water used for purification. ¹⁰ The person gathering up the ashes of the heifer must also wash both clothing and body, and will remain ceremonially unclean until sunset. This will be a perpetual ordinance both for the Israelites and for any foreigners living among you.

¹¹ "Those who touch the body of a dead person will be ceremonially unclean for seven days. ¹² They must purify themselves with the water on the third day and on the seventh day before becoming ceremonially clean. ¹³ Those who touch the body of a person who has died, and who have failed to purify themselves, have thereby defiled God's Tabernacle and must be cut off from Israel. Since the purifying water has not been sprinkled on them, they remain ceremonially unclean; their defilement remains on them.

¹⁴ "This is the law concerning people who die in their tent: those who enter the tent will be considered ceremonially unclean for seven days. ¹⁵ And every open container without a lid fastened on it will also be unclean.

¹⁶ "Anyone out in the open who touches the body of someone who was killed with a sword or who died from a natural death, or anyone who touches a human bone or a grave, will be ceremonially unclean for seven days.

¹⁷ "For such uncleanness they must put some of the ashes from the burned purification offering in a jar and pour fresh water over it. ¹⁹ They are to take some hyssop, dip it in the water, and sprinkle it on their tent and possessions, and anyone else who was there, as well someone who has touched a human bone, any dead body regardless of the cause of death, or a grave. ¹⁹ Then they are to sprinkle the unclean person on the third day and on the seventh day. On the seventh day the unclean person must wash their clothes and bathe with water, and will be considered ceremonially clean after sunset.

²⁰ "But those who become ceremonially unclean and do not purify themselves must be cut off from the community, for they have defiled the sanctuary of the Most High. The cleansing water has not been sprinkled on them, and they remain ceremonially unclean.

²¹ "This is a lasting ordinance for you: those who sprinkle the purification water must also wash their clothes. And anyone who touches the purification water will be ceremonially unclean until sunset. ²² Anything that an unclean person touches becomes ceremonially unclean, and anyone who touches it will become ceremonially unclean until sunset."

ଔ   ଔ   ଔ

20:1 The whole Israelite community entered the wilderness of Zin in the first month, and the people settled at Kadesh. It was here that Miriam died, and here that she was buried.

2 There was no water for the community, and they united against Moses and Aaron. 3 The people challenged Moses, and said, "It would have been better if we had died when our relatives died in God's presence! 4 Why have you brought the community of Our God into this desert, to die here with our livestock? 5 Why did you lead us out of Egypt, only to bring us to this wretched place that has no grain or figs or vines or pomegranates? There's not even any water to drink!"

6 Moses and Aaron left the assembly and went to the door of the Tent of Meeting, where they fell prostrate.

Then they saw the glory of the Most High, 7 and Our God said to Moses, 9 "Take your staff and assemble the community, you and Aaron, and in their presence speak to this rock, and order it to yield its water. You will make water flow for them out of the rock, and provide drink for the community and their cattle."

9 Moses took the staff from its place before God, as directed. 10 He and Aaron assembled the people in front of the rock, and Moses said, "Listen now, you rebels! Must we bring water for you out of this rock?" 11 Then, raising his hand, he struck the rock twice with the staff, and water gushed out in abundance, which the community and their livestock drank.

12 But Our God said to Moses and Aaron, "Because you did not trust me* to show forth my holiness before the Israelites, you two will not lead the community into the land I will give them!"

13 These are the waters of Meribah, "Quarrelling," where the Israelites quarreled with Our God, and where God was hallowed through them.**

ଓ   ଓ   ଓ

14 Moses sent emissaries from Kadesh to the ruler of Edom with the following message:

"This message is from your comrade Israel. You know of the hardships that have come upon us. 15 Our ancestors went down into Egypt, and we dwelled there for many years. The Egyptians mistreated us and our par-

---

* That is, because Moses struck the rock instead of simply speaking to it.
** God's promise to "show forth my holiness" in verse 12 and the affirmation here that God was "hallowed among them" underscore the name of the place, Kadesh, which means "holiness."

ents, ¹⁶ but when we cried out to our God, we were heard, and were sent an angel to lead us out of Egypt.

"Now we are here at Kadesh, a town on the border of your territory. ¹⁷ Please let us pass through. We will not trample any fields or vineyards, or drink water from your wells. We will travel along the ruler's highway, and not turn to the right or the left until we have passed through your land."

¹⁹ But Edom replied, "You will not pass through here. If you try, we will take up the sword and march out against you!"

¹⁹ The Israelites replied, "We will travel only on the main road, and if we or our livestock drink any of your water, we will pay for it. We ask you only to let us pass through on foot—nothing more."

²⁰ Again Edom answered, "You will not pass through!" and met them with a large and powerful army.

²¹ Since the Edomites would not let them pass through their territory, the Israelites turned away from that area.

²² The whole Israelite community left Kadesh and traveled to Mount Hor.* ²³ At Mount Hor, near the border of Edom, Our God said to Moses and Aaron, ²⁴ "Aaron will be gathered to his people. Your high priest will not enter the land I give the Israelites, for both of you rebelled against my command at the waters of Meribah. ²⁵ Take Aaron and his heir Eleazar, and take them up Mount Hor. ²⁶ Remove Aaron's vestments and put them on Eleazar, for Aaron is to be gathered to his people and will die there."

²⁷ Moses did as God commanded. They went up Mount Hor in the presence of the entire Israelite community. ²⁹ Moses removed Aaron's vestments and put them on Eleazar. And Aaron died there on top of the mountain. Then Moses and Eleazar came down from the mountain, ³⁰ and when the entire community learned that Aaron was dead, they mourned for the former high priest for thirty days.

21:1 When the Canaanite ruler of Arad, who lived in the Negev, learned that the Israelites were approaching Atharim, the Canaanites attacked the Israelites and took some of them captive. ² Then Israel made the following vow to Our God: "If you deliver these people into our hands, we will give their cities over to you for destruction." ³ God listened to Israel's plea and delivered the Canaanites to them. They completely destroyed them and their towns. It is for this reason that this place is called Hormah, "Destruction."

___

* Hor means "hill," so the place in effect was called "Hilly Hill."

⁴ The Israelites traveled from Mount Hor along the road to the Sea of Reeds in order to avoid Edom. But the people grew impatient along the way, ⁵ and they addressed their concerns to God and Moses: "Why have you brought us up out of Egypt to die in the desert? We have no bread! We have no water! And we are disgusted with this terrible food!"

⁶ Then Our God sent venomous snakes among the people. They fatally bit many of the people. ⁷ So the people came to Moses and said, "We sinned when we spoke against Our God and against you. Intercede for us, and ask that God remove the snakes from us."

So Moses prayed for the people. ⁹ And Our God said to Moses, "Make a snake and put it on the end of a pole.* Anyone who is bitten and looks at it will live." ⁹ So Moses made a bronze snake and put it up on a pole. Then whenever the people were bitten by a snake, they looked at the bronze snake and lived.

¹⁰ The Israelites moved on and came to Oboth, were they camped. ¹¹ Then they set out from Oboth and camped in Iye Ha-Abarim, in the desert east of Moab. ¹² Leaving that place, they moved on and camped by the Wadi Zared. ¹³ Then they moved on from there and camped alongside the Arnon, which is in the desert and extends into the Amorites' territory. The Arnon is the border between Moab and the Amorites. ¹⁴ It is for this reason that *The Book of the Wars of Our God*** says,

> "Waheb in Suphah, with its wadis,
>   the Arnon ¹⁵ and its canyon wadis—
> they stretch to the country of Ar
>   and lie along the border of Moab."

¹⁶ From there they continued on to Be'er, "The Well," which is the well where Our God said to Moses, "Call the people together and I will give them water."

¹⁷ It was there that Israel sang this song:

> "Spring up, O well!
>   Sing songs about it!
> ¹⁹   The well that our leaders dug,
>   that the nobles of our people created—
>   the nobles with their scepters and staffs."

¹⁹ Then they left the desert and traveled to Mattanah, ¹⁹ then to Nahaliel,

---

* This is the origin of the caduceus symbol used in the medical profession.

** An ancient text that has not survived.

then to Bamoth, ²⁰ and from there to the valley in Moab where the top of Pisgah overlooks the edge of the desert.

²¹ Israel sent emissaries to Sihon, ruler of Moab, with this message:
²² "Let us pass through your country. We will not trespass on your fields and vineyards. We will not drink from your wells. We will move through on the ruler's highway until we have passed through your territory."
²³ But Sihon refused to let Israel pass through Moab. The ruler mustered the entire army and marched out into the desert against Israel. When Sihon reached Jahaz, he fought with Israel. ²⁴ Israel, however, put them to the sword, and occupied their land only from the Arnon to the Jabbok—the territory of the Ammonites. Their border was fortified.
²⁵ Israel captured all the cities of the Amorites and occupied them, including Heshbon and all its surrounding villages. ²⁶ Heshbon was the city of the Amorite ruler Sihon, who had defeated the former ruler of Moab and annexed all the territory as far as the Arnon. It is for this reason that the ballad singers wrote,

²⁷ "Come to Heshbon! Let it be rebuilt!
    Let Sihon's capital be rebuilt!
²⁹ Fire blazed out of Heshbon,
    and there were flames from Sihon's city.
It devoured Ar and Moab
    and swallowed up the heights of the Arnon.
²⁹ Woe to you, Moab!
    You are no more, O people of Chemosh!
You made your sons fugitives;
    you made your daughters captives
    to Sihon, ruler of the Amorites.
³⁰ But we overthrew them;
    Heshbon is a desolation all the way to Dibon!
We destroyed them as far as Nophah,
    all the way to Medaba!"

³¹ So Israel settled in the land of Moab.

³² After Moses sent spies out to Jezer, the Israelites captured its surrounding villages and drove out the Amorites there. ³³ Then the Israelites wheeled around and advanced along the road to Bashan. Og, the ruler of Bashan, marched out to meet them with a large army in the battle at Edrei.
³⁴ The Most High God said to Moses, "Do not fear Og. I have handed the

ruler of Bashan over to you, as well as Og's army, and Og's territory. Do to Og what you did to Sihon, ruler of the Amorites, who ruled in Heshbon."

³³ So they struck Og down, together with Og's heirs and army, leaving no survivors. Then they took possession of the land.

22:1 Then the Israelites moved on to the plains of Moab and set up camp along the Jordan opposite Jericho.

℞   ℞   ℞

² Balak begot of Zippor saw all that Israel did to the Amorites. ³ And Moab was terrified by the number of them; they dreaded the Israelites.

⁴ The Moabites said to the elders of Midian, "Look, this horde will soon eat up everything around us, just as the ox eats up all the new grass in the meadow!"

So Balak begot of Zippor, then the ruler of Moab, ⁵ sent a delegation to the prophet Balaam begot of Beor, who lived in Pethor, close to the Euphrates in the land of the Ammon. They said, "A horde of people has come out of Egypt and settled next to me! ⁶ Please come and put a curse on these people, before they become too powerful for me. I hope to defeat them and drive them out of the country. For I know that those whom you bless stay blessed, and those whom you curse stay cursed."

⁷ The elders of Moab and Midian left, taking with them payment for the cursing. When they came to Balaam, they delivered Balak's message.

⁹ "Spend the night," Balaam said to them, "and I will give you the message of the Most High God in the morning." So the elders of Moab stayed the night.

⁹ That night God came to Balaam and asked, "Who are these people visiting you?"

¹⁰ Balaam told God, "Balak, begot of Zippor, ruler of Moab, sent me this message: ¹¹ 'A people that just came out of Egypt cover the face of the land. Come and put a curse on them for me! Then I might be able to engage them in battle and drive them away.'"

¹² But God said to Balaam, "Do not go with them! And you must not put a curse on them, for they are blessed!"

¹³ Balaam awoke at dawn and told Balak's delegation, "Return to your own country. The Most High God has refused to let me go with you."

¹⁴ So the Moabite delegation returned to Balak and said, "Balaam refused to come with us!"

¹⁵ Then Balak sent another delegation, more numerous—and more distinguished—than the first. ¹⁶ They came to Balaam with the message, "This is what Balak, begot of Zippor, says: ¹⁷ 'Do not let anything stand in the way of your coming to me, for I will reward you handsomely and do whatever you say. Just please come and put a curse on these people.'"

¹⁸ "Not even if Balak gave me a palace filled with silver and gold," Balaam replied. "No, no, of course I couldn't do anything great or small to disobey the command of the Most High, my God. ¹⁹ But perhaps—at least stay here the night as the others did, and I will find out what more God will tell me."

²⁰ That night God came to Balaam and said, "Because this delegation came to summon you, go with them—but do only what I tell you to do!"

²¹ The next morning Balaam got up, saddled his donkey, and left with the delegation for Moab.

²² But God was very angry because Balaam was going,* and God's angel stood in the middle of the road to bar the way. Balaam was riding on the donkey, with two assistants acccompanying him, one on either side. ²³ When the donkey saw the angel of Our God standing in the road holding a sword, she turned off the road into a field. Balaam started beating the donkey to get her to go back onto the road.

²⁴ But the angel of God stood on that narrow path, which was between two vineyards, with walls on each side. ²⁵ When the donkey saw the angel of God, she pressed close to the wall, crushing Balaam's foot against it. So Balaam beat the donkey again.

²⁶ Then the angel of God moved on ahead and stood in a place narrower yet, where there was no room to turn right or left. ²⁷ When the donkey saw the angel of God, she lay down under Balaam. This enraged Balaam, and he started beating the donkey severely.

²⁹ Then God opened the donkey's mouth, and she said to Balaam, "What have I done to you, to make you beat me three times?"

²⁹ Balaam answered the donkey, "You made a fool out of me! Why, if I had a sword in my hand, I would kill you this instant!"

---

* Why the divine wrath is kindled here, when God had just given Balaam permission to go, has been the subject of much debate. Many believe that since God had earlier said "No" unequivocally, Balaam's asking again is sinful, so God is in effect setting him up for a fall; and Balaam's waffling in verse 18 indicates his openness to being persuaded by the riches he was being offered. Certainly by the time the New Testament was written, the character of Balaam had become a false prophet and a greedy apostate, so it is likely there is more here than meets the eye; Balaam's name may mean "swallower" or "destroyer." Elaine Pagels points out the angel who stood "to bar the way" can be translated "as his [Balaam's] satan." Originally a *satan* was an adversary or obstacle of any sort, but soon came to indicate an angel sent by God to perform a specific task—often serving as a divine obstacle to turn one aside from the wrong path. Only in the Christian era did Satan become the personification of evil.

³⁰ But she said to Balaam, "Am I not your own donkey, which you have always ridden to this very day? Have I ever acted this way before?"

"No," Balaam replied.

³¹ Then the Most High God opened Balaam's eyes, and he saw the angel of God standing in the road with a drawn sword. And Balaam bowed low and prostrated himself before the angel.

³² The angel of God asked, "Why did you beat your donkey three times? I came here to bar your way, for your path is a reckless one before me! ³³ Three times your donkey saw me, and three times she turned away. In fact, if she had not turned away, I would certainly have killed you by now— though I would have spared her!"

³⁴ Balaam said to the angel of God, "I have sinned. I didn't realize it was you standing in the road to confront me. But if you so desire, I will turn back."

³⁵ God's angel said to Balaam, "Go with the delegation, but say only what I tell you." So Balaam traveled with Balak's delegation.

³⁶ When Balak learned that Balaam was coming, the ruler went out to meet him at the Ar-Moab near the Arnon, on the frontier. ³⁷ Balak said to Balaam, "Didn't I send delegations to you time and time again? Why didn't you come? Did you think I could not honor you with enough money?

³⁹ Balaam replied, "Well, now I am here. But are you presuming I have the power to say anything I like? I am only able to say what God tells me to say."

³⁹ Then Balaam went with Balak to Kiriath-huzoth. ⁴⁰ Balak sacrificed oxen and sheep, and sent portions to Balaam and to the delegation.

⁴¹ The next morning Balak took Balaam up to Bamoth-baal where he could see the full extent of Israelite camp. **23**¹ Balaam gave him these instructions: "Build me seven altars right here, and prepare for me seven bulls and seven rams." ² Balak did as instructed, and sacrificed a bull and a ram on each altar.

³ Balaam then told Balak, "Remain here near your sacrifices while I go off by myself. It might be that the Most High God will visit me. What God reveals to me, I will report to you." Then Balaam went off by himself.

⁴ And God met with Balaam. "I prepared seven altars," Balaam said, "and on each altar I had a bull and a ram offered."

⁵ Then Our God put a message in Balaam's mouth, and said, "Return to Balak and give my message to the ruler." ⁶ So Balaam returned to Balak, and found him standing next to the offerings, along with the delegation.

Then Balaam recited this oracle:

> "Balak brought me from Aram,
> the ruler of Moab from the mountains to the east,

'Come,' Balak said, 'curse the descendants of Jacob for me;
    come, denounce Israel!'
9 But how can I curse
    those whom God hasn't cursed?
How can I denounce
    those whom God hasn't denounced?
9 I see them from the craggy peaks;
    I view them from the heights.
I see a people living apart
    and not one of the nations.
10 Who can count the multitude of Jacob
    or number the masses known as Israel?
Let me die the death of the just,
    and may my leaving be as theirs!"

11 Balak said to Balaam, "What did you do to me? I have you here to curse my enemies! But you do nothing but bless them!"

12 Balaam responded, "Must I not speak what God puts in my mouth?"

13 Then Balak said to Balaam, "Come with me to another viewing area. You will see only part of them at that place. Curse that part of them for me." 14 So the ruler took Balaam to the field of Zophim on top of Pisgah, where he had built the seven altars and sacrificed a bull and a ram on each altar.

15 Balaam said to Balak, "Stay here beside your sacrifice while I meet with God."

16 God met with Balaam and put another message in his mouth and said, "Return to Balak and give that message to the ruler."

17 So Balaam went back and found the ruler standing next to the sacrifices, with the delegation. Balak asked him, "What did God say?"

19 So Balaam recited the second oracle:

"Arise, Balak, hear me;
    hear me, begot of Zippor:
19 God is not a human, able to lie,
    nor the offspring of humans,
    capable of retracting a promise.
Does God speak and then not act?
    Does God promise and not fulfill?
20 I received a command to bless;
    God blessed, and I cannot reverse it.
21 God finds no iniquity in the people of Jacob
    and finds no evil in Israel.

The Most High their God is with them,
and has acclaimed the ruler among them.
22 God, who brought them out of Egypt,
is what curved horns are to a wild ox.
23 There is no need for divination in Jacob,
no fortunetelling in Israel.
The moment God intends something,
all of Israel is told what it is!
24 A people rising like a lioness,
poised like a springing lion,
it stands until it eats its prey
and drinks the blood of its victim."

25 Then Balak said Balaam, "If you will not curse them, then at least don't bless them!"

26 Balaam answered, "Didn't I tell you I must do what God tells me?"

27 Then Balak said to Balaam, "Come, let me take you to a third place. It might please God to let you curse for me from there."

29 Balak took Balaam to the summit of Peor overlooking Jesimon. 29 Balaam told Balak to build seven altars and prepare seven bulls and seven rams. 30 Balak did as instructed and sacrificed a bull and a ram on each altar.

24 1 When Balaam realized that it pleased God to bless Israel, he did not resort to seeking God's will as at other times, but simply looked out at the desert. 2 Balaam raised his eyes and saw Israel encamped, tribe by tribe. Then the Spirit of God came upon him and 3 and he spoke this prophecy:

"The prophecy of Balaam begot of Beor,
the prophecy of one whose eyes are open,
4 the prophecy of one who hears the word of God:
I see what the Breasted One* makes me see;
God answers me, and opens my eyes.
5 How attractive are your tents, O Leah and Rachel and Jacob!
How attractive are your dwellings, O nation of Israel!
6 They are like valleys that stretch afar;
like gardens by the banks of rivers;
like aloes planted by Our God,
like cedars beside the waters!
7 Water will flow from your buckets,
and your descendants will live by running streams.

---

* Our translation for *El Shaddai*. See footnote at Genesis 17:1.

Your ruler is greater than Agag;
　　your ruler's majesty is exalted.
⁹　God brought you out of Egypt,
　　and you have the strength of a wild ox.
You devour hostile nations,
　　crushing their bones, breaking their backs.
⁹　You crouch and lie down like a lion,
　　or like a lioness—who dares to rouse them?
May those who bless you be blessed;
　　may those who curse you be cursed!"

¹⁰ Then Balak's anger burned against Balaam; beating his hands together, the ruler cried out, "I summoned you to curse my enemies! Three times you have insisted on blessing them! ¹¹ Leave! Go home! I said I would generously reward you, but the Almighty has kept you from being rewarded!"

¹² Balaam replied to Balak, "Didn't I tell the delegation you sent me, ¹³ 'Even if Balak gave me a palace filled with silver and gold, I could not disobey God's command by doing anything good or bad on my own? What God tells me to say, that is what I must say.' ¹⁴ So now I must return to my people; but allow me to give you some advice by telling you what this people will do to your people in days to come."

¹⁵ Then Balaam spoke as a prophet:

"The prophecy of Balaam, begot of Beor,
　　the prophecy of one whose eyes are open,
¹⁶　the prophecy of one who hears the word of God,
　　who has knowledge of the Most High:
I see what the Most High makes me see;
　　God answers me, and opens my eyes.
¹⁷　I see it—but not in the present,
　　I behold it—but not close at hand:
a star arises from Leah and Rachel and Jacob;
　　a scepter arises from the nation of Israel;
it will destroy the warriors of Moab, and
　　it will destroy the offspring of Sheth.
¹⁹　Edom will be conquered;
　　Seir, its enemy, will be conquered.
¹⁹　Jacob will dominate its foes
　　and destroy the fugitives of Ar."

²⁰ Then Balaam saw Amalek and prophesied:

"Amalek was the first of nations,
　　but its end will be utter destruction."

²¹ Balaam also saw the descendants of Cain and prophesied:

> "Your seemingly secure refuge,
>   your nest, seemingly secure too,
> ²² will be doomed, Cain, destroyed by fire,
>   when Asshur captures you."

²³ Balaam also prophesied,

> "Ah, who can remain alive whom God has condemned!
> ²⁴   Ships are coming from the coast of Kittim;
> Asshur and Eber they subdue,
>   only to be no more themselves."

²⁵ Then Balaam stood up and went home, and Balak went on his way as well.

ଔ   ଔ   ଔ

25:1 While the Israelites were camped at Shittim, they began to have sexual intercourse with the Moabites, ² who, in turn, invited them to the sacrifices of their gods, and the people ate and bowed before the gods. ³ In this way the Israelites yoked themselves to the Baal of Peor,* and God's anger blazed against them.

⁴ Our God said to Moses, "Take the elders of the people and impale them in the sun before me, in order that my fierce anger may turn away from Israel."

⁵ So Moses called together Israel's judges, saying to them, "Each one of you must execute those Israelites who joined in worshiping the Baal of Peor."

⁶ Then a male Israelite brought into his extended family a female Midianite, in open defiance of Moses and the whole community as they wept at the entrance of the Tent of Meeting. ⁷ When Phinehas, begot of Eleazar, begot of Aaron the priest, saw this, he stood up and left the assembly, and taking a spear ⁹ entered the nuptial tent and impaled the lovers—through the Israelite and into the Midianite. Then the plague attacking the Israelites stopped; ⁹ but by this time 24,000 had already died in the plague.

¹⁰ The Most High said to Moses, ¹¹ "Phinehas, begot of Eleazar, begot of the priest Aaron, has turned away my anger from the Israelites. For Phinehas was as zealous as I am for my honor among all of you, and therefore I didn't exterminate the Israelites in my fierce anger. ¹² Therefore, tell

---

*   Baal, the Canaanite storm and fertility god, was worshiped throughout the Middle East in numerous areas and communities, and was usually known as "the Baal" of that region.

Phinehas that I am making a covenant of peace with him and his family. 13 It will be for Phinehas and his descendants a covenant of perpetual priesthood, for his zeal for God and atonement for the Israelites."

14 The name of the Israelite who was killed with the Midianite woman was Zimri, begot of Salu, the leader of a Simeonite clan. 15 The Midianite woman's name was Cozbi, daughter of Zur, head of a clan, an ancestral house of Midian.

16 The Most High said to Moses, 17 "Consider the Midianites as enemies and kill them, 19 for they considered you enemies when they deceived you at Peor in the affair of Cozbi and Zimri, whose death caused the plague to end."

After the plague, Our God spoke to Moses and Eleazar begot of Aaron: 2 "Take a census of all of the Israelites, family by family, recording all able-bodied warriors, twenty years or older." 3 So on the plains of Moab, by the Jordan across from Jericho, Moses, together with Eleazar, Aaron's heir, met with the people and said, 4 "Take a census of all the able-bodied warriors, twenty years or older, as Our God commanded Moses."

These were the Israelites who came up out of Egypt:

5 The descendants of Reuben, firstborn of Israel, clan by clan: through Hanoch, the Hanochite clan; through Pallu, the Palluite clan; 6 through Hezron, the Hezronite clan; and through Carmi, the Carmite clan. 7 These were the clans of Reuben; those counted were 43,730.

9 The heir of Pallu was Eliab, 9 and the heirs of Eliab were Nemuel, Dathan and Abiram. These were the same Dathan and Abiram of the community who rebelled against Moses and Aaron and were among Korah's followers when they rebelled against Our God. 10 The earth opened up and swallowed them along with Korah, whose followers died when the fire devoured the 250 people. And they served as a sign of warning. 11 However, the line of Korah did not die out.

12 The descendants of Simeon, clan by clan: through Nemuel, the Nemuelite clan; through Jamin, the Jaminite clan; through Jakin, the Jakinite clan; 13 through Zerah, the Zerahite clan; and through Shaul, the Shaulite clan. 14 These were the clans of Simeon; those counted were 22,200.

15 The descendants of Gad, clan by clan: through Zephon, the Zephonite clan; through Haggi, the Haggite clan; through Shuni, the Shunite clan; 16 through Ozni, the Oznite clan; through Eri, the Erite clan; 17 through Arod,

the Arodite clan; and through Areli, the Arelite clan. ¹⁹ These were the clans of Gad; those counted were 40,500.

¹⁹ Er and Onan were heirs of Judah, but they died in Canaan. ²⁰ The descendants of Judah, clan by clan: through Shelah, the Shelanite clan; through Perez, the Perezite clan; and through Zerah, the Zerahite clan. ²¹ The descendants of Perez were: through Hezron, the Hezronite clan; and through Hamul, the Hamulite clan. ²² These were the clans of Judah; those counted were 76,500.

²³ The descendants of Issachar, clan by clan: through Tola, the Tolaite clan; through Puvah, the Puvite clan; ²⁴ through Jashub, the Jashubite clan; and through Shimron, the Shimronite clan. ²⁵ These were the clans of Issachar; those counted were 64,300.

²⁶ The descendants of Zebulun, clan by clan: through Zered, the Zeredite clan; through Elon, the Elonite clan; and through Jahleel, the Jahleelite clan. ²⁷ These were the clans of Zebulun, those counted were 60,500.

²⁹ The descendants of Joseph, clan by clan, through Manasseh and Ephraim:

²⁹ The descendants of Manasseh: through Machir, the Machirite clan; Gilead was begot of Machir; and through Gilead, the Gileadite clan. ³⁰ The descendants of Gilead: through Iezer, the Iezerite clan; through Helek, the Helekite clan; ³¹ through Asriel, the Asrielite clan; through Shechem, the Shechemite clan; ³² through Shemida, the Shemidaite clan; and through Hepher, the Hepherite clan. ³³ Zelophehad begot of Hepher had no sons; the names of his five daughters were Mahlah, Noah, Hoglah, Milcah and Tirzah. ³⁴ These were the clans of Manasseh; those counted were 52,700.

³⁵ The descendants of Ephraim, clan by clan: through Shuthelah, the Shuthelahite clan; through Becher, the Becherite clan; and through Tahan, the Tahanite clan. ³⁶ These were the descendants of Shuthelah: through Eran, the Eranite clan. ³⁷ These were the clans of Ephraim; those counted were 32,500.

These were the descendants of Joseph, by clans.

³⁹ The descendants of Benjamin, clan by clan: through Bela, the Belaite clan; through Ashbel, the Ashbelite clan; through Ahiram, the Ahiramite clan; ³⁹ through Sheshupham, the Sheshuphamite clan; and through Hupham, the Huphamite clan. ⁴⁰ The descendants of Bela through Ard and Naaman, clan by clan: through Ard, the Ardite clan; and through Naaman, the Naamite clan. ⁴¹ These were the clans of Benjamin; those counted were 45,600.

⁴² The descendants of Dan, clan by clan: through Shuham, the Shuhamite clan. These were the clans of Dan. ⁴³ All of them were Shuhamite clans; those counted were 64,400.

⁴⁴ The descendants of Asher, clan by clan: through Imnah, the Imnite clan; through Ishvi, the Ishvite clan; and through Beriah, the Beriite clan. ⁴⁵ For the descendants of Beriah: through Heber, the Heberite clan; and through Malchiel, the Malchielite clan. ⁴⁶ Asher's daughter's name was Serah. ⁴⁷ These were the clans of Asher; those counted were 53,400.

⁴⁹ The descendants of Naphtali, clan by clan, were: through Jahzeel, the Jahzeelite clan; through Guni, the Gunite clan; ⁴⁹ through Jezer, the Jezerite clan; and through Shillem, the Shillemite clan. ⁵⁰ These were the clans of Naphtali; those counted were 45,400.

⁵¹ The total number of the able-bodied in Israel was 601,730.

⁵² Our God said to Moses, ⁵³ "The land is to be allotted to them as an inheritance determined by the number of names. ⁵⁴ Give a larger inheritance to a larger group, and give a smaller inheritance to a smaller group. Each group is to receive its share of the inheritance based on the size of its group. ⁵⁵ You must distribute the land by lot. What each group inherits depends on the size of the group. ⁵⁶ Each inheritance must be distributed by lot among the larger and smaller groups."

⁵⁷ The descendants of Levi, clan by clan: through Gershon, the Gershonite clan; through Kohath, the Kohathite clan; and through Merari, the Merarite clan. ⁵⁹ These also were Levite clans: the Libnite clan, the Hebronite clan, the Mahlite clan, the Mushite clan, and the Korahite clan.

Kohath was the ancestor of Amram; ⁵⁹ the name of Amram's spouse was Jochebed, a descendant of Levi, who was born to the Levites in Egypt. To Amram she bore Aaron, Moses, and Miriam. ⁶⁰ Aaron begot Nadab and Abihu, Eleazar and Ithamar. ⁶¹ But Nadab and Abihu died when they made an offering before Our God with unauthorized fire.

⁶² All the able-bodied Levites one month or older came to 23,000. They were not included in the count of the other Israelites because they did not share in the inheritance.

⁶³ These were the lists prepared by Moses and Eleazar the priest when they counted the Israelites on the plains of Moab by the Jordan across from Jericho. ⁶⁴ Not one of them had been present when Moses and the priest Aaron had counted the Israelites when they were in the Desert of Sinai. ⁶⁵ For Our God told those Israelites that they would die in the desert, and not one of them remained except Caleb begot of Jephunneh, and Joshua begot of Nun.

ᛩ   ᛩ   ᛩ

27:1 A notice was presented by the daughters of Zelophehad begot of

Hepher, begot of Gilead, begot of Machir, begot of Manasseh, begot of Joseph. The daughters—Mahlah, Noah, Hoglah, Milcah and Tirzah— ² came to the entrance of the Tent of Meeting, stood before Moses, Eleazar, the elders, and the whole assembly, ³ and stated their case: "Our father died in the desert. But he was not one of those who joined up with Korah to conspire against Our God and were killed in the effort. Zelophehad died for his own sins, and left no sons. ⁴ But why should the name 'Zelophehad' disappear from the clan for lack of a son? Give us property equal to the share of our uncles!"

⁵ Moses brought the case to Our God, ⁶ who said to Moses, "What the daughters of Zelophehad claim is right and just. ⁷ You must allow them to inherit the share of property allotted to their uncles, and turn Zelophehad's inheritance over to them.

⁹ "Say to the Israelites, 'If a person dies without a son, give the inheritance to the daughter. ⁹ If there is no daughter, give the inheritance to the other heirs. ¹⁰ If there are no heirs, give the inheritance to the uncles. ¹¹ If there are no uncles, give the inheritance to the nearest relative in the clan, who will take possession of it.' " This is to be a legal statute for the Israelites, as Our God commanded Moses.

¹² Then God said to Moses, "Go up this mountain in the Abarim range, and view the land I have given to the Israelites. ¹³ After you view it, you will be gathered to your ancestors, as Aaron was, ¹⁴ because you rebelled against my command in the Desert of Zin, where the community quarreled, and you did not honor me as holy before them at the waters." These were the waters of Meribah Kadesh in the Desert of Zin.

¹⁵ Moses replied to the Most High, ¹⁶ "May you, the God of the spirits of all living creatures, appoint a person to lead the community— ¹⁷ one who will go out and come in before them, one who will lead them out and bring them in. Otherwise, your people will be like sheep without a shepherd."

¹⁹ So God said to Moses, "Lay your hands on Joshua, begot of Nun, on whom the Spirit rests. ¹⁹ Have Joshua stand before Eleazar the priest and the whole community, to commission him in their presence. ²⁰ Confer your authority on Joshua so that the Israelites will obey. ²¹ Joshua is to stand before Eleazar the priest, who will consult with God through the Urim,* and Eleazar will give instructions to Joshua and the people. At Eleazar's word, Joshua and the entire community of the Israelites will go out and come in."

²² Moses did as God commanded by having Joshua stand before Eleazar

---

* Priestly tools of divination, probably small stones.

and the whole assembly. ²³ Then Eleazar commissioned Joshua with the laying on of hands, as God had commanded Moses.

ભ   ભ   ભ

28:1 God said to Moses, ² "Command the Israelites and tell them this: Be sure to bring me my offerings—the food you offer to me by fire, my pleasing odor—at the appointed times.' ³ Tell them, 'This is the burnt offering you are to present to Your God:

"Every day, offer two yearling lambs without defect, as a regular burnt offering. ⁴ Prepare one lamb in the morning and the other at twilight, ⁵ as well as a grain offering of two quarts of fine flour mixed with a quart of oil from pressed olives. ⁶ This is the regular burnt offering established at Mount Sinai as a pleasing odor, an offering made to Your God by fire. ⁷ Its drink offering will be quart of wine for each lamb. Pour out the drink offering to Your God in the sanctuary. ⁸ Present the second lamb at twilight, along with the grain offering and the drink offering presented in the morning. This is an offering made by fire, an odor pleasing to Your God.

⁹ "On the Sabbath day, present an offering of two yearling lambs without blemish; a grain offering of a gallon of fine flour mixed with oil; and a drink offering: ¹⁰ this is to be the burnt offering for every Sabbath, in addition to the regular burnt offering and its drink offering.

¹¹ "At each New Moon you will offer a burnt offering to Your God: two young bulls, one ram, and seven yearling lambs without blemish; ¹² a drink offering, and a grain offering of six quarts of fine flour mixed with oil, for each bull; a gallon of fine flour mixed with oil as a grain offering for the one ram; ¹³ and two quarts of fine flour mixed with oil as a grain offering for each lamb—a burnt offering of pleasing odor, an offering by fire to Your God. ¹⁴ Offer a drink offering of two quarts of wine for each bull, three pints of wine for each ram, and one quart of wine for each lamb. This is the monthly burnt offering to be made at each New Moon during the year. ¹⁵ In addition to the regular burnt offering with its drink offering, one male goat is to be offered to Your God as a sin offering.

¹⁶ "In the first month, on the fourteenth day after the New Moon, the Passover of Your God is to be celebrated. ¹⁷ Then on the fifteenth day of this month there is to be a pilgrimage festival, and for next seven days, only unleavened bread is to be eaten. ¹⁸ On the first day of the festival there is to be a holy gathering, and no one is to do heavy labor on that day. ¹⁹ Present

to God an offering made by fire, a burnt offering of two young bulls, one ram, and seven yearling lambs, all without defect. ²⁰ Present grain offerings of fine flour mixed with oil—six quarts for each bull, one gallon for the ram; ²¹ and two quarts for each of the seven lambs. ²² Include one hairy goat as a sin offering to atone for you. ²³ Prepare these in addition to the regular morning burnt offerings. ²⁴ In this way prepare the food for the offering made by fire every day for seven days as an odor pleasing to Your God. It is to be prepared in addition to the regular burnt offering and its drink offering. ²⁵ On the seventh day hold a sacred assembly and do no heavy labor.

²⁶ "On Firstfruits Day, when you present to Your God an offering of new grain during the Feast of Weeks, hold a sacred assembly and do no heavy labor. ²⁷ Present a burnt offering, a pleasing odor to the Most High: two young bulls, one ram, and seven yearling lambs. ²⁸ Present grain offerings of fine flour mixed with oil—six quarts for each bull, one gallon for the ram, ²⁹ and two quarts for each of the seven lambs. ³⁰ Include one hairy goat as a sin offering to atone for you. ³¹ Do this in addition to the regular burnt offerings with their grain offerings. Make sure that all animals are without defect, and present drink offerings with them as well.

29:¹ "On the first day of the seventh month, hold a sacred assembly and do no heavy labor. It is the day to sound the trumpets!* Prepare a burnt offering of one young bull, one ram, and seven yearling lambs, all without defect. ³ Present grain offerings of fine flour mixed with oil—six quarts for each bull, one gallon for the ram, ⁴ and two quarts for each of the seven lambs. ⁵ Include one hairy goat as a sin offering to atone for you. ⁶ Do this in addition to the monthly and daily burnt offerings with their grain offerings and drink offerings according to the regulation—a pleasing odor, an offering by fire to Your God.

⁷ "On the tenth day of the seventh month, hold a sacred assembly. You must deny yourselves and do no work whatsoever. ⁹ Prepare a burnt offering to Your God, a pleasing odor: one young bull, one ram, and seven yearling lambs, all without defect. ⁹ Present grain offerings of fine flour mixed with oil—six quarts for each bull, one gallon for the ram, ¹⁰ and two quarts for each of the seven lambs. ¹¹ Include one hairy goat as a sin offer-

---

* Originally called the Feast of Trumpets, this is now known as Rosh Hashanah, the civil new year in the fall, which is still celebrated in synagogues with the blowing of the shofar. It is the first of the "Days of Awe," which culminate with Yom Kippur, the Day of Atonement, ten days later.

ing, in addition to the sin offering for atonement and the regular burnt offering with its grain offering and its drink offering.

¹² "On the fifteenth day of the seventh month,** hold a sacred assembly and do no heavy labor. You are to celebrate a pilgrimage festival to Your God for seven days. ¹³ Present an offering made by fire as an aroma pleasing to God, a burnt offering of thirteen young bulls, two rams, and fourteen yearling lambs,† all without defect. ¹⁴ Present grain offerings of fine flour mixed with oil—six quarts for each of the thirteen bulls, one gallon for each of the rams, ¹⁵ and two quarts for each of the fourteen lambs. ¹⁶ Include one hairy goat as a sin offering, in addition to the regular burnt offering with its grain offering and its drink offering.

¹⁷ "On the second day, prepare twelve young bulls, two rams and fourteen yearling lambs, all without defect. ¹⁹ With the bulls, rams and lambs, prepare their grain offerings and drink offerings according to the number specified. ¹⁹ Include one hairy goat as a sin offering, in addition to the regular burnt offering with its grain offering and its drink offering.

²⁰ "On the third day, prepare eleven young bulls, two rams and fourteen yearling lambs, all without defect. ²¹ With the bulls, rams and lambs, prepare their grain offerings and drink offerings according to the number specified. ²² Include one hairy goat as a sin offering, in addition to the regular burnt offering with its grain offering and its drink offering.

²³ "On the fourth day, prepare ten young bulls, two rams and fourteen yearling lambs, all without defect. ²⁴ With the bulls, rams and lambs, prepare their grain offerings and drink offerings according to the number specified. ²⁵ Include one hairy goat as a sin offering, in addition to the regular burnt offering with its grain offering and its drink offering.

²⁶ "On the fifth day, prepare nine young bulls, two rams and fourteen yearling lambs, all without defect. ²⁷ With the bulls, rams and lambs, prepare their grain offerings and drink offerings according to the number specified. ²⁹ Include one male goat as a sin offering, in addition to the regular burnt offering with its grain offering and its drink offering

²⁹ "On the sixth day, prepare eight young bulls, two rams and fourteen yearling lambs, all without defect. ³⁰ With the bulls, rams and lambs, prepare their grain offerings and drink offerings according to the number

---

* The Feast of Tabernacles.
** Note that double the number of rams and lambs are required for this sacrifice, indicating the solemnity of the festival. Thirteen bulls are required, coinciding with the number of New Moons in a year, again underscoring the importance of the lunar calendar.

specified. ³¹ Include one hairy goat as a sin offering, in addition to the regular burnt offering with its grain offering and its drink offering.

³² "On the seventh day, prepare seven young bulls, two rams and fourteen yearling lambs, all without defect. ³³ With the bulls, rams and lambs, prepare their grain offerings and drink offerings according to the number specified. ³⁴ Include one hairy goat as a sin offering, in addition to the regular burnt offering with its grain offering and its drink offering.

³⁵ "On the eighth day, restrain yourselves and do no heavy labor. ³⁶ Present a burnt offering, an offering by fire, as an odor pleasing to God, of one bull, one ram, and seven yearling lambs, all without defect. ³⁷ With the bull, the ram and the lambs, prepare the required grain offerings and drink offerings according to the number specified. ³⁹ Include one hairy goat as a sin offering, in addition to the regular burnt offering with its grain offering and its drink offering.

³⁹ "These are the offerings you are to present to Your God at your scheduled feasts: your burnt offerings, grain offerings, drink offerings, and peace offerings.'"

30·¹ Moses passed all these instructions on to the Israelites just as the Most High had commanded.

CR   CR   CR

² Moses spoke to the clan leaders of Israel and said, "This is what Our God commands: ³ When you make a vow to Your God or take an oath to bind yourself to an obligation, you must not break it, but do every word you vowed. ⁴ When a child, still living at home, makes a vow to God or takes a binding obligation, ⁵ and does so with the parents' knowledge and they do not forbid it, the vow stands. ⁶ But if the parents hear the vow and forbid the child, the vow does not stand. God will release the child from the vow because the parents are against it.

⁷ "If a young person gets married after having taken a vow or made some rash promise, ⁹ and the spouse or partner hears and is silent, the vow will be upheld and the young couple will be bound by the obligation. ⁹ But if the spouse or partner hears about it and protests, the spouse annuls the young person's vow and nullifies the rash promise, and God will release the couple from any obligation.

¹⁰ "Those who are widowed or divorced can freely bind themselves by vows.

¹¹ "If one member of a married couple has made a vow or bound themselves to an oath, ¹² and the spouse has heard and stood silent without pro-

test, the vows of the one will obligate and bind the couple jointly. ¹³ But if the spouse annulled the vow the moment it was spoken, everything that was said as a binding vow will not be upheld: the spouse has annulled it, and God will release the couple from any obligation. ¹⁴ Any vow, or any oath that might obligate a couple jointly, the spouse has the power to uphold or annul it. ¹⁵ If, however, the spouse says nothing about the vow for an entire day, all vows and binding obligations will be considered upheld, since the spouse was silent on the issue. ¹⁶ If the spouse attempts to annul the vow later, the obligation will stand."

¹⁷ These are the regulations Our God gave to Moses concerning married couples, and between parents and a child still living at home.

℞   ℞   ℞

31:1 Our God said to Moses, ² "Exact vengeance for the Israelites against the Midianites. After that you will be gathered to your ancestors."

³ So Moses said to the people, "Let the able-bodied among you come together to take up arms against the Midianites and carry out God's vengeance on them. ⁴ Put in the field 12,000 troops, 1,000 from each tribe of Israel." ⁵ So 1,000 troops were called up from each tribe of Israel, 12,000 in all, ready for active service. ⁶ Moses sent them into battle, 1,000 from each tribe, along with Phinehas, begot of Eleazar the priest, who carried into the field certain items from the sanctuary as well as the trumpets used to sound the battle cry.

⁷ They made war on the Midianites as God had commanded Moses, and they cut down every single male. ⁹ Over and above those dispatched in battle, they killed the five rulers of Midian—Evi, Redem, Zur, Hur, and Reba; they also dispatched Balaam begot of Beor. ⁹ The Israelites captured all the Midianite women and children, their herds, flocks and property. ¹⁰ They set fire to their towns, settlements, and camps. ¹¹ They gathered together the plunder, the captives, and the animals, ¹² and brought all of them to Moses and Eleazar the priest and the Israelite assembly, at their camp on the plains of Moab by the Jordan across from Jericho.

¹³ Moses and Eleazar the priest and the leaders of Israel met the troops outside the camp. ¹⁴ Moses was furious with the officers of the army, the troop and unit commanders who returned from the engagement. ¹⁵ "Why did you spare all the women?" he demanded. ¹⁶ "Recall, it was they who, after Balaam departed, set about seducing the Israelites into disloyalty to God in that business at Peor, culminating in a plague on God's people! ¹⁷ So now go and kill all the male children, and every woman who slept with a man, ¹⁹ but spare every woman who has not had intercourse.

¹⁹ "As for you, all of you who took a life or touched a dead body must remain outside the camp for seven days. Purify yourself and your captives on the third day and the seventh day, ²⁰ plus every piece of clothing, every leather article, everything woven with goat's hair, and everything made of wood."

²¹ Eleazar the priest told the soldiers, "This is the statute of the law which God ordained through Moses. ²² Anything that can withstand fire—gold, silver, copper, iron, tin, or lead— ²³ you must pass through fire to make it clean; you must also purify it with ritually pure water. And if it cannot withstand fire, it is to be purified with ritually pure water. ²⁴ You must wash your clothes on the seventh day to be made clean. Then you can enter the camp."

²⁵ The Most High said to Moses, ²⁶ "You and Eleazar the priest and the family heads of the community must count all the captured people* and animals. ²⁷ Divide the spoils between the combatants of the campaign and the rest of the community. ²⁸ As Your God's portion, set aside from the share of the troops who took part in the campaign one out of every 500—captives, sheep, donkeys or cattle— ²⁹ and turn them over to Eleazar the priest. ³⁰ Out of the Israelites' share, set aside one out of every fifty—captives, sheep, donkeys or cattle—and turn them over to the Levites who are in charge of Your God's tabernacle." ³¹ Moses and Eleazar the priest did as God commanded.

³² The totals of the plunder taken by the combatants were 675,000 sheep, ³³ 72,000 cattle, ³⁴ 61,000 donkeys, and ³⁵ 32,000 women who had not had intercourse with men. ³⁶ The half share of the combatants was 337,500 sheep, ³⁷ with a levy for God of 675; ³⁸ 36,000 cattle, plus a levy for God of 72; ³⁹ 30,500 donkeys, with a levy of 61; ⁴⁰ 16,000 people; with a levy of 32. ⁴¹ Moses gave Eleazar the priest God's levy, as the Most High had commanded him.

⁴² The community's share—the half share that Moses separated from the combatant's share—was ⁴³ 337,500 sheep, ⁴⁴ 36,000 cattle, ⁴⁵ 30,500 donkeys, ⁴⁶ and 16,000 people. ⁴⁷ Out of the people's share Moses selected one out of every fifty people and animals, as God had commanded Moses, and gave them to the Levites, who were responsible for the care of God's Tabernacle.

⁴⁹ Then the officers of the units of the army—the troop and unit commanders—went to Moses ⁴⁹ and said, "We have checked the roll of the combatants under our command, and every single one is accounted for. ⁵⁰ So we brought you as an offering to Our God the gold articles each of us ac-

---

* While the Hebrew here and in verses 40, 46 and 47 refers to captured "people," verse 19 reveals that the only people left alive were young virginal girls, and were treated as property, the spoils of war.

quired—armlets, bracelets, signet rings, earrings and necklaces—to atone for ourselves before Our God."

⁵¹ Moses and Eleazar the priest accepted the gold articles from the officers. ⁵² All the gold from the troop and unit commanders that Moses and Eleazar presented as a gift to Our God weighed 420 pounds, ⁵³ since every combatant had collected plunder. Moses and Eleazar the priest received the gold from the troop and unit commanders, and brought it to the Tent of Meeting as a memorial for the Israelites before the Most High God.

ଔ   ଔ   ଔ

32·¹ The Reubenites and Gadites, who had very large herds and flocks, noticed that the lands of Jazer and Gilead were more suitable for grazing than for cropland. ² So they came to Moses and Eleazar the priest and to the clan leaders of the community and said, ³ "Ataroth, Dibon, Jazer, Nimrah, Heshbon, Elealeh, Sebam, Nebo and Beon—⁴ the region God subdued before the advance of God's people—are suitable for livestock, and we have livestock. ⁵ If we deserve your friendship, let us have this land. Do not force us to cross the Jordan."

⁶ Moses exploded at the Gadites and the Reubenites. "Will you have other Israelites go to war for you while you sit here? ⁷ Why would you discourage the rest of the Israelites from entering the land Our God has given them? ⁹ Remember what your ancestors did when I sent them from Kadesh Barnea to look over the land. ⁹ After they went up to the Valley of Eshcol and viewed the land, they discouraged us Israelites from entering the land that God promised us. ¹⁰ Our God swore this oath in anger that day: ¹¹ 'Because you have not followed me wholeheartedly, not one of you twenty years or older who came up out of Egypt will see the land I promised by oath to Sarah and Abraham, Rebecca and Isaac, and Leah and Rachel and Jacob— ¹² none except Caleb begot of Jephunneh the Kenizzite and Joshua begot of Nun, for they followed me with their whole heart and soul.' ¹³ Our God's anger burned against Israel so much that God forced us to wander in the desert forty years, until that whole generation who did what was wrong in God's eyes died out.

¹⁴ "Now here you are, a brood of sinners, standing here in the place of your ancestors and making Your God even more angry with Israel! ¹⁵ If you turn your backs on God once more, God will abandon us in the desert, and you will be responsible for our destruction!"

¹⁶ Then they came to Moses and said, "We would like to build pens for our livestock here and towns for our families. ¹⁷ For we are ready to mobilize ourselves until we have brought the rest of the Israelites to their inheritance.

In the meantime, our dependents can live in the fortified cities, safe from the locals. ¹⁹ We will not return to our homes until all Israelites have received their inheritance. ¹⁹ We will not take part in their inheritance across the Jordan, for our inheritance has come to us on the east side of the Jordan."

²⁰ Moses said to them, "If you will do this—if you take up arms and go before Our God for battle, ²¹ and if you cross the Jordan in the presence of the Most High and stay with us until our enemies are driven out before us— ²² then when the land is subdued before Our God, you may return and be free from your obligation to God and to Israel. And this land will be your possession before God. ²³ On the other hand, if you fail to do this, you will be sinning against God Almighty. Be certain that your sin will find you out! ²⁴ So build towns for your families, and pens for your livestock, and carry out what you promised."

²⁵ The Gadites and the Reubenites said to Moses, "We, your subjects, will do as you command. ²⁶ Our families, our flocks and our herds will remain here in Gilead. ²⁷ But your subjects, all armed for battle, will cross the Jordan to fight for Our God, just as you say."

²⁹ Then Moses gave instructions to Eleazar the priest and Joshua begot of Nun, and to the clan leaders of the Israelites, and said, ²⁹ "If the Gadites and the Reubenites, all armed for battle, cross the Jordan with you before Our God, then once the land is subdued before you, give them the land of Gilead as their possession. ³⁰ But if they do not cross over armed, they must accept land with you in Canaan."

³¹ The Gadites and the Reubenites responded, "What God has spoken, we will do. ³² We will cross over before Our God into Canaan armed, but the land we inherit will be on this side of the Jordan."

³³ Then Moses gave to the Gadites, the Reubenites, and the half-tribe of Manasseh begot of Joseph, the realm of Sihon ruler of the Amorites and the realm of Og ruler of Bashan—the whole land with its cities and the surrounding territory. ³⁴ The Gadites and the Reubenites built up Dibon, Ataroth, Aroer, ³⁵ Atroth-Shophan, Jazer, Jogbehah, ³⁶ Beth-Nimrah and Beth-Haran as fortified cities, and they built pens for their flocks. ³⁷ And the Reubenites rebuilt Heshbon, Elealeh and Kiriathaim, ³⁹ as well as Nebo and Baal-Meon, which they renamed, and Sibmah. They also renamed the cities they rebuilt.

³⁹ The descendants of Makir begot of Manasseh went to Gilead, captured it, and drove out the Amorites who had dwelled there. ⁴⁰ So Moses gave Gilead to the Machirites, the descendants of Manasseh, and they settled there. ⁴¹ Jair, a descendant of Manasseh, captured their settlements and renamed them Fortified Villages of Jair. ⁴² And Nobah cap-

tured Kenath and its surrounding settlements and named it Nobah, after himself.

CR   CR   CR

33:1 These are the stages by which the tribes of Israel left Egypt under the guidance of Moses and Aaron. 2 Moses listed their starting points as God had commanded, stage by stage.

3 The Israelites left Rameses on the fifteenth day of the first month, the day after Passover. They defiantly left in full view of the Egyptians, 4 as the Egyptians buried all their firstborn struck down by God to render a judgment on their gods.

5 The Israelites left Rameses and camped at Succoth.

6 They left Succoth and set up camp at Etham on the edge of the desert.

7 They left Etham, turned back to Pi-Hahiroth, to the east of Baal-Zephon, and set up camp near Migdol.

9 They left Pi-Hariroth and passed through the Sea into the desert. They marched for three days through the desert of Etham and set up camp at Marah.

9 They left Marah and came to Elim, where there were twelve springs and seventy palm trees, and set up camp there.

10 They left Elim and set up camp by the Sea of Reeds.

11 They left the Sea of Reeds and set up camp in the Desert of Sin.

12 They left the Desert of Sin and set up camp at Dophkah.

13 They left Dophkah and set up camp at Alush.

14 They left Alush and set up camp at Rephidim.

15 They left Rephidim and set up camp in the Desert of Sinai.

16 They left the Desert of Sinai and set up camp at Kibroth-Hattaavah.

17 They left Kibroth-Hattaavah and set up camp at Hazaroth.

19 They left Hazaroth and set up camp at Rithmah.

19 They left Rithmah and set up camp at Rimmon-Perez.

20 They left Rimmon-Perez and set up camp at Libnah.

21 They left Libnah and set up camp at Rissah.

22 They left Rissah and set up camp at Kehelathah.

23 They left Kehelathah and set up camp at Mount Shepher.

24 They left Mount Shepher and set up camp at Haradah.

25 They left Haradah and set up camp at Makheloth.

26 They left Makheloth and set up camp at Tahath.

27 They left Tahath and set up camp at Terah.

²⁹ They left Terah and set up camp at Mithkah.

²⁹ They left Mithkah and set up camp at Hashmonah.

³⁰ They left Hashmonah and set up camp at Moseroth.

³¹ They left Moseroth and set up camp at Bene-Jaakan.

³² They left Bene-Jaakan and set up camp at Hor-Haggidgad.

³³ They left Hor-Haggidgad and set up camp at Jotbathah.

³⁴ They left Jotbathah and set up camp at Abronah.

³⁵ They left Abronah and set up camp at Ezion-Geber.

³⁶ They left Ezion-Geber and set up camp in the Desert of Zin, that is, Kadesh.

³⁷ They left Kadesh and set up camp at Mount Hor on the border of Edom.

³⁹ Aaron the priest went up Mount Hor and was gathered to his ancestors on the first day of the fifth month in the fortieth year after the Israelites came up out of Egypt. ³⁹ Aaron was 123 years old.

⁴⁰ The Canaanite ruler Arad, who dwelled in the Negev, which was in Canaan, got word that the Israelites were coming, ⁴¹ so they left Mount Hor and set up camp at Zalmonah.

⁴² They left Zalmonah and set up camp at Punon.

⁴³ They left Punon and set up camp at Oboth.

⁴⁴ They left Oboth and set up camp at Iye-Abarim, on the border of Moab.

⁴⁵ They left Iye-Abarim and set up camp at Dibon-Gad.

⁴⁶ They left Dibon-Gad and set up camp at Almon-Diblathaim.

⁴⁷ They left Almon-Diblathaim and set up camp in the mountains of Abarim, near Nebo.

⁴⁹ They left the mountains of Abarim and set up camp on the plains of Moab near the Jordan across from Jericho.

⁴⁹ Their camp near the Jordan extended from Beth-Jeshimoth to Abel-Shittim, in the plains of Moab.

⁵⁰ On the plains of Moab near the Jordan, across from Jericho, Our God said to Moses, ⁵¹ "Speak to the Israelites and say, 'When you cross the Jordan into Canaan, ⁵² drive out all those dwelling there before you. Destroy all their carved stone images, their images of cast metal, and their shrines. ⁵³ Take possession of the land and settle there: I give you that land to occupy. ⁵⁴ Apportion the land by lot, according to your clans, with each taking its share of the territory. Larger families will get a larger share and smaller families will get a smaller share. It is to be assigned by lot, each family of each tribe taking possession of its own territory.

⁵⁵ "'On the other hand, if you do not dispel the current dwellers as you

advance, those whom you leave behind will become a hooked barb in your eye and a thorn in your side. They will be troublemakers in the land where you are to live. ⁵⁶ And then I will do to you what I planned to do to them!'"

34:1 The Most High God spoke to Moses ² and said, "Once you enter Canaan, the land that will be allocated to you as an inheritance will have these borders:

³ "Your southern border will include a portion of the Desert of Zin along the border of Edom. On the eastern border, your southern point will start from the end of the Salt Sea, ⁴ cross south of Scorpion Pass, continue on to Zin and go south of Kadesh-Barnea. Then it will go to Hazar-Addar and over to Azmon, ⁵ where it will turn, join the Wadi of Egypt and end at the Mediterranean Sea.

⁶ "Your western boundary will be the coast of the Mediterranean, your frontier on the west.

⁷ "For your northern border, run a line from the Mediterranean to Mount Hor, ⁹ and then from Mount Hor to Lebo Hamath. Then the border will go to Zedad, ⁹ and continue to Ziphron and end at Hazar-Enan. This will be your northern border.

¹⁰ "For your eastern border, run a line from Hazar-Enan to Shepham ¹¹ to Riblah on the east side of Ain and continue along the slopes east of the Sea of Chinnereth.* ¹² Then the line will go down along the Jordan and end at the Salt Sea.

"This will be your land with all its borders laid out."

¹³ Moses gave these instructions to the Israelites: "This is the land you must assign by lot as your inheritance. Our God orders it to be distributed among the nine and one-half tribes. ¹⁴ For the families of the tribe of Reuben, the tribe of Gad and the half-tribe of Manasseh have received their inheritance. ¹⁵ These tribes received their inheritance on the east side of the Jordan, across from Jericho."

¹⁶ Our God said to Moses, "These are the names of those who are to assign the land for you as an inheritance: Eleazar the priest, and Joshua begot of Nun. Appoint one leader from each tribe to assist in assigning the land." ¹⁹ Those selected: from the tribe of Judah, Caleb begot of Jephunneh; ²⁰ from the tribe of Simeon, Shemuel begot of Ammihud; ²¹ from the tribe of Benjamin, Elidad begot of Chislon; ²² from the tribe of Dan, Bukki begot of

---

* Also known as the Sea of Galilee.

Jogli; ²³ from the tribe of Manasseh, begot of Joseph, Hanniel begot of Ephod; ²⁴ from the tribe of Ephraim, begot of Joseph, Kemuel begot of Shiphtan; ²⁵ from the tribe of Zebulun, Elizaphan begot of Parnach; ²⁶ from the tribe of Issachar, Paltiel begot of Azzan; ²⁷ from the tribe of Asher, Ahihud begot of Shelomi; ²⁹ from the tribe of Naphtali, Pedahel begot of Ammihud.

²⁹ These are the tribal leaders God selected to assign the inheritance to the Israelites in the land of Canaan.

          ℭℜ   ℭℜ   ℭℜ

35:1 On the plains of Moab by the Jordan, across from Jericho, Our God said to Moses, ² "Command the Israelites to give the Levites towns to live in from the inheritance the Israelites will possess, and provide them pastureland around their towns. ³ Then they will have towns to live in and pastureland for their cattle, their flocks and other livestock. ⁴ The pastureland you will provide to the Levites will extend outward 1500 feet from the town wall. ⁵ Outside the town measure 3000 feet on the east side, 3000 feet on the south side, three 3000 feet on the west side and 3000 feet on the north side, with the town in the middle. This land will be the pastureland for the towns.

⁶ "Six of the towns that you give to the Levites are to be cities of refuge, to which a person who kills someone may flee. Also give them forty-two other towns. ⁷ Give the Levites a total of forty-eight towns in addition to their pastureland. ⁹ The towns you give from the land that the Israelites possess will be in proportion to the size of the inheritance of each tribe. Provide many towns from a tribe that has much, and fewer towns from those who have less."

⁹ Then Our God said to Moses, ¹⁰ "Tell the Israelites that when they cross the Jordan into Canaan, ¹¹ they are to select some towns to be cities of refuge, to which a person can flee who has accidentally killed another. ¹² They will be places of refuge from the avengers, so that a person accused of murder may not die before standing trial before the community. ¹³ Six towns will be your cities of refuge. ¹⁴ Set aside three towns on this side of the Jordan and three towns in Canaan. ¹⁵ These six towns will be cities of refuge for Israelites, foreigners, and any other people living among you, so that anyone dwelling among you who has killed someone accidentally can flee there.

¹⁶ "If a person strikes someone with an iron object and that person dies, then that person has committed murder. The murderer must be put to

death. ¹⁷ If a person is holding a stone that could kill, and strikes someone with it and that person dies, the person striking is a murderer, and must be put to death. ¹⁹ Or if a person is holding a wooden object that could kill, and that person strikes another with the wooden object, and that person dies, the person striking the other is a murderer and must be put to death. ¹⁹ The avenger of blood must put the murderer to death. ²⁰ If anyone with malice aforethought shoves another or throws something at another intentionally, and the victim dies, ²¹ or if someone intentionally hits another with a fist and the victim dies, the perpetrator is a murderer and must be put to death.

²² "But if without hostility someone shoves another or throws something at another unintentionally ²³ or, not seeing the victim, drops a stone that kills, then since it was without malice and no harm was intended, ²⁴ the assembly must judge between the accused and the avenger of blood according to these regulations: ²⁵ The assembly must protect the one accused of murder from the avenger of blood, and remand the accused back to the city of refuge. The accused must stay there until the death of the high priest who was anointed with the oil of holiness. ²⁶ But if the accused ever leaves the city of refuge ²⁷ and the avenger of blood kills the accused, the avenger is not guilty of murder. ²⁹ The accused must stay in the city of refuge until the death of the high priest. Only after the death of the high priest may the accused return home. ²⁹ These regulations are to have the force of law for you and your descendants, wherever you may be.

³⁰ "In the case of murder, the accused must be put to death only upon testimony of eyewitnesses. But no one is to be put to death on the testimony of only one witness.

³¹ "Do not accept a ransom for the life of a murderer who deserves to die. The murderer must surely be put to death. ³² Do not accept a ransom for anyone who has fled to a city of refuge, since that would allow that person to return home and dwell there before the death of the high priest.

³³ 'Do not pollute the land where you dwell. Bloodshed pollutes the land, and no one can atone for the land upon which blood has been shed, except by the blood of the one who shed it. ³⁴ Do not defile the land where you dwell and where I dwell, for I, Your God, dwell among the Israelites.'"

ও   ও   ও

36¹ The family heads of the clan of Gilead begot of Machir, begot of Manasseh, who were related to the descendants of Joseph, came and spoke before Moses and the family heads of the Israelites. ² They said, "When Our God commanded Moses to give land as an inheritance to the Israelites by lot, Moses was ordered to give the inheritance of Zelophehad to his five daughters. ³ But what if they marry men from other Israelite tribes? Then their inheritance will be taken from our ancestral inheritance and added to that of the tribe they marry into. And so part of the inheritance allotted to us would be taken away. ⁴ When the Jubilee Year for the Israelites comes, their inheritance will be added to the tribe into which they marry, and their property will be taken from the tribal inheritance of our ancestors."

⁵ Then God commanded Moses to give this ruling to the Israelites, "What the descendants of the tribe of Joseph are saying is true. ⁶ This is what Our God commands for the daughters of Zelophehad: they may marry anyone they please as long as they marry within Zelophehad's tribe. ⁷ No portion in Israel will pass from one tribe to another tribe, but every Israelite will retain the family portion. ⁹ Any woman of a tribe of Israel who receives an interitance may marry a suitor from any family of her ancestral tribe. In this way the Israelites will retain the portion of their ancestors. ⁹ No portion may pass from one tribe to another, but every tribe in Israel will retain its own portion."

¹⁰ The daughters of Zelophehad acted according to God's command to Moses. ¹¹ Mahlah, Tirzah, Hoglah, Milcah and Noah, the five daughters, married cousins of Zelophehad. ¹² They married within the families of the tribe of Manasseh begot of Joseph, and their portion remained with the tribe of Zelophehad's family.

¹³ These are the commandments and decrees which Our God issued to the Israelites through Moses on the plains of Moab, near the Jordan across from Jericho.

deuteronomy

1:1 – 4:43

*t*hese are the words that moses spoke
to all the Israelites in the desert east of the Jordan—that is, in the Arabah
opposite Suph, between Paran and Tophel, Laban, Hazeroth and
Dizahab. 2 It is an eleven days' journey from Horeb to Kadesh Barnea by
the Mount Seir road. 3 On the first day of the eleventh month in the fortieth year, Moses spoke to the Israelites, as God commanded. 4 This was
just after the victory of the Israelites over Sihon the Moabite, who ruled
in Heshbon, and the defeat at Edrei of Og the ruler of Bashan, who ruled
in Ashtaroth. 5 It was in Moab, beyond the Jordan, that Moses began to
explain the Law.*

These were the words of Moses:

---

* The Hebrew word for "Law" is *Torah.* In the book of *Leviticus*, this word was translated "Instruction,"
which referred to a priestly ritual; here it refers to the broader structure of the law, and to portions
of the book of *Deuteronomy*. The Hebrew name for the book is "These are the words"; the English
name means "second law," because it repeats much of the law first expounded in *Exodus*. One
interesting feature is the phrase "Adonai, our God," which occurs with such regularity only in
Deuteronomy; it is meant to underscore both the reverence for the divine Name (usually "Our God"
in this translation, but "Adonai" throughout this book to echo Hebrew tradition) and the covenant
relationship between God and Israel.

⁶ Adonai, our God, said to us at Horeb,* "You have lived on this mountain long enough. ⁷ Begin your journey again: move to the hill country of the Amorites, and also of their neighbors in the Arabah, and to the Shephelah, and into the Negev and to the coast. Go into all of Canaan and Lebanon, as far as the Euphrates, the Great River. ⁸ I have opened this land for you. Enter this land and occupy it, the land which Your God swore to give to your ancestors: to Sarah and Abraham, to Rebecca and Isaac, to Leah and Rachel and Jacob, and to all their descendants after them."

⁹ At that time I said to you, "You are too great a burden for me to bear alone. ¹⁰ Adonai, our God, has multiplied you until you are as numerous as the stars in the sky. ¹¹ Your God, the God of your ancestors, will increase you a thousand times more and bless you, according to the promise that was given. ¹² How am I to bear the weight of all your quarrels by myself? ¹³ From each of your tribes, choose individuals of good reputation who are clear-sighted and wise to be leaders among you."¹⁴ You agreed that this was a good plan. ¹⁵ So I took leaders from your tribes, wise people of good reputation, and I gave them authority over you—some commanding units of a thousand, some of a hundred, some of fifty, some of ten—as officials throughout your tribes. ¹⁶ I appointed them to be judges for you: "Listen to the disputes between the Israelites, your sisters and brothers, and judge between them fairly, whether the dispute is between Israelites or Israelites and foreigners. ¹⁷ Listen to both the small and the great with impartiality. You must be intimidated by no one, for your judgment is God's judgment. Bring to me any case that is too difficult for you, and I will hear it." ¹⁸ Thus I told you the things that you should do.

¹⁹ Then we set out from Horeb in obedience to Adonai, our God, and made our way through the vast and unyielding desert to the hill country of the Amorites, until we reached Kadesh Barnea. ²⁰ There I said to you, "We have reached the hill country of the Amorites, which Our God promised us. ²¹ See for yourselves—God has given it to you, to possess as Our God, the God of our ancestors, promised. Don't be afraid, don't be dismayed."

²² You came to me and said, "Let us send out scouts to explore the countryside and report to us the route we should take and what cities we will find." ²³ Approving your plan, I picked twelve from among you, one from each tribe. ²⁴ They set out, traveling up into the hill country to the Valley of Eshcol to see what was there. ²⁵ They gathered samples of the produce of that place, which they brought back to us, and they reported, "The land that Adonai, our God, is giving us is good land."

---

* That is, Mount Sinai.

²⁶ But you would not go there; you rebelled against Our God's command. ²⁷ You grumbled in your tents that it was because Our God hated us that we had been brought up out of Egypt to be slaughtered by the Amorites. ²⁸ "What will we find up there?" you asked. "Our scouts made our hearts melt when they said, 'These people are stronger and taller than we; their great cities have walls up to the sky! We saw there the children of the Anakites.' " ²⁹ I said to you, "Let go of your dread and fear of them. ³⁰ Adonai, our God, who goes before us, will fight for us. Remember what Our God did in Egypt before your very eyes. ³¹ Remember in the desert, where Your God carried you, as one carries a child, all through our travels until we came to this place." ³² Still you had no trust in God, Your God, ³³ who went before you along the way to find a place for you to camp—fire by night, and a cloud by day, showing you what route to take."

³⁴ Hearing your words, God was enraged, and said, ³⁵ "Not one of you— not one of this evil generation—will see the good land I promised to your ancestors! ³⁶ Only Caleb begot of Jephunneh will see it. To Caleb and to Caleb's ancestors I will give this land where you now stand, for he has been unfailingly faithful to Your God." ³⁷ Our God was even angry with me because of you, and said, "You will not enter it either. ³⁸ But Joshua begot of Nun, who stands before you, will enter Canaan. Encourage Joshua, for he is the one who will secure Israel's possession of it. ³⁹ And your little ones, who you feared would be taken captive—your children who do not yet know right from wrong—they will enter the land. I will give it to them and they will take possession of it. ⁴⁰ But as for you, return to the desert in the direction of the Sea of Reeds."

⁴¹ You said, "We have sinned against Our God! We will go up and fight, as Our God commanded us!" So you put on your battle gear thinking it would be an easy task to go up into the hill country. ⁴² Our God told me to tell them, "Don't go up and don't fight, for I am not in your midst. You will be defeated by your enemies if you go." ⁴³ I told you this, and you would not listen. You spurned God's command and went presumptuously up into the hill country. ⁴⁴ The inhabitants of the hill country, the Amorites, came out against you and swarmed over you like bees. They beat you back from Seir as far as Hormah. ⁴⁵ You came back sobbing to Your God, who paid no attention to your crying and was deaf to your cries. ⁴⁶ That is why you remained in Kadesh as long as you did.

2:1 We traveled toward the desert in the direction of the Sea of Reeds, as Our God instructed me. ² Then Our God said to me, ³ "You have wandered long enough in this hill country. Go north, ⁴ and tell the people: 'You are about to pass through the territory of your kin, the descendants of Esau, who dwell in Seir. They will fear you, but be very careful, ⁵ and do not attack them; for I will not allow you so much as one square foot of their land, since I already gave Mount Seir to the descendents of Esau ⁶ You must pay them with money for the food that you eat and for the water that you drink. ⁷ Adonai, your God, has blessed you in everything you done. I have watched over you throughout your long journey through this uncharted desert. These forty years I, Your God, have been with you, and you have lacked nothing.' "

⁸ So we passed among our kin, the descendants of Esau who dwell in Seir. We traveled the Arabah road, which runs from Elath to Ezion Geber, and then moved on in the direction of the Desert of Moab. ⁹ When we came there God warned us, "Do not attack the Moabites or provoke them to fight, for I will give you none of their land. I gave Ar to the descendants of Lot as their possession."

¹⁰ The Emites—a numerous and strong people, and as tall as the Anakites—lived there at one time. ¹¹ Like the Anakites, they too were considered to be Rephaites, but the Moabites called them Emites—"the Frightful Ones." ¹² The Horites lived in Seir at one time, but Esau's descendants drove them out. They exterminated them as they advanced and replaced them by settling in their territory, just as the Israelites did in the territory Our God gave them.

¹³ "Go, then," Our God said, "cross over the Wadi of Zered." And we did so. ¹⁴ The journey from Kadesh Barnea to the crossing of the Wadi Zered took thirty-eight years—time enough for one generation of the able-bodied to live and die, as God had sworn would happen. ¹⁵ Our God's hand was against them, rooting them out of the camp until the last one was gone.

¹⁶ When the able-bodied were gone from among the people, ¹⁷ Our God said to me, ¹⁸ "Today you will cross into the land of Moab at Ar. ¹⁹ As you approach the frontier of the Ammonites, neither attack them nor provoke them to fight, for I will not give you the land of the Ammonites as a possession: I gave this to the descendants of Lot." ²⁰ This is also usually considered the territory of Rephaim. Rephaites formerly dwelt there, though the Ammonites called them Zamzummim—"Barbarians"— ²¹ a strong, numerous people and as tall as the Anakites. But God destroyed them before the advancing Ammonites, who dispossessed them and settled there. ²² God did the same for the descendants of Esau who lived in Seir—as they advanced, God destroyed the Horites, so that the descendants of Esau could take possession of the territory and live there, as they do still. ²³ It was the same for the Avvites who lived in villages as far as Gaza. The Caphtorites came out of Caphtor, destroyed them and settled there.

²⁴ Then God said, "Now set out and cross the Wadi Arnon, for I have put into your hands Sihon the Amorite, the ruler of Heshbon, and his territory. Arm yourselves, and attack. ²⁵ Beginning today, I will instill terror of you into all peoples under the heavens. If they so much as hear a rumor of you, they will quake in dread of you."

²⁶ So, from the desert of Kedemoth I sent this message to Sihon, ruler of Heshbon, offering peace: ²⁷ "Allow us to pass through your territory. We will travel the main road and not turn to the right or the left. ²⁸ Sell us food to eat and water to drink; we will pay in silver. We will only pass through your territory on foot— ²⁹ the descendents of Esau who now dwell in Seir granted us passage, as did the Moabites dwelling in Ar—until we cross the Jordan into the land which Adonai, our God, is giving to us."

³⁰ But Sihon, ruler of Heshbon, refused to grant us passage. For Our God had hardened the ruler's heart and spirit so as to put Heshbon at your mercy, as it has happened. ³¹ The Most High said to me, "Look: I have begun to turn Sihon and Heshbon over to you. Seize the territory."

³² When Sihon the ruler of Heshbon, and his army took to the field of battle at Jahaz, ³³ Our God delivered Sihon to us. We destroyed the ruler, the ruler's heirs and the entire army. ³⁴ We captured all the towns of Heshbon and killed them all—women, men, children—sparing none. ³⁵ The livestock we took as spoil, and we plundered the captured towns. ³⁶ From Aroer on the height above the Wadi Arnon, and the town which lies in the wadi itself, as far as Gilead, there was no town too strong for us. ³⁷ But as God had commanded, we did not encroach on any of the Ammonites' land, neither the land along the Yabbok River, nor the towns in the hill country.

3:¹ Then we turned up on the way toward Bashan, and Og, ruler of Bashan, came out with an army to meet us in battle at Edrei. ² The Most High said to me, "Do not fear Og, for I will deliver the ruler, with his army and his land into your hands. Do to Og as you did to Sihon, ruler of Heshbon."

³ So the Most High delivered Og, ruler of Bashan, into our hands. We wiped out his entire army, and left no survivors. ⁴ We took all the fortified cities of Bashan, sixty of them; there was not one that escaped us—the whole region of Arbob, Og's realm in Bashan. ⁵ These were fortified cities with high walls, gates and bars; and there were a great number of small unguarded towns as well. ⁶ We completely destroyed them all, as we had done with Sihon, ruler of Heshbon—killing women, men and children. ⁷ But all the livestock and plunder from the cities we carried off for our own use.

⁸ At that time we took from the two rulers of the Amorites the territory east of the Jordan, from the Wadi Arnon to Mount Hermon— ⁹ the Sidonians call Hermon Sirion, and the Amorites call it Senir. ¹⁰ We captured

all the towns on the plateau, all of Gilead, and all of Bashan as far as Salecah and Edrei; the towns belonging to Og, ruler of Bashan. ¹¹ Only Og ruler of Bashan remained, the sole survivor of the Rephaites. In fact, Og's bed, an iron bed thirteen feet long and six wide, may still be seen in the Ammonite town of Rabbah.*

¹² When we took possession of this territory, I gave to the Reubenites and Gadites the territory north of Aroer, which borders the Wadi Arnon and also the hill country of Gilead, with its towns. ¹³ The rest of Gilead and all of Og's realm of Bashan, I gave to the half tribe of Manasseh. The region of Argov in Bashan was once known as the land of the Rephaites. ¹⁴ Jair, a descendant of Manasseh, took the whole region of Argov up to the border with the Geshurites and the Maacathites, who named it, so that to this day Bashan is called the Tent Villages of Jair. ¹⁵ And I gave Gilead to Machir. ¹⁶ And to the Reubenites and the Gadites I gave the territory extending from Gilead down to the Wadi Arnon—the border was in the middle of the wadi—and out to the Yabbok River,** which borders the Ammonites. ¹⁷ Its western border is the Arabah and the Jordan, from Chinnereth down to the Sea of Arabah—the Salt Sea—below the slopes of Pisgah on the east.

¹⁸ At that time, I told you, "Although Adonai, your God, has given you this land to occupy, have all your able-bodied dress for battle, and cross over ahead of the Israelites. ¹⁹ Only your families and your livestock—you do have much livestock—may remain in the towns which I gave you. ²⁰ You are to do this until such time that Our God settles our sisters and brothers as you are now settled, and they too occupy the land which God, Your God, is giving to them across the Jordan."

²¹ At that time, I told Joshua, "You saw for yourself what God, Our God, did to these two rulers. Our God will do the same to all the realms which you are about to enter. ²² Don't be afraid, for God, Your God, fights for you."

²³ It was then I pleaded with Our God, and prayed, ²⁴ "O God, you have only begun to show me the immensity of your power and the strength of your hand. What god in heaven or on the earth can match your deeds, your mighty works? ²⁵ Let me cross over, I beg you, to view the good land lying beyond the Jordan, the excellent hill country and Lebanon." ²⁶ But Our God was angry with me because of you, and would not hear me. God said to me, "Enough! Never speak to me of this matter again. ²⁷ Climb to the top of

---

* This "iron bed" is particularly curious in that this was supposedly in the in the mid 15th century BCE, and archaeologists agree that iron working was in its earliest discovery stages at 1500 BCE. Rabbah is the modern city of Amman, the capital of Jordan.
** The Yabbok, which means "Crossroads," is the location of the great meeting between Jacob and the mysterious being who wrestled with him until daybreak.

Pisgah and look around you to the west, to the north, to the east and to the south. Look well, for you will not cross the Jordan. ²⁸ Instruct Joshua; encourage and strengthen him, for it is Joshua who will cross over the Jordan and lead this people, who will secure their possession of the land that you will see." ²⁹ So we remained in the valley opposite Beth Peor.

4¹ Now, Israel, hear the statutes and decrees which I am teaching you to observe, so that you may live, and may enter in and take possession of the land which Adonai, the God of your ancestors, is giving you. ² In your observance of the commandments of Adonai, your God, you must not add to nor subtract from that which I am giving to you. ³ You saw for yourselves what Our God did at Baal Peor—Adonai, your God, destroyed everyone who worshipped the Baal there. ⁴ But those of you who were faithful to Adonai, your God, are alive today. ⁵ I teach you the statutes and decrees of Adonai, your God, as it was commanded of me, so that you may uphold them in the land that you are about to enter and possess. ⁶ Observe them carefully, and demonstrate your wisdom and intelligence to the nations, who will hear of these statutes and say, "Surely this is a wise and intelligent people!" ⁷ For what other great nation has a god so near to it as Our God is to us when we call? ⁸ Or what great nation has statutes and decrees that are as just as this whole Law that I set before you today?

⁹ Take care and be diligent in guarding yourselves, that you do not to forget those things which your own eyes have seen. Do not forget them as long as you live, and teach them to your children and your children's children. ¹⁰ Never forget the day you stood at Horeb before Adonai, your God, and God said to me, "Assemble the people before me to hear my words, so that they may learn to revere me for as long as they dwell on this earth, and so that they may teach my words to their children." ¹¹ You came near and stood at the foot of the mountain, which was ablaze with fire reaching up to the heavens, surrounded by dark clouds and a heavy mist. ¹² When the Most High spoke to you from the midst of the fire, you could hear the words but saw no form. There was only a voice. ¹³ God announced to you the terms of the covenant, commanding you to observe the Ten Commandments,* written on two tablets of stone. ¹⁴ And God charged me then to teach you the statutes and decrees which you are to keep in the land which you soon will enter and possess.

¹⁵ On the day when God spoke to you from the fire at Horeb, you heard only words but saw no form whatever; ¹⁶ today you must take similar care,

---

* The Hebrew text is literally "the Ten Words," likely because they were more akin to guiding principles than mere commands.

and watch very closely that you do not fall into the corrupt practice of carving idols for yourselves. Make no figure that is male or female, 17 or looks like any earthbound animal or bird of the air, 18 or anything that creeps on the ground or swims in the waters below the earth. 19 And when you gaze up into the heavens and see the sun and the moon, and the stars and all the heavenly array, do not be led astray by them to bow down in worship. These are things God has given to all peoples everywhere under the heavens. 20 But you have been brought up out of Egypt, out of the fiery furnace, and been made Our God's own possession, which you are today.

21 Our God was angry with me because of you, and vowed that I would not cross the Jordan, but you will occupy and possess that good land. 22 I will die in this country. I will not cross the Jordan, which you will cross to take possession of that good land. 23 Take care that you do not forget the covenant that God, Your God, made with you. Do not make for yourselves a carved idol. Your God forbids it. 24 For Adonai, your God, is a devouring fire—a jealous God!

25 When you have had children and your children have had children, and they have grown old on the land—if you then corrupt yourselves by carving idols, and so do evil in the eyes of Adonai, your God— 26 I call upon heaven and earth as witnesses this day that you will vanish from the land which you are to occupy across the Jordan. You will not enjoy a long life; you will be swept away. 27 God will scatter you across the nations; only a few you will be remain in the nations where Our God will have driven you. 28 There you will serve gods made of wood or stone, made by human hands —gods who cannot see or hear, cannot eat or smell.

29 But when you seek Your God from those lands, you will find God where you are—if you search with all your heart and soul. 30 When you are filled with sorrow for all these things that will happen to you, you will turn back to Your God, and listen obediently. 31 Adonai God is a merciful God, one who will not fail you or destroy you, one who will never forget the Covenant that was made with your ancestors and sealed with a divine oath.

32 Ask this question, now, looking to the ages that are past, that went before you, from the time when God created people on earth forward: Was there ever a word so majestic, from one end of heaven to the other? Was anything like it ever heard? 33 Did ever a people hear the voice of the living God speaking from the heart of the fire, as you have heard, and live to tell of it? 34 Has any god before ever ventured to take one nation from the midst of another by ordeals, by signs and wonders, by war with a mighty hand and an outstretched arm, by the power of terror, as Your God did in Egypt before your eyes?

³⁵ You were allowed to see these things so that you might know that Your God is the only God; that there is no other. ³⁶ Out of the heavens God allowed you hear the divine voice to discipline you; on earth God let you see the great fire with the divine voice speaking from out of it. ³⁷ For the love of your ancestors, Your God chose you, their descendants, and led you out of Egypt by divine power, ³⁸ driving nations greater and mightier than you from your path, bringing you into their land and making it your legacy, as it is today.

³⁹ Know this today, therefore, and take it into your hearts: Your God is God indeed, in heaven above and on earth below, and there is no other. ⁴⁰ Keep the laws and commandments of the Most High as I give them to you this day, so that you and your children may prosper and live long in the land that Your God gives you forever.

ର ର ର

⁴¹ Then Moses set aside three towns to the east of the Jordan, ⁴² cities where people who had killed a person unintentionally—where there had been no malice or forethought—could take refuge. They could flee to one of these cities, and so save their lives. ⁴³ The cities were: Bezer on the desert plateau, for the Reubenites; Ramoth in Gilead, for the Gadites; and Golan in Bashan, for the Manassites.

4:44–11:32

*T*his is the code of laws that Moses set down for the Israelites. ⁴⁵ These are the precepts, statutes and decrees which Moses proclaimed to the Israelites, after they had come up out of Egypt ⁴⁶ while they were beyond the Jordan in the valley across from Beth Peor in the land of Sihon, ruler of the Amorites, who had lived in Heshbon. When they had come up out of Egypt, Moses and the Israelites had defeated Sihon, ruler of Heshbon, ⁴⁷ and Og, ruler of Bashan—the two Amorite rulers east of the Jordan. ⁴⁸ The territory that they occupied ran from Aroer on the rim of the Arnon Gorge to Mount Hermon, ⁴⁹ and included all the Arabah east of the Jordan, as far as the Sea of the Arabah, below the slopes of Pisgah.

5:1 Moses called together the Israelites, and told them the following:

Listen, O Israel, to the statutes and decrees I proclaim to you this day. Learn them and follow them with care. ² Adonai, our God, made a covenant with us at Horeb. ³ God did not make this covenant with our ancestors, but with us, who are yet living today. ⁴ God spoke to you face to face out of the blazing fire on the mountain, ⁵ and I stood between you and Our God to proclaim God's word, for you feared the fire and did not go up the mountain.

⁶ God said to you:

"I am Adonai, your God, who brought you out of Egypt, out of the land of bondage! ⁷ You must have no other gods before me.

⁸ "You must not make for yourselves idols formed like anything in the heavens above or on the earth below or under the waters. ⁹ You must not bow down to them or worship them. For I, Your God, am a jealous God. I punish my children for the sins of their parents who turn against me, until the third and the fourth generation. ¹⁰ But my love will flow unwaveringly for a thousand generations to those who love me and keep my laws.

¹¹ "You must not dishonor the Name of Your God, for Your God will not let go unpunished any who misuse it.

¹² "Honor the Sabbath day and keep it holy, as Adonai, your God, commanded. ¹³ For six days you will labor and do all your work, ¹⁴ but the seventh day is a Sabbath to Adonai, your God. You will do no work that day, neither you nor your daughter nor your son nor your workers—women or men—nor your ox nor your donkey, nor any of your animals; nor even foreigners among you. Thus your workers—both women and men—will rest as you do. ¹⁵ Remember that you were a slave in the land of Egypt and that Adonai, your God, brought you out from there with a mighty hand and outstretched arm; because of this, Adonai, your God, has commanded you to keep the Sabbath day.

¹⁶ "Honor your mother and your father, as Adonai, your God, commands you, so that you may live a long life, and that it will go well for you in the land that Your God is giving you.

¹⁷ "Do not murder.*

¹⁸ "Do not commit adultery.

¹⁹ "Do not steal.

²⁰ "Do not give false testimony against your neighbor.

²¹ "Do not lust for your neighbor's spouse. Do not crave your neighbor's house, or field, or female or male bonded worker, or ox, or donkey, or anything that belongs to your neighbor."

²² These are the words Our God spoke to the entire assembly on the mountain, from out of the fire, the cloud and the dark mist. There were

---

* Verses 17 through 20 in most English versions form only one verse in the Hebrew text, so there is a three verse discrepancy in the numbering through the end of the chapter.

these, and no more, and Our God wrote them on two stone tablets and gave them to me.

²³ When you heard the voice out of the darkness, while the mountain blazed with fire, the leaders of your tribes, your elders, came to me and said, ²⁴ "Today Adonai, our God, has shown us the divine glory and majesty, and we heard God's voice from the fire. Today we witnessed that someone can speak with God and still live. ²⁵ But now, why should we risk death? For the blazing fire will devour us; if we hear God's voice again, we will die! ²⁶ What mortals have ever heard the voice of the living God speaking out of the fire and lived to tell of it, as we have done? ²⁷ You should go alone, and listen to what Adonai, our God, says, and then come back to tell us what you have heard. We will listen, and obey."

²⁸ Hearing you, God said to me, "I have heard what these people have said to you. They are right. ²⁹ If only their hearts were inclined to hold me in awe and keep my commandments always, so that it might go well them and their children forever! ³⁰ Tell them to return to their tents. ³¹ But, you, stand here with me, and I will give you all the commandments, the statutes and decrees that you are to teach them to follow in the land that I will give over to them."

³² You must take care to do all that God commands of you. Do not turn from the road, either to the left or to the right. ³³ You must travel exactly where God, Your God, has commanded you to, so that you may live, and that all may go well with you, and you may long dwell in the land that you soon will occupy.

6₁ Here, then, are the commands, statutes and decrees which I will teach you. Obey them, so that you may enter into and occupy the land which Adonai, the God of your ancestors, gives to you. ² If you, and your children, and their children revere Adonai, your God, all the days of your life, and if you keep the laws and commandments which I lay before you, you will have a long life. ³ Listen then, Israel, and observe carefully what will bring you prosperity and will increase your numbers greatly, as Adonai, the God of your ancestors, has promised, giving to you a land that flows with milk and honey.

⁴ Hear, O Israel: Adonai, our God, Adonai is One!*

---

* This is the *Shema* (which means "hear"), an affirmation of the uniqueness and oneness of God that is expressed by Jews numerous times each day during morning and evening services and before retiring at night. The Shema is one of the two focal points of the morning and evening prayers; when the Shema is recited in the central part of the prayer service, the worshiper covers her or his eyes to concentrate on its meaning. Jewish martyrs have shouted these words with their last breath, and they are traditionally recited by any Jewish person as her or his life is ebbing away. Some scholars suggest that this paragraph begins an extended homily on the first commandment.

5 You are to love Adonai, your God,
        with all your heart,
    and with all your soul,
        and with all your strength.*
6 Let these words that I command you today
        be written in your heart.
7 Teach them diligently to your children,
        and repeat them constantly—
    when you are at home,
        when you are walking down a road,
    when you lie down at night
        and when you get up in the morning.
8 Tie them on your hand as a reminder;
        wear them as a circlet on your forehead;
9 write them on the doorposts of your house
        and on your gates.

10 When Adonai, your God, brings you into the land which was promised to your ancestors Sarah and Abraham, Rebecca and Isaac, and Leah and Rachel and Jacob, a land filled with good things—great and prosperous cities that you did not build, 11 houses full of good things that you did not gather, wells you did not dig, vineyards and olive groves you did not plant—and when you have eaten and are satisfied, 12 take care not to forget Your God who brought you out of the land of Egypt, out of the house of slavery.

13 You must revere Your God; you must worship Your God; and by the Name of Your God alone are you swear your oaths. 14 Do not follow other gods, the gods of the people around you; 15 for God, Your God who dwells with you, is a jealous God whose anger will then blaze up against you and wipe you from the face of the earth. 16 Do not test Adonai, your God, as you did at Massah. 17 You must keep the commandments stringently, the statutes and the decrees which Adonai, your God, gave to you. 18 Do what is right and good in the eyes of Your God, so that it may go well with you when you enter to occupy the good land which God swore to your ancestors that you would have, 19 driving out all your enemies before you, as Your God promised.

20 When, in times to come, your children ask you, "What is the meaning of the commandments, the statutes and the decrees which Our God gave us?" 21 say to them, "We were slaves of Pharaoh in Egypt, and God brought us out of Egypt with a strong hand. 22 God did wonders that struck terror,

---

* The word traditionally translated "strength" can also mean "wealth" or "substance."

signs that we could see, against Egypt and Pharaoh and Pharaoh's household. ²³ Adonai brought us out of there, leading us into the land promised to our ancestors. ²⁴ Then God commanded us to keep these statutes and to revere Adonai, our God, for our own everlasting benefit, that we may live, as we do now. ²⁵ For if we are to dwell in the light we must live in the commandments before God, Our God, as we were commanded."

⁷·¹ When Adonai, your God, brings you into the land that you are to enter and take possession of, and drives out multitudes before you—the Hittites, the Girgashites, the Amorites, the Canaanites, the Perizzites, the Hivites and the Jebusites, seven nations larger and stronger than you—² and when Adonai, your God, delivers them to you and you defeat them, you must destroy them entirely. ³ Make no treaties with them and show them no mercy. Do not intermarry with them. Do not give your daughters to their sons and do not take their sons for your daughters. For they will turn your daughters and sons from me, to serve other gods, and then Your God's wrath would be kindled against you and you would be quickly destroyed. ⁵ Treat them thus: Tear down their altars, smash their sacred poles, and burn their idols. ⁶ For you are a people holy in the sight of God, Your God, who chose you out of all the people on the face of the earth to be God's own, God's cherished belonging.

⁷ It was not because of your numbers among other nations that the Most High cared for you and chose you; for you were the least numerous of all peoples. ⁸ It was because God loved you, and held to the oath that was given to your ancestors, that you were freed with a hand of power, and redeemed from slavery, from the power of Pharaoh of Egypt. ⁹ Know then that Adonai, your God, is God, a faithful God who remembers the covenant of love that has been made with you so long you keep the commandments, to the thousandth generation. ¹⁰ But those who turn away from God will be repaid in kind. God is not slow, and rewards in their own way those who turn away from the divine will.

¹¹ So take care to follow the statutes, decrees and commandments that I give to you this day. ¹² If you are attentive to these laws and observe them with care, Adonai, your God, will keep the Covenant with you that was sworn to your ancestors. ¹³ God will love you, bless you and increase your numbers. God will bless the fruit of your womb, the crops of your land, your grain, your new wine, your oil, the calves of your herds and the lambs of your flocks, in the land that God swore to your ancestors would be given to you. ¹⁴ You will be the most blessed of peoples, without barrenness or sterility among you or among your livestock. ¹⁵ God will keep you free from dis-

ease; the terrible diseases that you experienced in Egypt will not be inflicted upon you; but God will inflict them on all those who hate you. ¹⁶ You must destroy all the peoples that God, Your God, is now giving over to you. Show them no pity, and do not serve their gods, for that would entrap you.

¹⁷ If you say in your heart, "These nations are so much stronger than we are! How can we dispel them?" ¹⁸ —do not be afraid. Only hold in your mind what God, Your God, did to Pharaoh and all of Egypt: ¹⁹ the trials you saw with your own eyes; the signs and wonders; the mighty hand and the outstretched arm by which God, Your God, freed you from there. God, Your God, will do the same to all that you fear. ²⁰ In a like manner God, Your God, will bring the pestilence to them until those that remain, even those in hiding, will perish. ²¹ Do not fear them, for God, Your God, who dwells among you, is a great God, worthy of awe. ²² God, Your God, will drive out those nations before you, step by step. You will not prevail against them all at once—wild animals, too many for you to cope with, would take their place around you.

²³ But God, Your God, will deliver them to you, filling them with panic until they are destroyed. ²⁴ God will deliver their rulers into your hands, and you will blot their names out from under heaven. No one will be able to withstand you; you will destroy them. ²⁵ Burn in the fire the images of their gods. Do not long for the silver and the gold that they are inlaid with, and do not take it for yourselves—it will entrap you, and it is detestable to God, Your God. ²⁶ Do not bring such a detestable idol into your home or you, like it, will be set aside for destruction. You must abhor it and revile it beyond redemption, for it is set apart for destruction.

8:1 Observe with great care every command that I give to you this day, so that you may flourish, and may take possession of the land that Our God swore to give to your ancestors. ² Remember how Adonai, your God, led you on a wandering path through the desert for forty years, humbling and testing you, to learn what was in your heart; whether you would keep God's commands or not. ³ God humbled you with hunger and then fed you manna, which was unknown to you and to your ancestors, to teach you that you cannot live on bread alone, but on every word that flows from the mouth of Our God. ⁴ Your clothes did not wear out, nor did your feet swell up during those forty years. ⁵ Understand within you that as a parent disciplines a child, so God disciplines you.

⁶ So keep the commandments of the Most High; walk with reverence in the ways of God, Your God. ⁷For Adonai, your God, is bringing you into a good land—a land with streams and pools of water, with springs flowing

in the valleys and in the hills, ⁸ a land of wheat, barley, vines, fig trees, pomegranates, olive oil and honey, ⁹ a land where bread will not be scarce and where you will lack for nothing, a land where rocks are iron and copper is dug out of hills. ¹⁰ You will eat and have your fill, and you will praise Adonai, your God, for the good land given to you.

¹¹ Take care that you not forget Your God by failing to observe the statutes, decrees and commands that are given you today. ¹² When you have had plenty to eat, and have built a fine house to live in, ¹³ when your flocks and herds, your silver and gold, and all your possessions increase, ¹⁴ do not grow proud and forget God, Your God, who brought you out of Egypt, from the land of slavery. ¹⁵ It was Your God who led you through the vast and desolate wilderness, a thirsty and waterless land, filled with poisonous snakes and scorpions. God made water spring forth for you out of solid rock, ¹⁶ and fed you in the wilderness with manna, which your ancestors had never known. God humbled you to test you, and in the end, to make you prosperous. ¹⁷ Do not say to yourself, "My own strength and the power of my hands brought this wealth to me." ¹⁸ Remember God, Your God, who enabled you to produce this wealth, to confirm the covenant that God swore to your ancestors, which is fulfilled today.

¹⁹ If it happens that you do not remember Adonai, your God, and turn to other gods, worshiping and bowing down to them, I swear to you today that you will surely be destroyed. ²⁰ Like the nations God will destroy before you, so will you be destroyed for not obeying God, Your God.

9:1 Listen, Israel! You soon will cross the Jordan, to take possession of territories and nations greater and stronger than you, whose vast cities are fortified to the heavens. ² The people are strong and tall—children of the Anakim: you know about them. You have heard it said, "Who can face the Anakim?" ³ But be assured that today it is Adonai, your God, who will cross over before you like a devouring fire. God will subdue them and destroy them before you. You will drive them out, taking possession of their lands and decimating them, as Our God has promised you.

⁴ When Our God has driven them so that they flee before you, don't vaunt yourself and say, "God brought me here possess this land because I am virtuous." No, it is because of these nations' own wickedness of that Your God scatters them in front of you. ⁵ It is not because of your righteousness or your integrity that you will take possession their land. It is because of their wickedness that Adonai, your God, will give their lands to you, to accomplish what God swore to our ancestors Sarah and Abraham, Rebecca and Isaac, and Leah, Rachel and Jacob.

⁶ Know this well: Adonai, your God, does not give this good land over to you because you are righteousness—no, you are a stiff-necked people! ⁷ Remember, and do not ever forget, how you provoked God, Your God, in the desert. From the day you left Egypt until you arrived here, you have rebelled against God. ⁸ At Horeb you so provoked God that your destruction was prepared for you. ⁹ When I went up the mountain to receive the stone tablets—the tablets of the covenant that Our God had made with you—I stayed on the mountain forty days and nights. I ate no bread, nor drank water. ¹⁰ Our God gave to me two stone tablets, inscribed by God's own finger, written with the words that God proclaimed out of the fire to you on the mountain, on the day of the assembly.

¹¹ When the forty days and forty nights were ended, God gave me the two stone tablets, the tablets of the Covenant. ¹² God said to me then, "Go down, hurry, for your people whom you brought out of Egypt are corrupting themselves. They have rushed to turn aside from the path which I gave them, and they have cast an idol for themselves." ¹³ Then God said to me, "I see now that these are an unbending people! ¹⁴ Leave me now, for I will obliterate them and their name from under the heavens. You I will make into a vast nation, and greater than them."

¹⁵ So I came down from the mountain, the blazing mountain, carrying in my hands the two stone tablets. ¹⁶ Then indeed I found that you had turned against Adonai, your God, having cast an idol for yourselves in the shape of a calf. It was so quick, how you turned from the ways that God commanded of you! ¹⁷ I took the two tablets from my hands and smashed them before you.

¹⁸ Then I threw myself down on the ground before the Most High. For forty days and forty nights, I ate no bread and drank no water, because of your offenses, because you did what was vile in God's eyes. ¹⁹ I was afraid that Our God's rage was so strong that you would be destroyed. But God listened to me. ²⁰ The Almighty was angry with Aaron so much that he would have been destroyed, but I prayed for Aaron too. ²¹ And I took that foul thing that had been made, the calf, and burned it in the fire, and crushed and ground it to dust, and the dust I threw into a stream running down from the mountain.

²² Again you also roused God's anger at Taberah, and at Massah, and at Kibroth Hattaavah. ²³ When God sent you out from Kadesh Barnea and said, "Go and take possession of the land I which give to you," you disobeyed God's command, without trust or deference to God. ²⁴ You have revolted against Your God as long as you have been known to God.

²⁵ Through the forty days and nights when I lay prostrate before God, who was intent on your destruction, ²⁶ I prayed, "O God, do not destroy

these people who are your very own, whom you redeemed by your great power, and brought up out of Egypt by the strength of your hand. ²⁷ Do not forget your servants Sarah and Abraham, Rebecca and Isaac, and Leah, Rachel and Jacob. Turn aside from the stubbornness of this people, and their wickedness and sin. ²⁸ The country from which you have freed us will say that our God was unable to deliver us into the promised land. They will say that our God hated us, and brought us out only to lead us to our death in the desert. ²⁹ But these are your people, your inheritance, whom you delivered by your might and by the reach of your arm."

10:¹ At the time Our God said to me: "Make two tablets like the first, and come meet me on the mountain. Make a wooden chest as well. ² I will write on the tablets the words which I had put on the first tablets, the tablets that you broke. Then you will put them in the chest."

³ So I made an chest of acacia wood, and carved two stone tablets like the first ones, and I went up the mountain carrying the tablets. ⁴ The Sovereign One wrote on these tablets what had been written before, the Ten Commandments which had been proclaimed to you out of the fire on the day when you were assembled, and these God gave to me. ⁵ Then I came down from the mountain and put the tablets into the ark which I had made, as God had commanded me—and so they are there now.

⁶ We traveled from the wells of Bene Jaakan to Moserah, where Aaron died and was buried. Eleazar his heir became high priest, ⁷ and from there we traveled to Gudgodah and on to Jotbathah, a land of many streams. ⁸ It was at this time that Our God set apart the Levites to carry the Ark of the Covenant of Our God, and to serve the Most High, blessing God's Name as they do to this day. ⁹ So it is that the Levites have no ancestral lands like other Israelites. Our God is their inheritance, as was promised by Adonai, our God.

¹⁰ Forty days and forty nights I stayed on the mountain, as I did the first time. And God listened to me again and agreed not to destroy you. ¹¹ Our God said to me, "Go—lead the people so that they may enter and take possession of the land I that promised to their ancestors that I would give to them."

¹²   And what now, Israel, does Your God ask of you?
        Only this:
     that you stand in awe of Your God;
        that you walk in all of God's ways;
     that you love and serve Your God
        with all your heart and soul,
¹³   and that you keep the commandments
        and obey the statutes of the Most High—

statutes which, for your good,
    I lay down today.
14 To God belongs heaven and the highest of heavens,
    the earth and all that it contains—
15 yet the Almighty so loved your ancestors
    that you, their descendants,
were chosen before all other peoples,
    and so it still is today.

16 Sensitize your hearts, therefore,
    and bend your will!
17 For Your God is the God of gods,
    the Sovereign of sovereigns,
the great God,
    powerful and awe-inspiring,
who has no favorites
    and cannot be bribed;
18 who brings justice
    to the orphan and the widowed,
and who befriends the foreigner among you
    with food and clothing.
19 In the same way, you too must befriend the foreigner,
    for you were once foreigners yourselves in the land of Egypt. 20
It is Your God, the God Most High,
    whom you must serve with awe;
whom you must cling to
    and by whom you must swear;
21 who is your praise;
    who is your God;
who has done great things
    which your eyes have seen with awe.
22 Your ancestors went down into Egypt seventy strong,
    and God has made you as numerous
    as the stars of the heavens.

11:1 So you must love God, Your God, and you must forever honor the responsibility given to you: the decrees, the statutes and the commandments. 2 Keep in your minds this day that it is you, not your children, who have known the discipline of Our God, and experienced God's great power, the surety of God's hand and the strength and reach of God's arm, 3 and the signs and wonders Our God worked in Egypt against Pharaoh the ruler, and all who lived under him; 4 how God destroyed the Egyptians' army with its horses and chariots when the waters of the Sea of Reeds engulfed them as they pursued you; how God's destruction of them affects them to this day. 5 You know the things God did for you in the desert before you came to this place; 6 and what God did to Dathan and Abiram, heirs of Eliab the Reubenite, when the earth opened up before you and swallowed them, together with their household, their tents, and all their livestock.

8 So observe the commandments I give you today, that you may have the courage to enter and take possession of the land which you are about to cross into, 9 and that you may live for many years in the land which Our God promised to your ancestors and their children, in a land flowing with milk and honey. 10 The land you are about to take possession of is not like Egypt, where you have come from—where after sowing your seed, you had to irrigate it, trudging through the fields like a vegetable garden. 11 This land which you will go into and occupy is a land of mountains and valleys, watered by the rain from the heavens. 12 It is a land which Our God nurtures, a land on which God gazes, from the beginning of the year to its end.

13 You have only to follow the commandments that I give you today—to love and serve Adonai, your God, with your whole heart and with your whole soul— 14 "and I will send rain for your land in its proper time, in the autumn and in the spring, and you will harvest your grain, your new wine, and your oil. 15 And I will provide pastures for your cattle, and you will have all that you need to eat." 16 Be cautious that you are not led astray in your hearts to worship other gods and serve them. 17 Do not arouse God's rage against you, for God will close up the heavens and there will be no rain. There will be no harvest from your soil, and you will wither away out this good land which Your God is giving you. 18 Put my words in your heart, and on your body. Tie them as a symbol on your hand, and fix them as a symbol on your forehead. 19 Instruct your children in these things, discussing them at home or on the road, before you go to bed and when you get up in the morning. 20 Write beside the doors to your homes, carve them on your gates, 21 so that your life and the lives of your children may grow long in the land that Your God promised to your ancestors, days as numerous as the days the heavens are above the earth.

22 If you are conscientious in keeping these commandments that I now charge you with—loving Adonai, your God; conforming to God's ways; and holding tightly to God— 23 then Our God will drive the nations out before you, nations larger and greater than you. 24 Every place where you walk will be yours. Your possessions will extend from the desert to Lebanon, and from the Euphrates to the western sea. 25 No one will have the

strength to resist you. Adonai, your God, will put the terror and the fear of you throughout the land, wherever you go, as it was promised to you.

²⁶ Look, I give you today the choice of a blessing or a curse: ²⁷ a blessing, if you keep the commandments of Adonai, your God, which I give you this day; ²⁸ a curse, if you ignore those commandments and turn from the way that I show you today, and seek out other gods unknown to you. ²⁹ When Adonai, your God, has brought you into the land you which you are to possess, you are to pronounce the blessing on Mount Gerizim, and the curse on Mount Ebal. ³⁰ These mountains are on the far side of the Jordan, in the west, in the direction of the setting sun, near the great Oaks of Moreh, in the territory of the Canaanites of the Arabah. ³¹ When you take possession of the land which Our God gives to you, across the Jordan, you must occupy it and settle there, and observe with care all the statutes and laws I have given you this day.

12:1–29:1

here are the statutes and laws that you must observe conscientiously in this land, which the God of your ancestors gives to you to be your possession for all of your earthly life:

² Completely destroy the sites high on the mountains and on the hills and under every spreading tree* where the peoples that you are dispossessing have worshipped their gods. ³ Smash their altars, crush their sacred pillars, burn their Asherah poles in the fire, cut down the idols of their gods and wipe out every trace of their name from those places. ⁴ You must not worship Adonai, your God, in the manner of their worship.

⁵ Seek out the place among all the tribes which Our God will choose as a dwelling, where the divine Name will be kept.* ⁶ To that place you are to go to bring your burnt offerings and sacrifices, your tithes and donations, your vow offerings and your voluntary gifts, and the firstborn of your flocks and herds. ⁷ There, in the presence of Your God, you and your families will eat and rejoice in everything you put your hand to, which will be blessed by Adonai, your God.

---

* A reference to the altars and sacred groves of the various nations they were supplanting. The Asherah poles in the next verse are the sacred phallic structures dedicated to the worship of the goddess Ashtoreth, also known as Astarte; later, to the Greeks, she was called Aphrodite.

⁸ You must not do in that land as we do now, where each one of us acts independently— ⁹ for you have not yet reached your resting place and come into the inheritance Your God gives you. ¹⁰ But when you are across the Jordan and settled on the land that God is giving you as your inheritance, and when God gives you peace from all your enemies surrounding you, so that you may live in security,¹¹ then you are to bring everything that I require of you to the place Your God will choose as a dwelling place for God's Name. Bring your burnt offerings and sacrifices, your tithes and donations, your vow offerings and your voluntary gifts that you promised to God. ¹² There you will rejoice in the presence of Your God, with your daughters and sons, your female and male bonded workers, and with the Levites living among you, for they have no allotment or inheritance of their own.

¹³ Be certain that you do not offer your burnt offerings wherever you please. Offer them only in the place Our God chooses from among one of your tribes, and observe there everything that I command you. ¹⁵ But you may slaughter your animals in any of your towns, and eat as much as you please. Both ritually clean persons and those ritually unclean may eat it as they would the gazelle or the deer,** according to the blessing God gives you. ¹⁶ But you must not eat the blood—pour it out on the ground as if it were water.

¹⁷ You must not eat in your own towns the tithe of your grain or new wine or oil, or the firstborn of your herds or flocks, or whatever you vowed to donate, or your freewill offerings of special gifts. Eat them, rather, in the presence or Your God at the place which Your God will choose—you, your daughters and sons; your workers, female and male; and the Levites from your towns—and rejoice before Our God in everything that you put your hand to. ¹⁹ Take care that you do not neglect the Levites as long as you live on your land.

²⁰ When Our God has increased your holdings as you have been promised, and you say to yourself, "I have a craving for some meat," you may eat it freely. ²¹ If the place that Our God chooses for the divine Name is too far from your home, and if you slaughter animals from your herds that I gave you in the manner that I have commanded,then you freely eat in your towns. ²²As with the gazelle or the deer, both the clean and the unclean may eat it. ²³ But you must be certain that you do not eat the blood, for the blood

---

* This will be a recurring phrase in this section; it refers to the as-yet-undesignated site of the Tabernacle, and provides for the twin possibilities that the site will move in the future, or that a more permanent structure like the Temple will be built.

** Only ceremonially pure individuals could eat from animals sacrificed at the altar; because the gazelle and the deer were not fit for the sacrificial rite, yet were allowed to be eaten, they could be eaten by all persons regardless of their ritual purity or impurity.

deuteronomy 12

is the life force, and you must not eat the life force with the meat. ²⁴ Do not eat it, but pour it out onto the ground. ²⁵ So long as you don't eat it, all will go well for you and your children after you, for you will be doing what is right in the eyes of Our God.

²⁶ But the sacred donations which are required of you, and your offerings in payment of a vow, must be offered at the place that God will select. ²⁷ You must present your burnt offerings on the altar of Adonai, your God, both of meat and of blood. The blood of other sacrifices must be poured out at the side of the altar of Our God, but you may eat the meat. ²⁸ Follow carefully all these regulations that I give you, so that both you and your progeny may have good lives, because you will have done what is correct and virtuous in the eyes of Adonai, your God.

²⁹ When Adonai, your God, separates for you the nations that you are to take possession of, and when you have driven them out and possessed their land, ³⁰ be careful not be become caught up in their ways, and do what they did, after you have destroyed them. Seek no knowledge about their gods, asking how they worshipped their gods and craving to do as they did. ³¹ You must not do those things for Adonai, your God, for these are detestable things which Your God despises—they would go so far even as to offer their children to their gods in a sacrificial fire.

³² See that you do exactly as I have commanded you. You must neither add to it or detract from this instruction in any way.

13:1 If a prophet, or one who foretells the future from dreams, comes among you and offers to do a sign or a wonder, ² and if the sign or wonder comes true, and that person says says, "Let us seek other gods—gods you have not known—and let us worship them," ³ you must not listen to the words of that prophet or of that dreamer. Adonai, your God, is testing you to see if you love Your God with your whole heart and soul. ⁴ It is Adonai, your God, whom you must follow, and Your God alone whom you must revere. You must keep God's commandments. You must obey God's voice; God alone you must serve and to God alone you must hold fast. ⁵ That prophet or that seer who comes among you must be put to death, for they preached rebellion against Adonai, your God, who brought you up out of Egypt and redeemed you from the land of slavery. These interlopers are trying to turn you from the way that Your God commanded you to follow. Cleanse this evil from among yourselves.

⁶ If anyone—even your own siblings, or daughters or sons, or the spouse you love, or your closest friend—secretly tries to seduce you and says, "Let's go off and worship other gods," gods that neither you nor your ancestors ever knew, ⁷ or gods of the peoples around you, either near or far,

from one end of the earth to the other, ⁸ you must not yield to them or listen to them. Show them no pity— ⁹ they must absolutely be put to death. You must be the first to bring them death, and all the people around you must participate. ¹⁰ Stone them, for they have tried to lure you away from Your God, who brought you up out of Egypt, out of the land of slavery. ¹¹ Then all Israel will fearfully hear of it, and fear it, and no one among you will attempt such evil again.

¹² If you hear that one of the towns Your God is giving you to live in ¹³ has been led away from the path by scoundrels among you, saying to the inhabitants of that town, "Let us go and worship other gods"—gods that you have never known— ¹⁴ then you must examine the matter carefully. If thorough investigation shows that this detestable thing has indeed happened in your midst, ¹⁵ you must kill the inhabitants of that town by the sword and utterly destroy all that is in the town, even the livestock. ¹⁶ Gather up all the spoils in the center of the town. Then burn the town and its spoils as a whole burnt offering to Your God. The town must remain in ruins forever; it must never be rebuilt. ¹⁷ Let nothing thus devoted to destruction dirty your hands, so that Your God may turn away from rage and show you mercy and compassion, and make you flourish as it was promised to your ancestors that it would be done ¹⁸ if you obey and kept all God's commandments that I give you today, so that you do only what is proper before God's eyes.

14¹ You are the children of Adonai, your God. Do not mourn for your dead by cutting yourselves or by shaving the front of your head, ² for you are a people holy to God. Out of all the inhabitants on the face of the earth, Your God has chosen you as a cherished inheritance.

³ You must eat nothing detestable. ⁴ The animals that you may eat are the ox, the sheep, the goat, ⁵ the buck, the gazelle, the roebuck, the ibex, the antelope, and the mountain sheep. ⁶ You may eat any animal which has split hooves and chews its cud. ⁷ Of animals that have split hooves or that chew the cud, you must not eat these: the camel, the rabbit and the rock badger—for they chew the cud, but do not have cloven hooves, and so are ceremonially unclean to you. ⁸ The pig, which has split hooves but does not chew its cud, is also unclean. You must not eat their meat, nor touch their carcasses.

⁹ Of the creatures that live in the water you may eat only those that have fins and scales. ¹⁰ Anything that does not have fins or scales you may not eat. It is unclean for you.

¹⁰ You may eat any clean bird, ¹² but these you may not eat: the eagle, the vulture, the osprey, ¹³ the red kite, the black kite, any kind of falcon, ¹⁴ any

kind of raven, ¹⁵ the ostrich, the screech owl, the gull, any kind of hawk, ¹⁶ the little owl, the great owl, the ibis, ¹⁷ the pelican, the white vulture, the cormorant, ¹⁸ the stork, any kind of heron, the hoopoe and the bat. ¹⁹ All winged insects are unclean to you, and must not be eaten. ²⁰ But you may eat any creature with wings that is clean.

²¹ Do not eat anything you find already dead. You may give it to a foreigner who lives among you, who may eat it; or you may sell it to a foreigner. You, however, are a people holy to God, Your God.

Do not cook a kid in its mother's milk.

²² Each year set aside a tithe of all that you produce from the land. ²³ This tithe of your grain, your new wine and your oil, as well as the firstborn of your herds and flocks, you are to eat in the presence of Adonai, your God, at the site God will choose as a dwelling for the holy Name, so that you may learn to revere Adonai, your God, for all times. ²⁴ But when Adonai, your God, blesses you with prosperity, if the place that is chosen as a dwelling place for God's Name is too far away and the journey is too great for you to carry your tithe there, ²⁵ then you are to sell it, and bring the money safely to the place that Our God has chosen. ²⁶ There you may spend the money on cattle, or sheep, or wine, or strong drink, or anything else you wish, and there present your offering with joy, both you and your family, in the presence of Adonai, your God.

²⁷ Do not neglect the Levites dwelling in your town, for they have no allotment or inheritance. ²⁸ Once in every three years you are to bring out the full tithe of your harvest and store them in your towns. ²⁹ There the Levites, who have no allotment or inheritance, and any foreigners, orphans, or widows and widowers who live in your towns may have plenty to eat. If you do this Adonai, your God, will bless you in everything which you set your hand to.

15:1 At the end of every seven years you must forgive all debts. ² This is how it is to be done: Every creditor must cancel all loans made to another Israelite. Payment of the debt cannot be demanded, for Our God's time of the forgiveness of debts has been proclaimed. ³ You may require repayment from a foreigner, but you must cancel any debt you owed by another Israelite. ⁴ But there are to be no poor among you, for in the land that Adonai, your God, is giving to you as your inheritance, Your God will bless you richly— ⁵ but only if you obey Adonai, your God, in all things, and conscientiously observe all the commandments that I give you this day. ⁶ For Adonai, your God, will bless you as it was promised, and you will lend to many nations, but borrow from none. You will rule over many nations, but be ruled by none.

⁷ If there is anyone among you who is need in any of the towns in the land that Adonai, your God, is giving you, you must not be harsh or stingy toward your sisters and brothers you are in need. ⁸ You must be generous, and ready to lend to those who need help of any kind. ⁹ Have care that you do not harbor the base thought, "The seventh year, the year of the forgiveness of debts approaches," and so show ill will toward your needy sisters or brothers and give them nothing. They might appeal to Your God against you, and you would be found guilty. ¹⁰ Be generous to them and not with a grudging heart; and in return, Your God will bless you in all things that you undertake and in all your endeavors. ¹¹ There will always be those among us in the world who are in need, so I require of you that you be always generous with the poor and needy in your land.

¹² If any Hebrews—be they women or men—are sold to you, and they serve six years, in the seventh year you must let them go free. ¹³ And when you release them, don't send them away empty-handed. ¹⁴ Give to them liberally from your flock, and from your threshing floor and your winepress. Give to them as Adonai, your God, has given to you. ¹⁵ Remember that you were once slaves in Egypt and Adonai, your God has bought your freedom. And so it that I give you this commandment today.

¹⁶ But if your indentured worker says to you, "I don't want to leave you," for love of you and your family, and is content to remain with you, ¹⁷ then take an awl and pierce it through the worker's earlobe and into your door, and that worker will be with you for life.* This applies equally to both women and men.

¹⁸ Don't think it a hardship to set your indentured worker free. For six years, the services rendered to you were worth what it would have cost you for a hired hand. And Adonai, your God, will bless you in everything you do.

¹⁹ Set aside for Your God every firstborn of your flocks and herds. Do not put the firstborn of your oxen to work, and do not sheer the firstborn of your sheep. ²⁰ Each year you and your family are to eat them in the presence of Your God at the place that God will choose. ²¹ But if an animal has a blemish—is lame or blind, or has any serious flaw—you must not sacrifice it to Your God. ²² You may eat it in your own towns; both the ceremonially unclean and the clean may eat it, as with the gazelle and the deer. ²³ But you must not eat the blood; pour it out on the ground like water.

---

* The custom of giving a lifelong household worker a pierced ear may have been symbolic: being attached physically to the doorpost of the owner's house represented the worker's emotional attachment there. The worker also likely wore an earring indicating her or his status.

16:1 Observe the month of Aviv by commemorating the Passover of Our God, for it was in the month of Aviv that God brought you up out of Egypt in the night. 2 You must sacrifice an animal from the herd of the flock as a Passover victim to Your God, in the place selected as a dwelling place for God's Name. 3 You must not eat with it any food that was made with yeast or any leavening agent. For seven days you must eat unleavened bread—the bread of affliction—for in haste you fled from Egypt. You are to remember all the days of your life the events of your departure from Egypt. 4 There must be no leavening in all your lands for seven days. Of the meat of the victim that you sacrifice on the evening of the first night, none must remain until the morning.

5 You may not slaughter the Passover victim in any town that Adonai, your God, gives you— 6 only in the place chosen as a dwelling place for the divine Name. There, you must sacrifice the Passover victim in the evening, when the sun goes down, at the time of your departure from Egypt. 7 Roast it and eat it at the place that Adonai, your God, has chosen, and then in the morning return to your tents. 8 For six days you must continue to eat unleavened bread, and on the seventh day hold a solemn assembly for Adonai, your God, and on this day, do no work.

9 Count off seven weeks from the time when you begin the harvest of the standing grain. 10 Then you must celebrate the pilgrim Feast of Weeks of Your God by sacrificing a voluntary offering in accordance with the blessings that God has given you. 11 Rejoice before Your God, with your spouse and your daughters and your sons, and with your indentured workers, female and male alike, and with the Levites who live in your towns—and with the foreigners who live among you, and the widows and widowers, and the orphans among you—at the place which Our God will choose as a dwelling place for God's Name. 12 Never forget that you were once slaves in Egypt, and take care to observe these rules.

13 You must keep the Feast of Tabernacles for seven days after you gather the bounty of your harvest from your threshing floor and from your winepress. 14 This is a feast of joy—be joyful with your spouse, and your daughters and sons, with your indentured workers, both female and male, and with the Levites that live in your towns, and with the foreigners that live among you, and the orphans, and the widows and widowers who live in your towns. 15 Celebrate the feast for seven days at the place that God will choose. For God will bless you in all your harvests and in all that you do, and your joy will be complete.

16 Three times a year all the heads of your households will gather before

Your God at a place that God will choose, at the Feast of Unleavened Bread, the Feast of Weeks and the Feast of Tabernacles. No one may show up emptyhanded; ¹⁷ every person must bring a gift in proportion to God's blessings upon you.

¹⁸ Appoint judges and officials for yourselves, within all your gates, in each of the town that Your God gives to you. They are to judge fairly. ¹⁹ and never pervert justice or show partiality. They must never accept bribes, for a bribe blinds the eyes of the wise and endangers the cause of the righteous. ²⁰ Follow the path of justice, and justice only, so that you might live, dwell on the land that Your God gives to you.

²¹ Do not set up wooden Asherah poles near the altar you build to Adonai, your God, ²² nor any standing stones, for these are detestable to Your God.

17:¹ Do not sacrifice to Your God an ox or sheep with any serious defect or flaw, for that would be abhorrent to Adonai, your God.

² If any person, man or woman, who lives among you is discovered to do what is wrong in the eyes of Your God, who violates the Covenant ³ and worships other gods against my command, bowing before them or before the moon, sun or stars of the sky— ⁴ should this be brought to your attention, then you must examine this person carefully. If it is true and proven that this detestable thing has happened in Israel, ⁵ then the person—woman or man—who has done this thing must be taken to the city gate and stoned to death. ⁶ Such a person will be put to death on the testimony of two or three witnesses, but never on the testimony of only one. ⁷ The witnesses must be the first to hurl stones at this person; then all the people will follow. In this way you must purge this evil from among you.

⁸ If there come cases before your judges that are too challenging for you to decide—cases of bloodshed, of lawsuits, or of assaults, or any such maters as may arise in your towns—then they must be taken to the place that Your God will choose. ⁹ Go to the Levitical priests and to the presiding judge to seek guidance. They will render a verdict for you. ¹⁰ Carry out the decision which they will give at the place which God will choose. Follow with care their instructions to you. ¹¹ Act in full accordance with the interpretation of the law that they hand down to you or the verdict they declare. Do not be diverted from what they tell you, either to the right or to the left. ¹² The person who goes against the ruling of the judge or the priest ministering to Adonai, your God, must be put to death. You must purge

evil from Israel. ¹³ All the people will hear of this with fear and their contemptuous behavior will end.

¹⁴ When you enter the land that Your God gives to you, and you settle on it and occupy it, and you then say, "Let us set up a ruler over us like all the peoples living around us," ¹⁵ you may do so, but appoint over yourselves the ruler whom Your God chooses. This ruler must be from among your own tribes. Do not place a foreigner over yourselves, one who is not an Israelite. ¹⁶ Your ruler must not acquire great numbers of horses, or send people back to Egypt for more horses; for Your God has said to you, "You are never to go back to that place." ¹⁷ Your ruler is not to acquire too many spouses and thus be led astray with lust, nor hoard great quantities of gold and silver.

¹⁸ After ascending the judgment seat, your ruler is to have a copy made of this Law in the presence of the Levitical priests. ¹⁹ Your ruler must keep it and learn from it every day, learning to live in the reverence of Our God, and assuring that this Law be always kept and its statutes always observed. ²⁰ Thus your ruler will avoid looking down with pride upon the people of Israel. Your ruler must not deviate from the keeping of the Law, either to the right or to the left. And if these things are done, your ruler and all rulers to come will have long reigns in Israel.

18:¹ The Levitical priests, all the tribe of Levi, will have no holdings to inherit in Israel. They will eat the food offerings of Our God as their share, ² but they are to have no birthright of property among the other members of the community. Our God is their inheritance, as it was promised to them.

³ The dues that are to be given to the priest by the people when they offer a sacrifice, whether a bull or a sheep, are the shank, the jawbone, and the stomach. ⁴ Also give them the firstfruits of your grain, your new wine and your oil, and the first fleece when the flock is sheared. ⁵ For it was they whom Our God chose out of all the tribes to stand before Our God, to perform the sacred duties and the blessings in the Name of Our God—they, and their heirs, for all time.

⁶ If a Levite comes from one of your towns anywhere in Israel where he has been living, to the place that will be chosen by God—any Levite may come there at any time— ⁷ then that Levite may minister in the Name of Our God, like all the other Levites who stand there to minister before God. ⁸ They are due equal portions to eat, even if they have income from the sale of family possessions.

⁹ When you come into the land that Your God is giving to you, do not adopt the abominable practices of the nations that were there. ¹⁰ There must

be no one found among you who makes their daughter or son pass through fire,* who practices divination or sorcery, or interprets omens, or engages in witchcraft, ¹¹ or casts spells, or who calls up spirits, or who consults the dead. ¹² Anyone who practices these acts is loathsome to Adonai, your God. Such abominable practices are the reason that Your God is driving these nations out before you. ¹³ You must be blameless before Your God. ¹⁴ These nations, whose lands you are about to take possession of, are disposed toward sorcery and divination. But for you, Your God will not permit such practices.

¹⁵ Adonai, your God, will raise up for you a prophet like me from among your own people; to that prophet you must listen. ¹⁶ It was this that you asked of Adonai, your God, at Horeb on the day of the assembly, when you said, "Let us not hear again the voice of Adonai, our God, nor see this great fire again, or we will die."

¹⁷ And Our God said to me, "This is well said. I will raise up for them a prophet like you from among their people, into whose mouth I will put my words, and that person will tell them all that I command. ¹⁹ If any person will not to listen to the words which my prophet speaks in my Name, I myself will call that person to answer for this. ²⁰ But if a prophet presumes to speak in my Name a message that I have not commanded to be spoken, or speaks in the name of other gods—that prophet will die."

²¹ You may say to yourselves, "How can we know when a message has not been spoken by Our God?" ²² If that which a prophet proclaims in the Name of God does shows itself to be untrue, or does not happen, then this is a message that God did not speak. Such prophets are presumptuous prophets. Do not listen to them.

19¹ When Adonai, your God, has destroyed the nations whose land is to be given to you, and when you have driven them out and taken possession of their dwellings and in their settlements, ² set aside for yourselves three cities in the land that Your God is giving to you. ³ Divide the land God is giving to you as your inheritance into three regions of equal distance from these cities, so that any Israelite who kills another may flee there.

⁴ This rule pertains to a person who kills another accidentally, when there was no quarrel between them, and so seeks to save his or her life by seeking refuge in one of these cities. ⁵ For instance, a person might go into a forest with another to gather wood, and when one person swings the ax, the head of the ax might come loose, flying off the handle and killing a

---

* A reference to human sacrifice, which was practiced by the Canaanites.

neighbor. That person may flee to one of these cities and so live. ⁶ Otherwise, the avenger of blood* could search out and find the killer on the road and, in a rage, could kill that person, even though the one who chopped the wood did not deserve death, because the killing of the neighbor was an accident and happened with no malicious intent. ⁷ Thus, you must set aside these three cities.

⁸ If Adonai, your God, enlarges your territory in fulfillment of the oath God swore to your ancestors, and you are given the whole land that was promised to your forebears ⁹ so long as you follow carefully all these commandments that I give you today—to love Your God and always walk in God's ways—then you are to set aside three more cities. ¹⁰ Do this so that innocent blood will not be shed in the land which Your God gives for your inheritance, and so that you will not be guilty of bloodshed.

¹¹ But if a one has a feud with a another and lies in wait to assassinate that person, and then flees to one of these cities, ¹² the elders of the slayer's town must bring the slayer home again, and surrender the slayer into the hands of the blood avenger to die. ¹³ Show no pity. Purge from Israel the guilt of shedding innocent blood, so that it may go well with you.

¹⁴ Do not move your neighbor's boundary marker, set up by previous generations, when you are settled on the property that you will be given, in the land Our God is giving you to possess.

¹⁵ One witness is not enough to convict a person accused of a crime or offense of any kind. All legal matters must be corroborated by the testimony of two or three witnesses.

¹⁶ If a witness comes forward and accuses a person of a crime, and does so with malice, ¹⁷ the two people involved in the dispute must stand in the presence of Our God before the priests and the judges who are in office at the time. ¹⁸ The judges must make a thorough examination of the matter, and if the witness is shown to have lied, ¹⁹ then do to the liar just what the liar had intended should be done to the accused. You must purge evil from among you. ²⁰ The rest of the people will hear of this case with fear, and never again will such an evil thing happen among you.

²¹ In judging, show no pity: take a life for a life, an eye for an eye, a tooth for a tooth, a hand for a hand, a foot for a foot.

20:1 When you go to war against your enemies and see horses and chariots and an army greater than yours, do not fear them. Adonai, your God,

---

* This is the victim's nearest relative, also called the blood redeemer; this person was obligated to avenge the victim's death.

is with you, the One who brought you up out of the land of Egypt. ² As you are about to go into battle, the priest will come forward and say, ³ "Listen, Israel! Today you are going into battle against your enemies. Do not lose heart; do not fear; do not panic in the face of them. ⁴ For Adonai, your God, will accompany you to fight for you against your enemies, to give you victory."

⁵ The officials are to say to the troops, "If any of you has built a house and not dedicated it, go back home and dedicate it; otherwise, if you are lost in battle, another will dedicate it. ⁶ If any of you has planted a vineyard and has not begun to enjoy its fruit, go back home; otherwise, if you are lost in battle, another might enjoy its firstfruits. ⁷ If any of you is pledged to another and not yet married, go back home, for if you are lost in battle, another might marry your betrothed." ⁸ The officers must also say to the troops, "If any of you is afraid and fainthearted, go back now, before you cause the hearts of your compatriots to melt like your own." ⁹ When the officers have finished talking to the troops, they will appoint commanders.

¹⁰ When you approach a town to attack it, first make an offer of peace. ¹¹ If the offer is accepted and the town gates are opened, then the residents living there will be put to forced labor and work for you. ¹² If the town refuses your offer of peace, and offers resistance, lay siege to it. ¹³ And when Your God delivers it into your hands, then all those who fought against you will die by the sword. ¹⁴ But you may take their spouses, their children, their livestock and any goods from the town as your spoils, which Your God delivers into your hands. ¹⁵ So it will be with all the towns that you take that are distant from you, and not part of the nations near you.

¹⁶ But in the towns of the peoples that Our God is giving to you as your inheritance, you must not let any living thing remain. ¹⁷ As Adonai, your God, commands you, you must destroy them—the Hittites, Amorites, Canaanites, Perizzites, Hivites and Jebusites—as Your God has commanded you, ¹⁷ so that they may not teach you to do the abominable things that they do for their gods, and so cause you to sin against Adonai, your God.

¹⁹ When in the course of war you lay siege to a town to capture it, you must not destroy the trees there by chopping them down. Eat from them, and do not destroy them. The trees in the field aren't people; do not make war on them. ²⁰ However, you may cut down any trees that you know do not provide food, and use them to build siege engines against the walls of a town at war with you, until it falls.

21:1 In this land which Adonai, your God, is giving to you to occupy, if a body is found in open country, and no one knows how the person died, ² your elders and your judges must come out to measure the distances to the towns nearest the body. ³ The elders of the town nearest the body must choose a heifer that has never been worked or worn a yoke, ⁴ and take it to a wadi with running water, one whose ground has never been plowed or sown, and there they must break the heifer's neck. ⁵ Then the priests, the Levites, must come forward, for Adonai, your God, chose them to minister and give blessings in the Name of Our God, and by their decision all cases of disputes and assaults must be settled. ⁶ All the elders of the town nearest the body must wash their hands in the wadi over the heifer with the broken neck, ⁷ and must proclaim, "Our hands did not shed this blood, nor were we witnesses to this bloodshed. ⁸ Accept this atonement for your people Israel, whom you redeemed, O God, and do not hold your people guilty of the blood of an innocent person." And the bloodshed will be atoned for. ⁹ Thus you will purge from yourselves the guilt of the shedding of innocent blood, since you have done what is right in the eyes of Our God.

¹⁰ When you go to war against your enemies, and Adonai, your God, delivers them into your hands and you capture them, ¹¹ if an Israelite man notices among the captives a woman he is attracted to, and whom he wishes to marry, ¹² he may bring such a captive into his home, and she must shave her head, cut her nails, ¹³ and take off her old clothes. She must stay inside the house and mourn for her parents for one month—then you may go to her and marry her. ¹⁴ If he is not happy with her, he must let her go free, and not sell her. He must treat her honorably, since she has shared his bed.*

¹⁵ If one of you has two spouses, and you love one but not the other, but you have children by both of them, and if your firstborn is the child of the spouse that you don't love, ¹⁶ then when the time comes for you to confer your property upon your children, you may not treat the child of the spouse you love as the firstborn, at the expense of the child of the spouse you don't love, who is the true firstborn. ¹⁷ You must acknowledge as firstborn the child of the spouse you don't love and give to this child a double portion of your estate, for this child is the firstfruit of your strength, and should enjoy all the rights of the firstborn.

¹⁸ If a couple has a child who is rebellious and unmanageable, and does not obey either parent, and does not heed punishment, ¹⁹ the parents are to

---

* Judith Antonelli explains that despite appearing to sanction the abduction and rape of women conquered in warfare, the intention of the commandment was in order to humanize captives, rather than allowing the soldier to participate in their systematic dehumanization. He must take her home, have her live in his part of the house, and see her every day; she had to be given all the rights of a wife, or be set free. The reference to cutting her nails and changing her clothes indicated ritual immersion—that is, religious conversion.

take the child to the elders of the town at the city gate. ²⁰ They are to say to the elders, "This recalcitrant child of ours is rebellious, and doesn't listen to us! Our child is a glutton and a drunkard!" ²¹ Then all the citizens of the town are to stone the child to death to rid the town of such wickedness. And all Israel will hear of this and be afraid.

²² If a person convicted of an offense that should be punished by death, and you do so by hanging that person from a tree, ²³ the body must not be left hanging from the limb overnight. You must bury this person on the same day, for anyone hung on a tree is accursed by God, and you must not desecrate the land that Adonai, your God, gives to you as your inheritance.

22:1 Should you see someone else's ox or sheep gone astray, don't ignore it but return it to its owner. ² But if the owner lives some distance away, or if you don't know who is the owner, take it home and care for it until the owner comes looking for it—then return it. ³ Do the same if you should find a donkey, or even a coat or anything lost. Do not ignore it. ⁴ If you see a donkey or an ox has fallen, you must not ignore it, but help the animal back onto its feet.

⁵ Don't wear the clothing of the opposite sex, for God detests those who do this.

⁶ If you come across a bird's nest, in a tree or on the ground, the young birds or eggs in the nest, do not take the parent bird with the young. ⁷ You may take the young, but let the parent bird go free, so that all may go well with you and that you have a long life.

⁸ When you build a new house, build a railing around your roof; otherwise, someone might fall off it, and you will bring the charge of bloodshed on your house.

⁹ You are not to sow any other seeds between your vine rows, or both crops will have to be forfeited to the sanctuary. ¹⁰ Do not plow with a team of an ox and a donkey together. ¹¹ Do not wear clothes of wool and linen woven together.

¹² Make tassels on the four corners of the cloak you wear.

¹³ If a woman and a man marry, and after the marriage is consummated, the man is not pleased with the woman, and fabricates accusations against her ¹⁴ of being not a virgin at the time of the marriage, ¹⁵ the parents of the woman will need to bring proof of their child's virginity to the elders at the city gate. ¹⁶ The parents of the slandered one must say to the elders, "We gave our daughter in marriage, but this slanderer doesn't like her. ¹⁷ Now

the slanderer is accusing her of not being a virgin as a pretext to end the marriage. But the evidence of virginity is here." Then, to prove the child's virginity, the parents will display the cloth before the elders of the town.*
¹⁸ If the elders accept the parents' charge of slander, ¹⁹ the man must pay one hundred silver shekels to the woman's parents. The slandered woman will continue to be married; and the slanderer cannot end the marriage by divorce. ²⁰ On the other hand, if the charge is true and no proof of the virginity of the accused can be found ²¹ the parents will be bring the woman to the door of their house and she will be stoned to death for the disgrace of having had sexual relations before marriage. You must purge this evil from Israel.

²² If a pair of adulterers are discovered, both must die. You must purge this evil from Israel.

²³ If a man has sexual relations with a virgin who is pledged to be married, and this happens in the town, ²⁴ you must take them both to the city gate and stone them to death—both the virgin who did not cry out for help in the town,** and the man who violated another's betrothed. You must purge this evil from your midst. ²⁵ But if a man rapes a woman who is engaged to be married, and this happens in the countryside, then only the rapist will die. ²⁶ Do nothing to the woman, who has done nothing to deserve death. This case is like that of someone who attacks and murders a neighbor, ²⁷ for the rapist came upon the woman out in the country, and even if she struggled and cried out, no one could hear and help her.

²⁸ If a man rapes an woman who is not engaged to be married, and is caught in the act, ⁵⁰ the rapist will pay one and a quarter pounds of silver to the parents of the woman. He must them marry her, and, as long as he lives, the rapist can never divorce her.

³⁰ No one must ever marry a spouse of his or her own parent: this is tantamount to incest.

23·¹ No male whose testicles are crushed or whose penis is severed may enter the assembly of Our God.

---

* This passage refers to the ancient custom in patriarchal societies of parents keeping the wedding night bed sheets of a couple as proof that the marriage had been consummated. If there was blood on the sheet, the woman was presumed to have been a virgin; if there was no blood, the young woman risked being labeled as promiscuous, even though her hymen may have been ruptured earlier without having had sexual relations. Such customs underscore the inherent inequality of women in this society, as there was no requirement that a man be a virgin when he married.

** This illustrates the high price women have had to pay because of sexism, since the argument is still offered in today's society: if the man puts his hand over his victim's mouth, or puts a knife to her throat so that she *cannot* cry for help, then she was "willing."

² No descendant born of a forbidden marriage, even down to the tenth generation, may enter the assembly of Our God.

³ No Ammonite or Moabite, even down to the tenth generation, may enter the assembly of Our God, ⁴ for they did not come to meet with you with food and water on your journey up out of Egypt, and because they hired Balaam, begot of Beor from Pethor in Aram Naharaim to curse you. Adonai, your God, refused to listen to Balaam and turned the curse into a blessing for you, because Adonai, your God, loved you. ⁶ You are not to seek their welfare nor their good will as long as you live. ⁷ Don't consider the Edomites to be abominable—for they are your kin—nor the Egyptians, for you lived as a foreigner in their land. ⁸ The third generation of children born of these may become members of the assembly.

⁹ When you are encamped at war against your enemies, keep clear of anything impure. ¹⁰ If one of the men is ceremonially unclean because of a nocturnal emission, he is to go outside the camp and stay there. ¹¹ As evening approaches he is to wash himself, and at sunset may return to camp.

¹² Designate a place outside the camp where you may go to relieve yourself. ¹³ Make trowels a part of your standard equipment; when you squat, you are to dig a hole with the trowel, and then turn and cover your excrement. ¹⁴ For Adonai, your God, moves about in your camp to protect you and to deliver your enemies to you. Your camp must therefore be holy, so that God will not see among you anything indecent and turn away from you.

¹⁵ You must not return escaped indentured workers who take refuge with you to their former owners. ¹⁶ Such indentured workers may freely choose where among your settlements he or she would like to settle; in all of your towns they may not be mistreated.

¹⁷ No Israelite, male or female, may become a temple prostitute. ¹⁸ You must not bring the fee of a female or the pay of a male prostitute into the house of Your God in fulfillment of a vow, for both of them are abominable to Your God.

¹⁹ You must not charge interest on what you lend to another Israelite, whether it be money, or goods, or anything else. ²⁰ You may charge interest on a loan to a foreigner, but never on a loan to an Israelite, so that Adonai, your God, will bless you in all you undertake in the land that you will soon possess.

²¹ When you make a vow to Adonai, your God, do not put off repaying that vow, or Your God will call you to account, and your vow will become

your downfall. ²² If you choose not to make a vow, you will guard yourself against sin; ²³ but should you make a vow to Adonai, your God, with your own words, you must be careful to fulfill what you have willingly promised to do.

²⁴ When you are in another's vineyard, you may eat as many grapes as you wish, but you may not put any grapes in a basket. ²⁵ When you enter the wheat field of another, you may pick the as many heads of grain as you can carry with your hands, but you must never cut another's uncut crop.

24:¹ If two people marry, but then one of them finds something offensive about the other and writes a certificate of divorce, ² and the spouse that was dismissed marries a second person, ³ and then the second spouse writes a certificate of divorce or simply dies— ⁴ in such a case, the first spouse may not remarry the divorced spouse; the divorced spouse is unclean to that person. This would be hateful in the sight of Your God, and you must not bring guilt on the land that Your God is giving to you as your inheritance.

⁵ A newly married person may not enter military duty, or be obligated to fulfill any similar service, for a period of one year, so that the couple may enjoy their happiness together.

⁶ No one may take a mill or a millstone in a pledge, for you are taking someone's livelihood.

⁷ If an Israelite kidnaps, another Israelite, or enslaves and sells one, the punishment is death. You must purge this evil from among you.

⁸ In cases of infectious skin diseases do exactly as the Levite priests tell you to do. You must diligently follow the commands I have given them. ⁹ Remember what Our God did to Miriam as you journeyed up from Egypt.*

¹⁰ When you make a loan of any sort to a neighbor, do not enter the neighbor's premises to receive the collateral. ¹¹ Stay outside the house and let the person to whom you are making the loan bring the item given as collateral out to you.** ¹² If the person is poor, and gives you a garment as collateral, do not keep it past the end the day—¹³ return a cloak by sunset so that the person may sleep in it. Then that person will thank you, and your good deed will be a righteous act before Adonai, your God.

---

* A reference to the incident in Numbers 12:9 in which Miriam was afflicted with a skin disease after challenging her brother Moses.

** This was done to ensure that the borrower was giving up the pledged item freely and without coercion.

¹⁴ Never hold back the wages a poor worker in need, whether an Israelite or a foreigner living in one of your towns. ¹⁵ Pay the hired worker's wages for that day before sunset, for the worker is poor and in need of that payment. Should you not do this, the hired worker might cry out against you to Our God, and you will be guilty of sin.

¹⁶ Parents may not be put to death in place of their children, nor may children be put to death in the place of their parents. No one may be put to death except for his or her own sins.

¹⁷ Do not deprive the foreigner living among you of justice, or the orphan either; nor take the cloak of the widow or widower as collateral. ¹⁸ Do not forget that you were slaves in Egypt, and Adonai, your God, redeemed you from that place. So it is that I command you to do these things.

¹⁹ When you are harvesting in your field and overlook a sheaf of grain, do not go back for it afterward. Leave it for the foreigner, the orphan, or the widowed, so that Adonai, your God, may bless you in all the work that you do. ²⁰ When you beat the olives from your trees, do not go over the branches a second time. Leave what remains to the foreigner, the orphan, or the widowed. ²¹ When you harvest grapes in your vineyard, do not go over the vines a second time. Leave what remains for the foreigner, the orphan, or the widowed. ²² Remember that once you were slaves in Egypt, and this is why I command you to do this.

25:¹ When two of you have a dispute, and you bring it before the judges, they will judge between you and find one of you justified, and the other not. ² If you are guilty and deserve to be flogged, the judge will have you lie down and be flogged with the number of lashes the crime deserves. ³ But you must not get more than forty. More than forty would bring you dishonor in your neighbor's eyes.

⁴ Don't muzzle the ox as it treads the grain on the threshing floor.

⁵ In an extended family, if one of the married men dies without an heir, his widow must not marry outside the family. It is her brother-in-law's duty to marry her himself. ⁶ The first child born from this union will carry on the name of brother who died, so that that his family name will not be blotted out from Israel.

⁷ If the man will not marry his sister-in-law, the widow is to go to the elders and tell them, "My brother-in-law will not perform the duty of perpetuating our family name in Israel." ⁸ The elders of the town will summon the brother-in-law to address the issue. If the man continues to refuse this marriage, ⁹ then the widow, in the presence of the elders, will approach

her brother-in-law, take off his sandal,* and spit in his face and say, "This is how to treat a person who refuses to build up his brother's line!" ¹⁰ The family of the recalcitrant one will be known through all of Israel as "the house of the one whose sandal was torn off."

¹¹ When two men are fighting and the spouse of one intervenes by reaching out and grabbing the genitals of the assailant, ¹² you must cut off the hand of the intervener. Show no pity.

¹³ Do not carry two weights in your bag—one light and one heavy.* Do not carry two measures in your house—one small and one large. ¹⁵ You must have accurate and honest weights and measures, so that you may live long in the land that Adonai, your God, gives to you. ¹⁶ For Adonai, your God, detests anyone who does such things, anyone who deals dishonestly.

¹⁷ Recall how the Amalekites treated you when you had left Egypt, ¹⁸ and you were weary and worn down; how they met you along the way and cut down those who were lagging behind. The Amalekites had no fear of God. ¹⁹ So when Adonai, your God, has given you rest from all the enemies that surround you in the land that God is giving to you as an inheritance, you must blot out the memory of the Amalekites from under the heavens. Do not forget!

26·1 Once you have entered the land that Adonai, your God, is giving to you as your inheritance, and you have taken possession of it and settled in it, ² take some of the firstfruits of all that you produce from the soil of the land that Adonai, your God, is giving to you, and put them in a basket. Take them to the place which Adonai, your God, will choose as a dwelling place for God's Name ³ and say to the priest in office at that time, "This day I declare to Adonai, our God, that I have come to the land Our God swore to our ancestors to give us." ⁴ The priest will then receive the basket from you and will set it in front of the altar of Our God.

⁵ Then you will declare before Our God, "My ancestor was a wandering Aramean who went down to Egypt with a small household and lived there

---

* In ancient Israel, sales transactions or acts of redemption were finalized by removing one's sandal and giving it to the other party, symbolically giving up one's right to ownership. Here, though the man wished to cede his right to raise a family by his brother's widow, it was seen as an insult to the woman, so the intention in the ceremony was to humiliate him: instead of his removing his own sandal and giving it to the woman in the normal way, she would show contempt by removing his sandal and spitting in his face.

** Travelling merchants would carry with them a standard weight that was used as a counterbalance on a scale; unbeknown to those doing business with them, duplicitous merchants would carry two different weights, and would use whichever one brought them a more favorable bargain.

as an alien. There they became a nation great, strong and numerous. ⁶ When the Egyptians mistreated and oppressed us, imposing hard labor upon us, ⁷ we cried to Adonai, the God of our ancestors, who heard our cry and saw our affliction, our toil and our oppression. ⁸ Our God brought us out of Egypt with a strong hand and outstretched arm, with terrifying power, with signs and wonders; ⁹ Our God gave us this land, a land flowing with milk and honey. ¹⁰ Therefore, I have brought now the first fruits of the products of the soil that you, O God, have given me." Then you must set them before Your God, and bow down before the Most High. ¹¹ Then you all, along with the Levites, and the foreigner that live among you, will feast on all the good things that Adonai, your God, has given to you and your household.

¹² When you have set aside the tenth of all your produce in the third year, the year of the tithe, give it to the Levite, the foreigner, the orphan, and the widowed, so that they may eat in your towns and be satisfied. ¹³ Then say to Adonai, your God, "I have removed from my house the sacred portion and given it to the Levite, the foreigner, the orphan, and the widowed according to all that you have commanded; I have neither neglected anything nor transgressed in anything. ¹⁴ I have not eaten any of the sacred portion while I was in mourning, nor have I separated any of it while I was unclean, nor have I offered any of it to the dead. I have obeyed Adonai, my God. I have done everything as you have commanded. Look down from heaven, your holy dwelling place, and bless your people Israel and the land which You gave to us as it was sworn to our ancestors, a land flowing with milk and honey."

¹⁶ Adonai, your God, commands you today to observe these decrees and laws. Take care to keep them in your heart and observe them with all your soul. ¹⁷ You have received today the promise that Adonai will be your God, and you will follow God's ways, listen to God's voice and keep all the statutes, commandments and ordinances. ¹⁸ And Our God has today declared, "You will be my very own people as I promised, but only if you keep all my commandments; ¹⁹ then for praise and renown and honor I will set you high above all the nations I have made, and you will be a people consecrated to me, as I promised."

ෲ ෲ ෲ

27:1 Moses and the elders of Israel commanded the people, "Keep all the commandments that I have given you today. ² Once you have crossed the Jordan into the land Adonai, your God, gives you, set up some large standing stones and coat them with plaster. ³ Write on them all the words of this Law when you have crossed over to enter the land that Adonai, your God, gives you, a land flowing with milk and honey, just as Adonai, the God of your ancestors, promised you. ⁴ When you have crossed the Jordan, set up these stones on Mount Ebal, as I command you today, and coat them with plaster. ⁵ Build an altar there to Your God—an altar of stone that no iron tool has touched. ⁶ Build the altar to Adonai, your God, of undressed stone, and sacrifice burnt offerings on it to Your God. ⁷ Make communal offerings there, eating them and rejoicing in the presence of Your God. ⁸ You must write very clearly all the words of this Law on these stones you set up."

⁹ Then Moses and the Levite priests said to all of Israel, "Be silent, O Israel, and listen! Today you have become the people of Adonai, your God. ¹⁰ You must listen to the voice of Adonai, your God, and follow the commandments and decrees I give you today."

¹¹ That same day, Moses commanded the people these things:

¹² When you have crossed the Jordan, these tribes will stand on Mount Gerizim for the blessing of the people: Simeon, Levi, Judah, Issachar, Joseph and Benjamin. ¹³ And these tribes will stand on Mount Ebal for the curse: Reuben, Gad, Asher, Zebulun, Dan and Naphtali. ¹⁴ The Levites will declaim to all the people of Israel in a great voice:

¹⁵   "Cursed are those who carve an images or cast an idol,
     the work of a crafter's hands—a thing detestable to Our God—
     and set it up in secret."
          Then all the people will say, "Amen!"
¹⁶   "Cursed are those who dishonor their mothers or their fathers."
          Then the people will say, "Amen!"
¹⁷   "Cursed are those landowners who move
     their neighbor's boundary stone."
          Then the people will say, "Amen!"
¹⁸   "Cursed are those who lead the blind astray on the road."
          Then the people will say, "Amen!"
¹⁹   "Cursed are those who withhold justice from foreigners,
     or from orphans or the widow or the widower."
          Then the people will say, "Amen!"
²⁰ "Cursed are those who sleep with their parent's spouse,
     and so dishonor the parental bed."
          Then the people will say, "Amen!"
²¹ "Cursed are those who have sexual relations with animals."
          Then the people will say, "Amen!"

²² "Cursed are those who sleep with their sister or their brother,
   or their half-brother or half-sister."
      Then the people will say, "Amen!"
²³ "Cursed are those who sleep with their in-laws."
      Then the people will say, "Amen!"
²⁴ "Cursed are those who kill their neighbor secretly."
      Then the people will say, "Amen!"
²⁵ "Cursed are those who accept a bribe to kill an innocent person."
      Then the people will say, "Amen!"
²⁶ "Cursed are those who do not uphold the words of this Law
   and observe them."
      Then the people will say, "Amen!"

28:1 Now, if you faithfully obey Adonai, your God, and carefully follow the commandments I give you today, Adonai, your God, will set you high above all the nations on earth. ² All these blessings will be with you always if you obey Adonai, your God:

³   Blessed will you be in the city,
       and blessed in the country.
⁴   Blessed will be the fruit of your womb,
       and of your land, and of the your livestock—
    the calves of your herds
       and the lambs of your flocks.
⁵   Blessed will be your basket
       and your kneading bowl.
⁶   Blessed will you be when you come in
       and when you go out.

⁷ Your God will hand over to you the enemies who attack you, and let them be routed before you. Though they come at you united, they will flee before you in seven directions.

⁸ Your God will bless you in your granaries and in all your labors; Your God will bless you in the land that is being given to you.

⁹ Your God will make of you a people consecrated to the Most High, as it was promised to you, so long as you keep the commandments of Your God and follow in God's footsteps. ¹⁰ All the peoples of the earth will know that you are called by the Name of Our God, and will live in fear of you. ¹¹ Your God will make you prosper greatly, in the fruit of your bodies, and that of your livestock, and of your soil, on this land which God swore to your ancestors to give you.

¹² Your God will open the heavens for you, a rich storehouse of bounty, to send rain on your land in the proper time, and to bless everything to

which you turn your hand. You will lend to many nations and borrow from none. [13] Your God will make you the head and never the tail. [13] If you obey the commandments that Adonai, your God, has given to you, you will be always at the top and never at the bottom. [14] Do not deviate, either to the right or to the left, from the things which I command you today, and do not go searching after other gods to serve.

[15] But if you do not obey Adonai, your God, by following carefully all of the commandments and statutes which I give to you this day, all these curses will overcome upon you and bring you down:

[16]   Cursed will you be in the city
            and cursed in the country.
[17]   Cursed will be your basket
            and your kneading bowl.
[18]   Cursed will be the fruit of your womb,
            and of your land, and over your livestock—
        the calves of your herds
            and the lambs of your flocks.
[19]   Cursed will you be when you come in
            and when you go out.

[20] Your God will send you catastrophes, confusion and fear in everything you attempt until you are destroyed and come to a quick ruin because of the evil you did in forsaking me. [21] Your God will plague you with diseases until you are destroyed and wasted from the land which you are entering to occupy. [22] Your God will plague you with wasting diseases, with fever and inflammation, with scorching heat and drought, with blight and mildew, which will plague you until you perish. [23] The skies above you will be unyielding as bronze and the earth below you hard as iron. [24] Your God will turn the rain in your land into dust, and dust will descend upon you from the heavens until you are blotted out.

[25] Your God will bring you defeat from your enemies. Though you go out against them united, you will flee them in seven directions. You will be a cause of revulsion among the realms of the earth. [26] Your remains will be food for the birds of the air and the wild beasts, and there will be no one to scare them away.

[27] Your God will strike you with afflictions such as you saw in Egypt—boils, tumors, scabs and itching—from which there is no cure. [28] Your God will strike you with madness, blindness and confusion of mind, [29] so that you will grope about in broad daylight, just as the blind grope about in darkness, and you will fail to find your way. You will be tormented and robbed, with no one to protect you.

³⁰ You may become engaged, but your betrothed will go lie with another; you may build a house, but will never live in it; you may plant a vineyard, but will never harvest its fruits. ³¹ Your ox may be slaughtered before your eyes but you will have nothing to eat; your donkey will be stolen in broad daylight, and will never be not returned to you; your sheep will be given to an enemy, and there will be no one to aid you.³² Your daughters and sons will be given away, while you look on, helpless—you my search for them all the day, but it will be useless. ³³ A nation of which you have never even heard of will eat the produce of your fields and of your toil, and you will exploited and brought to nothing. ³⁴ The sights that you see will drive you mad. ³⁵ Your God will afflict your knee and your leg with severe boils for which there is no cure; they will spread from the sole of your foot to the crown of your head.

³⁶ Your God will exile you, you and the ruler you appointed, to a nation that neither you nor your ancestors have known, and there you will serve other gods, gods of wood and stone. ³⁷ You will become a symbol of disgust, an object of scorn and ridicule to all the nations where Your God will send you.

³⁸ You will sow widely, but your harvest will be lean when the locusts have eaten their share. ³⁹ You will plant your vineyards and tend them, but eat the grapes nor drink any wine for the worms be there before you. ⁴⁰ Your olive trees will grow throughout your lands but you will never anoint yourselves with the oil, for your olive will fall off. ⁴¹ You will have daughters and sons, but they will be taken from you into captivity. ⁴² Swarms of locusts will swarm over your trees, and your crops and your land.

⁴³ The foreigners among you will rise high above you, higher and higher, while you sink lower and lower. ⁴⁴ They will become your lenders, and you will never lend to them. They will be the head, and you will be the tail.

⁴⁵ All these curses will bear you down; they will run you down until you are destroyed, for your disobedience to Your God, for not keeping the commandments and statutes that were given to you. ⁴⁶ They will be an omen and a warning among you and your descendants for all time, ⁴⁷ because you did not serve Adonai, your God, rejoicing gladly, and heartily grateful in all your blessings. ⁴⁸ In hunger and in thirst, nakedness and in terrible want, you will serve the enemies that Your God will send against you. They will put an iron collar around your neck until you are broken.

⁴⁸ God will bring against you from far off, from the end of the earth, a nation which will strike you from above like an eagle, a nation whose language is incomprehensible to you, ⁵⁰ a people of terrible countenance, a

nation without respect for the elderly or pity for the young. [51] They will devour your herds, and the fruit of your lands. They will leave you no grain, nor wine, nor oil; they will leave your herds and your flocks barren, and you will despair. [52] They will lay siege to all your towns until the mighty fortified walls that you trusted so well will collapse. They will besiege every city throughout the land which Your God is now giving to you.

[53] In the terrible suffering that your enemies will inflict on you during the siege, you will eat the fruit of your own bodies, the flesh of the daughters and sons which Adonai, your God, gave to you. [54] Even the most gentle and sensitive man among you will have no compassion on his sister or his brother, or even his loving spouse, or what children remain, [55] and he will not share even with them the flesh of his own children that he eats when nothing else remains for him, after the sufferings inflicted by your enemies in the siege of your cities. [56] The most gentle and sensitive woman among you, so sensitive and gentle she would not put her bare foot on the ground, will not share with her spouse or her surviving children [57] the afterbirth she expels or the child she bears during the siege, for she herself will eat them secretly in her terrible hunger, in the terrible straits to which the enemy will reduce you in your towns.

[58] If you do not fulfill every letter of the law written down in this book, if you do not revere this honored and dreaded Name, the name "Adonai, your God," [59] then God will strike you and your descendants with unimaginable plagues, virulent and chronic, and with severe and lingering diseases. [60] God will bring on you again all the diseases of Egypt which you dreaded, and they will cling to you. [61] Our God will bring upon you sickness and plague of every kind, kinds not even recorded in this book of the Law, until you are destroyed. [62] Then you who were as countless as the stars in the skies will be left few in number, because you did not obey Adonai, your God. [63] Just as Adonai, your God, delighted in you, making you prosper you and increasing your numbers, so now it will be God's delight to bring you to ruin and decimation. You will be uprooted from this land that you now are entering to occupy.

[64] Adonai, your God, will disperse you among all the peoples from one end of the earth to the other, where you will serve other gods, gods of whom neither you nor your ancestors have ever heard, gods of wood and stone. [65] You will find no peace among those nations, no place to rest your weary feet. In that place Your God will give you an worried mind, and your eyes will grow dim and your spirit will fade. [66] Your life will hang by a thread before you; fear will be your fare, by night and by day, and your life will have no security. [67] In the morning you will say, "If only it were evening!" and in the evening, "If only it were morning!" because of the terror that fills

your heart and the sights that fill your eyes. ⁶⁸ Your God will return you in ships to Egypt by the very road of which I said to you, "You will never see this road again." There you will offer yourselves, men and women alike, for sale as bonded workers to your enemies—but no one will buy you.

ဆ ဆ ဆ

29:1 These, then, were the terms of the Covenant that Our God commanded Moses to make with the Israelites in Moab, and the covenant God had made with them at Horeb.*

29:2–30:20

M̲oses summoned the Israelites and said these things:

You saw with your own eyes what Our God did in Egypt to Pharaoh, and to the Pharaoh's courtiers and to the whole land; you were witness to the great ordeals, the signs and wonders. ⁴ But until now, Our God has not given you the hearts to understand, or the eyes to see or the ears to hear.

⁵ "During the forty years that I led you in the desert," Our God says, "your clothes did not wear out, nor did the sandals on your feet. You have eaten no bread and drunk no wine, nor any other fermented drink. ⁶ I did this so that you might know that I am Adonai, your God." ⁷ When we reached this place, Sihon, ruler of Heshbon and Og, ruler of Bashan launched an attack on us. We defeated them, ⁸ took their land and gave it as an inheritance to the Reubenites, the Gadites and the half-tribe of Manasseh.

⁹ Follow carefully the terms of this Covenant, so that you may succeed in all that you do. ¹⁰ Today, all of you stand in the presence of Adonai, your God—the leaders of your tribes, your elders, all your officials, and all of the people of Israel, ¹¹ your children, your women and men, and all the foreigners living among you who draw your water and cut your wood. ¹² Your are about to enter into a covenant, sealed by an oath, with Adonai, your God. ¹³ Today, through this Covenant, Your God will make a nation of you, and Adonai will be your God, as it was promised to you and as it was sworn to your ancestors, Sarah and Abraham, Rebecca and Isaac, and

---

* In the Hebrew text, this is the final verse of chapter 28, and there follows a one-verse discrepancy through the end of chapter 29.

Leah, Rachel and Jacob. ¹⁴ It is not with you alone who stand here with us today before Adonai, our God, that I make this Covenant and take this oath, ¹⁵ but also with those who are not with us today.

¹⁶ You know how we lived in Egypt, and how we passed through other countries on our way here, ¹⁷ and saw among them detestable images—idols of wood and stone, of silver and gold. ¹⁸ Beware that there may be women or men among you today, even clans or tribes, whose heart is even now turning away from Adonai, our God, to go and worship the gods of those nations. There may already be a root growing among you that which produces such bitter poison.

¹⁹ If, even after you hear this oath, there is someone among you so foolish as to think, "All will go well with me, even though I follow my own path," sweeping disaster will come to the watered land as well as the dry; ²⁰ Our God will never be willing to forgive them. God's wrath and zeal will burn against such people. All the curses written in this book will fall upon them, and God will blot out their names from under heaven. ²¹ Our God will single them out from among the tribes of Israel for disaster, according to the curses of the Covenant written in this Book of the Law.

²² The next generation, your children who follow you, and foreigners who come from distant places, will witness the plagues of this land and the diseases which Our God has brought upon it and will cry, ²³ "The entire land is a burning waste of salt and sulfur! Nothing is planted, nothing is sprouting, no vegetation will ever grow on it again! It will be like Sodom and Gomorrah, Admah and Zeboiim, which Our God destroyed in fiery rage." ²⁴ They, and all the nations with them, will ask, "Why has Your God so afflicted this land? Why this specter of terrible wrath?"

²⁵ The answer will be: "It is because this people abandoned the Covenant of Adonai, the God of their ancestors, the covenant that was made with them when Their God brought them out of Egypt. ²⁶ They turned from their path to worship other gods and bow down before them—gods they did not know, and whom Their God had not assigned to them. ²⁷ The wrath of Their God was aroused against that land, so that God brought on it all the curses described in this book. ²⁸ The Most High God uprooted them from their soil in anger, in a rage and with great fury, and banished them to other lands, where they are to this day."

²⁹ Hidden things belong to Adonai, our God, but what is revealed belongs to us and our children forever, so that we may observe all that is prescribed in this Law!

30¹ When all these things have come into being—both the blessings and the curses which I have revealed to you—if you take them into your hearts, there among the nations to which Adonai, your God, will banish you; ² if you and your children turn your hearts back again to Adonai, your God, and obey God with all your heart and with all your soul, according to everything I command you today, ³ then Adonai, your God, will again restore you to your destiny, and will gather you again from all the nations to which you were banished. ⁴ Even though the banishment drove you to the ends of the earth, ⁵ Adonai, your God, will bring you back into the land which your ancestors occupied, and you will occupy it again. Then God will bring you prosperity and make you even more numerous than your ancestors were.

⁶ Adonai, your God will sensitize your hearts and the hearts of your descendants, so that you will love God with all your heart and with all your soul, and you will live. ⁷ Then Adonai, your God, will turn all these curses against your enemies, and on the foes who persecute you. ⁸ Then you will obey Your God once more and keep all the commandments which I give to you today. ⁹ Your God will make you prosper in all the work of your hands, and in the fruit of your body, of your livestock and of your lands. ¹⁰ Your God will once again delight in you and make you prosperous, just as God delighted in your ancestors and prospered them, if you obey Adonai, your God, and keep the commandments and decrees that are written in this Book of the Law, and return to the Most High with all your heart and soul.

¹¹ For this Law that I give to you today is not too difficult for you, nor is it beyond your reach. ¹² It is not up in heaven, so that you need to ask yourselves, "Who will go up to heaven for us and bring it down to us, so that we may hear it and keep it?" ¹³ Nor is it beyond the seas, so that you need to wonder, "Who will cross the seas for us and bring it back to us, so that we may hear it and keep it?" ¹⁴ No, the word of God is very near to you; it is in your mouth, and in your heart, so that you can keep it.

¹⁵ Today I have set before you life and success, or death and disaster. ¹⁶ For today I command you to love Adonai, your God, to follow God's ways and keep the commandments, the laws and the customs. If you do, you will live and increase, and Adonai, your God, will bless you in the land that you are entering to possess. ¹⁷ But if your hearts stray and you do not listen to me, if you let yourself be drawn into the worship of other gods, and serve them, ¹⁸ I tell you today, you will not survive. You will not live long in the land which you are now crossing the Jordan to enter and occupy.

¹⁹ I call heaven and earth to witness against you today: I set before you life or death, blessing or curse. Choose life, then, so that you and your descendants may live, ²⁰ by loving Adonai, your God, by obeying God's voice and by clinging to the Most High. For that will mean life for you, a

long life in the land which God swore to give to your descendants Sarah and Abraham, Rebecca and Isaac, and Leah and Rachel and Jacob.

31:1–34:12

*W*hen Moses had addressed these words to the whole of Israel, he said, ² "I am now one hundred and twenty years old, and I can no longer come and go as I will. Our God has told me that I will not cross the Jordan. ³ It is Our God who will lead you across and subdue these nations before you. And Joshua will cross over at your head, as it was foretold. ⁴ Our God will deal with these nations as with Sihon and Og, the rulers of the Amorites. Our God destroyed them, together with their country. ⁵ You must treat them exactly as I have ordered you. ⁶ Be brave and steadfast, have no fear of them, no terror, for Our God is the one who marches with you, and will never fail you or forsake you."

⁷ Then Moses summoned Joshua, and, in the presence of all Israel, said to him, "Be strong and courageous; you are going with this people into the land God promised to our ancestors. You must lead them to possess this land as their heritage. ⁸ Our God will march before you, and will never fail you or desert you. So do not fear and never be disheartened."

⁹ Then Moses wrote down this Law and gave it to the priests, the heirs of Levi—who carried the Ark of the Covenant of Our God—and the elders of Israel. ¹⁰ Then Moses commanded them: "At the end of every seven years, at the time set for the year of the forgiveness of debts, during the Feast of Tabernacles ¹¹ when all Israel comes to appear before Adonai, our God, at the place God chooses, you must read this Law before them in their hearing. ¹² Assemble the people—women, men, children, the foreigners living among you—so that they can listen to and learn to stand in awe of Adonai, our God, and follow with care every letter of this Law. ¹³ Their children who are not yet well-versed in this Law must hear it and learn to revere Adonai, our God, as long as you live in the land that you are now crossing the Jordan to possess."

¹⁴ Our God said to Moses, "Now the time of your death is at hand. Call Joshua and come to the Tent of Meeting so that I may commission him." Moses and Joshua went and presented themselves at the Tent of Meeting.

¹⁵ Then God appeared at the Tent in a pillar of cloud, and the cloud stood over the entrance of the Tent of Meeting. ¹⁶ God said to Moses, "You are going to rest with your ancestors, and these people are going to prostitute

themselves to the foreign gods of the land you are entering. They will abandon me and break the Covenant I made with them. ¹⁷ I will grow angry with them and will abandon them. I will hide my face from them, and they will be destroyed. Many disasters and misfortunes will come upon them, and the day will come when they will ask, "Are not these disasters and misfortunes because Our God has abandoned us?" ¹⁸ And I will assuredly not show my face on that day because of all the evil they have done by turning to other gods.

¹⁹ "Thus you must write down this song and teach it to the Israelites. Make them repeat it, so that it may be a testimony for me against them. ²⁰ When I have brought them into the land flowing with milk and honey, the land which I promised on oath to their ancestors, and when they eat their fill and thrive, they will turn to other gods and worship them, rejecting me and breaking my Covenant. ²¹ And when many disasters and misfortunes come upon them, this song will be a testimony against them because their descendants will never forget it. I know what they are disposed to do, even before I bring them into the land I promised them on oath." ²² So Moses wrote down this song on that day, and taught it to the Israelites.

²³ Then Our God gave this command to Joshua, begot of Nun: "Be strong and courageous, for you will take the Israelites into the land I promised them on oath, and I myself will be with you."

²⁴ After Moses had finished writing in a book the words of this Law from beginning to end, ²⁵ he commanded the Levites who carried the Ark of the Covenant of Our God, ²⁶ "Take this Book of the Law and place it beside the Ark of the Covenant of Adonai, your God. There it will stand as a witness against you. ²⁷ For I know how rebellious and proud a people you are. If you have been rebellious against Our God while I am still among you, how much more will you rebel once I am dead? ²⁸ Assemble before me all the elders of your tribes and all your officials, so that I may speak these words in their hearing and call heaven and earth to testify against them. ²⁹ For I am certain that after my death you are sure to become wholly corrupt and turn away from the way which I have commanded you. In days to come, disaster will fall upon you because you will do evil things in the sight of Our God and will provoke God's anger with your behavior."

³⁰ And Moses then recited the words of this song, from beginning to end, in the hearing of the whole assembly of Israel:

32:1 Listen, O heavens, and I will speak;
　　hear, O earth, the words of my mouth.

2 Let my teachings fall like rain
        and my words descend like dew,
     like rain on new grass,
        like abundant showers on new growth.
3 I proclaim the Name of Our God!
        Oh, praise the greatness of Our God!
4 Our God is a rock, whose works are perfect
        and whose ways are just—
     a faithful God who does no wrong,
        who is always upright and just.

5 You have acted corruptly toward Our God;
        to your shame you are no longer God's children,
        but a warped and crooked generation.
6 Is this the way you repay Your God,
        you foolish and stupid people?
     Is this not Your God, your Creator,
        who made you and formed you?
7 Call to mind the days of old;
        consider the generations long gone.
     Ask your parents, and they will tell you;
        ask your elders, and they will enlighten you.
8 When the Most High gave the nations their inheritance,
        when God divided all humankind,
     God set up boundaries among all the peoples
        according to the number of the gods;
9 but Our God's portion is you, the people of the Most High;
        Jacob is God's allotted inheritance.
10 God adopted you in a desert country,
        in a barren and howling waste.
     God shielded you and cared for you,
        guarding you as an apple of the eye.
11 Like the eagle that stirs up its nest,
        and hovers over its young,
     God spreads wings to catch you,
        and carries you on pinions.
12 Our God alone leads you;
        no foreign god is with you.
13 God gives you the heights of the land to ride
        and feeds you with the fruit of the mountains.

---

* A euphemism for Israel, here used ironically: it means "the upright one."

God nourishes you with honey from the rock,
  and with oil from the flinty crags,
14 with curds and milk from herd and flock,
  and the fat of lambs and goats,
  with choice rams from Bashan and the finest kernels of wheat,
  with red wine from the fermented grape.

15 Jeshurun* grew fat and kicked;
  filled with food, heavy and bloated.
  You abandoned the God who made you,
  rejecting the Rock, your Savior.
16 You made God jealous with your foreign gods
  and angered God with your detestable idols.
17 You sacrificed to demons who are not God,
  to gods you never knew,
  to gods you came to know,
  to gods that recently appeared,
  whom your ancestors did not fear.
18 You deserted the Rock who gave you life;
  you forgot the God who bore you.
19 Seeing this the Most High rejected you;
  angered by your sons and daughters, God said,
20 "I will hide my face from them, and see what their end will be;
  for they are a perverse generation, and faithless children.
21 They made me jealous with what are not gods;
  they have angered me with worthless idols.
  Therefore, I will make them envious
  with those who are not a people;
  I will make them angry
  with a nation that does not understand.
22 For a fire has been kindled by my wrath,
  one that burns to the realm of death below.
  It will devour the earth and its harvests
  and put to flame the foundations of the mountains.
23 I will heap calamities upon them,
  speeding my arrows against them.
24 I will send upon them wasting famine,
  consuming pestilence, deadly plague;
  I will send fangs of wild beasts against them,
  the venom of vipers gliding in the dust.
25 In the streets the sword will make them childless;
  terror will reign in the home.

Young women and young men will perish,
   infants and the gray-haired.
26 I said that I would scatter them
   and blot them out from the memory of humankind,
27 if I did not dread the taunt of the enemy,
   the adversary who might misconstrue,
saying, 'Our hand is triumphant;
   their God has not done all this.' "
28 They are a senseless nation;
   they have no discernment in themselves.
29 If only they were wise and able to understand all this
   and discern what their destiny will be!
30 How could one chase one thousand,
   or two rout ten thousand
unless their Rock had gotten rid of them,
   the Most High had given up on them?
31 For their rock is not like our Rock,
   as even our enemies concede.
32 Their vine comes from the vine of Sodom,
   and from the fields of Gomorrah.
Their grapes are filled with poison,
   and their clusters with bitterness.
33 Their wine is the venom of serpents,
   the deadly poison of cobras.
34 "Have I not kept this in reserve," God says,
   "and sealed it in my vaults?
35 Vengeance is mine—I will repay them!
   In due course their foot will slip;
their day of disaster is near
   and their doom rushes down upon them."

36 Your God will judge the faithful people
   and be compassionate with them
when God sees that their strength is gone
   and no one is left, bonded or free.
37 Your God will ask, "Now where are their gods,
   the rock they took refuge in,
38 the gods who ate the fat of their sacrifices
   and drank the wine of their drink offerings?
Let them rise up to help you!
   Let them give you shelter!

39 Now, see for yourself that I am that God!
　　There is no god besides me.
　I put to death and I bring to life;
　　I wound and I will heal,
　　and no one can deliver out of my hand.
40 I raise my hand declaring,
　　'As surely as I live forever,
41 when I sharpen my flashing sword,
　　I will take up the righteous cause;
　I will take revenge on my adversaries
　　and repay those who hate me.
42 I will make my arrows drunk with blood,
　　while my sword devours flesh:
　the blood of the slain and the captives,
　　the heads of the enemy leaders.' "

43 Rejoice, O nations, with God's people,
　　let the angels praise God's power!
　For God will avenge
　　the blood of the faithful believers;
　God will take vengeance on the enemies
　　and purify the land and the people.

44 Moses came with Joshua, begot of Nun, and recited all the verses of this song in the hearing of the people.

45 When Moses had finished reciting these words for the people of Israel, 46 he said to them, "Take to heart all the words I have solemnly declared to you today, so that you will command your children to heed and obey all the words of the Law. 47 They are not just idle words for you: they are your life, and by them you will live long in the land that you are crossing the Jordan to occupy."

48 On that same day Our God said to Moses, 49 "Go up into the Abarim Range to Mount Nebo in Moab, across from Jericho, and view the land of Canaan, the land I am giving the Israelites to occupy. There on the mountain you have climbed you will die and will be gathered to your ancestors, just as your brother Aaron died on Mount Hor and was gathered to his people. 51 This is because both of you broke faith with me in the presence of the Israelites at the waters of Meribath Kadesh in the desert of Zin and because you did not uphold my holiness among the Israelites. 52 Therefore,

---

* The Urim and Thummim were divination tools. See footnote at Exodus 28:30.

you will see the land only from a distance; you will not enter the land I am giving to the people of Israel."

33:1 This is the blessing Moses, God's own, pronounced over the Israelites before he died. 2 Moses prayed:

> You, Most High God, came from Sinai
>> and dawned over us from Seir;
>> you shone forth from Mount Paran.
> You came with hosts of holy ones
>> streaming along at your right hand.
> 3 Truly, you love the ancestors;
>> all the holy ones are in your hand.
> They have all bowed down at your feet,
>> and you instructed them
> 4 in the Law Moses gave us,
>> the possession of the assembly of Jacob.
> 5 You became the ruler in Jerusalem,
>> once the leaders of the people assembled
>> along with the tribes of Israel.

6 Of Reuben, Moses said:

> May Reuben live and not die out,
>> though few be Reuben's numbers.

7 And of Judah, Moses said:

> Hear, O God, the cry of Judah
>> and bring Judah back to their people.
> Be a strong defense for them,
>> and help them against their foes.

8 And of Levi, Moses said:

> Give your Urim to Levi,
>> your Thummim to your loyal ones*
> whom you tested at Massah,
>> and with whom you quarrelled at the waters of Meribah.
> 9 They said of their parents, "I don't know them";
>> they did not acknowledge their sisters and brothers;
>> who disowned their children.
> But they have kept your word;
>> they hold firmly to your covenant.
> 10 They teach your precepts to Jacob,
>> Your Law to Israel.

They send incense rising to your nostrils,
    And place the whole burnt offering on your altar.
¹¹ O God, bless their substance
    and accept the work of their hands.
Crush the loins of their enemies
    and of their foes, until they are subdued.

¹² And of Benjamin, Moses said:

The beloved of God dwell in safety.
Adonai protects them day by day
    and dwells between their hills.

¹³ And of Joseph, Moses said:

May God's blessing be on their land
    with choice dew watered from the heavens
    and from the Deep lying below,
¹⁴ with the best of what is ripened in the sun,
    choice fruit, the product of the months,
¹⁵ the first fruits of the ancient mountains,
    the best from the hills of old,
¹⁶ the best of the land and all it holds,
    by the favor of the One who dwells in the burning bush.
May the hair grow thick on the head of Joseph,
    of the consecrated one among the brothers—
¹⁷ the one like a firstborn bull in majesty,
    with horns like those of a wild ox,
with which to gore the nations
    and drive them to the ends of the earth.
Such are the thousands of Ephraim;
    such are the multitudes of Manasseh.

¹⁸ And of Zebulun, Moses said:

Rejoice, Zebulun, in your going out;
    and you, Issachar, in your tents!
¹⁹ On the mountains where the people come to pray
    they offer sacrifices for success,
for they taste the riches of the seas,
    and the treasures hidden in the sand.

²⁰ And of Gad, Moses said:

Blessed are they who give Gad enough space!
    They lie there like lionesses;
    they have savaged arm and face and head.

21 Then they took the first portion for themselves;
    they saw that there a leader's share was kept for them.
  They came leaders of the people,
    having executed the justice of Our God
    and God's judgments concerning Israel.

22 And of Dan, Moses said:

  Dan is a lion cub
    leaping from Bashan.

23 And of Naphtali, Moses said:

  Naphtali, sated with favors,
    filled with the favors of Our God:
    the sea and southward are their domain.

24 And of Asher, Moses said:

  Most blessed of the twelve
    may Asher be!
  Let them be privileged among the other eleven,
    and let them bathe their feet in oil!
25   May your bolts be of iron and of bronze
26   and your security as lasting as your days!

  There is none like the God of Jeshurun,
    who rides the heavens to your rescue,
27   who rides the clouds in majesty.
  The God of old is your refuge.
    Here below, Your God is the age-old arm
  driving the enemy before you;
28   it is God who cries, "Destroy!"
  Israel rests in safety
    Jacob dwells alone
  in a land of grain and wine
29   where the skies drip with dew
  Happy are you, O Israel!
    Who is like you, a people liberated by God?
  God is the shield that guards you;
    the Most High is your glorious sword.
  When your enemies come crawling before you,
    you will trample them underfoot.

ଓ୪   ଓ୪   ଓ୪

34:1 Moses went up from the plains of Moab to Mount Nebo, the head-land of Pisgah which faces Jericho, and Our God showed him all the land— Gilead as far as Dan, 2 all of Naphtali, the land of Ephraim and Manasseh, all the land of Judah as far as the Western Sea, 3 the Negev, and the stretch of the valley of Jericho, the city of palms, and as far as Zoar. 4 Then Our God said to Moses, "This is the land I swore to Sarah and Abraham, to Rebecca and Isaac, to Leah, Rachel and Jacob that I would give to their descendants. I have let you feast your eyes upon it, but you will not cross over."

5 So there in the land of Moab, Moses the servant of God died as Our God decreed, 6 and he was buried in the valley opposite Beth Peor in the land of Moab, but to this day no one knows the exact burial place. 7 Moses was one hundred and twenty years old when he died, yet his eyesight was strong and he was still quite vigorous. 8 For thirty days the Israelites wept for Moses in the plains of Moab, until they had completed the period of grief and mourning.

9 Now Joshua, begot of Nun, was filled with the spirit of wisdom, for Moses had laid his hands on him. And the Israelites gave him their obedience, carrying out the order God had given to Moses.

10 Since then, no prophet has risen in Israel like Moses, whom Our God knew face to face. 11 There is no equal to all the signs and wonders Adonai, our God, caused Moses to perform in the land of Egypt, against Pharaoh and all of Pharaoh's officials and the whole land. 12 How mighty the hand and how terrifying the displays of power that Moses wielded in the sight of all Israel!